Interest Group Politics in the Midwestern States

Interest Group Politics in the Midwestern States

EDITED BY

Ronald J. Hrebenar
AND
Clive S. Thomas

Iowa State University Press / Ames

1993

This book is dedicated to

Sarah McCally Morehouse,

a pioneer in the study of state interest groups.

Authorization to photocopy items for internal or personal use, or the internal or personal use of specific clients, is granted by Iowa State University Press, provided that the base fee of $.10 per copy is paid directly to the Copyright Clearance Center, 27 Congress Street, Salem, MA 01970. For those organizations that have been granted a photocopy license by CCC, a separate system of payments has been arranged. The fee code for users of the Transactional Reporting Service is 0-8138-1384-0/93 $.10.

⊗ Printed on acid-free paper in the United States of America

First edition, 1993

Library of Congress Cataloging-in-Publication Data

Interest group politics in the midwestern states / edited by Ronald J. Hrebenar and Clive S. Thomas.
        p.   cm.
    Includes bibliographical references and index.
    ISBN 0-8138-1384-0
    1. Pressure groups—Middle West. 2. Politics, practical—Middle West. I. Hrebenar, Ronald J. II. Thomas, Clive S.
JK1118.I5664   1993
322.4'3'0956—dc20   92-35679

Contents

Tables

Preface

When John F. Fenton published his book *Midwest Politics* in 1966, he organized his examination of midwestern politics around political parties.[1] The six midwestern states selected were divided into two categories (Michigan, Wisconsin, and Minnesota; Ohio, Indiana, and Illinois) based on whether their style of party politics was issue-oriented, as in the former group of states, or job-oriented, as in the latter group. The institution of political parties was the common thread in the understanding of politics in these states. When interest groups were mentioned by Fenton, such as the automobile industry in Michigan and the various reformer groups in Wisconsin and Minnesota, their significance was usually as a force that influenced the more significant institution of political parties.

During the decades that have elapsed since *Midwest Politics* was published, parties have declined in their importance as significant factors in our state and national public policy-making process, while more and more attention has been focused on interest groups. Still, in many states little is known about the number, types, significance, and roles played by interest groups in the state policy-making process. In many states no effort has ever been made to study in a systematic manner the interest group systems and their impact on state politics.

State politics research using a regional unit of analysis also has been unusual. Some exceptions are studies by V. O. Key, Jr., W. Duane Lockard, and Frank Jonas, which look at politics in the South, Northeast, and West, respectively, using the region to establish geographical boundaries of analysis.[2]

Interest groups have exerted enormous influence on the public policy-making process of all midwestern states. In most cases they have been the dominant political forces. This is not to say that the literature on midwestern politics ignores interest groups and their importance. There are many treatments of group systems in the literature on individual states. Yet in nearly all these studies interest groups are treated only incidentally. In a similar manner interest groups are one of many topics in each of the individual volumes in the University of Nebraska Press's series on government in the fifty states. We believe that by focusing on interest groups, this book provides a different perspective; and in so doing, we hope that it adds to the general understanding of the politics of the Midwest and of its individual states.

In all honesty, however, augmenting the general understanding of midwestern politics was not one of the major purposes we had in mind when we first considered a book on interest groups in the Midwest. This book was, in fact, conceived as the third in a series of four books that we are coediting on interest groups in all fifty states. Each book focuses on a region of the country. The first covers the thirteen western states, the second covers the South, this one focuses on the Midwest, and the fourth is on the northeastern states.[3] A fifth volume will compare all fifty states.[4] Seventy-eight political scientists were involved in the project, which took more than five years to complete and is the most extensive treatment of interest groups in the states yet produced. As with the other three regional books, this one on the Midwest grew out of a sense of frustration. Along with colleagues throughout the country who are primarily interested in teaching about and researching interest groups, we were particularly concerned about the dearth of material, especially hard data, on groups at the state level. These books seek to meet at least partially the need for a foundation of material on interest group politics in the states.

In planning for these regional books, we identified four primary objectives and one secondary objective. One major objective was to provide the first overall analysis of interest groups in states where there was no existing research on the subject. About twenty states fell into this category. Second, we wanted to provide an update on group activity in states where there was some previous work. Taken together, these first two purposes would provide an up-to-date data base for the comparative analysis of state interest groups to an extent that had never before been possible: our third major objective. Our fourth was to be able to measure our findings against previous research on state groups by scholars such as Harmon Zeigler, Sarah McCally Morehouse, Wayne Francis, and Belle Zeller. From such an assessment we could suggest modifications to existing theories and develop some new theories and propositions of our own.

As interest groups are so central a part of all political and governmental systems, we realized that, if our methodology and analysis were rigorous enough, our study would also throw light upon state and regional politics in general. This was our secondary objective. As our research progressed, we found that studying interest groups provided a perspective on the politics of the individual midwestern states and the region which had not been previously explored or, at least, had not been expressly treated. Hence our hope is that this book contributes to an overall understanding of midwestern politics. Nevertheless, it remains a book on state interest groups which focuses on the Midwest, not a treatment of midwestern politics which focuses on interest groups. First and foremost, we are interest group specialists and — despite immersing ourselves in the literature on the region for the last three years — do not claim to be experts on midwestern politics. We leave to such experts the task of discovering the deeper implications of our study for understanding politics in the Midwest.

A few words about the format of the book. The introductory chapter uses a conceptual framework combined with a historical methodology to set the scene for understanding the place of interest groups in midwestern state politics. It also explains our methodology. It is followed by the thirteen state chapters, ordered alphabetically. To provide some background for understanding the specifics of interest group activity in each state, each chapter begins with a brief overview of its state and its politics. The concluding chapter summarizes the story of midwestern interest groups. It does so by using the conceptual framework set out in the introduction and by drawing on the information in the state chapters to provide a comparative analysis of the current role, operating techniques, and power of midwestern state interest groups. It also compares and contrasts recent developments in midwestern interest group politics with those in other regions.

More so than most political science books, this volume is the result of the efforts of many people. At the top of the list are our nineteen contributors. In particular, we appreciate their willingness to bear the cost of their own research efforts. The contributors are listed with their chapter titles, and we have taken great care to ensure that they have received the recognition and appreciation that they deserve when we have cited their research in our other works. The University of Utah and the University of Alaska-Southeast provided us with some basic resources for our project, not least of which was regular employment. Our editor, Gretchen Van Houten, copy editor Kim Vivier, and the ISU Press staff were of immense help to us. Debbie Frye and Marilyn Miller helped type the manuscript and tables and taught us a few lessons in presentation and style. Finally, our families have been very understanding and supportive, and we express our appreciation and apologies for the time we have taken from them over the years.

Finally, a few comments about how we shared the work in putting together this book. At times each of us felt that it was he who was doing the bulk of the work and that the other was dragging his feet or was off working on his own projects. The truth of the matter is, however, that in the final tally we each did 51 percent of the work. That's not to say that we shared equally in each of the myriad tasks involved in producing an edited book, because, like all good partnerships, ours is based on the fact that we complement each other.

RONALD J. HREBENAR • CLIVE S. THOMAS

Notes

1. John F. Fenton, *Midwest Politics* (New York: Holt, Rinehart and Winston, 1966).

2. V. O. Key, Jr., *Southern Politics* (New York: Vintage, 1949); W. Duane Lockard, *New England State Politics* (Princeton: Princeton University Press, 1968); Frank Jonas, *Politics in the American West* (Salt Lake City: University of Utah Press, 1969).

3. Ronald J. Hrebenar and Clive S. Thomas, eds., *Interest Group Politics in the American West* (Salt Lake City: University of Utah Press, 1987); *Interest Group Politics in the Southern States* (Tuscaloosa, Ala.: University of Alabama Press, 1992); *Interest Group Politics in the Northeastern States* (College Park, Pa.: Penn State University Press, 1993).

4. Ronald J. Hrebenar and Clive S. Thomas, *Interest Groups in the Fifty American States: A Comparative Analysis* (New York: Harper-Collins, forthcoming).

Contributors

Fredric N. Bolotin is a lawyer and political consultant in Ohio. He received his Ph.D. from State University of New York-Binghamton and he was an assistant professor at Case Western Reserve University in Ohio.

William P. Browne is Professor of Political Science at Central Michigan University. He received his Ph.D. from Washington University (St. Louis). He is the author of five books on agricultural policy, including *Private Interests, Public Policy, and American Agriculture.*

Robert E. Burns is Professor of Political Science at South Dakota State University. He earned his Ph.D. from the University of Missouri-Columbia.

Gregory Casey is Associate Professor of Political Science at the University of Missouri-Columbia. He obtained his Ph.D. from Georgetown University.

Herbert E. Cheever, Jr., is Professor of Political Science and head of the department at South Dakota State University. He received his Ph.D. from the University of Iowa and is the former chair of the South Dakota Democratic party.

Allan J. Cigler is Associate Professor of Political Science at the University of Kansas. He is the coeditor of *Interest Group Politics* and received his Ph.D. from Indiana University.

John C. Comer is Professor of Political Science at the University of Nebraska. He received his Ph.D. from Ohio State University and is the coauthor of *American Government.*

Robert E. England is Associate Professor of Political Science at Oklahoma State University. He received his Ph.D. from the University of Oklahoma and is coauthor of *Desegregating Big City Schools* and *Oklahoma Government.*

David H. Everson is Professor of Political Studies and Public Affairs at Sangamon State University in Springfield, Illinois, and the former director of the Illinois Legislative Studies Center. He is the editor of *Comparative State Politics,* the author of *American Political Parties,* and a coeditor of *The Presidential Election and Transition, 1980.*

Samuel K. Gove is Professor of Political Science at the University of Illinois and the former director of the Institute of Government and Public Affairs. Among his many publications are *The Illinois Legislature, Policy Consequences in Higher Education,* and *State and Federal Impact: The Post-Daley Era.*

Craig H. Grau is Professor of Political Science at the University of Minnesota-Duluth. He received his Ph.D. from the University of Arizona. His various journal articles have focuses on state politics and lobbying.

David J. Hadley is Professor of Political Science and department chair at Wabash College in Crawfordville, Indiana. He received his Ph.D from Indiana University.

Keith E. Hamm is Associate Professor of Political Science at Rice University. He has published numerous articles and book chapters on state politics and is a past vice-president of the Southwest Political Science Association.

Ronald D. Hedlund is Professor of Political Science and Director of Research at the University of Rhode Island at Kingston. He previously taught at the University of Wisconsin-Milwaukee and has published many articles on state politics.

Ronald J. Hrebenar is Professor of Political Science at the University of Utah. He received his Ph.D. at the University of Washington. He is coauthor or coeditor of *Parties in Crisis, Interest Group Politics in America, The Japanese Party System,* and *Interest Group Politics in the American West.*

Dwight Kiel is Assistant Professor of Political Science at the University of Central Florida. He received his Ph.D. from the University of Massachusetts-Amherst and has also taught at the University of Kansas.

James D. King is Associate Professor of Political Science at Memphis State University. He received his Ph.D. from the University of Missouri-Columbia.

David R. Morgan is Professor of Political Science and Director of the Bureau of Government Research at the University of Oklahoma. He received his Ph.D. from the University of Oklahoma and is the author or coauthor of *Oklahoma Votes, Managing Urban America, Desegregating Big City Schools,* and *Oklahoma Government.*

Theodore B. Pedeliski is Professor of Political Science at the University of North Dakota. He received his Ph.D. from the University of Minnesota.

Delbert J. Ringquist is Associate Professor of Political Science and department chair at Central Michigan University. He received his Ph.D. from the University of Oklahoma. Among his various publications is *Congress and the President: Toward a New Power Balance.*

Clive S. Thomas is Professor of Political Science at the University of Alaska-Southeast in Juneau. He received his Ph.D. at the London School of Economics and has taught at Iowa State University. He is coeditor of *Interest Group Politics in the American West* and has several books in production on public policy and interest group politics.

Charles W. Wiggins is Professor of Political Science at Texas A&M University, where he also directs the masters of public administration program. He a former president of the Southwest Political Science Association and the author of several books, chapters, and articles on state politics and interest groups.

Interest Group Politics in the Midwestern States

Understanding
Interest Groups in
Midwestern Politics

CLIVE S. THOMAS

> The Midwest is both a geographical location and a state of
> mind. It is neither East nor West, neither South nor North. It is
> the population center of America and in many respects it is the
> heart of the nation. . . . Most Midwesterners think of them-
> selves as Americans. They do not live in the Midwest, they live
> in America, for the Midwest is America.
>
> — John Fenton, *Midwest Politics*

The Midwest as a region for examining political
patterns is, as John Fenton argued in 1966, a microcosm of American politics. Included within the
region's borders are some of America's most in-
dustrial states, some of the most agricultural states, states dominated by
metropolitan giants, states characterized by population scattered in
dozens of small cities and towns, and states with independent, moralistic, and traditional political cultures.

If one focuses on patterns of interest group politics, the entire range
of types of interest group systems and behavior emerges from the thirteen midwestern states. As one would expect from the variety of political
styles found in the Midwest, from the freewheeling and sometimes corrupt politics of Illinois to the "good neighbors" and squeaky clean politics of Minnesota and the Dakotas, lobbying styles run the gamut of the
"superlobbyists" of the megastates to the amateur citizen lobbyists of the
prairie states.

Some of the midwestern states have histories of periods of political domination by one or two powerful interests. North Dakota, as Theodore Pedeliski writes in Chapter 10, was dominated by the railroads up to the 1960s. Michigan politics, though more pluralistic than those of rural states such as North Dakota, were nonetheless dominated by automobile manufacturers and automobile labor unions until the 1980s. Missouri state politics, as Gregory Casey and James King relate in Chapter 8, were controlled in some periods by the Central Missouri Trust Company. Yet other midwestern states were sufficiently heterogeneous in population and economically diverse and thus tended to produce a pluralistic interest group system.

The stranglehold of interest groups on state politics was common in other regions, such as the South, in the 1800s. In almost every southern state, interest groups played a crucial and in most cases a dominant role. One reason why interest groups were more influential in southern state politics than in midwestern state politics is that the Democratic party's dominance in southern states failed to provide a check on interest group power. In the Midwest, interest group power historically was checked by competitive party systems operating in each of the states, and consequently, the overall influence of groups was less than in the South.

The Midwest is seen by many Americans as typical of the nation. The midwestern accent is often viewed by foreigners as the "standard American accent," and the values and behavior of the region's residents are considered archetypical of the nation. Expressions such as "Will it play in Peoria?" (a phrase used during the Nixon administration and subsequently by Madison Avenue advertising and product development agencies to indicate whether the American public will accept an idea or a product) are evidence of the centrality of midwestern values and behavior for the nation.

Yet despite the persistence of some aspects of midwestern values and behavior, change, and often significant change, has affected almost every aspect of midwestern life and culture. As the authors in the following chapters write, like all human systems, state politics and political behavior are changing in the Midwest. As integral and resilient features of midwestern political life, interest groups both have been affected by this change and have helped bring it about.

In each of the midwestern states the interest group systems have changed significantly in just a few decades. There has been a growth not only in the number of groups in state capitals, but also in the strata of the population represented by interest groups as well as in the professionalism of lobbyists and group leaders. Explaining exactly what the nature of this change, transition, and growth has been in recent developments in midwestern interest group politics forms the primary objective of this book.

To achieve this goal, we combine an in-depth analysis of individual states with a comparative analysis of the region as a whole. This approach involves four distinct but interrelated lines of inquiry. First, we provide an update on the types of groups operating in each state and the tactics they are using to achieve their goals. For several states, this analysis constitutes the first comprehensive treatment of interest groups — past or present. Second, we assess changes in interest group politics in the Midwest as a whole, especially the role that groups play in the public policy-making process. Third, we place the Midwest in context by comparing past and present trends with those in other regions. Finally, by combining the findings from these three lines of inquiry, we hope to enhance general theories of interest group activity in the states.

It should be noted that this book does not claim to be a comprehensive study of midwestern politics. That volume has yet to be written. Here we simply highlight those topics and themes of the region's politics that are essential for an understanding of the behavior and systems of midwestern interest groups.

The Midwest Defined

The Midwest is perhaps the most difficult region of the United States to define. In contrast, the West, South, and New England are all more or less distinctive as American regions. In our fifty-state study of interest groups we defined the West by drawing the boundary at the 100th meridian, which ends the farming culture of the prairie and begins the ranching culture of the West. The South was defined as the eleven states of the Old Confederacy plus Kentucky. Kentucky was added because it is predominantly more southern than midwestern in social, economic, and political terms. Oklahoma, Indiana, and Missouri were excluded because they were not primarily "southern" in these respects, although in some parts and in some cultural aspects significant "southern" characteristics were identified. Even clearly midwestern states such as Illinois in its southern region have a strong southern character due to the migration of many southerners into the states over the years.

From one perspective, it can be said that we determined the boundaries of the Midwest by defining the other three regions and keeping what was left over as the Midwest. Actually, our "Midwest" almost completely coincides with Neal R. Peirce's "Great Plains States" and "Great Lakes States," with the removal of Texas to the South.[1] An alternative scheme could use the regional and subregional categories of the U.S. Census Bureau (Oklahoma is a southern state in this classification). But we rejected that because we believed that Oklahoma fits better with the Great Plains states than with the South.

Existing Research on Midwestern Politics and Interest Groups

A review of published materials on politics and interest groups in the Midwest reveals that little has been written on either of these subjects. No book or article has ever been published to our knowledge on the subject of interest group politics in the Midwest. The Midwest is not unique in this dearth of material on interest groups. The West and South have had extensive publications on their politics, parties, and regional issues, yet little material exists on the regions' interest groups. The reason for this lack of focus on the states or regions is that the bulk of research on interest groups in the United States has concentrated on group activity at the national level. Such research, carried out in a single city, Washington, D.C., is comparatively easy to accomplish, as most of the major players are found within a few blocks of each other. Collecting information on state-level interest groups and lobbying in capitals thousands of miles apart in small, out-of-the-way cities is a nearly insurmountable research problem.

John Fenton's *Midwest Politics* and *Border State Politics* are the only major books that attempt to describe midwestern politics in a type of comparative framework.[2] As we note in the Preface, *Midwest Politics* focuses on political parties and only briefly mentions interest groups as they influence parties. As for midwestern interest group politics specifically, until now no comprehensive comparative analysis has been produced. However, five types of studies have touched on some aspects of interest group activity in the Midwest. First, there is the one book on midwestern politics, the Fenton volume already discussed. Second, there is the treatment of interest groups in books on the government and politics of individual midwestern states and in books that include chapters on midwestern states as examples or case studies.[3] Although at some time texts have been written on all thirteen states, the treatment of interest groups varies widely in length and approach, ranging from a few paragraphs to a separate chapter and from the purely anecdotal to the conceptual and quantitative. Most of these publications are now out of date, and though many chapters in books that include midwestern states as examples or case studies are well written, limitations of space preclude them from paying more than cursory attention to interest groups.[4]

Third, there is a small body of literature that has a public policy focus and has taken a case-study approach to investigating the impact of individual groups. William Browne's recent book on agricultural interest group politics, for example, provides a wealth of information on the nature of these agricultural groups and their roles in midwestern political, economic, and social life.[5]

A fourth category of literature on midwestern groups has taken what might be termed a micro approach to the study of group theory. These works have looked at either some specific aspect of the internal organization and operation of groups or how they affect some specific part of the political process such as the legislature. Sometimes these studies have been concerned solely with individual states, such as Samuel Patterson's article on lobbyists in Oklahoma.[6] Most often, however, this type of research has used one or more midwestern states as part of a larger study. For example, Charles Bell, Keith Hamm, and Charles Wiggins used Iowa in their recent three-state investigation of group impact on certain areas of public policy.[7]

Finally, a fifth category of books also contains information on midwestern interest groups. John Gunther's 1940s survey of politics in America, *Inside USA,* contained valuable insights on group activities in many states, including those in the Midwest.[8] The modern versions of the Gunther book are the nine volumes by Neal R. Peirce on the people, politics, and power in the various subregions of America. Peirce profiles each state and mentions in an informative but impressionistic manner the major interests that have influenced the state's politics.[9] Further information on the various states (and occasionally on their major interests) is found in the individual state profiles that introduce each state's congressional delegation in books such as the National Journal's *Almanac of American Politics.*[10]

These five categories are a useful starting point in a study of midwestern interest groups, particularly group activity in individual states, and numerous references are made to them throughout this book. Yet because of their great variation in methodology, scope, and depth, they have limited value for purposes of comparative analysis (and often for individual state studies as well). There is, however, a sixth category of literature that has been comparative in focus and has included the midwestern states as part of nationwide studies of state interest group activity. These works have taken what we might term a macro approach by attempting to understand interest groups in the context of the state as a whole and especially in relation to its political and governmental system. The most notable research in this category has been conducted by Belle

Zeller, Harmon Zeigler and Hendrik van Dalen, and Sarah McCally Morehouse.[11]

Despite the valuable contributions of these studies, all of them suffer more or less from the same weakness. Their attempts at comprehensive analysis of both the Midwest and other regions are based on original data from only a few states and draw on other information (such as that referred to above) that varies in its methodology from the impressionistic to the highly quantitative, a divergence that is not ideal for comparative analysis. Therefore, the theories and propositions developed from these studies were arrived at by extrapolation, by reliance on secondary sources, or sometimes, in the absence of data, by speculation.

Whatever their methodological weaknesses, these studies nonetheless made significant contributions. Each was a major source for the evaluation of interest groups at the subnational level — including the Midwest — at a time when little other data existed. Zeller was the first to categorize states into strong, moderate, or weak interest group systems. Zeigler, and Zeigler and van Dalen, developed several theories and propositions about how the economic, social, and political system in a state influences the composition, operation, and power of the state's interest group system. Most notably, they developed a four-category classification of group power within strong interest group states and advanced knowledge on the relationship between party strength and group power. More recently, Morehouse has built on this work. In particular, she has expanded on the relationship of parties and groups and has refined the threefold classification system of interest group power vis-à-vis a state's political system (strong, moderate, or weak). She also developed the first listing of the most "significant" groups in all fifty states. All this work has acted as a benchmark for scholars conducting subsequent research. It certainly provided us with an important point of departure for our study of midwestern interest groups.

Providing a Set of Common Terms and Definitions

Since each of the aforementioned researchers used different definitions, the usefulness of these studies of state-level interest groups was reduced for purposes of comparative analysis, whether comparisons within a state over time or among states at any point in time. Five of the most important terms are *interest group, lobby, interest, lobbyist,* and *group power.* The fact that previous works used various definitions of these terms is understandable, as disputes over their meaning have been common in the academic study of interest groups for years. For the purposes of methodological and analytical consistency, we developed a common set of definitions of these terms for use by our contributors in all fifty states. Here we define the first four, leaving *group power* for later when we explain our methodology in more detail.

In order of the most specific to the most general, the first term is *interest group*. Over the years researchers have used a variety of operational definitions of this term. Most commonly, they have employed the legal or regulatory definition, thus making their focus of study those groups required to register under federal and state laws and excluding those not required to do so. In certain limited cases such a definition may be adequate, but for most research on state interest groups, and particularly research with a comparative focus or component, it is clearly inadequate.

The major problem with this legal or regulatory definition is that the fifty states vary considerably in what groups and organizations they require to register as lobbying entities. Some states, such as Oregon, have relatively broad rules requiring even state agencies to register. Others, such as Georgia, have very narrow regulations.[12] Many of the groups that are not required to register in Georgia are active in the state capital. Consequently, the exclusion of these nonregistered, or "hidden," groups and lobbies, and especially state government agencies, greatly distorts an understanding of the role in and impact of interest groups in such a state's public policy-making process. For these reasons, using group registration lists as the sole basis for comparative state interest group research is unsatisfactory.

We attempt to overcome these problems by the use of the following definition of *interest group* in our fifty-state study: *any association of individuals or organizations, whether formally organized or not, that attempts to influence public policy.* The South Dakota Association of County Commissioners is an example of a specific interest group, as is the University of Nebraska. This definition is a variation of what is probably the most widely used definition of an interest group, that of David Truman. Our definition is shorter and more concrete, however. It embraces the various concepts that Truman included and, at the same time, eliminates some of the shortcomings of his definition.[13] Since all definitions have some weaknesses, ours is no exception. It is very broad, and as some of our contributors discovered, it creates some problems in securing data. However, the findings from this project demonstrate that this definition produces a comprehensive and balanced view of interest group activity in the states, including many aspects previously unnoticed or only superficially treated in some previous studies.

Lobby has a much broader connotation than *interest group*. In our study we use it as a collective term as follows: *two or more individuals, groups, or organizations that are concerned with the same general area of public policy but that may or may not be in agreement on specific issues.* For example, the education lobby in most states, including those in the Midwest, comprises state boards of education, PTAs, education associations, boards of regents of higher education, student groups, vocational education institutions, special education groups, and lobbyists for major individual institutions such as research universities. These groups share a general interest in promoting legislation and funding to enhance the quality of education. Yet on any given issue members of this lobby may be on opposite sides. Since education makes up half or more of many state government budgets, education lobby members agree that this proportion should continue or be increased, but they may intensely disagree about how the funds should be distributed.

The term *interest* has a broader connotation than *interest group* but is more specific than *lobby.* We can again use education groups as an example. Individual universities such as the University of Wisconsin, Nebraska, or Illinois often lobby directly and thus can be considered specific interest groups. These groups, as we noted above, are also members of the education lobby in their states. But they can also be considered part of the interest category of higher education. Higher education also includes community colleges, vocational education, and other institutions depending on the state. Exactly where an interest ends and a lobby begins is not always clear. But it is often a useful distinction to make for two reasons. Public officials frequently refer to similar types of interest groups that often act in concert as an interest, and the term is helpful for categorizing similar types of groups for purposes relating to such activities as the types of groups that are active in state capitals, group tactics, and group power.

Finally, we define *lobbyist* as *a person designated by an interest group to represent it to government for the purpose of influencing public policy in that group's favor.* From our definition of an interest group, we know that the interest represented by the lobbyist need not necessarily be a formal organization such as the Central Missouri Trust Company or the Michigan State Chamber of Commerce. It includes informal and ad hoc groups such as neighborhood residents dissatisfied with their community leaders or an informal association of business people concerned with a specific issue. Lobbyists, as we define them, are not limited just to those representing groups required to register under state law, but include all those who lobby, whether they are required to register or not.[14]

Not all lobbyists are the same, just as not all lawyers perform the same roles in our nation's judicial system. Lobbyists can be divided into five major categories:

Contract lobbyists: Those hired on contract for a fee specifically to lobby. They may represent more than one client.

In-house lobbyists: Employees of an organization, association, or business who as all or part of their jobs act as lobbyists. They represent only one client — their employer.

Government lobbyists or legislative liaisons: Employees of state, local, and federal agencies who as part or all of their jobs represent their agencies to the legislative and executive branches of state government. They represent only one interest.

Citizen or volunteer lobbyists: Persons who, usually on an ad hoc and unpaid basis, represent citizen and community organizations or informal groups. They rarely represent more than one interest at a time.

Private individual, "hobbyist," or self-styled lobbyists: Those acting on their own behalf and not designated by any organization as an official representative.

These five categories of lobbyists are viewed differently by those they seek to influence. This is because although all lobbyists have the identical goal of influencing public policy, their backgrounds, experiences, resources, and the organizations they represent are different, and thus different types of lobbyists will probably lobby in different ways.

A Framework for Understanding Interest Group Activity in the States

To understand interest group activity in the states, including the midwestern states, it is useful to consider the basic factors that influence that activity; that is to say, what determines (1) the types of groups that are active in the states; (2) the methods that they use in pursuing their goals; and (3) the role that groups play within state political systems and, in particular, the power that they exert within those systems.

Although little research has been conducted on this topic, scholars agree that the answers lie in a complex set of economic, social, cultural, legal, political, governmental, and even geographical variables. These factors vary in their combinations from state to state, giving each state a unique interest group system. Nevertheless, we have identified seven specific sets of factors that appear to be of particular importance in all states (Table 1.1).

Table 1.1. Seven major factors influencing the makeup, operating techniques, and impact on public policy of interest group systems in the states

1. State Policy Domain: Constitutional/legal authority of a state affects which groups will be politically active. Policies actually exercised by a state affect which groups will be most active. The policy priorities of a state affect which groups will be most influential.

2. Political Attitudes: Especially political culture, and political ideology viewed in terms of conservative/liberal attitudes. Affect the type and extent of policies performed, the level of integration/fragmentation and professionalization of the policy-making process, acceptable lobbying techniques, and the comprehensiveness and stringency of enforcement of public disclosure laws, including lobby laws.

3. Level of Integration/Fragmentation of the Policy Process: Strength of political parties; power of the governor; number of directly elected cabinet members; number of independent boards and commissions; initiative, referendum, and recall. Influences the number of options available to groups: greater integration decreases them, whereas more fragmentation increases them.

4. Level of Professionalization of State Government: State legislators, support services, bureaucracy, including the governor's staff. Influences the extent to which public officials need group resources and information. Also affects the level of professionalization of the lobbying system.

5. Level of Socioeconomic Development: Increased socioeconomic diversity tends to produce a more diverse and competitive group system; a decline in the dominance of one or an oligarchy of groups; new and more sophisticated techniques of lobbying, such as an increase in contract lobbyists, lawyer-lobbyists, multiclient/multiservice lobbying firms, grass-roots campaigns, and public relations techniques; and a general rise in the professionalization of lobbyists and lobbying.

6. Extensiveness and Enforcement of Public Disclosure Laws: Including lobby laws, campaign finance laws, PAC regulations, and conflict-of-interest provisions. Increase public information above lobbying activities, which influences the methods and techniques of lobbying; in turn, this affects the power of certain groups and lobbyists.

7. Level of Campaign Costs and Sources of Support: As the proportion of group funding increases, especially that from PACs, group access and power increases.

Source: Developed by the authors from the fifty state chapters of the Hrebenar-Thomas study.

This conceptual framework for understanding the environmental influences on group activity in the states is a synthesis of previous research and of findings from our fifty-state study. Though all seven factors and their various elements are not new, what is original is the way that many of these elements have been used here and the integration of the seven factors into a single framework. These factors and their components are very much interrelated in that they influence each other. A change in one factor may result in a change in one or more of the other factors. Any change at all is likely to affect the nature of group activity, and major changes will have a significant impact on the interest group and lobbying scene in a particular state or the states as a whole.

Midwest Politics and Their Interest Group System

Midwest politics are difficult to generalize about. The region is a study in both homogeneity and considerable complexity. Its political traditions span the range from socialism and populism to strong liberalism and fundamental conservatism. The wide range of political ideologies within the Midwest continues today and is perhaps more varied than ever, as the chapters in this book show. Nevertheless, we can briefly identify certain themes common to midwestern political life.

Isolationism and conservatism in foreign policy and fiscal matters tended to differentiate the Midwest from the rest of the nation throughout this century. Much of its isolation and conservatism can be traced to the region's economic dependence on agriculture and its significant rural sector. On the other hand, its radical and liberal traditions are derived from the tenuousness of prairie agricultural life and the peculiar mix of northern European ethnic groups.

The interest group patterns of midwestern states during the late 1800s were, like those in most states, very narrowly based in terms of both the types of interests represented and those that wielded power. Railroads were important both as employers and because for several decades they held a transportation monopoly. Even after the advent of the truck and the airplane, railroads were (and in many instances remain) the only feasible means for moving freight and farm produce in the large region of the Midwest. In most states agricultural interests were also significant economically. In states such as Ohio, Illinois, and Michigan strong industrial bases were built and came to overshadow the agricultural sector. A laissez-faire philosophy of state government up to the mid-1950s meant that the role of the states was far less extensive than it is today. As a consequence, state bureaucracies were small and the level of state civil service professionalism was low. Professionalism exhibited a mixed pattern among state elected officials, especially legislators, as some states (such as Illinois) developed traditions of professional legislators and other states (such as the Dakotas) revered the "citizen legislator" as their model.

Once-dominant business and agricultural interests have been joined in recent years by local government groups, labor unions, and education interests, especially schoolteachers. Together these five interests—business, agriculture, labor, local government, and education—formed the major interests operating in state capitals in the Midwest, and in statehouses across the nation, down to the 1960s.

All the midwestern states to one degree or another developed the most famous, or perhaps notorious, of stereotype lobbying styles—the wheeler-dealer. This style is easier to recognize than to define. But in general, it involves a powerful lobbyist who operates in an aggressive and flamboyant manner and is willing to use a variety of methods, some of which may be suspect, to achieve his goals. As with many other aspects of the pre-1960s lobbying community, it is impossible to determine how widespread wheeler-dealers were in the states. The nature of politics at the time, resulting in part from the lack of both public disclosure and professionalism, lead to the conclusion, however, that this was the dominant lobbying style.

Methodology

If we could have designed the perfect methodology for this study of interest groups on the state level, we would have used identical research procedures, including identical survey instruments, in each of the fifty states. The real world does not permit such absolute methodological consistency on such a scale, however. In fact, the practical problems of conducting identical social science research in fifty state capitals has kept other state-level researchers from achieving absolute methodological consistency for all fifty states.

In each state we first attempted to find a contributor who was a qualified political scientist as well as an interest group specialist. Even when we had secured contributors for all fifty states, certain factors precluded the imposition of an identical methodology. First, in some states literature on interest groups already existed, but in others—the majority—our contributors had to start from scratch. Second, because the registration and reporting requirements vary so much among states, some information (lobbyists' fees or the percentage of campaign funds contributed by political action committees) is simply not available. Third, a demand for an identical and restrictive methodology might have prevented contributors from identifying certain unique and perhaps crucial aspects of their states' interest group systems which would be valuable both for an understanding of that system and for comparative purposes.

We strongly believe that a purely quantitative approach would be inadequate even if we could mandate it. This is because, unlike in other areas of political science such as voting behavior, we have not yet reached the stage of being able to understand the role, influence, and impact of interest groups by simply quantifying their activities. This approach would fail to convey the highly personalized and dynamic nature of several of the key aspects of interest group activity. One of the most important of these is the interaction between lobbyists and group leaders on the one hand and policy makers, both elected and appointed, on the other. Much of the dynamics of this relationship, and especially what ultimately determines influence, requires a qualitative as opposed to a quantitative methodology. A purely quantitative approach has similar shortcomings when it comes to assessing the various aspects of group power. Quantitative methods need to be combined with a qualitative approach: "soaking and poking," as Richard Fenno would say—interviewing, observating, and associating with lobbyists, group leaders, legislators, and bureaucrats. Accordingly, we encouraged our contributors to use qualitative methods in conjunction with quantitative research and to place both within a conceptual framework.

Keeping in mind the aforementioned practical problems, we devised a methodology that would obtain as much quantitative and usable qualitative data as possible to maximize our ability to make comparisons among states. We also wanted to give the contributors sufficient flexibility to identify the unique aspects and nuances of interest group activity in their respective states. To achieve this objective, we developed a set of guidelines that required each contributor to use a methodology incorporating certain specified elements. These guidelines are presented in the appendix.

We previously presented common definitions for *interest group, interest, lobby,* and *lobbyist.* Now we explain our approach to defining *group power.* The concept of interest group power can denote two separate though interrelated ideas. It may refer to the ability of an individual group, coalition, or lobby to achieve its policy goals. Alternately, it may be used to refer to the strength of interest groups as a whole within a state's political and governmental systems or the strength of groups relative to other organizations or institutions, particularly political parties.

Those acquainted with interest group theory know that individual group and lobby power is a problematic concept. The problem focuses on methods of assessment rather than definition. So many variables affect both long- and short-term group power that it is difficult to develop a methodology to assess and predict it in more than a general way. Three methods have been used for assessing individual group power: the use of purely objective criteria; the perceptual method, relying on the perceptions of politicians, bureaucrats, and political observers; and a combination of these two approaches.

We decided to adopt the combination approach. Along with using the perceptual method, we attempted to inject a high degree of objectivity and consistency into the research by using quantitative techniques to analyze the responses. This study's definition of *individual group power,* which also incorporates our method of assessment, is *the ability of any particular interest group or lobby to achieve its goals as it defines them and as perceived by the various people directly involved in and observing the public policy-making process (e.g., present and former legislators, aides, bureaucrats, other lobbyists, journalists, etc.).*

The admission that there are weaknesses in both our methodology and the results is unavoidable. Yet despite these weaknesses, our findings represent the first comprehensive assessment, based on a consistent research method, of the most effective interest groups and lobbies in each of the fifty states.

Assessing group power as a whole within a state's political system is even more problematic. In fact, it is probably the most difficult aspect of interest group activity to assess, primarily because there are so many variables to consider, many of which have not yet been identified, let alone defined. Consequently, assessments of overall group power are crude at best. Many scholars, however, have taken a valiant stab at the question. As we mentioned earlier, Zeller, Zeigler and van Dalen, and Morehouse have developed a classification of states as strong, moderate, or weak in regard to the overall impact of their interest group system. One of the key factors in these studies is the inverse relationship between party strength and group strength. This relationship does not always stand up to more detailed investigation, however.

No definitions or methodologies involving overall group power and its assessment were mandated by the editors. We saw this study as a golden opportunity to develop some new approaches to assessing group power. With nearly eighty researchers involved in our fifty-state study, we decided to turn our contributors loose on the problem, since no other acceptable alternative was available. As a starting point, we asked them to consider existing methods and the findings on overall group impact. The authors were to critique these methodologies and assessments and offer alternatives. To our knowledge, this is the largest number of people who have ever focused on this problem at any one time. The individual state chapters and the book's conclusion explain the results.

State-Level Interest Group Politics in Comparative Perspective

Since the central theme of this book is change and transition in midwestern interest group politics, as a basis for comparison it is useful to identify the major changes and trends that are occurring in the other three regions: the South, the West, and the Northeast. Then, as the analysis of the individual states in this book proceeds, the changes and trends in the Midwest can be measured against those of the other regions.

These overall developments in state-level interest groups have been examined in detail in other writings.[15] For our present purposes, however, we need only discuss the highlights. Ten such changes and trends appear to be of major importance in the other regions.

1. The number of groups active in state capitals has increased substantially.

2. Simultaneously, the range of groups that attempt to affect public policy in the states has expanded.

3. Most notable in the broadening of interests is the rise of public service unions (especially teachers and public employee associations), state and local government agencies as lobbying forces, and public interest and citizens' groups.

4. The first three developments have led to an increased intensity of lobbying as more and a wider range of groups are spending more time and money on lobbying than ever before in the history of state government.

5. Interest group tactics are becoming more sophisticated. They now include public relations campaigns, networking (using member contact systems) and grass-roots lobbying, as well as coalition building, newsletters, and more active participation in campaigns.

6. The use of political action committees (PACs) by certain groups as a means of channeling money to favored candidates has risen dramatically. Business, labor, and professional groups account for the bulk of PACs and their contributions.

7. Some notable changes have occurred in the background and style of contract lobbyists (those hired for a fee specifically to lobby). The wheeler-dealer is being replaced by the technical expert lobbyist. And more and more contract lobbying is being taken over by multiservice lobbying firms, law firms, and public relations companies.

8. Public monitoring of interest group activity has increased through the passage and strengthening of lobby laws, as well as campaign finance and conflict-of-interest regulations.

9. Major shifts in interest group power in the states have occurred, involving both individual groups and groups as a whole. Business is having to share power with an increasing range of groups, and group influence overall appears to have benefited from, among other factors, the decline of political parties.

10. Overall, and partly because of this decline in parties, the role of

interest groups within state political systems has expanded. In particular, they have become more important as vehicles of political participation.

In summary, interest group activity outside the Midwest is becoming much more professionalized and increasingly like the interest group system operating in Washington, D.C. As we examine the extent of change and growth in midwestern interest group politics, we also address the following broad political questions: (1) Is the midwestern interest group system significantly different from those found in the other three regions? and (2) Are there common elements in midwestern interest group politics?

Notes

1. Neal R. Peirce, *The Great Plains States of America: People, Politics, and Power in the Nine Great Plains States* (New York: W. W. Norton, 1973); Neal R. Peirce and John Keefe, *The Great Lakes States: People, Politics, and Power in the Five Great Lakes States* (New York: W. W. Norton, 1980).
2. John Fenton, *Midwest Politics* (New York: Holt, Rinehart & Winston, 1966); John Fenton, *Politics in the Border States* (New Orleans: Houser Press, 1957).
3. Austin Ranney, *Illinois Politics* (New York: New York University Press, 1966); James D. Nolan, ed., *Inside State Government* (Illinois) (Urbana, Ill.: University of Illinois Press, 1982); Philip S. Wilder and Karl O'Lessker, *Introduction to Indiana Government and Politics* (Indianapolis: Indiana Sesquicentennial Commission, 1967); Charles W. Wiggins, *The Legislative Process in Iowa* (Ames: Iowa State University Press, 1972); James W. Drury, *The Government of Kansas* (Lawrence: Regents Press of Kansas, 1980); Marvin Harder and Carolyn Rampey, *The Kansas Legislature* (Lawrence: University of Kansas Press, 1972), and also by Harder, *Interest Groups and Lobbyists in Kansas State Government* (Lawrence: Center for Public Affairs, University of Kansas, 1983); Ferris E. Lewis, *State and Local Government in Michigan* (Hillsdale, Mich.: Hillsdale Educational Publishers, 1968); G. T. Mitau, *Politics in Minnesota* (Minneapolis: University of Minnesota Press, 1960 and 1970); Richard J. Hardy and Richard R. Dohm, eds., *Missouri Government and Politics* (Columbia: University of Missouri Press, 1985); Robert F. Karsch, *The Government of Missouri* (Columbia, Mo.: Lucas Brothers, 1971); Robert D. Miewald, ed., *Nebraska Government and Politics* (Lincoln: University of Nebraska Press, 1984); Robert D. Thomas Howard, ed., *The North Dakota Political Tradition* (Ames: Iowa State University Press, 1981); Carl Lieberman, ed., *Government and Politics in Ohio* (Lanham, Md.: University Press of America, 1984); Stephen Jones, *Oklahoma Politics in State and Nation* (Enid, Okla.: Haymaker Press, 1974); Alan L. Clem, *Prairie State Politics* (Washington, D.C.: Public Affairs Press, 1967), on South Dakota; Wilder Crane and A. Clarke Hagensick, *Wisconsin Government and Politics* (Milwaukee: Department of Governmental Affairs, University of Wisconsin-Milwaukee, 1987).
4. See, for example, Samuel C. Patterson, "Iowa," in Alan Rosanthal and Maureen Moakley, eds., *The Political Life of the American States* (New York: Praeger, 1984); Leon D. Epstein, *Politics in Wisconsin* (Madison: University of Wisconsin Press, 1973).

5. William P. Browne, *Private Interests, Public Policy, and American Agriculture* (Lawrence: University of Kansas Press, 1988).

6. Samuel Patterson, "The Role of the Lobbyist: The Case of Oklahoma," *Journal of Politics,* 25 (February 1963), 77–92.

7. Charles G. Bell, Keith E. Hamm, and Charles W. Wiggins, "The Pluralistic Model Reconsidered: A Comparative Analysis of Interest Group Policy Involvement in Three States" (Paper presented at American Political Science Association meeting, New Orleans, August–September 1985).

8. John Gunther, *Inside USA* (New York: Harper & Row, 1947 and 1951).

9. Neal Peirce's regional books, in addition to the two in note 1, are *The Megastates of America* (1972), *The Pacific States of America* (1972), *The Mountain States of America* (1972), *The Deep South States of America* (1974), *The Border South States of America* (1975), *The New England States of America* (1976), and *The Mid-Atlantic States of America* (1977; with Michael Barone), all published by W. W. Norton of New York City. Also see Neal R Peirce and Jerry Hagstrom, *The Book of America: Inside Fifty States Today* (New York: W. W. Norton, 1983).

10. *Almanac of American Politics 1988* (Washington, D.C.: National Journal, 1989).

11. Belle Zeller, *American State Legislatures,* 2d ed. (New York: Thomas Y. Crowell, 1954), 190–91 and chap. 13, "Pressure Group Influence and Their Control"; L. Harmon Zeigler, "Interest Groups in the States," in Virginia Gray, Herbert Jacob, and Kenneth N. Vines, eds., *Politics in the American States: A Comparative Analysis,* 4th ed. (Boston: Little, Brown, 1983), chap. 4; L. Harmon Zeigler and Hendrik van Dalen, "Interest Groups in State Politics," in Herbert Jacob and Kenneth N. Vines, eds., *Politics in the American States: A Comparative Analysis,* 3d ed. (Boston: Little, Brown, 1976), chap. 4; and Sarah McCally Morehouse, *State Politics, Parties and Policy* (New York: Holt, Rinehart & Winston, 1981), chap. 3, "Pressure Groups versus Political Parties."

12. For the provisions of the lobby laws in the fifty states, see COGEL, *Campaign Finance, Ethics & Lobby Law Blue Book 1988–89: Special Report* (Lexington, Ky.: Council on Governmental Ethics Laws through The Council of State Governments, 1988), 157–68.

13. Truman's definition is: "An interest group is any group that is based on one or more shared attitudes and makes certain claims on other groups or organizations in the society for the establishment, maintenance or enhancement of forms of behavior that are implied by the shared attitudes" (David B. Truman, *The Governmental Process* [New York: Alfred A. Knopf, 1951], 33). Despite its insight, the Truman definition has been criticized on the basis of its emphasis on "shared attitudes" and the modes of political behavior that result. Subsequent works, especially those by Clark and Wilson and by Olson, persuasively challenge the notion that group members share common reasons for joining or maintaining membership in a group, or that all members are concerned or aware of the political goals of the group. See Peter B. Clark and James Q. Wilson, "Incentive Systems: A Theory of Organizations," *Administrative Science Quarterly* 6 (1961), 219–66; Mancur Olson, *The Logic of Collective Action: Public Goods and the Theory of Groups* (Cambridge: Harvard University Press, 1965); also see Terry M. Moe, *The Organization of Interests* (Chicago: University of Chicago Press, 1980).

14. COGEL, *Campaign Finance,* 157–68.

15. See Clive S. Thomas and Ronald J. Hrebenar, "Interest Groups in the States," in Virginia Gray, Herbert Jacob, and Robert Albritton, eds., *Politics in the American States: A Comparative Analysis,* 5th ed. (Glenview, Ill.: Scott, Foresman; Boston: Little, Brown, 1990), chap. 4.

ILLINOIS

Political Microcosm of the Nation

DAVID H. EVERSON and SAMUEL K. GOVE

Illinois is a political microcosm of the nation. The state has a history of backing winners in presidential elections. In this century it has failed to do so only twice, in 1916 and 1976. Even more significantly, the shape of the two-party presidential vote in Illinois faithfully follows that of the nation.[1] Illinois reflects national political trends because of its social, economic, and political pluralism.

The state's inhabitants number slightly over 11.5 million, with a minority population of about 21 percent including blacks (15 percent) and Hispanics (6 percent). This minority population is concentrated in Chicago and East St. Louis. Illinois has long had an individualistic and patronage-oriented political culture. In the past the state was afflicted with periodic episodes of political corruption. At the state level such has not been the case recently. The relationship of Chicago, with its legendary political machine, to the rest of the state has tended to dominate the political agenda. Illinois has had strong, but nonideological, two-party competition, and its interest group system likewise exhibits the politics of pragmatism.

Socioeconomic and Political Environment

Illinois is the 6th largest state, according to the 1986 census. It has a striking economic and demographic diversity. Because of the mix of industry and agriculture, the state was once a microcosm of the nation's economy as well. In recent years Illinois has lost jobs from its industrial and manufacturing base, and its economy is in transition.

Within its boundaries can be found one of the nation's major urban areas—Chicago (Chicago is the only city in the state with more than 150,000 inhabitants); a fast-growing suburban area—the "collar counties"—encircling Chicago; a rich corn and soybean farming belt in downstate Illinois; and a far southern coal-mining region more reminiscent of Kentucky than the Midwest. As a whole the state is wealthy; the median income (over $22,000) is 6th in the nation. There are pockets of extreme poverty, however, in Chicago, East St. Louis, and far southern Illinois. Moreover, the recent slump in the farm economy has hurt downstate cities (such as Peoria and the Quad Cities) because of their dependence on the manufacture of farm implements.

Illinois has a complex economic and political structure with sharp regional divisions. The current splits involve Chicago, the suburban collar counties, and the rest of the state (labeled *downstate*). Within these regions there are other subdivisions: pluralism within pluralism. The state is divided politically, and regional politics affect most decision making, especially in the legislature. Alliances between regions are often necessary to break policy deadlocks.

Illinois's political parties vary in effectiveness. On a statewide basis the Republicans are stronger and better organized than the Democrats. The Cook County Democratic party historically tended to dominate the state organization and has been more concerned with Cook County than with the state as a whole. In the General Assembly, however, the Chicago bloc was the most cohesive unit, taking its directions from Mayor Richard J. Daley. In the 1980s the Cook County Democrats splintered and the state Democratic organization seemed to be more active. However, neither party would come close to meeting the stringent cohesiveness requirements of the responsible parties model.[2]

Two-party competition is alive and well in Illinois. Republican James R. ("Big Jim") Thompson was governor from 1977 to 1992. From 1982 to 1992 the Democrats controlled both houses of the General Assembly. Until 1984 the parties usually divided control of the state's U.S. Senate seats. Then Democratic Congressman Paul Simon defeated Republican incumbent Charles Percy, leaving the state with two Democrats in the Senate. After the 1986 elections the Democrats controlled thirteen U.S. House seats and the Republicans nine. Illustrative of the generally close party competitiveness in recent years is the striking fact that "of the more than 19 million votes cast for Illinois congressional candidates . . . from 1972–1980, only slightly more than 20,000 votes separate the two parties."[3]

In the 1986 general election, the voters did not seem to follow the lead of either party. They continued to show much independence. Ticket splitting has been rampant in statewide elections since the early 1970s.[4] Voters seem to vote for candidates more as individuals than as party standard bearers. In 1986 incumbent Republicans won two statewide offices (governor and secretary of state); the Democrats won the others, including the three low-visibility seats on the Board of Trustees of the University of Illinois. (This vote is often used as a rough indicator of basic party support.) A factor that helped the two incumbent Republicans win reelection was the presence of two LaRouche candidates for lieutenant governor and secretary of state on the Democratic ballot (they had beaten organization-supported candidates in the Democratic primary). In addition to winning most statewide offices, the Democrats retained control of both houses of the legislature.

In the executive branch of Illinois state government the appointment process involves a mixture of professionalism and patronage. Politics play an important role in many decisions; despite civil service, patronage is not dead in Illinois. Hiring freezes have been used to control the appointment process, because the governor's office has to approve exemptions.

The legislature is also quite political. It is organized on a partisan basis, and many decisions are made on partisan roll calls. The partisan staff—assigned and controlled by leadership—is divided equally between the majority and minority parties. If a 1970 study of state legislature effectiveness were replicated, Illinois would still receive high marks for legislative modernization in comparison with other state legislatures.[5] The Illinois General Assembly would be clearly at the "professional" end of the citizen-professional state legislative continuum. In fact, nearly half of the legislators describe themselves as "full time" in the *Illinois Blue Book*.

Illinois's political culture is mixed, but the predominant strand is "individualistic" and patronage-oriented. And as Jack Van Der Slik and Kent Redfield point out, "The most obvious example of individualistic political culture . . . [has been] the regular Democratic party of Cook County."[6] The recent splits in the Chicago Democratic organization have meant that a solid bloc of votes is no longer automatically deliverable by the machine in the legislature.

The individualistic political culture emphasizes politics as a professional activity with material goals.[7] For the most part, that description fits the interest groups in the state as well. Interest groups in Illinois are numerous and diverse. They represent an astonishing variety of perspectives. They spend large sums of money, especially on campaigns, but they are not closely regulated by the state government. There have been scandals involving interest groups as recently as the 1970s,[8] but in the early 1990s they are not particularly controversial. There is no single dominant interest group and no dominant lobbyist such as the legendary Arthur H. Samish in California.

The interest group system in Illinois fits neatly into the pragmatic and bargaining political culture of the state. Interest groups are widely regarded as legitimate actors by other players in the game. Ideological conflicts between groups are downplayed. "Let's cut a deal" is the name of the game. Ultimately, compromise of competing interests — brokered by the politicians — is assumed.

The Legal and Political Environment of Interest Group and Lobby Activity

Consistent with its individualistic political culture, Illinois is not a reform-minded state with respect to the political rules of the game. This attitude is illustrated by the weak laws regulating lobbyists and lobbying. Moreover, in contrast to many progressive or moralistic states, Illinois does not have the general initiative and referendum mechanisms. Initiatives are limited to changes in the structure and procedures of the legislative article of the 1970 constitution. Any further efforts to strengthen regulatory legislation would have to be enacted by the legislature. And the majority of the legislators are not unhappy with the present law. Only a major scandal accompanied by intense lobbying from an organization like Common Cause could move the legislature to strengthen the law.

The first Illinois law regulating interest groups was adopted in 1957 — after the Orville Hodge scandal in the auditor's office — when illegal actions by lobbyists were uncovered. The 1957 law was quite weak and was replaced by the current law in 1969. It has not been amended since.

The current law provides that a person has to register with the secretary of state if "for compensation, or on behalf of any person other than himself, [he] undertakes to promote or oppose the passage of any legislation." But the law contains a long list of people who do not have to register, including those who lobby but not for compensation, employees of the media, and government employees, among others. For example, Phyllis Schlafly, who led the fight against ratification of the Equal Rights Amendment in Illinois, did not register as a lobbyist. There is little enforcement, although the secretary of state publishes a list of registrants. The Legislative Research Unit of the General Assembly reorganizes the information provided by the secretary and categorizes interest groups in a separate publication.

A provision of the law that many would consider weak concerns the financial reporting requirements. Lobbyists are required to submit reports listing expenditures made to influence the legislative process. The person benefiting from each expenditure must also be listed. Enforcement is again almost nonexistent, primarily because of loopholes in the statute that exempt most common lobbying expenses from reporting requirements. For example, the law does not require the reporting of funds used for salaries of lobbyists and staff, or for research, advertising, travel, and office expense. A minority of lobbyists even bother to report expenditures, and virtually none report any exceeding $1,000. The *State Journal Register* reported on March 24, 1992 (p. 26), that according to figures compiled by Common Cause, the nine hundred registered lobbyists reported spending only $297,000 in Springfield in 1990, a little over $300 per lobbyist! The existing law is so weak that strengthening legislation is regularly introduced, as it has been again in the 1991 session.

Although not much can be learned from the lobby registration reporting requirements, helpful information is available from the campaign finance law requirements, the source of much of the data we use in this chapter on interest group expenditures. Again, the reports filed by candidates and campaign committees are not published but are available in the office of the State Board of Elections.

Like the lobby registration law, the campaign finance law is weak compared to laws in some other states. There is no limit on campaign expenditures. Nor is there any limit on contributions from PACs, other organizations, or individuals. Illinois law does not require businesses or labor unions to form PACs to give contributions.

The key to the Illinois campaign finance law is disclosure. Campaign finance reporting requirements in Illinois are relatively uncomplicated. Campaign committees or candidates who raise or spend more than $1,000 must file reports with the state board. Campaign committee receipts must be listed. Periodic reports must be filed during an election year. Annual reports must include all income reportable under the law and most expenditures for the year. Only contributions of $150 or more must be attributed to the giver. The legislature has not allowed computerization of campaign finance records, making research difficult. One must search every legislator's reports to find out the amount of special interest money received.

Not surprisingly, there is no provision for public funding of state campaigns, although in 1983 and 1985 bills to so fund the gubernatorial campaigns were introduced and passed by the Democratically controlled General Assembly. In both cases the Republican governor vetoed the bills, and the vetoes were sustained. In the spring of 1987 proponents of partial public funding of gubernatorial elections introduced the legislation again. The sponsors expressed cautious optimism that Governor Thompson might sign this bill, in part because it was thought unlikely he would seek a fifth term. Of course, this view assumed that the bill would pass the General Assembly again. It did not. In June two partial public financing bills were assigned to "interim study" in the House Election Law Committee.

The only recent "scandal" involving lobbying was the very unusual case of Wanda Brandstetter, a supporter of the Equal Rights Amendment who was convicted of attempting to bribe a state legislator. She had handed to a legislator a card which made an "offer of help in your campaign + $1000 for pro ERA vote." Apparently, it was the explicit quid pro quo that made this action a bribe: "The court upheld Brandstetter's conviction for offering a $1000 campaign contribution to a state representative in 1980 in exchange for a favorable vote on the Equal Rights Amendment. Under the law, it's illegal to make or request the campaign contribution in exchange for a specific vote or action. But it's legal to make a contribution to support a cause, or in unspoken hopes of gaining access."[9] The maximum penalty for bribery is a $10,000 fine and seven years in jail. Brandstetter was given a one-year conditional discharge and fined $500.

Illinois has an interest group system to match its social and political diversity. In 1985, 486 groups were registered to lobby the General Assembly. But as noted above, registration pertains to a legal definition of *interest group* which does not include all organizations that attempt to influence public policy in Illinois. For example, more than sixty legislative liaisons are employed by the code departments, the constitutional officers, and other state offices to represent the interests of the various state agencies. These liaisons function for all practical purposes as lobbyists.

Contrary to Harmon Zeigler's general assertion that "the range of lobbying in state legislatures is rather narrow,"[10] the spectrum of groups represented by registered lobbyists in Illinois is wide. It extends from the Illinois State Acupuncture Association to the township of Zion. The registrants include single-issue groups such as the National Rifle Association, legislative consulting firms, and large multipurpose organizations such as the Illinois State Chamber of Commerce. It also includes public interest groups such as the Coalition for Political Honesty and social welfare groups such as the Coalition for Governmental Concerns. Local units of governments are also well represented.

The variety of interests seeking access in Springfield is illustrated by an article in the *Chicago Tribune* which noted that "some of Chicago's top sports moguls . . . are sending teams to Springfield this week. But there are no athletes on these squads and they aren't going Downstate to play games. They are political lobbyists. And depending on which sports enterprise they work for, they will be asking the General Assembly for help in building a stadium, for public works money, for tax breaks and perhaps for permission to play at night."[11] (It is only in Illinois that night baseball could become a legislative issue because, as all baseball fans know, until 1989 Wrigley Field had no lights.)

At the national level the recent interest group literature calls attention to dramatic change: the growth of public interest groups, the explosion of the number of PACs, and the increase in single-issue groups. Despite these developments, business and corporate interests tend to predominate in the Washington pressure system in terms of sheer numbers and resources.[12] As might be expected, given the claim that Illinois is a political microcosm of the nation, the state shows parallels to the national picture. Consider the growth of PACs. At the national level the number of PACs increased by 684 percent from 1974 to 1986. In Illinois the number increased by "a whopping 1,171%."[13] In just one year, 1986, 108 new PACs were created in the state.

Moreover, PACs have become an increasingly important element in the financing of state legislative elections in Illinois. In 1986 the top six PACs in contributions "contributed roughly $1.5 million to legislative candidates in Illinois, . . . approximately three times the amount contributed by these same PACs only ten years earlier."[14] And just as PAC spending tends to favor incumbents at the national level, so it does in Illinois, and the gap is widening.[15]

About two out of every five groups registered to lobby in Illinois are businesses or are business related (Table 2.1). Less than 10 percent represent social welfare or public interest groups. These figures are consistent with national trends. Zeigler notes that "about 58 percent of the registered lobbyists in the American states represent business."[16]

The 1985 data on lobbyists (see Table 2.2) support and extend the conclusions arrived at via Table 2.1. Business predominates in representation in the Illinois pressure system. Six out of every ten lobbyists in Illinois represent some form of business, a figure very close to Zeigler's.

The sheer number of lobbyists representing various interests is an index of the changing shape of the interest group system in Illinois. In 1986 a "record number of lobbyists, 678, registered with the state. . . .

Table 2.1. Illinois interest groups, by type, 1985

Type	No.	%
Business or business-related	198	41
Agriculture	13	3
Education	37	8
Health associations	47	10
Professional associations	35	7
Labor unions	39	8
Local governments	31	6
Contract lobbying firms	40	8
Public interest groups	29	6
Social welfare	12	2
Unclassified	5	1
Total	486	100

Source: Illinois Legislative Research Unit, Directory of Registered Lobbyists, 1985.

That was nearly 300 more than were registered 10 years ago."[17] Between 1961 and 1973 the total number of lobbyists actually declined, and the number representing business associations declined as a percentage of the total and as an absolute number (Table 2.2). Note that public interest and education groups did not rate separate categories in either 1961 or 1973.

Table 2.2. Illinois lobbyists, by type of group represented, 1961, 1973, and 1985

Type of Group	1961		1973		1985	
	No.	%	No.	%	No.	%
Agriculture	9	2	35	11	20	2.9
Business	270	56	152	49	413	60.9
Labor	84	17	47	15	50	7.3
Professional	37	8	29	9	81	11.9
Local government	85	17	45	15	33	5.8
Public interest					28	4.1
Education					41	6.0
Other					12	1.8
Total	485	100	308	99	678	101

Sources: James Andrews, "Interest Groups in Illinois Government," in Edgar G. Crane, ed., Illinois: Political Processes and Governmental Performance (Dubuque, Iowa: Kendall/Hunt, 1980), 194; Illinois Research Unit, Directory of Registered Lobbyists, 1985.
Note: Because of rounding, percentages may not add to 100.

Illinois Lobbyists

About 40 percent of Illinois lobbyists work full time at their job. They are "recruited most commonly from law or business and, especially among business lobbyists, are likely to have had background experience similar to the legislators themselves. They are also likely to be middle-aged, white and male and relatively well-educated."[18] Among the 678 registered lobbyists in Springfield in 1985, 14 were former legislators. In addition, two former legislators served as liaisons for state agencies. These figures are consistent with the averages for the recent past.

Although the backslapping, wheeler-dealer type of lobbyist can still be found hanging out at the brass rail in the capitol or at a local watering hole, a new breed of professional lobbyist has emerged. In the new breed, information and expertise are the keys to influence. Illustrative of the trend is Saul Morse—election law lawyer, lobbyist, member of the state Human Rights Commission, and a paraplegic. Morse previously had experience with the Illinois Commerce Commission and as a Senate Republican staffer. This law firm represents several major clients in Illinois, including the Illinois Medical Society, which has its own highly competent lobbying staff. Morse rejects the stereotype of influence peddler and emphasizes the "educator" aspects of the role. In 1987 the General Assembly passed a major revision of the Medical Practice Act: "The 123-page bill was drafted entirely in Morse's office."[19] (The bill passed both houses as an agreed bill after the governor's staff and legislative leaders reached a compromise that deferred hard decisions on other medical issues—a characteristic mode of resolving group conflict in Illinois.)

Several writers have attempted to classify various types of Illinois lobbyists. One such classification divides lobbyists into four types: administrators, watchdogs, informants, and contact people.[20] This classification suggests the roles that Illinois lobbyists play. An "administrator" is likely to be the executive vice-president of an association "with general responsibility for the group's activities." "Watchdogs" help "keep their associations informed on the actions taken by the legislature rather than persuade lawmakers to act on the group's behalf." Watchdogs can be seen at committee hearings and floor sessions taking copious notes on yellow legal pads. Naturally, lobbyists who are primarily watchdogs work in tandem with other, more active lobbyists. "Informants" direct communications, especially information, toward legislators. Finally, there are the "contact men," who "interact most frequently with legislators and spend most of their time in the hallways and galleries of the legislative chamber."

Groups that can hire large lobbying staffs, such as the Chamber of Commerce, may be able to specialize and designate specific roles for their lobbyists. Lobbyists for small organizations lacking financial resources may find themselves playing all four roles.

Veteran Illinois lobbyist Robert Cook has provided another breakdown of types of lobbyists. His list includes executive directors of associations, governmental relations representatives of large associations, contract lobbyists, legal firm lobbyists, and governmental lobbyists. Cook's first category, the executive director, is very similar to the "administrator": "This person is . . . responsible for membership services, conference planning, and all activities required to sustain the organization." Governmental relations lobbyists represent "a large association, major company or union." Contract lobbyists, whose ranks are growing, represent "several clients."[21] Cook, a longtime lobbyist for realtors, recently opened such an agency.

In a 1984 survey ranking individual lobbyists in influence, four of the top ten were contract lobbyists, including the top lobbyist, Gerald Shea, a former Democratic leader in the House. Shea illustrates the old and the new in Illinois lobbying: "A blunt man who favors dark suits and slender, filter-tipped cigars, [he] is a fixture at the statehouse: along the brass railing outside legislative chambers, in the recesses of hearing rooms . . ., or at closed sessions in legislative leaders' offices."[22] Shea combines the skills of the behind-the-scenes power broker with the latest developments in contract lobbying. In a recent session Shea's firm represented thirty-three separate clients.

Cook's next category—the law-firm lobbyist—is a subcategory of the contract lobbyist. Saul Morse is an example. Law-firm lobbyists are often retained because of a "combination of legal skills and contacts in government." Next, there are the "lobbyists representing government." In this category one might find the Illinois Municipal League lobbyists, representatives of the Illinois Association of School Boards, and the many legislative liaisons representing state agencies. It is common for these liaisons to move from agency to agency or from liaison to private interest group and back. Cook's last category is the "volunteer lobbyist," who "spend[s] time in Springfield in behalf of students, senior citizens, and cultural and other groups."[23] For example, until the mid-1980s the lobbyist of the state League of Women Voters was such a volunteer.

Interest Group Tactics

Illinois's interest groups use the full range of standard tactics in trying to influence public policy. Their actions are focused on, but not limited to, the Illinois General Assembly.

Clearly, campaign contributions to legislative candidates, legislative leaders, and candidates for governor—to gain access—is one tactic that deserves scrutiny. In Illinois, as elsewhere, the costs of political campaigns have skyrocketed. From 1984 to 1986 the cost of House elections rose 22 percent and Senate elections an astonishing 135 percent (the latter figure is probably due to the close division in partisan control of the Senate, which has led both sides to invest resources in tight races).[24] As elsewhere, a major reason for the rise is the increasing use of television for campaigning. This development has led to a sharp upturn in the flow of PAC money to candidates as they "go hunting where the rabbits are."[25] It has been reported that "an estimated $16 million was poured into state election campaigns . . . in the past two and a half years by the political action committees."[26] Such contributions are, as noted above, heavily targeted to incumbents and are, therefore, bipartisan in nature. Contributions to challengers by major PACs are sharply down in the 1980s,[27] and it is increasingly difficult to defeat incumbent legislators.[28] This means that the major groups are backing winners a substantial percentage of the time.

In 1983–84 the Illinois State Medical Society topped the list of contributors: "Jeffrey Holden, lobbyist for the clout-heavy Illinois State Medical Society, said contributions simply mean 'you'll at least have the opportunity to talk. . . . There aren't any members of the legislature we can't at least talk to.' "[29]

The top three PAC contributors in 1983–84 legislative elections were the Medical Society, the Manufacturers' Association, and the Education Association (Table 2.3). In 1984–85 a similar pattern was evident except that two labor organizations joined the list of the top ten—the Teamsters Volunteers in Politics and the Association of Federal, State, County and Municipal Employees. In that year fifteen groups contributed more than half of the special interest money given to legislative candidates. Business groups would be quick to point out, however, that such lists do not take into account in-kind contributions (for vote mobilization and the like) made by large member organizations such as unions.

The pattern of contributions in the 1986 gubernatorial election was much different from that in the legislative elections. Most of the large

Table 2.3. Top ten interest group contributors to legislative candidates in Illinois, 1983-84 and 1984-85

July 1983-June 1984	July 1984-June 1985
Illinois Medical Society	Illinois Manufacturers' Association
Illinois Manufacturers' Association	Illinois Medical Society
Illinois Education Association	Illinois Education Association
Illinois Bankers Association	Illinois Trial Lawyers' Association
Illinois Dental Society	Certified Public Accountants Society
Illinois Association of Realtors	Illinois Bankers Association
Illinois Hospital Association	Teamsters Volunteers in Politics
New Car & Truck Dealers Association	State Bar Association
State Bar Association	Association of Federal, State, County,
Certified Public Accountant Society	and Municipal Employees
	Illinois Dental Society

Sources: Chicago Tribune, February 9, 1986, p. 18; "Rating the Clout of Lobbying Groups," State Journal-Register, November 25, 1984, p. 4.

contributions tended to come from individuals, law firms, and specific businesses, not from PACs. Again, there are no limits on the size of contributions by corporations, individuals, and PACs. And there were sharp differences between the candidates. According to Common Cause, Governor Thompson received 46 percent of his $7.11 million contributions from special interests (including PACs) and 30.9 percent from individuals. (The remainder came from nonitemized contributions and from Republican party organizations.) Senator Adlai E. Stevenson III received 12 percent of his less than $2.39 million from special interests and a whopping 55.9 percent from large (over $150) individual contributions—primarily from a few sources, including $480,000 from one individual.[30] After the election the governor received a $100,000 contribution from an agribusiness company that had previously received a $6 million grant from the state government to build a coal-fired furnace at its plant.[31]

One of the significant recent developments in Illinois politics is the formation and widespread use of legislative campaign committees controlled by the legislative leadership.[32] In moving to this practice, Illinois has followed the lead of other states such as California. In essence, contributors give money to the personal campaign committees of the leaders or to PAC committees controlled by the leaders. These committees in turn distribute the money to candidates in selected races. This system began to develop in the late 1970s but mushroomed in the 1980s. Presumably, this method of financing campaigns should strengthen the legislative parties vis-à-vis the interest groups, because winning legislative candidates owe a major obligation to the party leadership. The stakes in this game can be seen by the fact that in 1986 the Republican House campaign committee contributed as much as $49,000 and $33,000 to single campaigns. Along with the financial assistance comes technical assistance and manpower, as both sides struggle for control of the legislature in time for the 1990 reapportionment.

Legislative leaders actually have control of two types of funds: legislative campaign committees and their personal campaign war chests. In 1985 House Speaker Michael Madigan and House Minority Leader Lee Daniels received $127,050 (out of a total of $474,000) and $74,250 (out of a total of $220,000), respectively, from special interests for their personal campaign treasuries. Senate President Phil Rock raised $52,000 (out of a total of $112,000). Since none of the leaders faces strong opposition in his or her district, this personal campaign money can be diverted to other legislative races.

In 1984–85 the leadership committees raised the following amounts: Senate GOP, $383,000; Senate Democrats, $140,000; House GOP,

$323,600; and House Democrats, $428,000. The House Republicans had about $500,000; the House Democrats, about $900,000; the Senate Democrats, about $250,000; and the Senate Republicans, almost $400,000.

Some of this money directed to leaders seems to be quid pro quo. In 1986, after the tort reform legislation favorable to the legal profession was engineered by House Speaker Madigan, more than $200,000 was contributed by lawyers' groups to the Friends of Michael Madigan fund.[33]

A dubious practice that has developed recently is the holding of fundraisers during the legislative session close to the time of crucial votes. For example, in 1985, "nine days before the House Financial Institutions Committee took a crucial vote on a banking bill, the Illinois Bankers Association, which strongly backed the measure, contributed $2,000 to House Democrats. When the committee voted on the proposal, Democrats helped defeat a Republican-sponsored amendment opposed by the bankers association. The committee then passed the banking measure."[34] The appearance of a quid pro quo in such circumstances is difficult to avoid.

The development of legislative campaign committees appears to strengthen the hand of legislative leaders because members elected to the General Assembly owe a debt to the leadership, especially those in tight races. House Speaker Madigan has been particularly deft in converting these committees into influence on policy, although not without causing some restlessness in the ranks.

In 1986 some interest groups began contributing large amounts of money directly to the campaign committees: the Illinois Manufacturers' PAC gave $107,900 to Senate Republicans, and the Illinois Trial Lawyers' Association contributed $32,000 to Senate Democrats. In all, the four legislative leaders, through legislative campaign and personal committees, funneled about $2.8 million to legislative candidates in 1986. The net result was a standoff—almost no change in the partisan composition of the General Assembly.

By reputation, and by dollars expended, professional and business groups, along with some labor organizations, appear to have the most clout in the General Assembly. That is often true, but it is not the whole story. There are other resources of influence in the legislative process, such as the reputation for accurate research and information. In addition, reform and public interest groups also have some impact on the process through the power of ideas as well as the demonstration of grassroots support.

For example, the Illinois Taxpayers' Federation has maintained a reputation for nonpartisan and valuable research on revenue issues.

"Some lobbies win legislative battles simply by informing and persuading without campaign contributions or legislative endorsements. The Taxpayers Federation of Illinois, a bipartisan tax watchdog, is one."[35] The reputation of the federation is so high that both candidates for governor in 1986 claimed that its executive director, Doug Whitley, supported their respective positions on the tax situation in the state. After the election Whitley was named by the governor to head a special study commission on the state tax system. And when Governor Thompson proposed a major tax increase, Whitley's reservations were often cited by opponents of the plan.

The number of lobbyists representing public interest and consumer groups in Illinois has expanded in recent years. Some of the more active groups are the Illinois Political Action Council, Common Cause, the League of Women Voters, the Coalition for Political Honesty, and the Environmental Council.

Of course, these groups are outgunned in terms of resources: "The Illinois Municipal League . . . spends $10 for every $1 spent by Common Cause–Illinois. The Illinois Manufacturers' Association has six registered lobbyists it can use to battle the stricter environmental laws sought by the Illinois Environmental Council."[36] Nonetheless, the Environmental Council has 30,000 members, and Common Cause has 10,000. These public interest and proconsumer groups have achieved some recent successes. In 1980, a citizens' petition drive launched by the Coalition for Political Honesty resulted in the reduction of the size of the Illinois House. With the assistance of House Speaker Michael Madigan, a Freedom of Information Act was passed in Illinois in 1984. A Citizens Utility Board (CUB) was created in 1983. A broad coalition of public interest and social welfare groups and unions, again with the assistance of the Speaker, achieved the passage of voter registration reform in 1984. The Illinois Political Action Council and CUB were both involved in the rewriting of the public utilities act in 1985.

During the legislative session Illinois interest groups use a wide range of tactics to attempt to influence the course of legislation. They include one-on-one meetings with legislators, testifying before legislative committees, and stimulating grass-roots (constituency-based) pressure on legislators. As noted above, interest groups are often directly involved in the drafting of legislation. Groups participate in building coalitions and plotting legislative strategies. Several groups have legislative networks back in the districts which can quickly generate communication to legislators.

Illinois interest groups are also aware of the pressure points in a modern legislature. For example, a manual on how to lobby notes that "many lobbyists . . . mistakenly forget about legislative staff."[37] Because Illinois has a highly developed system of professional staff, access to these individuals may be as significant in terms of the details of legislation as access to legislators themselves.

Because of the nature of legislative decision making in Illinois—particularly the relatively weak committee system[38]—interest groups must remain alert throughout the "dance of legislation." It often said around the General Assembly that "we should all have the life expectancy of an Illinois bill." Many legislators introduce innocuous "vehicle bills" that can be amended at later stages in the process. The "nine lives" of Illinois bills present both opportunity and danger for interest groups—opportunity to get a bill passed that earlier seemed dead, and danger that something you thought was buried got slipped into an amendment or a conference committee report. Illinois's rules governing the subjects of conference committee reports are generous. It is even alleged that some sharp lobbyists have conference committee reports written in March for use in June.

The Illinois governor has the amendatory veto, which means, in practice, that he or she can make substantive changes in legislation as well. Thus the job of lobbying legislation does not end when it passes the General Assembly. Indeed, the amendatory veto means that the governor need not be as active in trying to shape legislation in the legislative process during session. He or she can afford to sit back, amend legislation at the veto stage, and because it takes 60 percent to override, leave bill sponsors with a take-it-or-leave-it choice in the veto session.

Interest groups also lobby state agencies that implement policy and write administrative regulations. In 1977 the General Assembly created the Joint Committee on Administrative Rules (JCAR), which monitors administrative regulations to determine if they are consistent with legislative intent. Interest groups are somewhat active in seeking favorable interpretations from JCAR, which has the power to file objections to rules and to seek new legislation.

Illinois is not immune from more unconventional lobbying as well. The state was a prime battleground in the effort to ratify the Equal Rights Amendment in the late 1970s. No recent issue has seen more intense and drawn-out lobbying. Efforts ranged from conventional actions such as testimony, to demonstrations, to disruption and civil disobedience. Those opposed to the ERA, led by the redoubtable Phyllis Schlafly, distributed baked goods to lawmakers. Frustrated advocates of the ERA chained themselves to a statue in the capital, went on hunger strikes, and disrupted sessions. As noted above, one pro-ERA lobbyist was convicted of attempted bribery. In the end, the Illinois Legislature's requirement of an extraordinary majority (three-fifths) frustrated the movement.

One way to get a sense of how interest groups fare in Illinois is to examine characteristic modes of resolving conflict. One recurring pattern of legislative decision making is the "agreed bill" — decision making by "treaty" between organized interest groups "ratified" by the legislature. Other typical Illinois patterns of policy making include consensus between the governor and the mayor of Chicago and the more recent practice of decision making at the summit by the governor and the four legislative leaders.[39]

The agreed-bill practice is of special interest because it places decision making directly in the hands of organized groups, in effect delegating legislative power to private groups. Illinois has a long history of using the agreed-bill process to arrive at policy decisions, especially in the labor-management area. In 1965, after noting that Illinois legislative committees often seek informal agreed bills (a practice that continues), James Andrews described the agreed bill as "legislation by 'collective bargaining,' the procedure by which representatives of two strong counter-interests negotiate as if they were diplomats, entirely outside the legislature, and then submit their treaty for ratification."[40]

The agreed-bill tradition in the Illinois General Assembly goes back at least as far as the 1920s. According to Gilbert Y. Steiner, the practice started well before the passage of federal unemployment compensation legislation in the 1930s: "The use of the agreed bill technique was well known prior to the development of unemployment compensation legislation. . . . Indeed, by 1937, when unemployment compensation first became an important issue here, there had been more than twenty years of experience both with an explicit statutory demand for an agreed bill in mining, and with informal arrangements leading to agreement."[41]

In his study of "legislation by collective bargaining," Steiner made several points about the practice in Illinois. First, the requirement of a constitutional majority (a majority of the elected membership) to pass legislation in Illinois "appears to be a strong argument in favor of the use of the agreed bill"[42] because such majorities are not easy to obtain when there is balanced conflict among interested parties. This may have been more true in the Illinois House when multimember districts and cumulative voting meant that partisan control tended to hover around the 50–50 mark, thereby making bipartisan coalitions necessary for passing bills. In 1980 Illinois voters cut back the size of the General Assembly and eliminated cumulative voting and multimember districts. Second, an agreed bill is more likely when a principle, such as unemployment compensation, has been agreed on and the question is how to implement it.

In the absence of such fundamental agreement, the parties may simply deadlock on first principles. Third, an important factor leading to agreement is the perception that "sooner or later, the legislation is going through anyway."[43] In Illinois as elsewhere, when the perception spreads that there's only one train leaving the station, individuals and groups figure they had better get on board and not get left behind.

After extensive use from the 1930s to the late 1950s, the agreed-bill practice lapsed somewhat until the mid-1970s. In 1977 the outlines of a new agreed-bill procedure emerged on the issue of product liability, a forerunner of the broader tort liability issue of 1986. The legislature used its subcommittee structure to bring contending groups together and undertook the research necessary to make policy.

> In the Spring of 1978, the Legislature adopted new product liability legislation with only three negative votes in the House and none in the Senate. It was the result of demanding and careful negotiations over several weeks. Among the groups involved were representatives of manufacturers, insurers, trial lawyers, Chicago and State bar associations and the State Chamber of Commerce. Presiding at the several meetings were subcommittee chairmen and legislative sponsors, assisted by committee staff. The final negotiating meeting was held in the office of the Speaker of the House with his participation.[44]

The new agreed-bill process differs in one important respect from that of the past. The active involvement of elected officials at the negotiation stage is characteristic of the process as it has evolved.

In the 1980s the agreed-bill technique has been revived in the area of labor-business negotiations, the subject of Steiner's 1951 work. The ten-year history (1976–86) of efforts to deal with problems in unemployment insurance and workers' compensation illustrates the practice. The story starts with a policy change that business regarded as one-sided. In 1975 the Illinois workers' compensation law had been on the books for sixty years. Democrats controlled both houses of the General Assembly and the governorship. Labor pushed for and the General Assembly passed a major overhaul of the law which was clearly pro-labor. The changes expanded employer liability and raised benefits.

By 1980 workers' compensation costs for employers had tripled. Along with the soaring costs, by 1981 Illinois business was paying $130 million a year in federal penalty tax in the unemployment compensation area and Congress was threatening to charge interest on what the state fund borrowed from the federal government. Added to these pressures, a recession loomed as the state moved into harsh economic times. These realities, along with prodding by the governor and legislative leaders, forced the two sides into negotiations. At first, progress was halting: "Business and labor produced a pseudo reform of UI [unemployment insurance] in 1979, but nothing on WC [workers' compensation]. They produced at least the preliminaries to lasting WC reform in 1980, but nothing on UI."[45]

There was a breakthrough on UI in 1981. "In an eleventh hour effort," the General Assembly passed and the governor signed a "historic UI reform bill . . . after business and labor negotiated an unprecedented agreement . . . [the agreed bill] was reinstated in the mid-1970s, chiefly to resolve the workers' compensation . . . and unemployment insurance issues that arose in 1975 when the then-Democratically controlled General Assembly radically liberalized WC and UI benefits."[46]

But the UI story was not over. The positive impact of the agreement in 1981 was short-lived. In 1981, "business and labor went to the executive mansion . . . and emerged with a $500 million settlement two days later. . . . But in 1982 the federal government started charging the state interest; in 1983 Congress removed a temporary cap on the federal UI penalty tax. And the recession went on."[47] Consequently, the agreed-bill process continued into 1983, again with nudging from the governor and legislative leaders. At a press conference in mid-March Governor Thompson announced an agreement: "We have achieved the unachievable . . . I think we have set the pattern for leadership in the nation."[48] Next the Senate amended the compromise onto a "vehicle bill" and passed it 51–0; the House followed suite 107–1, and the governor signed it into law.

The success of the unemployment compensation agreed bill was remarkable. By the end of 1984 there was a net operating surplus of $550 million in the fund. And in 1986 Governor Thompson signed "an agreement negotiated during the spring by representatives of the state's business and labor communities. The next pact extends through the end of 1987 most of the provisions of past unemployment insurance agreements and should allow the state to pay back the remaining . . . it owes to the federal trust fund."[49]

The sailing was not so smooth in workers' compensation. In 1982 a temporary compromise was reached to save business $80 million a year. In 1983 the parties were unable to reach agreement. Business ended the negotiations and opposed the legislation that was passed. However, in 1984 the sides came back to the bargaining table and the signs were more favorable. None of the participants would talk about the state of the negotiations: "That's the usual strategy when two interest groups are serious about producing an 'agreed' bill, which is designed to reflect a compromise by legislative parties as well as interest groups."[50] Indeed, an agreement was reached in 1984 in which labor accepted reduced WC benefits in exchange for reform of the administration of WC by the Illinois Industrial Commission.

In these two related areas the agreed-bill process has reemerged and has worked relatively well, although there was a breakdown in 1987 — in all probability because these issues got intertwined with Governor Thompson's tax increase proposal.[51] A major difference with past practice is that the governor and the legislative leaders now take a much more active role in the process in terms of bringing the opposing sides together and participating in negotiating the compromise.

On a smaller scale, aspects of the agreed-bill idea can be observed in Illinois legislative committees or subcommittees. For example, in 1983 a subcommittee of the Senate Judiciary Committee, along with staff, met with representatives of legal groups, prosecutors, and various women's groups to hammer out an agreed bill on reform of the state's criminal sex laws: "Representatives of the Illinois State Bar Association . . . pointed out some potential problems in the amendments to clarify definitions and redefine some of the terms of the crimes."[52] The whole group acted much like a legislative committee marking up a bill, and at times it was difficult to distinguish who were legislators and who were not. Nine hours were spent in subcommittee before an agreed bill was reached. That bill eventually passed the Senate overwhelmingly.

In other policy areas the agreed-bill formula has not been as successful, and other means of breaking interest group deadlocks have developed. Medical malpractice insurance reform is a case in point. In 1983, negotiations designed to produce an agreed bill between medical and legal groups failed. The governor then created a special task force. Both of the contending groups found things in the report that supported their positions. In the 1985 legislative session, however, the efforts of the governor and the legislative leaders to reach a "treaty" agreement between doctors and lawyers broke down. Lobbying on the issue was intense, with both sides lining up high-powered contract lobbyists to augment their own staffs. In the midst of strong grass-roots lobbying (which included a doctors' rally at the capitol), "legislative leaders, the governor and medical society representatives — but not representatives from the lawyers' groups — ironed out a proposal for medical malpractice reform."[53] This agreement gave the doctors nearly everything they wanted except a cap on jury awards for noneconomic losses due to malpractice. As would be the custom if this had been a true agreed bill, it passed both houses by overwhelming margins. But the president of the Chicago Bar Association declared: "There is no agreement to which the . . . Association is a party."[54]

Strong protests from outraged lawyers caused House Minority

Leader Lee A. Daniels to ask for some modifications in the legislation. The lawyers participated in this rump agreed-bill process and won some concessions. However, "although the lawyers were involved in the negotiations of the refined agreement, they did not endorse the final provisions."[55] Indeed, they carried the fight to the courts. In 1987 an agreed bill on the revision of the state's Medical Practice Act passed, by postponing other, more divisive issues—another frequent practice in Illinois.[56]

The medical malpractice case illustrates the fact that if the agreed-bill process does not work, the governor and the legislative leaders are willing to make hard decisions even if it means offending powerful interest groups. In the 1980s a practice of "summiteering" has replaced negotiations between the governor and the de facto leader of the Democratic party (the mayor of Chicago) as a means of making high-level policy decisions. The passage of the temporary income tax increase in 1983 is clearly an example of such decision making and stands in sharp contrast to what happened when the tax was initially adopted in 1969—when the old system was in place[57]—and to the failure to reach agreement on the governor's 1987 tax increase proposal when summitry did not work.

Tort reform provides a second illustration of the breakdown of the agreed-bill process and the substitution of another mode of conflict resolution in Illinois. Tort reform was perhaps an even tougher issue than medical malpractice because of the range of powerful interests involved: the insurance lobby, various business groups, local governments, and, again, the legal profession. The legislature finally passed a package that had few supporters. According to one lobbying newsletter, "it contained something to displease everyone. The 125-member coalition of businesses, local governments, and professional groups that had called for massive changes in the civil justice system called it 'a victory of the narrow, special interests of personal injury lawyers and their allies.' " This legislation was "largely crafted by Democratic leadership, and the vote in both houses reflected the partisan nature of the opposition to it."[58]

In other areas of intense interest group conflict, such as banking reform, the agreed-bill process has also floundered. With respect to the banking issues discussed earlier, "Illinois bankers are the first to admit they should break the deadlock in their three-way turf war, [but] neither Citicorp, the IBA [Illinois Bankers Association] nor the ICBI [Independent Community Banks of Illinois, representing downstate banking interests] is willing to give more than an inch. This throws the whole geographic deregulation issue into the laps of the governor and the legislative leaders."[59]

In the recent instances in which the agreed-bill process has failed, the reason seems to be that the parties involved have not really agreed with the basic premises needed for the process to work: (1) that there is a problem of sufficient magnitude that change is inevitable, (2) that the only question is how the change is to be implemented, and (3) that a stalemate is not preferable to any likely agreement. In the absence of the conditions for an agreed bill, Illinois most often relies on delaying the tough decisions until a consensus of the governor and the legislative leaders emerges to break the policy logjams.

Interest Group Power in Illinois

Which interest groups have the most clout in Illinois? Zeigler asserts that "business groups have no peers in reputed influence."[60] Note the word "reputed." The direct measurement of group power or influence has always been problematic. It is no less difficult than demonstrating "cause." Because of the difficulty, political scientists are usually left with a secondary question: Which groups are perceived to have the most influence? Such perceptions, of course, may also be a resource of power.

In 1981 Sarah McCally Morehouse listed "significant interest groups" in Illinois (Table 2.4). She did not rank these groups with respect to influence. She classified Illinois as a state with "moderately strong" groups. She derived her state rankings and the list from "the recent state literature,"[61] and she acknowledged the hazards of such an enterprise. Of the sources she cited, the latest publication date is 1975, and she relied on John Fenton's major work on midwestern politics, published in 1966.[62]

Nevertheless, Morehouse's list turns out to be a good beginning in identifying the most influential groups in Illinois. There appears to be

Table 2.4. Significant interest groups in Illinois

Morehouse (1981)	Strong (1984)
Illinois Manufacturers' Association	1. Illinois Medical Society
Illinois Chamber of Commerce	2. Illinois Education Association
Coal Operators' Association	3. Illinois Manufacturers' Association
Insurance companies	4. AFL-CIO
Illinois Education Association	5. Illinois Chamber of Commerce
Illinois Medical Society	6. Illinois Association of Realtors
AFL-CIO (Steelworkers)	7. Illinois Bankers Association
Illinois Retail Merchants' Association	8. Illinois Trial Lawyers' Association
Racetracks	9. Illinois Retail Merchants'
Illinois Farm Bureau	Association
Chicago Tribune	10. Illinois Farm Bureau

Source: Sarah McCally Morehouse, State Politics, Parties and Policy (New York: Holt, Rinehart & Winston, 1981); William Strong, "Rating the Clout of Lobbying Groups," State Journal-Register, November 25, 1984, p. 4.

considerable stability in such rankings from decade to decade. A 1984 survey asking Illinois legislators to assess group influence turned up similar results (Table 2.4).

The groups in this survey were ranked from one to ten in terms of influence. The two lists agree on seven groups – the Illinois Medical Society, the Illinois Education Association, the Illinois Manufacturers' Association, the Illinois Chamber of Commerce, the Illinois Retail Merchants' Association, the AFL-CIO, and the Illinois Farm Bureau. The most significant interests missing from the more recent list are the insurance lobby, which has continued to demonstrate its clout by blocking mandatory auto insurance in Illinois, and the racetracks, which recently gained limited off-track betting in the state. These omissions may show the somewhat artificial and restrictive nature of "top ten" lists more than any real diminution of influence. Why not a top twenty or fifty?

In total, fourteen interests were mentioned on the two lists. Of those fourteen, two are professional associations, two are labor organizations, and eight represent some kind of business orientation. The remaining two are the Farm Bureau and the *Chicago Tribune*. (The presence of the *Tribune* on Morehouse's list is a vestige of an era when Colonel McCormick's paper wielded considerable clout in Illinois. For a vivid description, see the oral history of George Tagge compiled by the Oral History Office of Sangamon State University.) The tilt toward representation of business interests in the total universe of Illinois groups, discussed earlier, is also present when we look at lists of "significant" or "influential" groups.

The interests of the business community are not necessarily in harmony, however. The policy preferences of retail merchants, used-car dealers, and high-tech manufacturers are not always the same. The perennial Illinois issue of branch banking can provide an illustration. As Diane Ross expressed it in *Illinois Issues: "Rape? Pillage? Plunder?* You bet. Illinois bankers don't mince words when it comes to what could be the bloodiest and bitterest of the blockbuster economic battles raging at the statehouse this June. . . . It's a life and death struggle for Illinois' hopelessly divided bankers, who have been locked in a turf war of their own for 15 years."[63] That ongoing war pitted large Chicago-based banks, represented by the Illinois Bankers Association, versus smaller downstate banks, represented by the Independent Community Banks of Illinois. More recently, the interstate banking issue has brought banking interests from outside Illinois into the fray to make it a three-cornered dispute. The smaller downstate banks want protection from expansion by the larger Chicago banks, and the out-of-state banks want to get into the Illinois market.

Moreover, big business does not always win its fights. In 1986 the tort liability reform bill was opposed by both the Illinois Chamber of Commerce and the Illinois Manufacturers' Association, supported by the Democratic Speaker of the House, passed by the Illinois General Assembly, and signed by a Republican governor. One cannot simply assume an identity of interest among the business community nor conclude that business interests always dominate in Illinois.

A closer look at some of the organizations listed in Table 2.4 suggests some of the sources of interest group influence. The Illinois Medical Society represents about 17,000 doctors and has been a leading PAC contributor to legislative campaigns in recent elections (see Table 2.3). The society runs a "key contact" system designating colleagues, sometimes legislators' own physicians, as grass-roots lobbyists. Legislators have been known to complain about being lobbied on the medical malpractice issue in hospital emergency rooms.

The Illinois Education Association (IEA) represents about 60,000 teachers and 5,000 other school employees. For several years the organization's chief lobbyist was the brother of the Senate Assistant Majority Leader (who is now a congressman). The IEA provides legions of teachers and substantial sums of money for legislative candidates. The association is a potent force on the legislative committees dealing with school policy. It also sponsors an annual lobbying day, which brings hordes of teachers to Springfield.

The Illinois Manufacturers' Association represents about 5,300 manufacturing companies, 4,000 of which employ 100 people or fewer, and sees itself in a defensive posture—attempting to prevent legislation inimical to its interests or, as their lobbyists put it, "killing other people's weird ideas." The Illinois Chamber of Commerce represents about 6,000 businesses, and fields the biggest team of lobbyists in Springfield. Its lobbyists even specialize in policy areas. Although these two business groups share many goals, it is alleged that they "often work at cross-purposes."[64]

The state AFL-CIO represents about 920,000 workers in Illinois. Its strength is in numbers and in-kind contributions of manpower to candidates. The AFL-CIO contributes a fraction of the money compared to the medical society or the manufacturers' association. The organization is moderate and politically pragmatic. In the 1986 governor's race it endorsed Republican incumbent Thompson for reelection over Democrat Stevenson.

Table 2.5 arrays the several imperfect indicators of group influence in Illinois: Morehouse's "significant" groups, the perceptual data on interest group influence, the campaign finance data from three recent peri-

Table 2.5. Convergence of measures of Illinois interest group influence

Morehouse List[a]	Legislators' Perceptions[b]	Top Contributors 1983-84	Top Contributors 1984-85	Top Lobbyists
IMA	IMS	IMS	IMA	Shea (CL)
ICC	IEA	IMA	ISM	Holden (IMS)
Coal Op	IMA	IEA	IEA	Dart (IMA)
Ins Co	AFL-CIO	IBA	TL	Bruce (IEA)
IEA	ICC	IDS	CPA	Duffy (CL)
IMS	IAR	IAR	IBA	Walsh (AFL-CIO)
AFL-CIO	IBA	HA	TEAM	Gibson (AFL-CIO)
RMA	ITLA	New Car	ISBA	Fletcher (CL)
Racetracks	RMA	ISBA	AFSCME	Vite (RMA)
IFB	IFB	CPA	IDS	Swan (CL)
Tribune				

Source: See Tables 2.3, 2.4, and William Strong, "Shea Leads in Clout, Survey Shows," State Journal-Register, November 26, 1984, p. 4.

[a]List of "significant" pressure groups; no order implied.

[b]Most influential lobbying groups in the Illinois General Assembly as rated by lawmakers (in order from one to ten).

Note:
- CL = Contract lobbyist
- IMA = Illinois Manufacturers' Association
- ICC = Illinois Chamber of Commerce
- IEA = Illinois Education Association
- IMS = Illinois Medical Society
- RMA = Illinois Retail Merchants' Association
- IFB = Illinois Farm Bureau
- IAR = Illinois Association of Realtors
- IBA = Illinois Bankers Association
- ITLA = Illinois Trial Lawyers' Association
- IDS = Illinois Dental Society
- HA = Hospital Association
- ISBA = Illinois State Bar Association

ods, and a ranking by legislators of the Illinois lobbyists with the most clout. The purpose of the table is to examine the degree to which these imperfect indicators converge on a consensus. Three groups are on all five lists: the Illinois Medical Society, the Illinois Manufacturers' Association, and the Illinois Education Association. As noted above, "the AFL-CIO does not rank among the top twenty campaign contributors. . . . The labor organization's clout comes in part from the political connections of its leaders and the manpower it can offer in elections."[65] However, the AFL-CIO is the only group to have two lobbyists make the top ten, and thus it seems reasonable to add the AFL-CIO to the top three. Adding the AFL-CIO to the list gives us four groups in the very top rank of the most influential in Illinois. Morehouse and Strong also agree on three other groups that would then rank in the next echelon: the Farm Bureau, retail merchants, and the Chamber of Commerce. It should be kept in mind that special circumstances may alter the influence of groups in specific cases. Support or opposition of any of these top groups on a bill does not make victory certain.

"Strong" and "weak" pressure systems seem to be defined by some authors in terms of the conditions associated with them rather than in terms of what they actually are. Zeigler, for example, asserts that "economically more advanced states—those with strong parties, professionalized legislatures, and well-developed public service components—tend to have weak interest groups. . . . When states are economically simplex, with poorly developed political parties, unprofessional legislatures, and a weak public service component, groups flourish."[66] By these standards, one would predict that the Illinois interest group system would be weak. But close contact with that system does not leave the observer with the impression of weakness. In fact, Morehouse classifies it as a "moderately strong" system—a classification we would not quarrel with. Something seems amiss with the theory.

The current literature suggests that strong pressure group systems are characterized by social, economic, and political homogeneity; premodern or unprofessionalized legislatures; weak political parties; and poorly developed bureaucracies. It further suggests that interest group strength is likely to be maximized where there is one dominant industry (such as coal or lumber), a relatively simple socioeconomic profile, and weak political parties. Zeigler says that "the most important aspect of a state's socio-economic structure (and one might add: political) is its level of complexity."[67] In this formulation the literature seems to equate a strong interest group system with a single predominant interest or a small set of such interests that hold sway in the legislature. A plurality of strong interest groups seems to be considered inconsistent with a strong pressure system: "Pluralism in the distribution of group influence is *not* a characteristic of strong interest group states."[68] Consequently, strong interest group systems are found in small states, particularly in the South and West.

In contrast, large, complex states with multifaceted interest groups, strong party cohesion, competitive two-party politics, professionalized legislatures, and highly developed public bureaucracies are thought to have moderate or weak pressure politics. Illinois is clearly a state that has socioeconomic diversity, a professionalized legislature, a developed public bureaucracy, and two-party competition with at least moderately strong parties. On these grounds, Illinois should not have a strong pressure system.

A key assumption of the literature on the strength of interest group systems is that strong and competitive parties will guard access to policy makers. Another is that a high degree of pluralism will result in a kind of balance-of-power standoff between the contending groups. This pluralism extends to the public sector as well, with a large, complex bureaucracy and professional legislative staff: multiple sources of information to legislators reduce the need to rely on groups for advice.

But is it not possible that pluralism and a strong pressure system may coexist? As difficult as it may be, it is necessary to try to assess interest group strength in terms of the total impact of groups on the policy process. The central issue is whether one judges the strength of an interest group system by the probability of the dominance of the system by a single, or narrow, range of interests, or whether one considers the combined impact of a range of competitive interests on public policy. In classical interest group theory, public policy is the result of the clash of group forces. As Earl Latham argued, "The legislature referees the group struggle, ratifies the victories of the successful coalitions, and records the terms of the surrenders, compromises, and conquests in the form of statutes."[69] This sounds like a literal description of Illinois's agreed-bill process — with the qualification that official groups play a significant role in the negotiations, a fact recognized by Latham. However, *no single interest* necessarily dominates. Theoretically, the balance of group interests would be determined in the struggle, and the political system would merely ratify the results. If policy makers primarily play the role of "Moses the registration clerk" and not "Moses the lawgiver," wouldn't we want to call that a strong pressure system?

Interest groups in Illinois are diverse and highly competitive. In the area of labor versus business, the balance of power is such that an agreed-bill process has periodically emerged. Illinois legislators are continually seeking a (formal or informal) consensus of the affected groups in conflict over specific issues. The net effect of the group struggle may be compromise or a temporary tilt in one direction or the other. But no single set of interests consistently predominates.

Strong pressure systems may take many forms. If, as is the case in Illinois, many interests in the state are well organized, well financed, active and sophisticated in lobbying and campaigns, and regularly involved with policy makers in decisions, even to the point of agreed bills, is this necessarily a weak or even moderate pressure system? Is, in fact, such a designation not confusing levels of analysis by assuming that small sets of dominant interests define a strong pressure system and that many competing strong interests, resulting in policy compromises, define a moderate or weak pressure system? Is it not possible that social and economic diversity and relatively strong parties are also compatible with strong pressure groups? For example, do legislative campaign committees of the type that have developed in Illinois enhance only party leadership or do they indirectly strengthen groups (such as the lawyers' association) as well by enhancing group access to those same leaders? We conclude that Morehouse's assessment of Illinois interest groups as "moderately strong" is correct.

Conclusion

Illinois is clearly a pluralistic state in terms of social, economic, and political diversity. The political culture is individualistic. The face of Illinois politics is shifting with the decline of the Chicago Democratic organization and the increase in independence in the electorate. The parties are still relatively strong, however, and party leadership in the legislature is a significant element in policy making. The system of regulation of interest groups and campaign finance is weak. The growing costs of campaigns, the increase in PACs, and the development of strong legislative campaign committees all signal the interdependency of relatively strong interest groups and political parties. In the legislative process Illinois is notable for the use of the agreed bill, particularly in connection with labor-management issues. In an informal way Illinois legislators instinctively seek the consensus of the affected groups. The case of Illinois clearly shows that complex social-economic-political systems with relatively strong parties are in no way inconsistent with moderately strong interest groups.

Notes

1. James Przybylski, "As Goes Illinois . . . The State as a Political Microcosm of the Nation," in *Illinois Elections* (Springfield, Ill.: Sangamon State University, 1979), 34–38. Also see David Everson, "Illinois: A Bellwether," in Jack R. Van Der Slik, ed., *Almanac of Illinois Politics—1990* (Springfield, Ill.: Illinois Issues, 1990), 1–5.
2. Peter W. Colby, "Illinois Politics and the Ideal of Responsible Party Government," in Edgar G. Crane, ed., *Illinois: Political Processes and Governmental Performance* (Dubuque, Iowa: Kendall/Hunt, 1980), 177–90.
3. David H. Everson and Joan A. Parker, "Congressional Elections: The Advantage of Incumbency," *Illinois Elections III* (Springfield, Ill.: Sangamon State University, 1986), 58.
4. David H. Everson and Joan A. Parker, "Ticket Splitting: An Ominous Sign of Party Weakness," *Illinois Elections III* (Springfield, Ill.: Sangamon State University, 1986), 110–13.
5. In 1971 the Citizens Conference on State Legislatures ranked Illinois as the third most capable state legislature. *The Sometime Governments* (New York: Bantam, 1971), 49.
6. Jack R. Van Der Slik and Kent D. Redfield, *Lawmaking in Illinois* (Springfield, Ill.: Sangamon State University, 1986), 23.
7. For a general discussion of state political culture, see Daniel Elazar, *American*

Federalism: A View from the States (New York: Crowell, 1972). For a discussion of Illinois's mixed political culture, see Elazar, "Competing Political Cultures in Illinois," in Elazar and Joseph Zikmund II, eds., *The Ecology of American Political Culture* (New York: Crowell, 1975), chap. 13.

8. See Mike Lawrence, "Cement Bribery Trial," *Illinois Issues,* December 1976, pp. 10–16.

9. William Strong, "Concern Voiced over Clout of PACs," *State Journal-Register,* November 27, 1984, p. 4. For an account that stresses the ironies of the conviction, see Sandra Martin, "Wanda Was Wronged," *Illinois Times,* August 20, 1980.

10. L. Harmon Zeigler, "Interest Groups in the States," in Virginia Gray, Herbert Jacob, and Kenneth Vines, eds., *Politics in the American States,* 4th ed. (Boston: Little, Brown, 1983), 99.

11. John McCarron, "Sports Lobby Chooses Up Sides in Capitol," *Chicago Tribune,* November 16, 1986, p. 1.

12. Allen J. Cigler and Burdett A. Loomis, "Introduction," in Cigler and Loomis, eds., *Interest Group Politics* (Washington, D.C.: CQ Press, 1983), 1–30. Kay Lehman Schlozman and John T. Tierney, *Organized Interests and American Democracy* (New York: Harper & Row, 1986), 70–71.

13. Larrv Sabato, *PAC Power* (New York: Norton, 1984), 117; quotation is from Ronald D. Michaelson, "The PAC Man Cometh in Illinois," *Illinois Issues,* May 1987, p. 10. Michaelson, who has a Ph.D. in political science, is the executive director of the Illinois State Board of Elections.

14. Michaelson, "PAC Man Cometh," 11.

15. Schlozman and Tierney, *Organized Interests and American Democracy,* 231. Michaelson, "PAC Man Cometh," 12.

16. Zeigler, "Interest Groups in the States," 98.

17. Tim Franklin, "In State Politics, Special Interest Rate Is 40%," *Chicago Tribune,* February 9, 1986, p. 18.

18. Robert Maple, "Role Orientations of Registered Lobbyists" (Master's thesis, Illinois State University, 1976), 102–3.

19. Toby Eckert, "Legislative Lawyer: Burying Stereotypes while Building a Reputation," *Weekend Journal, State Journal-Register,* August 21, 1987, p. 11a.

20. Terry Campo, "Lobbyists and How They Work," *Illinois Issues,* June 1980, pp. 11–12. The quotations in this paragraph are from this article.

21. Robert Cook, "Lobbyists and Interest Groups," in James D. Nowlan, ed., *Inside State Government* (Urbana: University of Illinois Press, 1982), 113–22.

22. William Strong, "Shea Leads in Clout," *State Journal-Register,* November 26, 1984, p. 4.

23. Cook, "Lobbyists and Interest Groups," 117.

24. Michaelson, "PAC Man Cometh," 11.

25. William Strong, "Concern Voiced over Clout of PACs," *State Journal-Register,* November 27, 1984, p. 4.

26. Strong "Clout of PACs," 4.

27. Michaelson, "PAC Man Cometh," 12, Tables 6, 7.

28. David H. Everson, "1986 Elections: The Crime that Didn't Happen," *Illinois Issues,* March 1987, pp. 15–17.

29. Strong, "Clout of PACs," 4.

30. Chris Gaudet, "Financing Gubernatorial Campaigns: Via Special Interests or Public Financing?" *Illinois Issues,* May 1987, p. 13.

31. Chuck Neubauer and Deborah Nelson, "Thompson Gets Biggest Campaign Gift—$100,000," *Chicago Sun-Times,* February 3, 1987, p. 6.

32. Richard R. Johnson, "Partisan Legislative Campaign Committees: New Power, Old Problems," *Illinois Issues,* July 1987, pp. 16–18.

33. Peter Ellertsen, "Legal Groups Backing Democrats," *State Journal-Register,* October 29, 1986, p. 5.

34. Franklin, "In State Politics," 2A.

35. John Dowling and William Strong, "Money Buys Power in Capital—But Is That Bad?" *State Journal-Register,* November 25, 1984, p. 3.

36. Don Sevener, "The Do-Gooders Do Better," *Illinois Issues,* July 1984, p. 8.

37. Illinois Association of School Boards, *Lobbying for the Public Schools* (Springfield, Ill.: 1985), 18.

38. David H. Everson, "Committees in the Legislative Process: The Illinois General Assembly," in Thad L. Beyle, ed., *State Government: CQ's Guide to Current Issues and Activities, 1985–86* (Washington, D.C.: Congressional Quarterly, Inc., 1985), 67–72.

39. Joan A. Parker, *Summit and Resolution* (Springfield, Ill.: Sangamon State University, 1984), 75–89.

40. James H. Andrews, *Private Groups in Illinois Government* (Urbana, Ill.: Institute of Government and Public Affairs, 1965), 25–26.

41. Gilbert Y. Steiner, *Legislation by Collective Bargaining* (Urbana: University of Illinois Press, 1951), foreword.

42. Ibid., 48.

43. Ibid., 50.

44. James H. Andrews, "Interest Groups in Illinois Government," in Crane, ed., *Illinois,* 197–98.

45. Federal Threat Forces Action on Unemployment Insurance," *Illinois Issues,* August 1981, p. 24.

46. Ibid., p. 24.

47. Diane Ross, "Unemployment Insurance Reform," *Illinois Issues,* May 1983, p. 27.

48. Ibid., 26.

49. Jeff Brody, "Jobless Debt To Be Repaid by the End of '87," *State Journal-Register,* September 10, 1986, p. 15.

50. Diane Ross, "Worker's Compensation on the Table," *Illinois Issues,* June 1984, p. 35.

51. See Michael D. Klemens, "Impasse: Unemployment Insurance and Workers' Comp," *Illinois Issues,* August–September 1987, p. 57.

52. Katherine Lawson, "Sex Crimes: Revised," *Illinois Issues,* February 1984, p. 8.

53. Debbie Willard, "Medical Malpractice," *Illinois Issues,* October 1985, p. 25.

54. Ibid., 25.

55. Ibid., 26.

56. Chris Gaudet, "Medical Practice, Malpractice and Medicare," *Illinois Issues,* August–September 1987, p. 58.

57. See Parker, *Summit and Resolution,* 1–10.

58. *Cook-Witter Report 2* (7); 2.

59. Diane Ross, "Banking Battles at the Statehouse," *Illinois Issues,* June 1985, p. 10.

60. Zeigler, "Interest Groups in the States," 99.

61. Sarah McCally Morehouse, *State Politics, Parties and Policy* (New York: Holt, Rinehart & Winston, 1981), 110, 107, 112.

62. John H. Fenton, *Midwest Politics* (New York: Holt, Rinehart & Winston, 1966).

63. Ross, "Banking Battles at the Statehouse," 6.

64. *State Journal-Register,* November 25, 1984, p. 4.

65. John Dowling and William Strong, "Money Buys Power in Capital," 3.

66. Zeigler, "Interest Groups in the States," 129–30.

67. Ibid., 111.

68. Ibid., 99.

69. Earl Latham, "The Group Basis of Politics," in Frank Munger and Douglas Price, eds., *Political Parties and Pressure Groups* (New York: Crowell, 1964), 48.

INDIANA

Interest Groups in a Changing Party Environment

DAVID J. HADLEY

As the 1989 session of the Indiana General Assembly began, two men standing ten yards apart outside the House chamber symbolized the changing nature of interest group and party politics in the state. The one, an aging, longtime, rural-county, Democratic party chairman; the other, a younger, impeccably attired, former House Speaker who is widely identified as one of the new breed of multiclient "Superlobbyists." The county chairman stood silently observing House business, killing time before an appointment with someone on the staff of the recently inaugurated Democratic governor. He was there to see about jobs for "my people." His people had been waiting since the Democrats lost the governor's office in 1968, and they were impatient with what they regarded as an unnecessarily slow hiring process. He hoped to "speed things up a bit." As the county chairman waited, Phillip Bainbridge, Democrat, Speaker-turned-lobbyist, carried on quiet conversations with a stream of legislators, both Democrat and Republican, as they returned from lunch. Two weeks passed, and as Bainbridge continued his hushed conversations on behalf of one of his fourteen clients, the county chairman reported no real progress on jobs for his people. He did, however, have a promise of license plates numbered 1 to 100 "in the 'D' series – for Democrat" to distribute among his party's faithful. Thirty years earlier, after a change of party control of the governor's office, a county chairman would have delivered jobs, not low-numbered license plates, and may well have been able to boast of some input into the governor's program, while the interest groups' and lobbyists' effectiveness would have depended, in part, on their abilities to work through county chairmen and other party leaders.

No one in Indiana would argue that interest groups and lobbyists have supplanted political parties as the key actors in Indiana politics. After all, the change in party control of the governor's office in January 1989 had directly affected lobbyist Bainbridge's work, as well as the county chairman's. But Indiana's midwestern conservatism and archetypical, traditional, party-organizational politics have been giving way to candidate-centered, media-oriented, PAC-financed campaigns and a more professionalized state government that addresses a broad, complicated agenda. The new setting offers interest groups substantial independence from local party organizational structures but still requires them to operate in a context in which party control of state policy-making machinery makes a difference.

The Sociopolitical Setting

Indiana's rural agricultural image is built more on James Whitcomb Riley's poetry and on nostalgic movies like *Hoosiers* than on reality. In fact, the Hoosier state, 12th in population, provides a good mix of metropolitan and rural residents.[1] Indiana ranks 22d and 21st, respectively, in percentages of its population who live in these environments. And the state is far from being dominated by its farm population: in 1987 only 2.8 percent of the civilian labor force was employed in agriculture, ranking Indiana 26th among the fifty states.

Indiana's most serious problems in the 1980s came not from its agricultural character, but from the fact that it ranked 6th in manufacturing employment and had become heavily dependent on the manufacture of durable goods. The state could hardly avoid deep economic trouble as the national economy underwent transition, then major recession, in the 1970s and early 1980s. As manufacturing employment as a percentage of total employment in the United States dropped from 24 percent in 1976 to 19 percent in 1986, the percentage of the Indiana workforce employed in manufacturing fell from 34 to 27.[2] The index of manufacturing activity estimating total industrial output for the state as a percentage of 1967 manufacturing production tells the tale of manufacturing decline in the state. In 1973 the index peaked at 124.0 percent of 1967 manufacturing output, then fell to a low of 90.5 in 1982. By

1986 it had recovered to only 104.4 percent of 1967 industrial output.[3] This output decline and the associated loss of 160,000 manufacturing jobs between 1977 and 1983 propelled economic development issues, which crossed traditional geographical and partisan divisions, to the top of Indiana's political agenda in the 1980s.

Although Indiana has been a predominantly urban state since 1920, it has lacked a dominant urban center. Its cities are a diverse lot separated by economic profiles, geography, culture, and character of populations. They range from cities such as Gary and East Chicago, whose economies rose and fell with the domestic steel industry and whose populations, once significantly of Eastern European descent, are increasingly black and Hispanic, to Indianapolis, the "Capital in a Corn Field," with its lighter industrial, government, and service-centered economy. They range from Fort Wayne, which for many years functioned as an agricultural service center, to Richmond, Anderson, and Kokomo, cities whose fates are tied closely to the automobile industry, and to Evansville, tucked along the banks of the Ohio River in the southwest corner of the state, culturally, geographically, and economically separated from the northern half of the state. This diversity seriously disadvantaged urban Indiana in the political arena, particularly during the state legislature's long refusal (1921–63) to redistrict itself and the county party organizations' domination of the conventions that nominated candidates for statewide office.

Socially, Indiana has its share of diversity. Its 7.6 percent black and 1.6 percent Hispanic populations rank it near the middle of the American states in minority residents. There are no other dominant ethnic populations in the state, though the concentrations of Eastern European groups in the northwestern industrial cities give those areas a political flavor missing from much of the rest of the state.

The most famous division in Hoosier state politics separates northern and southern Indiana.[4] The roots of that division, symbolized by the Old National Road, or U.S. 40, which bisects the state from east to west through Indianapolis, are embedded in geologic prehistory and in early settlement patterns. Glaciers pushed south in Indiana, scouring and flattening the northern half of the state, leaving it well suited to rich agricultural development. To the south, beyond the reach of the glaciers, the land remained rugged and hilly, ill suited for the farming activity of the north. Communities there sat isolated from one another and economically less developed than the rest of the state. Settlers from Virginia and Kentucky spread throughout the southern half of the state, while people moving from New York, Pennsylvania, and Ohio later settled the northern half. The differing perspectives in which the two halves of the state viewed the Civil War made for firm partisan divisions that survived into the mid–twentieth century. The regional division has occasionally cut across the political parties. Indiana Democrats, for example, have had to contend with split versions of their party as southern Indiana Democrats regularly cast a suspicious eye toward the more liberal, union-oriented Democrats in northern counties, where steel and automobile workers are concentrated.

Indiana's party system and recent changes in it provide the most important focus for understanding what is happening to interest group politics in the state. The strong, two-party system developed in an essentially individualistic political culture in which private concerns were central, government served limited utilitarian purposes, and politics was a line of work through which one pursued personal, social, and economic advancement.[5] This cultural orientation has been evident in the conservative cast to Indiana public policy over the years, in Hoosiers' suspicion of government and government programs,[6] and in an apparent tolerance for what would be considered in many other states corruption or unacceptable partisan practices.[7]

Although Indiana has a well-deserved reputation for delivering large margins of victory to Republican presidential candidates and in recent years the Republican party has regularly controlled statewide offices and the General Assembly, a strong, highly organized, competitive, two-party system stands at the center of Indiana politics. Republicans traditionally hold an advantage, but Democrats always challenge and with some regularity win. In 1988, after a twenty-year control of the governor's office by Republicans, Democrats elected Evan Bayh, thirty-two-year-old son of a former three-term U.S. Senator, to that office. In 1990 they won control of the state House of Representatives and elected twenty-four of the fifty members of the Senate. Although strong partisanship, particularly at the organizational level, has always characterized Indiana politics, an impressive amount of split-ticket voting aided the Democrats' comeback in 1988.[8]

County party organizations and their chairmen (they have usually been men and will be so referred to here) have historically been the backbone of the strong party system in Indiana. Traditionally, strong parties at the state level have depended on the existence of strong organizations at the county level and below. Political patronage, rather than a well-defined ideology or program, held together the entire system from top to bottom.

At least part of the state's reputation for rural conservatism through the first seven decades of the twentieth century can be traced to the place of county party organizations and their chairmen in both legislative and

executive electoral politics. As the state became increasingly maldis-
tricted under the 1921 districting plan, rural county chairmen assumed
great influence. County organizations provided convenient, effective,
and relatively inexpensive campaign support for legislative candidates;
their chairmen became natural links between legislator and district and
points of access to the policy-making process for interest groups and
lobbyists.[9]

Similarly, convention nomination of statewide candidates worked
against major urban areas and in favor of the most conservative elements of the Hoosier population. Because of the diversity among them,
urban Indiana counties had great difficulty uniting to compete with the
more conservative rural counties in choosing gubernatorial candidates.
Between 1924, when both gubernatorial candidates came from Marion
County (Indianapolis), and 1976, when these nominations were placed in
the hands of party voters, not a single additional candidate for governor
came from any of the three most populous counties in the state. During
this time Indiana governors owed their nomination to party organizations of rural counties. They expressed their gratitude with jobs, control
over automobile license branches, and by being accessible to those responsible for their nomination and election.

The place of the county organizations and their chairmen in legislative and executive arenas has changed in recent years, however. Court
decisions[10] and economic change that reduced the attractiveness of political jobs undermined the patronage system. Furthermore, change in the
agenda of state government and politics subverted county chairmen's
involvement in legislative and executive politics. As issues of economic
development, environmental management and protection, and education replaced questions of who would hire employees in the highway
department, state hospital, and parks, the burning interest of county
chairmen in state politics declined.[11] At the same time, the change in
agenda raised the stakes in state politics for a variety of interest groups.
Consumer and environmental groups contest with utility companies over
the need for the regulation of new power-generating facilities, while the
Chamber of Commerce and the Indiana Manufacturers' Association
work to moderate demands of environmental, consumer, and union
groups for the labeling of workplace hazards, issues in which local party
organizations have little direct interest.

Court-ordered redistricting and a change from convention to pri-
mary-election nomination of gubernatorial candidates also reduced the
role of county chairmen and shifted power in state government toward
the less conservative urban and suburban areas. Recent districting plans,
constructed to achieve population equality and partisan advantage, have

abandoned county units as building blocks for districts. Legislators now represent bits and pieces of four, five, or more counties. Their dependence on single-county organizations for campaign and electoral purposes evaporated with redistricting, to be replaced by the candidates' abilities to establish and fund personal organizations that link fragments of several counties. Interest group connections and political action committees stepped in to provide important campaign resources once available through local party organizations. In the process, county party chairmen lost much of their value as intermediaries or pressure points between interest group and legislator.[12]

County organizations and their chairmen lost another key to the doors of state government when in 1973 the primary replaced conventions for nominating gubernatorial candidates. Statewide recognition, access to media markets, and money replaced good relations with rural-county party people as crucial to these nominations. Again, interest groups and their PACs touted resources that could serve candidates in this new nominating process.

The Setting for Interest Group Activity

Although restructured and less dependent on grass-roots, patronage-based organizational structures, parties continue to shape government and public policy making at the state level. Interest-group representatives understand that party control of the governor's office and of the General Assembly fundamentally affects the strategic situation they face. Party control of the governor's office, even with a decline in patronage positions, still influences a broad range of executive-administrative appointments. In addition, the governor's legislative program sets much of the General Assembly's agenda.

The issue of collective bargaining for government employees illustrates how important it is to interest groups which party controls the governor's office and the fact that party control does not mean their automatic, immediate success. State and municipal employee unions, which had worked for years to gain bargaining rights, were confident in 1989 that the first Democratic governor in twenty years would place their item on his legislative agenda. Governor Bayh, however, announced early in the first General Assembly session of his term that he needed more time to study the problem and formulate a sound legislative proposal. He thus postponed until 1990 the key agenda item of one group of his strongest supporters, but party and gubernatorial support was so important to them that they publicly accepted delay.

Similarly, even with the changes in intraparty relationships, the Indiana General Assembly is, first and foremost, a partisan body. Party leadership plays a central role, and party caucuses meet regularly to discuss positions on major issues and strategies. The President Pro Tem of the Senate and the House Speaker appoint members of standing and conference committees and their chairs and have great flexibility in assigning legislation to committees.[13] So powerful has the Speaker been that he is routinely identified as the most powerful person in the state during the last ten days of a legislative session. Until 1989, when a 50–50 party split resulted in a unique cospeakers arrangement, the Speaker had the sole power to call legislation to the floor for action.[14] Such powers have always been used to the advantage of the majority party, but they have also made the Speaker, the President Pro Tem, and their parties central foci for interest groups.

The political environment and the institutional setting within which party-mediated interest group activity occurs has, however, changed markedly since 1970. The "citizen" or amateur character of the General Assembly, which for more than a century enhanced the influence of both party leadership and interest groups, has been undermined by the move to annual sessions, reduced legislative turnover,[15] and a modest increase in caucus-hired legislative staff. At the same time, however, as the legislature confronts an expanded agenda of complex issues, legislators depend heavily on the expertise offered by representatives of interest groups.

Many key elements of the system that once operated out of public view and to the advantage of party organizations and organized interests have been brought into the sunshine or distributed more broadly. Although party caucuses remain tightly closed to all outsiders, standing and conference committees have operated under open-meeting requirements since the early 1970s. Expertise in bill drafting, once handled by a single person in the legislative service agency or by a few lawyers in private practice in Indianapolis, is now available to all members from the increasingly professional Legislative Services Agency. Even something as pedestrian as low-cost photocopying has dramatically changed the flow of information about pending legislation. Before the advent of photocopying, bill texts were in short supply until they were ready for final passage. At the crucial committee stage, frequently only the bill's sponsor, the presiding officer of the chamber, the committee chairman, and perhaps a key interest group representative had copies of bills and knew the details of the legislation. Now groups opposing parts of bills, sponsoring groups, and rank-and-file committee members, as well as the chairman, can follow along as legislation is discussed and amended.

Finally, conference committees, keys to any bicameral legislature, today remain important, if somewhat less powerful, components of party and interest group influence in the Hoosier legislature. As recently as 1980, however, they embodied not only the enormous influence of party leadership, and opportunities for influence by interest groups working in conjunction with party leaders, but also the ever-present potential for corruption and abuse of power.

Conference committees are small, powerful, and controlled by the party leadership. Appointed by the Speaker and President Pro Tem, they consist of four members—a Democrat and Republican from each chamber. The small, bipartisan groups must produce unanimous reports, which makes it possible for any member to hold legislation hostage or kill it. Little wonder that interest group representatives focus strong efforts on appointments to conference committees. Since bill sponsors usually gain appointment to conferences, it is essential for a group to get "dependable" legislators to carry its bill. The party leaders who appoint the conferees, however, remain in a position to restrain them. The Speaker or President Pro Tem can replace a rogue committee member with someone more cooperative.

Until 1982 the power of the conference was virtually unlimited. Through a process called "bill stripping," the committee could replace the content of the bill that had necessitated the conference with any subject matter on which all the conferees agreed. The new content of the bill need not have passed either chamber, nor indeed even have been introduced as a bill.

The stripping procedure figured prominently in federal investigations of influence peddling in the Indiana General Assembly in the early 1980s. In one incident the Senate leader used his appointments to a conference committee on bills to reorganize the State Highway Commission and to set bonding authority for the Toll Road Commission in order to insert content requiring the state to pay half the cost of installing railroad-crossing signals. The federal investigation revealed that the Senate leader, his predecessor, and another Senate colleague had been paid by the state railroad trade association a $55,000 legal fee for which no work was done. The railroad trade association also had paid for the President Pro Tem's hotel room during the legislative session.[16]

Criminal convictions of two consecutive Senate leaders led to changes in conference committee procedures. New guidelines limit bill stripping by requiring that the content added to a gutted bill have passed at least one house. But the small conference committees operating under the unanimity rule continue to function as magnets attracting lobbyists' strongest efforts. Here interest can be defended and compromise forced, but on most issues it must be done within parameters acceptable to party leadership.

Regulation of Interest Groups

Consistent with its individualistic political culture, Indiana's statute on lobby regulation is bareboned. Passed in 1981, replacing legislation that had been in effect since 1916, the statute requires registration of lobbyists and their employers and semiannual reporting of expenditures to influence legislation. A lobbyist is "any person who engages in lobbying and who receives or expends an aggregate of $500 for lobbying in any registration year, whether the compensation or expenditure is solely for lobbying or the lobbying is incidental to that individual's regular employment."[17] *Lobbying* covers any attempt to communicate with a legislative official for the purpose of influencing a legislative action. Activities directed at executive agencies, boards, commissions, and regulatory agencies are not covered by the act. In their semiannual reports lobbyists must state total reimbursed expenditures for personal sustenance, the cost of receptions and entertainment (except when the occasions are open to the entire General Assembly by invitation), and gifts and expenditures directed to individual legislators, their staff, or families. Gifts and expenditures to legislators, staff, and families must be reported only if they exceed $100 in a day or $500 during a session.[18]

The statute requires the secretary of state randomly to select 5 percent of the reports for inspection and audit each year. That official may require that corrected reports be filed. Failure to file may result in the case's being turned over to the relevant prosecuting attorney or the state attorney general for further action. As of 1991, no prosecutions had occurred since the law was passed in 1981.

In interviews with legislators and lobbyists during the 1989 General Assembly session,[19] the vast majority (about 75 percent) considered the lobby statute to be "fair." No one considered it too strict. A number of lobbyists commented that although it was fair, it was also "useless," "stupid," or simply "a pain." One public interest group lobbyist, however, argued that the legislation was too vague and depended too heavily on the secretary of state for interpretation. He said it could have a chilling effect on the activities of those "not connected with the power" in the state.

Legislation passed in 1976 regulates campaign finance in Indiana.[20] As one might suspect in this party-oriented, individualistic state, public funding of elections does not exist. Rather, the state regulates campaign finance through public disclosure of contributions and expenditures by donors and recipients. Any contribution of $100 or more must be itemized on campaign finance reports. Although there are no limits on amounts of contributions by political action committees or individuals, corporations and labor organizations are limited to a $3,000 maximum of contributions to all statewide candidates and a $3,000 total to all party state central committees. They are also limited to total contributions of $1,000 to all legislative, district, and local offices and to a $1,000 total to all party committees other than state central committees. Statewide and state legislative candidates must file their reports with the State Election Board. The staff of the election board maintains files of reports by political action committees, party committees, and candidate committees and issues an annual report of their receipts, expenditures, and balances.

The law on campaign finance and financial disclosure has been criticized for its lack of teeth. Violations of the law are to be referred to county prosecutors for action. One former director of the State Election Board argued that "as long as violations of the law are referred to county prosecutors, who are often political allies of those accused, the law will have no teeth."[21]

Indiana's efforts to use public disclosure to monitor and limit interest group activity fall short on several fronts. First, to get a clear picture of the activity one must look for information in several different sources. The secretary of state's office maintains files on lobby registrations and lobbying expenditures. The election board gathers reports of political action committees and campaign receipts and expenditures, and it compiles a mimeographed annual report from each active committee of its total receipts, expenditures, and balances carried forward. Legislators' conflict-of-interest reports, another piece of the whole picture of interest group activities, are filed with the clerks of the House and Senate. Getting a full picture of interest group activity, even in the General Assembly, requires drawing information from three disparate sources. In addition, none of the reports is electronically coded, nor do they give all the detail one might want. One cannot determine, for example, how much multiclient lobbyists are paid by their employers, nor can one determine in much detail how lobbying funds are expended.

Interest Groups in Indiana Politics

Number and Types of Groups

Indiana has experienced the proliferation of interest groups so thoroughly documented at the national level and in other states. In 1963 an

Indianapolis newspaper reported that 346 lobbyists representing 139 organizations had registered with the secretary of state. In 1965, 413 lobbyists representing about 175 groups registered.[22] By 1989 these numbers had grown to 518 lobbyists representing 367 organizations (Table 3.1).[23] In 1965, corporate or trade associations accounted for 51 of the organizations registered; by 1989, 225 of the 368, or 60 percent of lobbyist employers, fit into this category. Professional associations registered increased from 17 to 36 between 1965 and 1989, while the number of unions that employed lobbyists declined from 22 to 16. Sixty-five organizations (18 percent of those that employed lobbyists) were from outside the state in 1989. In most cases these out-of-state groups (lottery equipment manufacturers, insurance companies, breweries) had very specific economic interests.

Among the interests not showing up in lobby registrations are elected public officials who contact state government as part of their official duties and public employees acting within the scope of their employment. Each of the public officials selected statewide has at least one person designated as a legislative liaison. The governor's staff includes four persons whose chief responsibilities involve legislative liaison work. Other executive assistants to the governor engage in legislative liaison activity connected with specific issues. At least the last three governors have made serious efforts to control contact between executive departments and the legislature from their office. Shortly after taking office in 1989, the Bayh administration announced, for example, that all testimony by executive department personnel should be cleared through the governor's office.

Among the public employees specifically exempted from lobby-registration requirements are state university personnel, identified by some legislators as among the most influential groups during a legislative session. In the basketball-crazed Hoosier state it is significant that being exempted from lobby registration and reporting requirements, university

Table 3.1. Classification of organizations employing lobbyists in Indiana, 1989

Type	No.
Corporations, businesses, trade associations	225
Professional associations	36
Public interest groups	30
Unions	16
Government groups	11
Utilities	11
Religious groups	5
Farm associations	7
Education/Universities	3
Miscellaneous	23

Source: Employers of Lobbyists (1989) (Indianapolis: Indiana Secretary of State).

personnel are free to give legislators tickets to their schools' basketball games without reporting them as gifts.

Volunteer "advocates" for a variety of interest groups (League of Women Voters, Retired Hoosiers, youth services agencies, motorcyclists opposing compulsory helmet laws) also fail to show up on lobby registrations filed in the secretary of state's office. The number of these individuals is unknown, as is their overall influence. They remain, however, a part of the regular flow in the corridors of the statehouse, managing to capture the ears of legislators as they come and go.

The Cost of Interest Representation

Good records of lobbying expenditures are not available over an extended period, and those that exist obviously exclude expenditures for seeking to influence executive-branch operations. Records available, however, do show the expected increases in the costs of interest group efforts (Table 3.2). Between 1983 and 1985 alone, organizational expenditures for lobbying increased 37 percent and lobbyists' expenditures rose 50 percent. These increases occurred while the number of groups represented rose only 14 percent.[24]

Table 3.2. Interest group and lobbying expenditures in Indiana, 1979-85

Year	No. of Groups	Organization Expenditures (millions $)	Lobbyists Expenditures (thousands $)
1979	265	1.0 +	not reported
1983	321	2.68	448
1984 (short session)	320	2.52	446
1985	367	3.68	672

Source: Summary of Lobbyist Statements and Reports (1983, 1984, 1985) (Indianapolis: Indiana Secretary of State).

In 1987, the last long session of the General Assembly for which lobbying expenditures are available, the Indiana State Teachers' Association ranked as the top spender ($88,088) among employers of lobbyists. It was followed closely by Northern Indiana Public Service Company ($87,799) and Charter Medical Corporation ($84,278). The top ten spenders among employers of lobbyists included professional associations, public utilities unions, businesses and industries, and business associations (Table 3.3).

As one might expect, the objects of these expenditures reveal both stability and change. Laws concerning utility regulation, energy, alcoholic beverages, and banking and finance annually attract the attention

Table 3.3. Top ten spenders among Indiana employers of lobbyists, 1987

Employer	Amount Spent ($)
Indiana State Teachers' Association	88,088
Northern Indiana Public Service	87,799
Charter Medical Corporation	84,278
Lincoln National	67,825
Indiana Trial Lawyers Association	64,702
Indiana UAW-CAP	54,404
ALCOA	53,538
Indiana State Medical Association	50,059
Indiana Forum for Civil Justice	48,283

Source: Compiled from Employers of Lobbyists Reports (Indianapolis: Indiana Secretary of State).

of groups spending the most money to influence legislative actions (Table 3.4). Between 1983 and 1985, health-care issues emerged as another area that drew substantial attention. Other issue areas that showed a large percentage growth in expenditures included local government (105 percent) and motor vehicle sales and safety (160 percent). Since 1985, however, banking issues and utility regulation have receded as a focus of legislative attention after several major policies concerning them moved through the legislative arena.

Table 3.4. Lobbying expenditures by Indiana interest groups, by area of legislative interest

	1983		1984		1985	
Rank	Policy Area	Expenditure (thousands $)	Policy Area	Expenditure (thousands $)	Policy Area	Expenditure (thousands $)
1	Utilities	268	Energy	277	Energy	334
2	Energy	232	Utilities	207	Health care	314
3	Alcoholic beverages	170	Alcoholic beverages	206	Utilities	303
4	Banking	168	Banking	191	Insurance	256
5	Insurance	164	Health care	171	Alcoholic beverages	252

Source: Summary of Lobbyist Statements and Reports (1983, 1984, 1985) (Indianapolis: Indiana Secretary of State).

Legislative Lobbying in Indiana

The Lobbyists

The typical lobbyist in Indiana is well educated (80 percent of those interviewed have a bachelor's degree and 40 percent have a graduate or professional degree), experienced (an average of 6.8 years of lobbying), and male. The number of women lobbyists has, however, doubled, from 51 in 1983 to 102 in 1989.[25] Most Indiana lobbyists (456 of the 518 registered in 1989) represent a single organization, of which they are either members or employees.

According to Indiana legislative observers, contract lobbyists representing multiple clients have increased in numbers in recent years. Sixty-two of the lobbyists registered in 1989 represented two clients or more. The largest number of separate clients represented by contract lobbyists in 1989 was sixteen. A cursory review of the registered contract lobbyists reveals two kinds of background. Most are associated with Indianapolis law firms. The other group—at least twenty of the sixty-two contract lobbyists in 1988—had previous political or governmental experience at the state level. Ten were former legislators, six had served on the governor's staff, and four had held significant positions in the state party organizations.

Perhaps the most prominent contract firm is built around Phillip Bainbridge and John Hammond. Bainbridge, identified as one of Indiana's "superlobbyists,"[26] served as Democratic Speaker of the House of Representatives in 1975–76. John Hammond, a Republican, served as Governor Robert Orr's legislative liaison until 1988, a position in which he had gained a great deal of respect as chief coordinator of the effort to pass the governor's educational reform package. Bainbridge and Hammond offer a broad range of services to their clients, including representation in both legislative and executive branches, good access to both sides of the aisle, and help in creating and maintaining "an appropriate organizational image" in the policy-making process. They also help to establish and then manage clients' political action committees.

James and Susan Smith, also identified as superlobbyists, both served as executive assistants to popular two-term Governor Otis Bowen (1973–80). Jim Smith entered private legal practice and began lobbying when Bowen left office. Susan Smith remained as special counsel in Governor Orr's office until 1984, when she joined her husband in private practice and interest representation in the policy process. Others identified as contract superlobbyists include Nelson Becker, former six-term member of the House of Representatives; John Frick, who served two terms in the Indiana House and one in the Senate; and Edward Treacy, former administrative assistant to the Democratic state party chairman. Another prominent contract lobbyist is Kermit Burrous, Republican and former Speaker of the Indiana House.[27]

Lobbying in Indiana

Legislators, contract lobbyists, and in-house lobbyists and legislative liaisons show substantial agreement about where influence on public policy making in Indiana rests. The three groups ranked the governor and the legislature very close to one another in terms of their influence over policy. Legislators ranked the governor slightly more influential than the legislature, while contract lobbyists ranked the legislature slightly higher, and in-house and legislative liaisons showed the legislature and the governor tied for influence over public policy. Among the remaining groups ranked, interest groups emerged as third, departments and agencies ranked fourth, and the judiciary rated last (Table 3.5).

Allocations of time and resources by lobbyists do not, however, follow influence rankings. Lobbyists report that they concentrate their efforts and resources on the General Assembly and devote considerably fewer resources to the governor and executive branch.[28] The difference between influence attribution and resource allocation is understandable, even in light of numerous assertions by interest-group representatives that lobbying the executive branch has become more important as the agenda and the scope of Indiana government have expanded and administrative rule making has increased. Lobbying the executive branch remains a relatively focused activity, aimed at particular executive agencies and departments or at the governor's office. In contrast, legislative lobbying is perceived to be a much more diffuse process. Gubernatorial or majority-party leadership support for a group's interest may assume great importance on some small percentage of bills, but insiders claim that the basic task of interest representation in the Indiana General Assembly has become more complex since 1970. Increasingly, lobbyists see their jobs as involving the communication of factual information about the issues and their groups' interests and positions on them to a wide range of individual legislators. This communication is now less mediated by party leadership, committee chairpersons, or a few other key individuals than in the past. Many lobbyists also feel that their effectiveness during the legislative session is more related to what they or their groups do during the election campaign.

The sense of the legislative process as increasingly individualized and uncertain helps to account for the relatively low profile of volunteer,

Table 3.5. Most influential groups in public policy making in Indiana, as identified by legislators, contract lobbyists, and in-house lobbyists, 1989

Group	Legislators	Lobbyists In-House	Lobbyists Contract	Overall Rank
Legislature	3.9[a]	3.7	4.0	1
Governor	4.1	3.7	3.6	2
Interest groups	2.9	2.8	3.1	3
Press	2.4	2.6	2.5	4
Departments and agencies	1.9	1.4	1.4	5
Judiciary	.9	.4	.3	6

Source: Questionnaires administered by the author and his students to legislators, lobbyists, and legislative liaisons during February and March of 1989 session of the Indiana General Assembly.

[a]Cell entries are average rankings assigned by respondents within each of the three groups and are calculated by assigning 5 points to a first-place ranking, 4 points to a second-place ranking, etc. A high score indicates a group indentified as very influential.

part-time interest advocates in the Indiana legislative process. Full-time lobbyists judge the part-time lobbyists and volunteer advocates to be of little consistent influence because they are not continuously on hand to monitor and influence the legislative process, a task said be as difficult as "pushing a rope."

That the focus of interest group activity is on the legislative arena may also derive from the very conservative view of government in Indiana. Even though it is recognized that times have changed, that there is, of necessity, more administrative rule making today, the legislature remains jealous of its policy-making role. It protects this role, to some extent, by resisting steps that would establish legislative intent behind the legislation it passes.[29] Although the lack of a record of legislative intent gives executive agencies latitude in rule making and administration, the legislature jealously reserves its power to step back into the process if the rules are not to its liking. Interest groups understand this and regularly appeal to the General Assembly to fine-tune administrative rules.

The State Board of Education learned this lesson quickly in 1985. Shortly after being broadly empowered to make rules affecting Indiana public schools, the board promulgated rules carefully defining what constituted an "instructional day." For many rural school corporations, the changes would have meant considerable inconvenience and additional expense for transportation, as elementary and high schools would be operating under significantly different time requirements. When the board refused to respond to outcries from the local school corporations, the Indiana School Boards Association and the Indiana Association of Public School Superintendents turned their attention to the General Assembly, which quickly granted waivers from the rules to all schools requesting them and sent the board back to redraft the regulations.

The legislature's importance to interest groups is also enhanced by the conservative role the Indiana court system has traditionally played. The Indiana Supreme Court has, in the past, steadfastly resisted the temptation to create "new" law through liberal interpretation of statutes.[30] The legislature, not the court, changes law in Indiana.

The Indiana legislature has, over the years, been the arena to which major conflicts between competing interests are brought for resolution. Occasionally, as in Illinois, this resolution takes the form of "agreed bills," in which the legislature ratifies a compromise reached by the interested parties.[31] The 1989 effort to increase the award ceilings for medical malpractice cases is an example of an agreed-bill process. As the whole House debated the legislation, the sponsors of the bill took pains to call the members' attention to the "letter of agreement" circulated with copies of the bill. The letter, signed by representatives of the Indiana Medical Association and the Indiana Trial Lawyers' Association, could be used by representatives to justify their votes to lawyers and doctors from their districts, the sponsors said.

Campaigns to mobilize public opinion behind legislative proposals have not been prominent weapons in interest groups' arsenals in Indiana. In part, this may be the result of the traditional strength of political parties in the state. In addition, absent any provision for initiatives and referenda, except for approval of constitutional amendments, large-scale public opinion campaigns outside regular electoral politics have never become established. As a lobbying tactic, public opinion mobilization ranked low among both in-house and contract lobbyists. None of the contract lobbying firms emphasizes its advertising or grass-roots mobilizing capabilities. In 1989 only the retail grocers and their allies launched a major effort publicly to activate grass-roots action regarding legislation. They ran newspaper advertisements calling on beer drinkers to oppose legislation that would establish exclusive distribution territories for beer wholesalers and result in increased prices to consumers. Their effort failed at the last minute when the two black state senators voted for the legislation after having told opponents they would vote "nay." Senator Carolyn Mosby, Democrat from Gary, said she changed her mind on the bill after officials of the major breweries agreed to consider the creation of a black-owned distributorship in the Gary area.[32] The governor eventually vetoed the legislation.

Interest Groups and Campaign Finance

Indiana runs with the national mainstream in campaign finance. Campaign costs have skyrocketed in recent years, and political action committees have assumed a central role in underwriting those costs. Between 1986 and 1988 alone, the average cost of Republican Senate campaigns rose from $18,762 to $33,939, while the average cost of Democratic Senate campaigns increased from $14,316 to $28,939. Spending in all House campaigns rose from $1.5 million in 1986 to $2.5 million in 1988. Jean Leising, a Republican contesting for an open state Senate seat, spent $105,210 in her successful campaign, the most ever spent in a General Assembly contest. The record for a House race was $74,213 spent by Republican candidate William F. Morrison in a losing effort in 1988.[33] Between 1978 and 1986 the average campaign expenditure by House candidates rose from $2,775 to $7,020.[34]

Political action committees, too, have become commonplace in campaign funding in Indiana. In 1976, 84 PACs spent $1.5 million on elections in the Hoosier state; by 1988, 240 committees had spent more than $7 million on state elections.[35] In 1976 the ten highest-spending, nonparty PACs spent $1,108,380 in Indiana elections. In 1986, with no gubernatorial elections to draw interest, the top ten nonparty PACs pumped just over $4 million into state contests (Table 3.6).

A study of fifteen House districts selected to represent a variety of situations — multi- and single-member districts, races with and without incumbents, urban and nonurban districts — found PAC contributions to constitute about 41 percent of all candidate receipts in 1984 and 1988.[36] In 1984 the incumbent candidates received about 50 percent of their funds from PACs, but this figure dropped to 45 percent in 1988. Challengers increased the percentage of their receipts coming from PACs from 28 to 33 percent between 1984 and 1988. The average cost of the campaigns studied rose from $8,000 to $21,000 over this time, while the gap between incumbent and challenger campaign receipts grew from about $1,500 to $8,000.

Legislators and lobbyists alike admit that PACs and changes in campaign finance have had a significant impact on interest group activity in Indiana. More than 50 percent of the lobbyists interviewed during the 1989 General Assembly session identified PAC contributions as "very important" in gaining access in the Hoosier policy-making process. Another 35 percent said they were "important." Indeed, several veteran lobbyists reported that some legislators had suggested to them that groups worked at a disadvantage during the legislative session if they had not operated a PAC during the campaign. The four party caucuses in the two chambers of the Indiana General Assembly have themselves

Table 3.6. Top ten spending PACs in Indiana, 1984 and 1986

1984		1986	
PAC	Expenditure ($)	PAC	Expenditure ($)
Transportation Political Action League	988,026	Transportation Political Action League	1,229,067
United Steelworkers	900,791	United Steelworkers	901,524
General Motors	334,647	Railway and Airline Clerks	432,000
Bear Stearns	162,390	Bear Stearns	315,575
U.S. Steel	154,615	Chrysler	235,650
Indiana Medical	132,986	United Rubber, Cork, Linoleum, Plastic Workers	233,336
Eli Lilly and Co.	130,168	General Motors	231,663
Railway and Airline Clerks	117,176	Indiana State Teachers' Association	205,902
Indiana Realtors	116,619	Indiana Realtors	153,246
Coal Miners	109,555	Eli Lilly and Co.	141,313

Source: Summary of Political Action Committees Receipts and Expenditures Reports (1984 and 1986) (Indianapolis: Indiana State Election Board).

maintained PACs since the mid-1970s. All subtlety about expectations of PAC contributions in Indiana legislative politics disappears when the caucuses hold fundraisers during the assembly session. Several lobbyists and journalists argue, however, that publicly reported PAC contributions have replaced the hidden influence buying and influence peddling of the past. Money in Indiana politics, they say, is now up front, out in the open, and everyone can expect to pay to play the game.

Because the legislative party caucuses maintain PACs and have developed greater sophistication over the years in using campaign funds to protect threatened incumbents and to fund challengers against vulnerable incumbents of the other party, political parties remain important actors in the legislative process. Now, however, the important party mechanism is the House or Senate party campaign committee, rather than county chairmen and the local organization.

Interest Group Power in Indiana

Both stability and change are evident in looking at perceptions of interest-group power in Indiana across time. Five of the top eight groups identified as powerful by legislators in 1961[37] remained on the list in 1989 (Table 3.7). All four of the groups Morehouse identified in 1981 as influential in Indiana are among the top five groups identified in 1989.[38] Most significant among the changes seems to be the relative decline of organized labor and the emergence of the Indiana State Teachers' Association (ISTA) as the group recognized by legislators and lobbyists alike as the most powerful in the state. Labor's decline may well be associated with the decline in labor union membership in the state.[39] In 1961 labor's influence was attributed to the size of its membership and its potential electoral impact. Obviously these interrelated factors have changed in the intervening years.

ISTA, which ranked very close to labor as the most influential group in 1961, stood clearly alone in that position in 1989. About two-thirds of the lobbyists and legislators interviewed placed ISTA first, both in influence at election time and during the legislative session. No other group received first-place rankings from more than 10 percent of those interviewed in 1989. In 1961 legislators attributed the teachers' association's influence to its prestige, the number of its members, and organizational and leadership factors.[40] In 1989, though its numbers and prestige were important, legislators and lobbyists attributed its influence to electoral efforts. ISTA's election involvement was extensive during the 1980s, ranging from encouraging members to become delegates to both parties'

Table 3.7. Indiana interest groups ranked by influence, 1961 and 1989

Rank	1961	During Elections	During Legislative Session (1989)	Combined Ranking (1989)
1	Labor	ISTA	ISTA	ISTA
2	Indiana State Teachers' Association (ISTA)	Chamber of Commerce	Chamber of Commerce	Chamber of Commerce
3	Chamber of Commerce	Labor (AFL–CIO)	Trial Lawyers' Association	Trial Lawyers' Association
4	Farm organizations	Trial Lawyers' Association	Farm Bureau	Labor (AFL–CIO)
5	Truckers' Association	Manufacturers' Association	Manufacturers' Association	Farm Bureau
6	Medical Association	Farm Bureau	Labor (AFL–CIO)	Manufacturers' Association
7	Township Trustees	Insurance industry	Insurance industry	Insurance industry
8	Manufacturers' Association			

Sources: Ranking of interest groups in 1961 taken from Kenneth Janda, Henry Teune, Melvin Kahn, and Wayne Francis, "Legislative Politics in Indiana," in James B. Kessler, ed., Empirical Studies of Indiana Politics (Bloomington Indiana University Press, 1970), 40. Rankings for 1989 calculated from responses to questionnaires administered to legislators and lobbyists during 1989 session of the General Assembly.

state conventions and recruiting or encouraging teachers to run for state legislative seats, maintaining a well-financed PAC, making large contributions to supportive candidates, and targeting and working for the defeat of unfriendly state legislators. ISTA is feared in the electoral arena because of its numbers, its capacity to drive up the cost of legislative campaigns, the organizational and electoral sophistication it brings to campaigns it supports, and its successful opposition to several prominent incumbent legislators, including William Long in 1982, a five-term Republican and chairman of the House Ways and Means Committee, and three-term Speaker of the House J. Roberts Dailey in 1986.

ISTA may also have assumed a more prominent role in state politics in the 1980s because the map of educational policy making in Indiana has changed. State budgetary adjustments necessitated by the property tax freeze imposed in 1973 have resulted in a complete reversal of the state-local shares of educational funding. Today the state meets about 60 percent of the costs of education, whereas before the freeze it contributed only about 30 percent. Local school corporations now provide about one-third of the funds for education. In 1973 the legislature also approved collective bargaining for public schoolteachers, making them the only public employees ever accorded that opportunity in Indiana. ISTA and its local affiliates became the teachers' bargaining agent in most school corporations. Thus, just as the change in financial power shifted the locus of educational policy making to the state level, collective bargaining enhanced the structure of ISTA, strengthening its local organizations and tying them more closely to the state organization.

The Indiana Chamber of Commerce also remains among the groups identified as influential by persons throughout the policy-making system. As organized labor moved down the list, the chamber moved up. Although the gap between ISTA and the chamber is wide in terms of numbers of people ranking each as most powerful in the state, the chamber occupies second place by broad consensus. Its reputation for influence rests on the fact that its conservative viewpoint is widely shared within Indiana government, on the expertise its lobbyists and members bring to policy questions, and on its ability to stimulate its members to contact their legislators.

The Indiana Chamber of Commerce and the state business community are, however, reacting to what they perceive to be a changing pattern of influence and policy making. The chamber created a political action committee in 1986, having become aware of the increasing role campaign finance seemed to be playing in Indiana politics. Expenditures from that PAC increased from $20,000 in 1986 to more than $120,000 in

1988. The Hoosier business community, with the Chamber of Commerce as a participant, has also begun to coordinate its campaign spending more effectively. These efforts appear to be tacit recognition of the changing face of interest politics in Indiana. The business community can no longer rely on exercising influence through established party leadership. It must be concerned with protecting individual officeholders who have supported it in the past, building a base of support for the future, and seeking to influence individual legislators.

New to the list of powerful groups in Indiana is the Indiana Trial Lawyers Association. Its place on the list seems to be a function of abiding interest in a range of profession-related issues; an actively involved membership; a group of lawyer-legislators who can function as inside lobbyists; a lobbying team that includes Ed Treacy, one of the best-known contract lobbyists in the state; and effective use of PAC contributions to reward supporters and maintain access. The Trial Lawyers Association, for obvious reasons, has also taken an active interest in judicial politics. The association is credited with having managed to fill with its members all three legal-profession seats on the state judicial nominating commission.[41]

The fact that Indiana banks, utility companies, realtors, the medical association, and the health-care industry are not listed among the most influential groups does not mean that they are unimportant. These groups are always present and well represented. Their issues come and go, however, and with them the groups' perceived influence fluctuates. All these groups would have been listed among the five to ten most influential groups in Indiana at some time during the 1980s, and all are capable of achieving that reputation during future legislative sessions, but the issues of the 1989 General Assembly did not warrant their most aggressive efforts.

Some groups also find it more in their interest to operate outside the more publicly visible policy-making arenas. Public utilities traditionally have been in this situation. According to one lobbyist, for example, Public Service Company of Indiana generally finds it safer to pursue its interests through the Public Service Commission. Policies that would make it possible for utilities to charge customers for construction work in progress or for telephone companies to provide "local measured service" rather than charge a flat fee for local calls can generate widespread public opposition under the leadership of public interest groups.[42] If such issues can be confined to the less public, more legalistic and formalistic policy-making environment of the Public Service Commission, so much the better for the utility. Public interest groups, such as the Citizens Action Coalition, however, have worked with increasing diligence and visibility in recent years to bring these issues into the more public arena of the General Assembly.

Conclusion

Morehouse classified Indiana among the "moderately strong" interest group states.[43] This classification, made in the early 1980s from available and sometimes impressionistic information, seems still to fit today, perhaps in part because the category covered so broad a range of possibilities. A more useful classification, however, is provided by Thomas and Hrebenar. Their "complementary" interest group system includes those states "where groups tend to have to work in conjunction with or are constrained by other aspects of the political system. More often than not this is the party system."[44] Indiana fits comfortably into this category, and the classification communicates important information about interest group politics in the state. No single group dominates Indiana state politics, but a number of identifiable groups are influential, regular players in the policy-making process. In that process, those influential groups understand that they often face significant opposition.

Nonetheless, the interest groups operate within a system in which party politics cannot be ignored, in either the short or the long run. The 1989 legislative session illustrates the importance of the short-run partisan context. With the Democratic party controlling the governor's office for the first time in twenty years and neither party controlling the House, interest groups and lobbyists spent much time learning to play the policy game with a new alignment of players, under some new rules, and on a different playing field. The long-run party context is important to interest group influence and operations as well. And it, too, has changed, with consequences for group politics. Although the party system is still strongly competitive and the organizations remain strong and vital compared to parties in many American states, the nature of those organizations and their involvement in politics have changed. Interest groups have had to adapt to a system in which party control of the governor's office remains important, but one in which gubernatorial nominations are no longer effectively controlled by county party organizations meeting in convention. Interest groups continue to operate in a system in which party-selected legislative leaders exercise important powers and party caucuses continue to meet regularly. But it is a system in which PAC-financed legislative caucuses, rather than local party organizations, provide the party presence in increasingly candidate-centered legislative elections.

Notes

1. Demographic and comparative state data in this section are taken from *State Policy Data Book, 1988* (McConnelsberg, Pa.: Bruzius & Foster, 1988).
2. United States manufacturing employment figures are taken from U.S. Department of Commerce, Bureau of Economic Analysis, *Business Statistics, 1986* (Washington, D.C.). Indiana figures appear in Bob J. Lain, "Indiana 1986: The Economic Year in Perspective," *Indiana Business Review,* 62 (April 1987), 11.
3. *Perspectives on the Indian Economy,* no. 13 (January 1988), p. 12 (Indianapolis: Division of Economic Analysis, Indiana Department of Commerce).
4. John Fenton, *Midwest Politics* (New York: Holt, Rinehart & Winston, 1966), 155–63. See also V. O. Key, Jr., and Frank J. Munger, "Social Determinism and Electoral Decision," in Eugene Burdick and Arthur Brodbeck, eds., *American Voting Behavior* (Glencoe, Ill.: Free Press, 1959), 281–99.
5. Daniel J. Elazar, *American Federalism: A View from the States,* 3d ed. (New York: Harper & Row, 1984), 115.
6. Many readers are familiar with the Indiana General Assembly's famous resolution declaring that it "needs no guardian and intends to have none" and asking its congressional delegation to "vote to fetch our county courthouses and city halls back from Pennsylvania Avenue" (Indiana Acts, 1947, chap. 337, vol. 2, pp. 1509–10). Less well known is Indiana's near-withdrawal in 1951 from the federally funded social welfare program in a dispute over an attempt to reduce its welfare rolls by publicizing welfare recipients' names. Kan Ori, "Basic Ideas in Federal-State Relations: The Indiana 'Revolt' of 1951" (Ph.D. dissertation, Indiana University, 1961).
7. Neal Peirce, *The Great Lakes States* (New York: Norton, 1980), 252–57, provides a good description of these practices.
8. In 1988, for example, Republican presidential candidate George Bush, with favorite son Dan Quayle on the ticket, won the state with 39.9 percent of the vote, while Democrat Bayh beat the incumbent lieutenant governor with 53.2 percent of the vote. Three-term U.S. Senator Richard Lugar won 31.9 percent of the vote statewide, but Democrats carried six of the state's ten congressional seats, despite the Republican party's elaborate efforts to construct those districts to their advantage.
9. Ernest T. Williams, longtime lobbyist for the Indiana Chamber of Commerce, cites the "time in Indiana politics when, if we wanted to influence legislators, one of the great levers we had . . . was the county chairman." Their influence declined with the appearance of multicounty legislative districts. Ernest T. Williams, interview with author, November 4, 1983.
10. The U.S. Supreme Court, for example, ruled that "patronage dismissals severely restrict political belief and association" and thus violate First Amendment protections. *Elrod v. Burns,* 427 U.S. 347 (1976).
11. I am indebted to William J. Watt, former executive assistant to Governor Otis Bowen, for this observation. William J. Watt, interview with author, November 4, 1983.
12. Ernest T. Williams, interview, November 4, 1983.
13. In the mid-1970s one senior Republican representative, a committee chairman, learned the hard way about the powers of the Speaker to assign and reassign legislation to committees. This chairman had publicly opposed a key element of the Republican governor's program. For this action, the Speaker reassigned to other committees nearly all legislation previously assigned to the committee chaired by the offender.
14. Under the power-sharing agreement, each cospeaker appointed his own party members to cochair standing committees, and the cospeakers alternated days presiding

over the House. To make the sharing arrangement work, the power to call legislation down for floor action passed from the Speaker to the members. Cochairs of committees also alternated days presiding. Any legislation that received a tie vote in the partisanly balanced committees was automatically reported favorably to the House.

15. Between 1965 and 1976 an average of 41 percent of the members of the House in each session were serving their first term. This figure dropped to 18 percent for the period 1977–86, after longer annual sessions were instituted. Calculations made from Justin E. Walsh, *The Centennial History of the Indiana General Assembly, 1816–1978* (Indianapolis: Indiana Historical Bureau, 1987), Appendix A, Table 5, p. 705.

16. See Patrick T. Morrison and Patrick J. Traub, "Special Interests Comprise Legislature's 'Third House,' " *Indianapolis Star,* April 5, 1981, pp. 1 and 14, for a fuller account of these activities. This article is part of a series by Morrison and Traub, appearing April 5–10, 1981, which examined in detail interest group activities in Indiana state politics.

17. *Indiana Code* 2-7-1-10.

18. *Indiana Code* 2-7-3-3.

19. Data on which much of the remainder of this discussion is based were collected by the author and students in two of his classes at Wabash College. They conducted interviews with 86 individuals: 39 legislators, 17 contract lobbyists, and 30 in-house lobbyists or legislative liaisons. Although a systematic sample was not drawn, the legislators interviewed reflect the partisan makeup of the Indiana General Assembly, and the proportion of House and Senate members in the sample closely parallels the numerical composition of the two chambers. The legislators in the sample also reflect the range of tenure and experience in the Indiana assembly. Lobbyists interviewed represent a significant range of experience: 24 percent had lobbied for two years or less; 29 percent, three to five years; 16 percent, six to nine years; and 32 percent, ten or more years.

20. *Indiana Code* 3-4, Acts 1976, P.L. 6.

21. Patrick T. Morrison and Patrick J. Traub, "Weak Enforcement Enables Legislators to Ignore State Financial Disclosure Law," *Indianapolis Star,* April 9, 1981, pp. 1 and 8.

22. Philip S. Wilder and Karl O'Lessker, *Introduction to Indiana Government and Politics* (Indianapolis: Indiana Sesquicentennial Commission, 1967), 24–29.

23. These data are taken from lobbyist and lobbyist employer registration lists maintained by the Indiana Secretary of State.

24. Figures taken from 1983 and 1985 "Summary of Lobbyist Statements and Reports," prepared by the Indiana Secretary of State, Indianapolis.

25. Several lobbyists expressed the view that men and women lobbyists operate on about equal footings within the confines of the state House, in testifying before committees and making personal contacts with legislators. They felt, however, that women operate at a disadvantage in the after-hours exchanges over drinks and dinner at the Columbia Club, in hospitality suites, and other places frequented by policy makers when the General Assembly has adjourned for the day.

26. The lobbyists discussed here were identified in "The Super Lobbyists," *Indiana Business* (December 1988), 14–20. Editors of *Indiana Business* sent questionnaires to all Indiana General Assembly members and all lobbyists registered in 1988. Return rates for the mailed questionnaire were about 20 percent for lobbyists and 30 percent for legislators.

27. At one time in the mid-1980s, when utilities issues were high on the assembly's agenda, Northern Indiana Public Service Company employed as lobbyists both Burrous and Bainbridge, former Speakers of the House, one a Republican, the other a Democrat.

28. Fifty-nine percent of the lobbyists interviewed in 1989 reported spending 75 percent or more of their time lobbying in the General Assembly, while only a quarter reported

spending 25 percent or more of their time lobbying in the executive branch.

29. No records of committee or floor debates are kept. Committee reports contain only the details of amendments passed and a recommendation for passage of the legislation.

30. Joseph T. Hallinan, "A Court Divided: Part One," *Indianapolis Star*, March 12, 1989, sec. A, p. 6.

31. See David H. Everson and Samuel K. Gove, "Illinois: Political Microcosm of the Nation," Chapter 2 of this volume.

32. James G. Newland, Jr., "Senate Passes 'Beer Baron' Bill by 1 Vote," *Indianapolis Star*, April 5, 1989, sec. A, p. 1. The legislation would have repealed an administrative rule promulgated by the Alcoholic Beverage Commission. The bill passed the House, then the Senate, but only after newly elected Democratic Lt. Gov. Frank O'Bannon cast a tie-breaking vote. Observers expected the governor to sign the legislation into law, but he vetoed it after several major beer distributors raised prices substantially just days before he was to take action on the bill. By raising prices before the bill became law, the distributors circumvented, but violated the spirit of, an informal agreement between the beer industry and the administration which would have limited price increases to 10 percent over the next two years.

33. Peter L. Blum, "Election Spending Hits Record High," *Indianapolis News,* January 27, 1989, sec. A, p. 1.

34. Sameer A. Bade, "Campaign Finances in Indiana" (unpublished manuscript, Wabash College, 1989).

35. These comparative figures are calculated from mimeographed annual reports produced by the Indiana State Election Board.

36. Scott Alexander, "The Impact of PAC Contributions on Indiana Politics" (unpublished manuscript, Wabash College, 1989).

37. Kenneth Janda, Henry Teune, Melvin Kahn, and Wayne Francis, "Legislative Politics in Indiana," in James B. Kessler, ed., *Empirical Studies of Indiana Politics* (Bloomington: Indiana University Press, 1970), 40.

38. Sarah McCally Morehouse, *State Politics, Parties and Policy* (New York: Holt, Rinehart & Winston, 1981), 110.

39. James H. Madison, *The Indiana Way* (Bloomington: Indiana University Press, 1986), 285–86, notes that during the 1970s, union membership as a percentage of the nonagricultural workforce declined from 38 to 30 percent.

40. Janda et al., "Legislative Politics in Indiana," 41.

41. James T. Hallinan, "A Court Divided: Part Two," *Indianapolis Star*, March 13, 1989, sec. A, p. 6.

42. Public interest groups also fail to make the "most influential" list. They, too, intermittently occupy positions of prominence, depending on the issues on the agenda and, perhaps, on the existence of conflict within or among established special interest groups. For example, public interest groups may gain prominence when investor-owned and cooperatively owned rural electric companies become locked in conflict over service territories or when beer brewers and beer wholesalers engage beer retailers in combat over exclusive distribution territories.

43. Morehouse, *State Politics,* 110.

44. Clive S. Thomas and Ronald J. Hrebenar, "Interest Groups in the States," in Virginia Gray, Herbert Jacob, and Robert Albritton, eds., *Politics in the American States: A Comparative Analysis,* 5th ed. (Glenview, Ill.: Scott, Foresman; Boston: Little, Brown, 1990), 147–48.

IOWA
Interest Groups and the Politics of Moderation

CHARLES W. WIGGINS and KEITH E. HAMM

An Iowa novelist once noted that her state "combines the qualities of half a dozen states, and perhaps that is the reason why it so often seems, and
more to its own people than to others, the most
undistinguished place in the world."[1] Although somewhat of an over-
statement, this observation captures much of the essence of a state that
so represents the mainstream of American political life that it generally
lacks the political personalities, processes, and behavior patterns that
often make examinations of other states more interesting. And it is
within this broad cultural context that the state's interest groups operate
and attempt to influence public policy outcomes.

Socioeconomic and Political Environment

Iowa stands at the crossroads of America, not only in a geographical sense, but also in a demographic and political sense. Geographically,
it is located in the middle of the United States, between the two large
rivers that drain the Upper Middle West. In 1980 its population stood at
2.9 million residents, placing it 27th among the fifty states. Unlike that
of many other states, this population is not concentrated in either one or
a handful of metropolitan communities. Instead, it is well dispersed,
with slightly over 50 percent located in fifteen semimetropolitan com-

munities. Thus, no major metropolitan-outstate conflicts have defined the state's politics.

Homogeneity tends to characterize the state in terms of religion, ethnicity/nationality, and race. With regard to religion, the state is primarily Protestant (84 percent), with only 15 and 1 percent, respectively, indicating a Catholic and Jewish affiliation among those who identify with a religious organization. Among Protestants, Methodists (35 percent) and Lutherans (30 percent) are the two largest denominations, with the remainder scattered across other denominations. Spatially, these religious denominations are well dispersed, with at least some representation in most counties. Only three of ninety-nine counties have major concentrations (60 percent or more) of a particular denomination: Dubuque (Catholic), Carroll (Catholic), and Winnebago (Lutheran). Homogeneity has also characterized the ethnicity/nationality origins of the state's population, with the majority being U.S. natives. No more than 17 percent of the people living in the state during any period in its history, even during settlement, have been foreign-born. Of the few who have been foreign-born, most were from northern Europe (Germany, England, and the Scandinavian countries) and immigrated during the 1840–1890 period. Racially, minorities constitute only around 1 percent of the state's population.

Economically, the typical Iowan tends to enjoy average prosperity in relation to citizens in other states, with per capita income frequently hovering around the U.S. average. A similar pattern is present with regard to the distribution of this income. The occupational structure of the state also tends to mirror that of the nation, with slightly less than 10 percent employed in the agriculture sector, 22 percent in manufacturing, and 68 percent in service industries. Of course, many of the manufacturing and service industries are agriculturally related. For example, Deere and Company has been the state's largest employer in recent decades. Thus, the economic prosperity of both manufacturing and service industries is closely linked to the vitality of the state's agricultural sector.

Overall, Iowa's political milieu can best be described as bland, low-keyed, and in many ways dull.[2] Political interactions, including those between lobbyists and public officials, occur on the basis of honesty and trust. Consistent with a moralistic political culture,[3] political corruption is not tolerated, since the primary motive for taking part in politics should be public service and not private gain. Political discourse is conducted in a very civil manner, with those involved addressing what they perceive to be the major problems confronting the state. Participation in the political process on the part of all Iowans, regardless of means, is encouraged and actually occurs in several respects, whether in precinct caucuses or general elections. Ideologically, Iowans tend to be quite moderate and hold an extreme dislike for more radical perspectives at either end of the political continuum.[4]

After an initial brief period of Democratic dominance, Iowa became a primarily Republican state with the advent of the Civil War. It remained this way until the mid-1950s, although the Democratic party gained somewhat in strength during the Great Depression and New Deal years. Today, Iowa can be characterized as a two-party state. This is reflected in both voter registration records and polls of the Iowa electorate, although at least one-third regard themselves as falling into the Independent category. It also is reflected in the frequent divided party control of legislative and executive branches of state government, which has occurred since the late 1950s.

Iowans expect their governmental institutions to be efficient and effective. Because Iowa's residents also perceive these institutions for the most part as conforming to their expectations, state and local governmental bodies normally enjoy a high level of diffuse support among the state's populace.[5]

Thus, a major dose of blandness tends to characterize the political environment within which interest groups operate. Overall, Iowans expect their politicians and governments to operate fairly, openly, moderately, honestly, competitively, efficiently, and effectively. Extremism, even in the defense of liberty, is more often than not suspect. It is within this context that Iowa interest groups pursue their public policy objectives.

Interest Group Power Structure:
A Historical Perspective

Three types of interest group power structures have been present on the Iowa political scene since statehood in 1846. The first, or single dominant interest pattern, was present during the state's formative years, from the mid-1800s until around the turn of the century. The population growth and economic development that occurred during this period was directly linked to the coming of the "Iron Horse," or railroad industry, to the state.[6] The major incentive employed by the fledgling legislature to encourage the railroads to enter and cross the state was the land grant, whereby large amounts of land were donated to railroad corporations that, in turn, would sell such property to settlers and use the proceeds to support the construction of new routes or tracks. More than 4 million acres of Iowa land was granted to the railroad industry for this purpose, a truly impressive amount when compared to the rather paltry 200,000-acre federal land grant used to support the construction of an agricultural and technical college in Ames in the early 1860s. The major railroads that eventually crossed the state (Burlington, Rock Island, Chicago Northwestern, Illinois Central, and Milwaukee) acknowledged the need for a close, friendly working relationship with state and local officials, at times, by issuing complimentary passes. This practice was a departure from the more dominant moralistic political orientation of the state throughout its history. The legislature also tended to be supportive of railroad interests when confronted with periodic agrarian demands for railroad regulation, especially in the area of rates, by passing weak and ineffective measures.

After the turn of the century a second type of interest group power structure gradually evolved: the alliance of dominant interests. This alliance, consisting of the Iowa Farm Bureau Federation and the Iowa Manufacturers Association, appeared as the character of the Iowa economy changed.[7] The structure of the agricultural sector of the state's economy shifted from one that emphasized small and self-sustaining units to one that emphasized larger units oriented toward commercial production and markets. In addition, the nonagricultural sector of the Iowa economy experienced significant development and growth during this period. Of the two main players in this alliance, the senior partner was definitely the Iowa Farm Bureau Federation (IFBF). Key political resources available to the IFBF to influence public policy outcomes were size of membership (it eventually became the state's largest group), member dispersion throughout the state, organization (each county had a farm bureau legislative committee to oversee and interact with local lawmakers), and financial resources. Together with the Iowa Manufacturers Association, the IFBF wielded much influence in legislative decision making in such issue areas as taxation, business regulation, education, and state government reform. For example, this alliance was quite successful during the 1950s and early 1960s in defeating increasing urban demands for reapportionment of the state legislature.[8]

Today the interest group power stucture of Iowa can best be described as pluralistic. The roots of the present power structure lie in the increasing urbanization and industrialization of the state, plus the coming of competitive two-party politics during the late 1950s and 1960s. As long as the state was dominated by the Republican party, the Iowa Farm Bureau and Iowa Manufacturers Association partnership was able to operate within this single-party framework to be the main initiator and promoter of major public policies. The initial crack in this alliance occurred in 1956, when the Democratic candidate for governor, Herschell

Loveless, surprisingly unseated the Republican incumbent, Leo Hoegh. Major fissure, however, was delayed until the mid-1960s, when federal and state court rulings mandated the reapportionment of the state legislature along population lines. No longer would the legislature be inordinately dominated by farmers, many of whom had been officers in their local county farm bureaus as well as small-town businessmen. Instead, the lawmaking body became more reflective of a more diversified state, with labor, consumer, environmental, public official, and other interests wielding more influence.

In the present pluralistic structure of Iowa interest group politics, more and more groups are making demands on the legislature and the administration. Individually, group demands are more selective than indiscriminate and are targeted toward a limited number of issues debated each session.[9] Group coalitions, to the limited extent that they appear, tend to be shifting and occur on an ad hoc basis. Most group leaders are cognizant of the fact that their success is closely linked to the support or at least acquiescence of the governor's office, as well as the majority party leadership's groups in both chambers of the legislature.

Within this context, which particular groups tend to wield the most influence within the Iowa political system? Although to our knowledge no systematic survey of Iowa lawmakers, media representatives, or other knowledgeables has been conducted in recent years to answer this question, casual conversations with several observers of the capitol scene suggest the following groups: Iowa State Education Association, Iowa Farm Bureau Federation, Iowa Association of Business and Industry, Iowa Federation of Labor, AFL-CIO, Iowa Bankers Association, and the Iowa Academy of Trial Lawyers. It should be emphasized, however, that none of these groups can necessarily carry the day on its favorite public policy proposals, especially when confronted with opposition from other interest groups or party leaders in state government. As indicated above, the interest group power structure is too pluralistic to accommodate steady dominance by a handful of organizations.

Interest Groups and Elections

Interest groups are deeply emeshed in Iowa state elections through political action committees. In terms of sheer numbers the growth of PACs parallels general trends in other states, increasing roughly 40 percent between 1978 and 1986. Somewhat surprisingly, in the 1980s the number of PACs tended to be higher in gubernatorial election years (with 184 in 1982 and 180 in 1986) and smaller in presidential election years (only 151 in 1984). In Table 4.1 the nonpolitical party PACs during the 1984 election are categorized by type. Overall, a slight majority (52.9 percent) are statewide organizations, roughly one in four are regional or local PACs, and about one in five involve a single company.

In terms of type of organizations, business-related PACs appear most often, but they account for slightly less than 50 percent of the total. PACs representing the financial/insurance (13.9 percent) and utilities/ telecommunications (9.3 percent) sectors are by far the most frequently occurring business PACs. It is worth noting that slightly less than one-half of the business PACs are associated with a single company (e.g., Central Life Insurance Company, John Deere, Iowa Power and Light). An interesting finding, at least in comparison to other states, is the relatively large number of PACs related to public and private (non-management) employees. In Texas, for example, these "labor" PACs accounted for only roughly one in ten of the total, whereas in Iowa they

Table 4.1. Political action committees in Iowa, by type and scope, 1984

Type	Total %	Total No.	Statewide	Regional/ Local	Single Company
Business	45.0	68	33	3	32
Financial/ Insurance	13.9	21	13		8
Energy/Chemicals	2.6	4	1		3
Building/Construction	3.3	5	4	1	
Transportation	2.6	4	2		2
Utilities/Telecommunications	9.3	14	3		11
Real estate/Apartments/Hotels	2.0	3	3		
Alcohol related	.7	1	1		
Aerospace/Steel & iron/High technology	.7	1			1
Business-General	2.6	4	2	2	
Commercial-Miscellaneous	4.0	6	3		3
Manufacturing-Miscellaneous	3.3	5	1		4
Professions	11.9	18	18		
Attorneys	1.3	2	2		
Health-care related	6.7	10	10		
Architects/Engineers/CPAs/Surveyors	1.3	2	2		
Miscellaneous	2.6	4	4		
Employees	26.5	40	14	26	
Private sector	21.9	33	9	24	
Public sector					
Education	3.3	5	4	1	
Local government					
Miscellaneous	1.3	2	1	1	
Agriculture/Ranching/Forestry	2.6	4	4		
Noneconomic	14.0	21	11	10	
General	7.3	11	3	8	
Specific issue					
Nationality/Ethnicity					
Education	.7	1		1	
Taxation	.7	1	1		
Morality (i.e., gambling, abortion)	2.0	3	3		
Conservation/Natural resources					
Miscellaneous	3.3	5	4	1	
Total	100	151	80	39	32

Source: Iowa Common Cause, 1986.
Note: Excludes political party PACs.

comprise slightly more than one in four, with the bulk being regional or local in scope.[10]

Noneconomic-oriented PACs account for another 14 percent of the total PACs, with roughly one-half being the single-issue variety (for example, the Pro-Life PAC). In addition, in terms of scope, there is roughly an even split among such PACs between statewide organizations and those that are regional or local in nature. Professional PACs, all statewide in scope, constitute another 12 percent of the total, with a majority associated with health-care specialists (doctors, chiropractors, nurses). Finally, and somewhat unexpectedly, given the reliance of the Iowa economy on farming, PACs associated with agriculture, ranching, and forestry comprise only 4 out of the 151 non–political party PACs.

To what extent do nonparty PACs fund candidate campaigns in Iowa? Although PACs tend not to play an overly significant role in statewide races, their major impact is in state legislative races. In 1984 nonparty PACs contributed 50.7 percent of the $1,641,374 raised by candidates for the Iowa Legislature.[11] PAC contributions are a larger percentage of contributions for candidates than in past years. For example, the average Iowa Senate winner in 1976 received roughly 23 percent of the $6,314 in total contributions from nonparty PACs, whereas in 1984 the figure was roughly 67 percent out of an average of $13,032.[12] Thus, while campaign contributions increased slightly more than two-fold in the eight-year period, PAC contributions increased six-fold.

Perhaps more significantly, fourteen PACs accounted for more than 50 percent of all PAC money contributed. Ten of the key PACs involve a single statewide industry or union, including two professional associations (doctors, optometrists), six trade associations (realtors, bankers, construction industry, savings and loan, automotive retailers, life underwriters), one public sector organization (educators), and one private sector union (the UAW) (Table 4.2). Two PACs represent employees and management of individual companies dealing with banking and telephones. The two remaining PACs are more broadly based, one being a coalition for tax relief and the other representing the somewhat influential Iowa Association of Business and Industry (formerly the Iowa Manufacturers Association).

Who is the recipient of the PACs' largesse? Incumbents in both parties received the largest absolute amounts of campaign contributions from PACs, followed by candidates of both parties for an open seat, and then the challengers (Table 4.3). Particularly striking is the comparison of the paucity of challengers relative to incumbents who received a total of $5,000 from PACs. Of course, since incumbents generally tend to raise more money, perhaps there are no significant differences among the can-

Table 4.2. Leading PAC contributors to state legislative candidates in Iowa, 1984

PAC	Amount Contributed ($)	% of Candidate Receiving Money[a]					
		Incumbent		Challenger		Open-Seat	
		D	R	D	R	D	R
Taxpayers United	50,900	7.6	82.2	3.2	40.0	0.0	71.4
Iowa Realty	41,750	86.0	91.1	0.0	15.6	42.9	64.3
Iowa Bankers	40,600	89.4	93.3	9.7	4.4	50.0	67.1
Construction Survival Club	39,850	59.1	91.1	3.2	40.0	0.0	71.4
Iowa Medical	30,650	51.5	64.4	3.2	17.8	42.9	57.1
Hawkeye Bank	29,451	48.5	68.9	9.7	33.3	42.9	64.3
Northwestern Bell-Iowa	28,296	87.9	86.7	3.2	11.1	35.7	64.3
Professional Optometric League	28,200	75.8	75.6	19.4	36.7	64.3	42.9
Iowa State Education Association	25,250	60.6	4.4	38.7	2.2	71.4	21.4
Iowa State UAW	23,000	48.5	0.0	41.9	0.0	71.4	7.1
Savings & Loan	21,745	72.7	84.4	0.0	22.3	14.3	50.0
Iowa Committee of Automotive Retailers	20,550	39.4	64.4	6.5	26.7	21.4	57.1
Iowa Life Underwriters	20,000	24.2	53.3	3.2	15.6	35.7	35.7
Iowa Industry	18,300	33.3	88.9	0.0	31.1	0.0	71.4

Source: Iowa Common Cause, 1986.

[a]Entries are percentages of specific types of legislators receiving any contribution from the particular PAC.

didates in terms of PAC reliance. However, even when PAC contributions are used as a percentage of the total funds raised, these differences still emerge. Overall, in 1984, incumbents and winners in open-seat races received 67 and 57 percent of their contributions from PACs in Senate and House elections, respectively. Challengers and losers in open-seat races in the Senate were least reliant on PACs, with a still respectable 25 percent of their funds coming from this source, while in the House elections challengers and losers in open-seat races garnered 38 percent from PACs.[13]

Do different individual PACs pursue different strategies in dispensing contributions?[14] The answer is both yes and no for the fourteen leading PAC spenders (see Table 4.2). Similarities emerge in terms of contributions to candidates within a particular political party. That is, in terms of the percentage of candidates receiving contributions (but excluding the amount of those contributions), twelve of the fourteen major PACs are most likely to contribute to an incumbent, then to an open-seat candidate, and least of all to a challenger among each political party's candidates. The two exceptions—the Iowa State Education Association

Table 4.3. PAC contributions to Iowa legislative candidates, 1984

Candidate Status	Party	PAC Contributions ($)			% Greater than $5,000
		Mean	(Median)	Range ($)	
Incumbent	Democrat	4,711	4,352	0-21,786	43.4
Incumbent	Republican	5,690	4,875	0-27,499	46.7
Challenger	Democrat	1,073	725	0-4,500	0.0
Challenger	Republican	2,186	645	0-16,275	11.1
Open-seat	Democrat	2,805	2,117	0-7,775	14.3
Open-seat	Republican	5,525	3,962	900-14,455	42.9

Source: Iowa Common Cause, 1986.

and the UAW—contribute to a larger percentage of open-seat candidates than to incumbents in each party.

The major difference among the fourteen PACs involves the extent to which there is a partisan bias in the distribution of contributions. At one end of the spectrum, the Taxpayers United PAC provides funding almost exclusively to Republicans, including 40 percent of the Republican challengers. The Iowa Industry PAC and the Construction Survival Club lean toward Republicans, but not as exclusively as the Taxpayers United PAC, while the Automobile Retailers PAC, the Iowa Life Underwriters PAC, the Savings and Loan PAC, and the Hawkeye Bank PAC are more modestly Republican-oriented. Four PACs—optometrists, bankers, realtors, and Northwestern Bell—provide funding to at least three-fourths of the incumbents in each party and give few challengers any money. The doctors' PAC displays no major partisan preference, but it tends to be much more discriminating in terms of the number of candidates who receive contributions. Finally, two PACs—the Iowa State Education Association and the Iowa State UAW—give almost exclusively to Democrats, including about four in ten Democratic challengers. In summary, the fourteen largest PACs use a wide spectrum of campaign contribution strategies, although there generally is a tendency not to provide challengers with significant resources.

Regulation of Lobbyists

The rules of the Iowa House and Senate provide for the registration of lobbyists and regulation of some of their activities. Both chambers define a lobbyist as one who (1) is paid to influence the legislature, (2) spends money to influence the legislature, or (3) represents an organization that has as one of its purposes influencing the legislature. Also included in this definition are (4) representatives of state agencies, as well as those representing units of local government. Each lobbyist must register his or her name, address, and the name(s) of the groups he or she represents with the chief administrative officer of each chamber. Registration must occur before the individual begins lobbying activities.

During the course of a session, lobbyists must also register the numbers of the individual bills on which they are lobbying, a situation we explore in a later section. Although it is not mandated, some group representatives indicate the positions—pro or con—that their groups are taking with regard to individual measures. In some cases, lobbyist registration on individual bills is a "protective action," in that the lobbyist wants to be in a position to lobby immediately on a relevant measure if an amendment affecting his or her group's interests is subsequently introduced and considered during committee markup or floor consideration.

Both House and Senate rules prohibit lobbyists or their employees from making open-end, or charge-free, accounts available to lawmakers. In addition, a lobbyist cannot offer a legislator an economic or investment opportunity with the intent of influencing his or her legislative actions. The payment of contingency fees to lobbyists based on the success of their lobbying efforts is effectively prohibited. Lawmakers must report the value (above a $15 threshold) of gifts and entertainment received from lobbyists, while lobbyists must report monthly aggregate expenditures for lobbying, including expenditures for individual lawmakers above $15.

Formal charges against lobbyists for violating lobbying rules are filed with the ethics committee of either chamber. After conducting a hearing, and only if the findings warrant, the committee prepares specific recommendations for disposition. Although such a case has never occurred, a lobbyist found to have violated a regulatory provision may be suspended or banned from lobbying.

In recent history only two hearings have been held by the ethics committees over an alleged violation. A House member in the late 1960s filed charges against a lobbyist for the Iowa Farm Bureau Federation, arguing that the lobbyist had made comments to him about a bill on which he was not registered. The committee ruled that the lobbyist's comments did not represent or reflect a position on the measure, and the charges were dropped. This event, however, had the effect of further sensitizing many lobbyists to the requirement that they had to register on individual bills before lobbying on them.

The other formally alleged violation occurred in early 1987 when a group of House members filed charges against a representative of the Iowa Chemical and Fertilizer Association. Involved House members argued that the lobbyist was guilty of distributing misinformation about circumstances surrounding the consideration of a proposed water measure. After a preliminary hearing the House Ethics Committee dismissed the charges, concluding that no rule existed prohibiting lobbyists from spreading, intentionally or unintentionally, misleading information about pending bills.

Annually, a high level of compliance is achieved in Iowa with regard to lobbyist regulation requirements. This compliance level is reflective of the broader moralistic cultural environment within which lobbyist and legislator interactions occur in Iowa's political system.

Groups and Lobbyists: Trends and Variations

What types of groups are actively involved in promoting or protecting their interests via representation by lobbyists during sessions of the
Iowa General Assembly? According to 1986 data, business groups, as is
generally the case at the national and state level, tend to dominate the
Iowa legislative scene, with more than one-half of all groups falling into
this category (Table 4.4). These groups range from the once-powerful
general business organization, the Iowa Association of Business and
Industry; to such trade associations as the Iowa Petroleum Council, the
Iowa Bankers Association, and the Iowa Wholesale Beer Distributing
Association; to such prominent individual corporations as John Deere
and Company (Iowa's biggest single employer), Meredith Corporation
(publisher of *Better Homes and Gardens,* in addition to other publications), and Ruan Industries (the state's major trucking company).

Table 4.4. Types of groups with registered lobbyists in Iowa Legislature, 1970 and 1986

Type of Group	Composition of Group	1970 No.	1970 %	1986 No.	1986 %	% Change
Business	General business groups, trade associations, individual corporations, professions, etc.	147	56.0	282	57.0	+ 92.0
Governmental	State governmental agencies, local governments, governmental officials' associations, etc.	23	8.9	74	14.9	+221.7
Citizens or causes	Permanent and ad hoc groups interested in such issues as gambling, liquor, welfare, highway safety, governmental reorganization, environment, etc.	21	8.0	69	14.2	+228.6
Educational	School employees and officials, community school districts, private colleges, alumni associations, etc.	20	7.7	29	5.9	+ 45.0
Labor	International unions and brotherhoods, state federations, local unions, special union conferences, etc.	18	6.9	19	3.8	+ 5.6
Farm	General farm organizations, commodity producer groups, etc.	7	2.9	7	1.4	0.0
Miscellaneous	Veterans, political party organizations, etc.	25	9.6	15	3.0	- 40.0
Total		261	100.0	495	100.2	+ 90.0

Sources: For 1970 data, Charles W. Wiggins, The Legislative Process in Iowa (Ames: Iowa State University Press, 1972); for 1986 data, Iowa Common Cause, 1986.

Other types of groups trailed far behind the business category. Collectively, two types of organizations, state and local governmental official groups and citizen-cause groups, make up approximately 30 percent
of those with registered lobbyists. Examples of the former are the very
active Iowa League of Municipalities, the Iowa Association of Counties,
the Iowa Association of County Conservation Boards, and the Iowa
Sheriffs' Association. Examples of the latter are the Sierra Club, the
League of Women Voters, Common Cause, the Iowa Citizen Action

Network (a recent arrival on the state interest group scene), and a host of other groups representing battered women, neglected children, the retarded, blind, and disabled, and parents with adopted children, among others.

Educational groups, such as the Iowa State Education Association, the Iowa Board of Regents, the Iowa Association of School Boards, and the Iowa Chapter of the American Association of Christian Schools, constitute slightly less than 6 percent of all groups, while labor groups (Iowa Federation of Labor, AFL-CIO, UAW, CWA, etc.) provide an even smaller amount (3.8 percent). Trailing even those are the farm groups, ranging from the general farm organizations (the Iowa Farm Bureau Federation is still the only one that really counts); to the various commodity groups representing producers of beef, pork, corn, soybeans, and poultry; to individual farm corporations. The limited representation of farm groups before the Iowa Legislature is somewhat surprising, given the important role that agriculture has played over the years in the state's economy. Perhaps the individualistic propensities of farmers, as well as the dominant representative role of the Iowa Farm Bureau Federation in the agricultural sector, help account for this phenomenon.

From the data in Table 4.4 one can also see an increasing concern and involvement by interest groups in state legislative affairs. From 1970 to 1986 the number of groups with registered lobbyists increased almost two-fold. Furthermore, this increase in group representation has not been uniform across all types of groups. Two types of groups — governmental and citizen-cause groups — increased about three-fold during the sixteen-year period, a phenomenon that is probably consistent with national trends. While business groups increased proportionally at the statewide rate, educational, labor, and farm group increments lagged significantly behind. Overall, these mixed trends are probably related to the static nature of the Iowa population and economy, the communications revolution, and national forces that encouraged the formation of many citizen-cause groups from the mid-1960s into the 1970s.

Concomitant with the overall leap in group representation before the Iowa Legislature has been an increase in the number of registered lobbyists. Whereas 297 men and women registered as group representatives during the 1970 session, 497 individuals were registered in 1986. While most lobbyists continued to represent a single group in 1986, the proportion representing more than one group increased marginally (from 14.8 to 18.3 percent). Thus, it seems that multiclient lobbyists, most of whom are Des Moines attorneys, are representing more groups than was previously the case.

Several multiclient lobbyists are generally regarded as quite effective in influencing legislative action. Foremost among them is Gene Kennedy, a former Democratic senator from Dubuque, who in 1986 represented nineteen clients ranging from the State Association of Beverage Retail Establishments to the Iowa Funeral Directors' Association. Kennedy has been especially effective in recent sessions on measures establishing a state lottery, pari-mutuel betting on horses and dogs, and private retail package liquor outlets (formerly a state-run monopoly). Other former lawmakers enjoying recent successes in the lobbying business are Craig Walter and Ted Anderson. Walter, a former Democratic representative from Council Bluffs, represented fourteen groups in 1986 ranging from the Iowa Hotel-Motel Association to Adventureland (a Des Moines amusement park). He allegedly has played a key role in opposing efforts by school interests to change the public primary and secondary school starting date in the fall to an earlier date. Anderson is a former Democratic senator from Waterloo and has the reputation for effectively representing senior citizens' groups and agencies, as well as state employees.

Several lobbyists without legislative backgrounds are also noted for their prowess. Among them is George A. Wilson, the son of a former Republican governor, whose Des Moines law practice represents several groups (eleven in 1986), including tobacco distributors, small loan companies, police chiefs, pharmaceutical manufacturers, and wine producers. Richard Bergland, another highly regarded lobbyist, represents several insurance companies, as well as the Iowa Hospital Association and the Iowa Independent Bankers Association. He has been deemed particularly effective in recent sessions in opposing proposals to legalize interstate banking. Russell "Rusty" Laird, another veteran multiclient lobbyist, is especially active in representing wholesale beer and wine distributors, among others.

All of these multiclient lobbyists are considered effective because of their personal acumen in interactions with relevant lawmakers. In other words, their effectiveness is a function more of their personalities and approaches to the legislative process than of the power of the various individual groups they represent.

Interest Group Involvement and Influence

How involved are interest groups in the Iowa legislative process and how much influence do they actually wield? Political scientists have traditionally used three means of determining the role and influence of groups. First and foremost has been the case study method, whereby the analyst selects a key issue (or a narrow range of issues) before a legislative body and focuses intensively on the activities and impacts of groups on the issue.[15] Issues involving a high level of public awareness, conflict, media attention, *and* group involvement have frequently been the subjects of such case studies. The second method is the survey of knowledgeables' *perceptions* of group influence in the legislative process.[16] Knowledgeables frequently tapped for assessments of group influence, whether that of individual groups or groups overall, are legislators, reporters, legislative staff, executive agency personnel, lobbyists, and even political scientists. In the third approach, researchers rely primarily on an overall review of the results of studies employing the first two methods.[17]

In the late 1970s the authors began a study of interest group activities in Iowa, as well as two other states, employing a significantly different methodology. The regulatory requirement referred to above, that lobbyists must register on bills before they begin lobbying on them, provided an opportunity for examining interest group involvement and influence. Immediately after the 1977–78 session we drew a 15 percent random sample of all bills that had been introduced. We next consulted the lobbyist bill registration lists of both legislative chambers and identified those lobbyists registered on our sample of bills. All identified lobbyists were interviewed in person or via telephone to ascertain the specific positions (pro or con) that their groups had taken on bills falling into our sample. ("Protective registrations," referred to above, were also ascertained and eliminated from further consideration.) In addition to group positions, we determined the final legislative disposition (passed or not passed) of each proposal in our sample by consulting appropriate legislative records.

Thus, what follows is a brief analysis of the involvement and influence of interest groups in a state legislature which employs a methodology significantly different from those used previously, as well as elsewhere in this volume. This methodology approaches the questions of group involvement and influence from more of a legislative decision-making perspective; that is, we start with a broad range of proposed legislation considered in Iowa in 1977–78, and then, using bill registration lists, lobbyist interviews, and legislative records, we determine lobbying structures and group impacts. It should be emphasized that state agency lobbying is excluded in this analysis.

How involved are groups in the Iowa legislative process? Table 4.5 lists the number of groups taking pro or con positions on the 287 bills falling into our random sample. On the one hand, our measures of central tendency displayed at the bottom of the table suggest that groups

Table 4.5 Number of interest groups taking positions on bills in Iowa, 1977-78

No. of Groups	No. of Bills	%
0	62	21.6
1	73	25.4
2	55	19.2
3	32	11.1
4	25	8.7
5-6	23	8.0
7-9	10	3.4
10	7	2.3
Total	287	99.9

Mean no. of groups per bill: 2.3

Mean no. of groups per bill
with at least 1 group taking
a pro/con stand: 4.4

Note: Pro or con lobbying by state agency lobbyists is not included.

are quite active in the Iowa legislative process, with two to four groups taking a pro or con position on measures. On the other hand, a closer examination of the distribution of group involvement across all bills indicates that our mean indicators tend to exaggerate the degree of group activity. For example, *no* interest group took a pro or con position on one-fifth of the bills, and only a single group took a position on one-fourth of the bills. Thus, limited group activity occurred on almost one-half of the measures. These findings support the more general observation, referred to previously, that the Iowa interest group system is loosely structured, with group activity targeted toward a limited number of measures deemed of major importance.

How successful were these interest groups in gaining passage of bills they favored or in defeating bills they opposed? Generally, our analysis suggests that groups are successful 50 percent of the time when one or more groups take a position, measured by determining which side of the question (pro or con) had more interest groups lobbying on it and then ascertaining whether the bill passed or failed. Thus, when more groups favored a measure than opposed it and the measure passed, it was scored as a success; similarly, when more groups opposed the measure than favored it and the bill was not passed, group lobbying was also scored as a success.

This 50 percent success rate of groups appears to raise some doubts about previous classifications of Iowa as a strong interest group state.[18] A comparison of the group success score in Iowa with those of two other states (55 percent for Texas and 67 for California) further reinforces the perspective that Iowa might be more accurately classified as a state where interest groups play a moderately influential role within the state's political system.[19]

Further support for the notion that groups are not as influential in the legislative process is provided by the information presented in Table 4.6. The data deal with the success rates of groups when their positions are in opposition to or in agreement with three other types of influence agents within the Iowa Legislature: governor, majority party leadership, and minority party leadership. (In personal interviews representatives of these groups had indicated to us their positions on our random sample of bills.) Generally, we see that two influence agents, the governor and majority party leadership, can have a significant impact on the influence of groups when they are mutually involved. For example, when the dominant group position on a bill runs counter to that of the governor, groups are successful only slightly more than 27 percent of the time, a decrease of almost 19 percent in relation to situations in which the governor has no position. Furthermore, groups are successful only 33.1 percent of the occasions when running up against the majority party leadership, a success rate reduction of almost 20 percent compared to when the majority party leadership is not involved. Agreement with the governor or majority leadership, on the other hand, results in a significant increase in interest group success (27.8 and 30 percent, respectively). These findings lend additional support to the position that Iowa can be best characterized as a state where interest groups play a moderately influential role.

Table 4.6. Success of Iowa interest groups when in conflict/agreement with other influence agents

Influence Agent	Conflict		Neutral[a]		Agreement	
	%	No.[b]	%	No.	%	No.
Governor's office						
Success	27.3	11			73.8	42
No governor involvement			46.0	150		
Gain/Loss[c]	-18.7				+27.8	
Majority leadership						
Success	33.3	21			83.7	92
No majority leadership involvement			53.2	171		
Gain/Loss	-19.9				+30.0	
Minority Leadership						
Success	81.8	11			86.7	45
No minority leadership involvement			55.7	228		
Gain/Loss	+26.1				+31.0	

[a]Does not include situations in which group positions were balanced or in which there was no group involvement.

[b]Represents the total number of situations in which groups and other influence agents took a conflicting or the same position.

[c]Success of groups when in conflict or agreement with other influence agents versus success when other influence agents were not involved in the situation.

Conclusions

In many ways the approaches groups pursue in attempting to influence public policy-making decisions are a reflection of the prevailing
moralistic political culture of the state, which in Iowa's case is one that
emphasizes openness, fairness, honesty, and integrity. Thus, the "booze,
women, and bribes" syndrome has never been characteristic of the interaction between lobbyists and public officials in the state. The Iowa populace expects its public officials to operate with the highest standards of
conduct, and the state's dominant newspaper, the *Des Moines Register,*
performs an effective role as the keeper, or enforcer, of this public expec-
tation. Thus, Iowa politicians tend to be so honest that they are at times
characterized as "dull"!

The changing character of the interest group power structure reflects the changing nature of the Iowa economy and its political institutions. From its early history of initial settlement when railroads dominated the scene to a fairly lengthy period of dominance by two groups
(the Iowa Farm Bureau Federation and the Iowa Manufacturers Association) as a result of the commercialization of agriculture and industrialization, the contemporary power structure can be best characterized as
interest group pluralism, with no group or set of groups dominating
public policy decisions. This pluralism has been associated with further
socioeconomic diversification, as well as the arrival of two-party competition and court-mandated legislative apportionment. Not only have
more groups organized to pursue public policy goals, but more groups
now have a reasonable chance of being heard and responded to within
the decision-making agencies of state government.

Overall, groups play a moderately influential role within the state's
political system. Although most have only recently become active in the
campaign finance field via the formation and operation of PACs, their
impact on election outcomes cannot be characterized as inordinate. Iowa
has a well-educated and informed electorate, as well as a tradition of low
to modest spending in political campaigns, so the role of PACs in electioneering can be described at best only as modest. Interest group lobbying initiatives in the legislative arena also result in moderate success, with
the governor and majority party legislative leaders capable of exerting a
significant impact on the chances for such success. Thus, overall, interest group power in Iowa is consistent with the politics of moderation that
characterize the state.

Notes

1. Samuel C. Patterson, "Iowa," in Alan Rosanthal and Maureen Moakley, eds., *The Political Life of the American States* (New York: Praeger, 1984), 97.
2. Ibid., 83–98.
3. Daniel Elazar, *American Federalism: A View from the States,* 2d ed. (New York: Harper & Row, 1972), 90–120.
4. Arnold A. Rogow, "The Loyalty Oath Issue in Iowa, 1951," *American Political Science Review* 55 (1951), 861–69.
5. Samuel C. Patterson, Ronald D. Hedlund, and Robert G. Boynton, *Representatives and Represented: Bases of Public Support for the American Legislatures* (New York: John Wiley, 1975), 42–44.
6. Harlan Hahn, *Urban-Rural Conflict: The Politics of Change* (Beverly Hills, Calif.: Sage, 1971), 47–48.
7. Ibid. See also Charles W. Wiggins, "Interest Group Power within State Legislative Systems: The Case of the Iowa Farm Bureau Federation" (Ph.D. dissertation, Washington University, St. Louis, Mo., 1964).
8. Charles W. Wiggins, "The Post–World War II Legislature Reapportionment Battle in Iowa Politics," in Dorothy Schwieder, ed., *Patterns and Perspectives in Iowa History* (Ames: Iowa State University Press, 1973), 403–30.
9. Charles W. Wiggins and William P. Browne, "Interest Groups and Public Policy within a State Legislative Setting," *Polity* 14 (1982), 548–58.
10. "Texas," in R. J. Hrebenar and C. S. Thomas, eds., *Interest Group Politics in the Southern States* (Tuscaloosa, Ala.: University of Alabama Press, 1992).
11. Iowa Common Cause, written communication to Charles Wiggins, October 1986.
12. Iowa Common Cause, "Fact Sheet on H. F. 2476," prepared by Peggy Huppert, 1986.
13. Iowa Common Cause, written communication to Charles Wiggins, October 1986.
14. John R. Wright, "PACs, Contributions, and Roll Calls: An Organizational Perspective," *American Political Science Review* 79 (1985), 400–414.
15. Andrew Hacker, "Pressure Politics in Pennsylvania: The Truckers vs. the Railroads," in Alan Westin, ed., *The Uses of Power* (New York: Harcourt, Brace & World, 1962), 324–76.
16. Belle Zeller, *American State Legislatures* (New York: Thomas Crowell, 1954); Wayne L. Francis, *Legislative Issues in the Fifty States: A Comparative Analysis* (Chicago: Rand McNally, 1967).
17. Sarah McCally Morehouse, *State Politics, Parties and Policy* (New York: Holt, Rinehart & Winston, 1982).
18. Ibid.; Zeller, *American State Legislatures.*
19. Wiggins and Browne, "Interest Groups and Public Policy," 556–58.

KANSAS

Representation in Transition

ALLAN J. CIGLER and DWIGHT KIEL

Traveling west across Kansas on Interstate 70 in the summer on the way to the Colorado Rockies, it is easy to see how the Sunflower state has developed its national image. The landscape is vast and largely treeless, at times looking like an ocean of wheat. The weather is hot and muggy, windy, but with little rain. Except along short stretches of the highway near Lawrence and Topeka, the livestock appear to outnumber the human inhabitants of the land. But inferring the nature of politics from what appears to be a homogeneous, rural landscape is misleading. Early Kansas political history was anything but dull, and contemporary Kansas politics are as conflictual as those in many urban industrial states.

Kansas, from before statehood in 1861 until World War II, was considered a crystal ball for many political and social developments in the country.[1] Kansans played prominent leadership roles in a variety of movements, including abolition, populism, progressivism, and Prohibition. During the last half century, however, Kansas has been less a leading indicator of national trends than a reflection of them, while the state has undergone the slow process of urbanization and the diversification of its economic base.

When one hears of Kansas today, "usually it's either a tornado one thinks of, or the Wizard of Oz or the inability to get a drink."[2] But the rural and farm-based image of the state has been overdrawn in the popular press. Urbanization has taken place at a fairly rapid rate since World War II. In 1940 more than 58 percent of the citizens of the state lived in rural areas, but by the mid-1980s the figure was less than 25 percent. The traditional view of Kansas as a state dominated by rural and farm interests is now a shadow image, although the shadow remains active and lively. Agricultural interests are strong politically, but their role in the state economy has been steadily declining. In the 1940s, farm commodities alone generated 20 percent of the state's economic product, while manufacturing contributed just 8 percent. By the 1980s these figures had been reversed. Wholesale and retail trade is now the largest component of the Kansas economy.

The growth in the state's population and its business and industry has not been uniform across the state. Many of the counties in rural western Kansas actually have fewer residents than in the 1890s. In general, most new enterprises and accompanying population growth are concentrated in a northeastern corridor from Kansas City, Kansas, to Topeka (the capital) and in the south central region around Wichita. The Wichita aerospace industry, in particular, is a major component of the state's changing economic base.

Despite economic diversification, however, Kansas still remains very dependent for economic growth on agriculture and the rural-based oil and gas industry, two sectors that did not experience economic recovery in the 1980s. As in the other Plains states, many small towns in Kansas based on the farm economy are in deep trouble, as grain commodity and energy prices remain low. The expansion of manufacturing enterprises, though helpful, has not provided enough employment for both displaced farm workers and young Kansans entering the labor force.

Perhaps the leading "growth" industry in Kansas since 1970 has been higher education, which was supposed to provide the knowledge for new directions in economic growth. Unfortunately for the state, higher education has become an "export" business. Between 1970 and 1984 Kansas experienced an out-migration of 31,000 of its citizens, mostly among young adults with higher than average education and skill levels.

Many in Kansas believe that the state is at a social and economic crossroads, as it tries to evolve from a relatively narrow economic base to one far less dependent on the rural economy. Political leaders are struggling to generate a vision of what a "new economic Kansas" might look like, creating a situation that increasingly pits rural against urban interests, on both economic and life-style issues. The state has a long tradition of nonintervention in economic and social areas (in 1986 Kansas ranked 42d in governmental expenditures per capita), and accepting activist government does not come easily for many citizens. The ongoing debate over the state's future, coupled with the current lack of political direction, has contributed to a situation in which special interests are at the forefront of state politics.

The Political Context:
A Setting for Interest Group Influence

At first glance, Kansas appears to be a state quite susceptible to interest group domination. With the notable exception of the Populist interlude, the Republican party has dominated state electoral politics and Kansas government. Further, state and local party organizations in Kansas have been and continue to be very weak.[3] The parties play a relatively minor role in the recruitment of candidates, and "legislative candidates are pretty much on their own in running for office."[4] The traditional understanding of an inverse relationship between party and interest group strength leads one to expect that a few strong groups could have substantial influence over Kansas electoral and legislative processes.

Accounts of Kansas politics before the late 1960s and early 1970s support the traditional understanding. These studies report the impressive influence of certain economic interests, particularly the banks, the gas and electric utilities, pipeline companies, the railroads, and farm groups.[5] However, the Supreme Court's reapportionment decisions in the early 1960s began to generate a new set of electoral and legislative conditions.

Kansas entered the 1960s with both houses severely malapportioned. Urban areas were especially underrepresented. Between 1910 and 1959 the population of the state increased by 27.4 percent. While many rural areas declined in population or grew at slow rates, the urban areas of the state experienced major growth. During the same 49-year period Johnson County (suburban Kansas City) experienced a growth rate of 671 percent; Shawnee County (Topeka), 109 percent; and Sedgwick County (Wichita), 388 percent.[6] Yet according to the state Agricultural Census in 1959, one rural county with 2,061 people had one representative, while urban Sedgwick County (Wichita), with a population of 321,503, was entitled to only five representatives.[7] Compared to other states before the reapportionment cases of the 1960s, both houses of the Kansas Legislature ranked low in population representativeness,[8] high in terms of rural bias,[9] and high in the advantage accorded the Republican party.[10]

By the 1970s both houses had experienced a sharp decline in members from rural constituencies and a huge increase in the number of urban and suburban members. In 1963 urban legislators held 7.5 percent of the seats in the Kansas Senate, at a time when 30.8 percent of the state's population resided in urban areas. By 1973 urban legislators held 32.5 percent of the Senate seats. Suburban representation in the Senate likewise grew from 4 percent of the seats in 1963 to 12 percent in 1973. A large decline in legislators with agricultural occupations accompanied the changes.[11]

The diminution of rural bias in the legislature did not affect Republican party domination, because of Republican strength in suburban areas and in some of the state's major cities. Although Democrats made major gains in the House and Senate in the middle and late 1970s and have done well in recent gubernatorial elections, they remain the minority party.

Perhaps the major impact of reapportionment was to exacerbate a cleavage between suburban Republicans concentrated in eastern Kansas and their rural western colleagues. Republican factionalism has enabled conservative Democrats to win the governorship on a number of occasions. Urban Democrats often join their suburban Republican colleagues in voting against rural interests. In Kansas the most progressive statewide candidates are often Republicans from the Kansas City suburbs. Successful statewide Democrats often are more conservative than their Republican opponents.

Despite these changes the Kansas Legislature remains a "citizen" forum, meeting for only ninety days each year. The legislator's job is still a part-time one. Parties are important in structuring legislative conflict,[12] but Kansas legislators are rather independent and/or constituency-oriented.[13]

Interest Group Regulation

Regulation of special interests in Kansas is not especially harsh, though it is rather complex. Kansas has had a law requiring the registration of lobbyists since 1909. In 1974, in the post-Watergate reform climate, a comprehensive governmental ethics law was enacted through a bipartisan effort. Besides mandating the registration of lobbyists, the law requires special interest representatives to file a financial report in any month in which expenditures exceed $100, showing the amount paid for such items as entertainment, gifts, honoraria or payments, and mass media expenditures. In a given calendar year a lobbyist may not offer or

pay any "economic opportunity" gifts, loans, special discounts, or hono-
raria that have an aggregate value of more than $100. Interest group
expenditures such as salaries or fees paid to lobbyists, however, are not
recorded, making the disclosure laws greatly understate the true financial costs of lobbying efforts. Lobbyists are required to wear group identification name tags when they are in the state capitol building. Individuals coming to Topeka on a one-time basis to petition their
representatives and state officials attempting to influence the legislature
on an agency's behalf are not considered lobbyists under Kansas law and
do not register.

The post-Watergate era also saw the adoption of a state campaign
finance law. The current law calls for the registration of political action
committees, and limits each PAC to contributions in legislative races up
to $500 in the primary and $500 in the general election. PACs may contribute up to $2,000 for a primary and $2,000 in a general election for
candidates for statewide office. Candidates are also required to report
periodically their campaign expenditures.

In 1975 the Kansas Governmental Ethics Commission was established to enforce the campaign finance laws, and the agency soon got
into difficulty because of its vigorous enforcement efforts, including
some directed at the Majority Leader of the Kansas Senate. The result
was the creation of a new enforcement agency in 1981, the Public Disclosure Commission, with a diminished capacity to enforce the laws. The
commission is composed of five political appointees, four selected by
legislative leaders and one by the governor. The position of its executive
director has been deliberately left vacant since 1981, and the small staff
lacks the resources to audit all but a few campaigns each election, and
then only when a majority of the commissioners approve. Individual
campaign reports and PAC data are available for public and media use
but have not been computerized for easy access.

Perhaps the biggest change in the interest group climate in Topeka
since the reform era of the 1970s is one of style and nomenclature rather
than of rules and regulations. "Image" in legislator-lobbyist relations has
become crucial. Although interest group tactics in the state continue to
range from formal testimony before committees to wining and dining
legislators, "the ground rules and 'watering holes' have changed."[14] For
example, before the late 1970s a variety of important interest groups
maintained "hospitality" rooms at a downtown Topeka hotel, providing
drinks for legislators after working hours each day of the session. In
1978 legislative leaders stopped the practice in the face of adverse publicity. Today one hospitality night a week during the legislative session is
sponsored by a group of special interests.[15]

Whether legislators and lobbyists are scrutinized more than previously is an open question. What is perhaps more important is that both legislators and lobbyists are acutely aware of image concerns, and act accordingly. Kansas has never been a state where the undue or corrupt influence of special interests dominated the political climate, nor is it today.

Group Representation in Kansas Politics

The sheer number and diversity of special interests active in contemporary Kansas politics run contrary to the stereotype of politics in the Plains as largely limited to agriculture, utility, and railroad interests. Like the national political arena, Kansas has experienced a proliferation of groups and interests, at a pace that has quickened since the early 1970s. For example, in 1971, 211 lobbyists registered with the secretary of state, all but a few representing only one group.[16] By 1987, a decade and a half later, 843 registrations were made by more than 600 lobbyists.[17] The number of "lobbyists" is even greater, since some individuals go to Topeka as "citizen" participants rather than registered representatives of a group.

Table 5.1 presents a summary of special interest representation, by type of organization and number of registered lobbyists. As one might expect, various business organizations, the oil and gas industry, and the highly regulated professions (particularly banking, medicine, health care, and insurance) are well represented in Topeka, a situation that has existed for years. But the aggregate figures tell little about the significant changes since the mid-1970s in Kansas interest group politics.

For example, in 1971 nearly one-eighth of the registered lobbyists in Kansas represented insurance companies, and more than half were representatives of only six interests: medicine, business/industry, insurance, liquor (brewers and dealers), railroads and transportation, and utilities.[18] Although the interest group universe has nearly tripled in size since 1975, the number of lobbyists representing these interests has grown more slowly.

The causes of the tremendous growth of new interests in Kansas parallel those at the national level in three important ways. First, and most important, organizations now lobby through more than interest-wide coalitions, that is, through peak associations. In recent years many organizations, including individual corporations, state and local governments, and universities, have sought additional representation.[19] For example, the League of Kansas Municipalities has represented cities for

Table 5.1. Special interest representation in Kansas, by category, October 1986

Category	No. of Interests Registered	No. of Lobbyists Registered[a]
Business/Industrial	84	108
Medical/Health care	41	61
Professional	16	35
Insurance	29	49
Education	30	70
Energy, oil & gas	30	43
Banks/Savings and loan	13	28
Utilities	7	16
Agriculture/Rural	12	27
Cities	14	17
Religious	6	10
Environment	6	9
Chambers of commerce	12	19
Civil rights/Ethnic	1	3
Intergovernment relations	22	33
Labor/Unions	7	12
Real estate	4	4
Railroads	4	8
Construction/Land development	11	20
Telephone & communications	14	30
"Sin" & morality groups	2	10
Aged	5	11
Legal profession	11	15
Liquor interests	11	17
Highways/Safety	9	23
Social problems	15	26
Women's groups	4	5
Registered individuals	15	15
Other/Unclassified (including single issue, pubic interest)	24	27
Total	459	751

Source: List of lobbyists registered with the Kansas Secretary of State as of October 1986.

[a]A total of 584 individuals registered, some in more than one category.

years, but beginning in the 1980s some smaller cities have sent lobbyists to Topeka to fight for their specific interests. And though the Kansas Chamber of Commerce and Industry is an important organization representing "all business and industry, large and small," twelve local, county, or city chambers or promotional agencies are now active in the capital. Companies, too, increasingly send their own corporation executives to lobby or hire professional lobbyists to represent their interests. For example, Anheuser Busch is represented by the U.S. Brewers Association as well as by an Anheuser Busch lobbyist.

The second cause of the growth of new interests is the changing role of Kansas government in certain policy sectors. Nowhere is the change more evident than in education, where expenditures now take up more than half the state's general fund, or nearly $770 million of the $1.3 billion in state expenditures. The key factor was the passage of the

School Foundation Finance Act in 1965, reflecting the state's recognition that reliance on local school district property taxes could not keep up with the demand for increasing educational services and spiraling costs.[20]

The educational policy sector is currently the most visible and highly competitive policy area in state politics. Various interests are highly involved, ranging from organizations of teachers like the Kansas National Education Association (KNEA) and the Wichita chapter of the American Federation of Teachers, to the Kansas Association of School Boards and the United School Administrators of Kansas. The Kansas Congress of Parents and Teachers, the state PTA, plays an active role in the political process, as do a number of "alternative" education groups, "special" education groups, and those representing religious schools. Competition for the public educational dollar is so intense that, increasingly, individual school districts send registered lobbyists to Topeka, as do some local NEA chapters. With the decline of rural property values in the 1980s, the state aid formula has been a major source of rural-urban tension; rural school systems have attempted to maintain quality by greatly increasing their share of state support, often at the expense of urban and suburban school systems.

Kansas government is also deeply involved in higher education, supporting six state universities and nineteen junior colleges. Two other institutions, the Kansas Technological Institute and Washburn University of Topeka, receive partial state funding, and even private college students are eligible for certain state aid. Many of the state-supported universities and junior colleges have lobbyists who are quite active in Topeka. On the bigger campuses, such as the University of Kansas in Lawrence, the faculty has its own registered lobbyist, who acts independently of the school's institutional lobbyists. Students at the public institutions are similarly organized, with a peak association called Associated Students of Kansas (ASK); the student bodies of some of the individual universities have their own registered lobbyists. Classified employees, mostly clerical and maintenance staff, also have their own lobbyists. The State Board of Regents, a government agency, has traditionally been a key player in lobbying on behalf of funding for higher education.

The increasing federal and state role in the social services and welfare areas likewise has spawned a tremendous growth of special interest activity. For example, though groups of service deliverers such as doctors, nurses, and nursing home owners have long played an important role in Kansas politics, since the mid-1970s there has been a rise in the number of recipient groups or "public interest" groups that claim to speak for recipients. A good example is Kansans for Improvement of Nursing Homes (KINH), a group founded in 1975 by a wealthy Lawrence resident concerned with the lack of meaningful state supervision of nursing home personnel. KINH was influential in developing the state's program for the training of nursing home aides and the monitoring of nursing homes by county public health nurses. KINH, along with a number of recently organized groups, is a member of the Kansas Coalition on Aging, a collection of advocacy groups viewed as speaking for senior citizens' interests. Groups representing the disabled, children with specific health and education problems, and the financially disadvantaged are now a regular part of the Topeka scene.

The third cause of the proliferation of Kansas special interests has been the rise of "single issue" politics in the 1980s. Morality issues have always had a central place in Kansas politics, and the state until the 1980s had among the most restrictive liquor and "sin" laws in the country. But the declining rural influence in the legislature and the deteriorating economic condition of the state have combined to create a new context for morality issues. Now such issues are largely debated as matters of economic development, with such groups as Kansans for Pari-Mutuel and the Kansas Greyhound Owners Association challenging long-established traditional interests such as Kansans for Life at Its Best. Both prochoice and prolife groups are very active in Kansas, including the National Organization for Women (NOW), Planned Parenthood, Right to Life of Kansas, and Kansans for Life. Traffic safety groups have also become active, especially groups such as Traffic Safety Now and Kansas Women for Highway Safety. Motorcyclists have become involved in preventing helmet laws, in a classic case of quiescent interests forced to respond when social issues are politicized.

In their 1971 study of the Kansas Legislature, Marvin Harder and Carolyn Rampey commmented that "what is notable about the list of lobbyists is that few of the major social and political issues of our times — poverty, civil rights, ecology, consumer protection — are represented by interest groups in Topeka."[21] They could not make the same claim in the 1990s, although both the legislators and the lobbyists we surveyed mentioned such issue areas as still being "underrepresented." In the environmental and social service areas the "public interest" seems to be increasingly better represented. Common Cause now has a paid lobbyist, as does Amnesty International USA. With the exception of the organized labor sector, limited by the existence of right-to-work laws in the state, the number and kind of groups participating in the contemporary political arena in Kansas reflect those found in many urban industrial states.

Many observers of Kansas politics believe that political decision making is much more complex and more scrutinized than even in the early 1980s, because of the increasingly large number of groups active in the process. More special interest representation, however, does not necessarily mean that group power has been significantly altered in the policy-making process. Representation may open up the possibilities for the diffusion of power among interest groups but does not translate into immediate and effective power.

The "Powerful" Interests

In the fall and early winter of 1986, lobbyists and legislators who participated in the 1986 session of the Kansas Legislature were surveyed by mail questionnaire to assess the influence of special interests in the policy-making process. The survey instruments were a mix of open- and closed-ended questions. All legislators were sent the questionnaire, and 86 out of 165 responded, a response rate of 52 percent. The survey was sent to 282 lobbyists (half of the registered lobbyists), and 156 returned usable questionnaires, a response rate of 55 percent.[22]

The questionnaire and cover letter encouraged respondents to think of special interests and groups in the broadest sense and to include government agencies and individual companies as special interests. The key question asked both legislators and lobbyists to name the five most consistently influential interests, defined as influential beyond one session in the Kansas lawmaking process. Respondents noted special interests in broad policy sectors, such as education, and specific groups, such as the KNEA. Both types of information are included in Table 5.2.

Legislators and lobbyists were in fundamental agreement concerning the most consistently influential interests. Agriculture, banking, and education were ranked among the top three interests by both groups of respondents, clearly ahead of the fourth-ranking interest (business and commerce).

The importance of agricultural interests in the state is hardly a surprise. The Kansas Farm Bureau, with its large membership, professional lobbying staff, and automatic access to sizable rural contingent at the state House has long been a dominant force in Kansas politics. The Kansas Livestock Association is viewed as quite powerful as well. The strength of agricultural interests in politics is best illustrated by the State Board of Agriculture, the agency that regulates farming activity, including such matters as control of products used on the farm. The agency also deals with what some see as consumer protection activities, such as

Table 5.2. Most "consistently influential" interests in Kansas politics, as named by legislators and lobbyists, 1986

Policy Sector[a]	No. of Times Mentioned	
	By Legislators	By Lobbyists
Education (KNEA, Kansas Assoc. of School Boards)	48	53
Agriculture/Rural (Farm Bureau, Kansas Livestock Assoc.)	45	66
Banks (Kansas Bankers Assoc., Independent Bakers Assoc.)	40	74
Business (KCCI, Boeing)	23	43
Utilities (Kansas Power and Light, rural electric co-ops)	21	33
Lawyers (Kansas Bar Assoc., Kansas Trial Lawyers Assoc.)	20	34
Medical and health (Kansas Medical Society)	18	36
Insurance	13	15
Cities	12	13
Local chambers of commerce	11	8
Labor (AFL-CIO)	11	11
Oil and gas	11	28
Telephone and communications (Southwestern Bell)	9	15
"Sin" and morality groups (Kansans for Life at Its Best)	9	8
State agencies (Dept. of Social and Rehabilitation Services, Board of Regents)	9	18
Real estate	7	0
Motor carriers (Kansas Motor Carriers Assoc.)	5	16
Railroads	5	14

[a]Interests noted by a minimum of five legislators or lobbyists are listed.

dairy product inspection, product labeling, inspection of soft-serve ice cream establishments, and meat and poultry inspection.

Members of the board are elected by delegates from various farm organizations rather than appointed by the governor, the method of selection for other state boards. "The Board of Agriculture may be viewed as an association that is recognized by law, financed by the state, and authorized to administer certain state laws, but one that is responsible in a theoretical sense to the delegates who are elected from private farm associations."[23] By statute, 60 percent of the board's budget comes from state funds and 40 percent from fees collected from those regulated.

Some respondents in both surveys, however, noted that agricultural interests are less influential than often thought and that even groups like the Farm Bureau can no longer bully the legislature. Farm groups must engage in coalition activity with nonfarm or even urban groups to achieve their goals today. For example, agricultural interests have worked closely with senior citizen groups to keep property taxes down.

Further, in large measure because of the economic crisis facing many farmers since the mid-1970s, farming interests have become less cohesive. To some Kansas farmers, the Farm Bureau is just an insurance company, out of touch with farmers' needs. Kansas was one of the hotbeds of the radical American Agriculture Movement in the late 1970s, and the Farm Bureau has evidently lost credibility as a representative of agricultural policy interests in some quarters.[24]

Even the privileged position of the State Board of Agriculture has recently been challenged. The two previous governors, one of each party, made major efforts to change the selection procedure for the body, including an attempt to make the secretary of agriculture a gubernatorial appointee. In 1987 Governor Mike Hayden, a Republican, "invited" the current agriculture secretary to become a member of his cabinet, revealing continued gubernatorial insistence on executive control of the "independent" board.

Many in our survey saw banking interests as the most dominant special interest in Topeka, and the Kansas Bankers Association (KBA) as perhaps the single most powerful group in the state. Kansas banking interests possess impressive financial resources, highly professional lobbying staffs, and a reputation for social lobbying. The KBA, in particular, always is among the leaders in "entertainment" expenses reported to the secretary of state. The banking groups have active PACs and the advantage of an "inside" lobby of bankers who sit as elected legislators on the banking regulation committees.

The KBA is the dominant group in this policy sector, but banking interests, like agriculture interests, are less monolithic than they were. A major issue in the late 1980s was a proposal to allow statewide branch banking, permitting Kansas banks to buy other banks throughout the state and convert them to branches. The Kansas Independent Bankers Association, made up of smaller local banks, vigorously opposed the bill, which was the work of the KBA, on the grounds that it would result in banks' "taking control of the capital out of the community where it was created."[25] Savings and loan associations and credit unions are also active participants in banking policy making.

The third major "consistently influential interest," education, represents a relative newcomer to the list of special interests with political power. Like agriculture and banking groups, however, educational interests are often divided and compete with each other. While all interests want more money from the state for education, groups such as the KNEA and the Kansas Association of School Boards are often in opposition on issues such as caps on teacher salaries and compulsory arbitration. Though no educator in the state likes to admit it, the higher education lobby and public school interests are, in reality, competitors for government funds, especially when funds are scarce.

The KNEA clearly emerged in the 1980s as a force to be reckoned with in Kansas politics. The group relies on grass-roots lobbying, an aggressive PAC effort, and an extensive membership throughout the state (more than 20,000 dues-paying members). The KNEA represents the faculty at Pittsburg State University and is active in trying to become the recognized bargaining agent for the faculty at other state schools. Like the NEA in many states, the group is most closely related to the Democratic party (though it endorses members of both parties) and seems particularly influential when there is a Democratic governor.

Certain business interests are also viewed as influential in Kansas politics, including the Kansas Chamber of Commerce and Industry, a variety of local chambers of commerce, and a few companies, especially Boeing Aircraft. The Kansas Medical Society and the Kansas Trial Lawyers Association were among the most-mentioned of all groups in our survey. Both groups were given high marks for their professional lobbying staffs and their vast resources. The Kansas Trial Lawyers Association, with fewer than 1,000 members, is another group greatly aided by its "inside lobby." Group members in both houses frequently sit on committees that deal with legislation affecting the legal profession. The insurance lobby, which is composed of a large number of individual insurance companies, was mentioned by quite a few of our respondents as the strongest lobby in the state.

When our findings are compared with previous research on Kansas politics, it appears that some interests are decreasing in influence. The railroads, utilities, and the oil and gas industry, though still quite important in the state, are no longer unchallenged. The railroads now face tough competition from the motor carriers. The politics of utility regulation has become much more visible since 1980, as consumers have mobilized in the face of the large energy cost increases. The utilities, once able to secure passage of bills effectively overturning rulings of the Kansas Corporation Commission, recently have had less success. The oil and gas industry, which for years avoided a severance tax, now must pay the tax, in no small measure because of the efforts of educational interests, which aggressively campaigned for the increased state revenue. The "sin" groups, which for so long prevented the state from modernizing its liquor laws, have also lost influence, as the state seeks to attract new business by creating the impression that it is now in the American mainstream.

Organized labor has a presence in Kansas, though its political influence has been hampered by the existence of the state's right-to-work law. There are an estimated 80,000 members of organized labor in Kansas, most affiliated with the AFL-CIO in some way.[26] The United Auto Workers, the International Machinists Association, and the Brotherhood of Airway and Airline Clerks are among the largest affiliates. Labor interests in Topeka are closely identified with "reform measures and the liberal side of social-welfare issues" but have a record of "intensive involvement with both parties."[27] Labor's impact is enhanced, however, when a Democrat is governor.

Perhaps the biggest change in the overall patterns of special interest influence in Kansas is that group competition is simply keener than before. Few policy sectors are dominated by only one group as thoroughly as in the past, though clearly groups are not equal in the influence process. As the Kansas economy diversifies, the scope of what used to be narrow policy sectors broadens. One result is that strong groups are pitted against other strong groups more often, as when the Kansas Medical Society, the insurance companies, and the Kansas Trial Lawyers Association clash over the limits of liability in a malpractice suit.

The Kansas Lobbyists

Given the diversity of the Kansas group universe, comprised of long-standing groups, new groups, and ad hoc groups, it is not surprising to find Kansas lobbyists and their activities reflecting diversity as well.

Tables 5.3 and 5.4 present summary data on the backgrounds of Kansas lobbyists from our survey, as well as information related to the job of the Kansas lobbyist. It is clear that Kansas lobbyists are drawn from the most highly educated sector of society; all but a handful have college degrees. More than 60 percent of our respondents had either done graduate work or received a graduate degree. A degree in law is the most common educational background. Most lobbyists are males, but women have substantially increased in number in recent years and comprise 23 percent of the registered lobbyists in Topeka. Women are the primary lobbyists for some highly influential groups, including the Kansas Motor Carriers Association and the Kansas Trial Lawyers Association. The mean number of years our respondents had registered to lobby

Table 5.3. Backgrounds of Kansas lobbyists

Characteristic	%
1. Gender	
Female	23.1
Male	76.9
2. Education	
Less than high school	2.6
High school graduate	2.6
Some college	9.6
College graduate	23.7
Graduate work or graduate degree	61.5
3. Is primary occupation lobbyist?	
Yes	30.8
No	69.2
4. Years lobbyist in Kansas	
Fewer than 3	29.5
3 to 5	28.8
5+ to 10	23.8
More than 10	17.9

Table 5.4. Level of lobbying activity of Kansas lobbyists

Characteristic	%
1. Lobby in other states?	
Yes	12.2
No	87.8
2. Member of the organization for which they lobby?	
Yes	60.3
No	39.7
3. Number of groups or interests lobbied for	
One	80.1
Two	7.7
Three or more	12.2
4. Number of days a week lobby during session	
One or fewer	30.1
More than one/fewer than three	13.7
More than three	56.2
5. Amount of time lobbying directed toward legislature	
Less than 80%	30.1
80% or more	69.9

in Kansas was 6.6, but our survey revealed wide variation in lobbying experience in the state. More than half of the survey respondents had lobbied 5 years or less, and nearly 18 percent had been active for more than 10 years.

Examination of our findings suggests that the lobbyists represent a mix of "types": full-time, "contract" lobbyists, often hired by groups or companies to lobby for them; association executives, whose major activity is lobbying during the ninety-day legislative session; and part-time "amateurs," who lobby only occasionally, usually without payment. In our survey we asked, "All things considered, what do you consider to be your primary occupation?" Nearly one-third of the respondents indicated "lobbyist" or "special interest advocate." Among the other two-thirds were a number of executive directors of associations, whose job descriptions included the coordination of the groups' lobbying activities and who during the legislative session served as primary lobbyists for the groups.

The level of activity of the lobbyists varied tremendously, with more than 30 percent lobbying one day or less a week during the session, and more than 55 percent lobbying for three or more days per week during the session. Lobbying in Kansas is concentrated on the legislative branch; nearly 70 percent of our survey respondents indicated that 80 percent or more of their time is spent lobbying legislators; more than 17 percent indicated that all their time is directed toward the legislative branch; 38.5 percent estimated that less than 5 percent of their time involves nonlegislative lobbying. Group representatives most likely to get involved in lobbying activity directed toward the governor's office and executive activities appeared to be concentrated among representatives of regulated industries and professions. More than 80 percent indicated that they were active at least occasionally between legislative sessions, reflecting the increase in interim legislative committees created to study state problems between sessions.

In recent years in American politics there has been growth in the number of group consultants, so-called "guns for hire," professionals paid by special interests to lobby in their behalf, often on a contingency basis. A variety of questions on our survey lend some insight into how this phenomenon has affected Kansas. For example, nearly 40 percent of the lobbyists are contract lobbyists and are not members of the group for which they lobby, while nearly 20 percent lobby for two or more groups. Both figures are far higher than those of the early 1970s.[28] Twelve percent of the respondents lobby in states other than Kansas, and a few even mentioned lobbying at the federal and local levels.

Although the typical Kansas lobbyist lobbies for only one group, the multiple-group lobbyist is becoming an increasingly important part of the policy-making landscape. In our survey of lobbyists we asked them to name the three most effective lobbyists in Kansas. Twenty-seven different individuals were named by at least one respondent. Not surprisingly, many of the most-named individuals were long-time lobbyists for some of the state's most influential groups, including the Farm Bureau, the Kansas Medical Society, the Kansas Bankers Association, and the Kansas Trial Lawyers Association. But also prominent on the list were the new breed of professional lobbyists, most often ex-legislators or past members of a governor's staff or executive team.

According to our respondents, the most prominent lobbyist in Topeka is Pete McGill, who heads the firm of Pete McGill and Associates. McGill, ex-Speaker of the Kansas House and a seven-term legislator who retired in 1977, has developed a reputation as an effective representative of business interests. For the 1987 legislative session, McGill had registered to lobby on behalf of eighteen different interests; still others, ranging from the Kansas Independent Bankers Association and the Kansas Funeral Directors Association to Iowa Beef Processors and R. J. Reynolds Tobacco Company, are represented by members of his firm. McGill is the epitome of the political insider, and his move from legislator to lobbyist has been compared to that of a doctor who goes to school first and then goes out to practice his skills.[29] The firm offers a variety of services to clients, from help with research and testimony before the legislature and help with the state bureaucracy, to analysis of legislator voting records and help with group PAC decisions.[30] According to one astute lobbyist respondent, McGill is influential "because everyone thinks he is – and perception is power." In addition to McGill, we identified sixteen registered lobbyists from the secretary of state's list who had either served in the legislature or in the governor's office; most lobbied for more than one group.

The second most-mentioned "effective" lobbyist in Topeka, according to our respondents, was an administrative official, Robert Harder, secretary of the Kansas Department of Social and Rehabilitation Services. A former Methodist minister and a Democratic member of the Kansas House of Representatives, Harder has served as the secretary of the department for eighteen years, under both Democratic and Republican governors. Considered by one legislative respondent to be a "strong, quiet, almost humble man," Harder has combined an open, nonaggressive style with a reputation for hard work and caring (including writing personal notes of thanks to individual legislators at the close of the legislative session), as well as, in the words of one legislator, "an incredible capacity for detail."

Managing one of the most diverse and controversial departments in the state, Harder has effectively mobilized the increasingly influential social service recipient and service delivery groups in the state. He has so gained the trust of legislators that budget cuts and reallocations within his agency are usually, by law, left to his discretion. Not surprisingly, this power has made him an enemy or two as well. As an ex-legislator, he is allowed on the House floor and uses his privilege to great advantage. According to one lobbyist respondent, the chief executive officer of a community-based mental health association, "Robert Harder has become an artist. Lobbying is an art form."

If our survey results are any indication, however, Harder is the exception rather than the rule in terms of the influence of state officials as particularly effective lobbyists. Indeed, some respondents commented that most state agencies and their officials are less influential than in the past. Most mentioned were officials of the State Board of Regents, who in previous years were perhaps the key figures in higher education funding. Kansas appears to be one of those states with a rather high turnover of state officials, and entrenched administrators like Harder tend to be anomalies.

While the number of professional Kansas lobbyists is undoubtedly growing, so too is the number of "grass-roots" lobbyists. Certain Kansas groups, most notably the state Chamber of Commerce and the Kansas Bankers Association, have long been involved in "subtle" grass-roots lobbying, urging their members to contact legislators as constituents or having "eggs and issues" breakfasts for legislators in their home communities. The 1970s, however, seemed to spawn a new kind of grass-roots lobbyist. Farmers coming to Topeka en masse or "fastings" by groups of welfare and social service recipients in front of the capitol and similar activities are a part of almost every legislative session. Most often such individuals do not register as "lobbyists" but act rather as "citizens" attempting to petition their legislators or the governor.

According to our survey, with few exceptions legislators view interest groups as an essential part of the process of governing. Lobbyists are perceived as generally trustworthy members of the political process whose key function is to relieve the informational burdens placed on part-time, understaffed legislators; lobbyists provide information on drafting legislation, pending bills, and the "pulse" of the state's population.

Legislators' chief concern about interest groups in Kansas is not their (undue) influence on policy, but rather the public perception that special interests are antithetical to the pursuit of the public good. A Democrat who had served ten years in the Senate summed up the comments of many legislators: "[special interests are] highly misunderstood by citizens of the state partially because of media coverage. Spending time and/or money does not necessarily 'influence' a legislator." Legislators realize the danger interest groups can pose for sound policy making but believe that the current system is working well.

The professionalization of lobbyists was seen by most legislators as a positive development. Though some legislators regard the emergence of full-time, privately owned lobbying firms as threatening grass-roots organization and potentially stifling the average citizen's voice in government, most find important benefits in dealing with professional lobbyists. To the question, "What is the most negative thing about special interests in Kansas?" the two most common responses were (1) a failure by lobbyists to see the bigger policy picture and (2) an unwillingness by lobbyists to understand that losing is also a part of the political process. Many legislators feel that the more professional lobbyists are able to avoid these two pitfalls.

The professionalization of lobbyists has occurred during a period of increasingly strict regulation. The wining and dining of legislators, though still part of the process, is now closely monitored, and the old system of largely informal contacts and "old boy" networks has been replaced by a more formalized and open system.[31] Most legislators and lobbyists in our survey believe that the regulatory framework is "effective" and contributes to a better image of the political process. A twenty-four-year veteran of the Senate explained it this way: "Yes, before regulation, rumor talked of how much certain legislators' votes cost. If this [buying of votes] goes on now, it is buried much deeper. This means that it is harder for favors to be bargained for and delivered." That is not to say that once-powerful interests are now without sway; rather, special interests must rely on more open and more sophisticated techniques and information to be successful.

A Note on PACs in Kansas

Special interest political action committees play an increasingly important role in Kansas politics. By 1984, 281 PACs were registered in Kansas, and 211 of them filed reports indicating that legislative candidates received more than $1.1 million during the 1984 election cycle, a figure representing more than a 400 percent increase since 1978. Less than 5 percent of PAC contributions came from out-of-state groups.

For members of the Kansas House elected in 1984, 63 percent of all campaign contributions came from special interests; for members of the

Senate, 71 percent. PAC contributions were concentrated on the House and Senate leadership, where those in the twelve top positions accepted more than 82 percent of their campaign contributions from special interest lobbies.[32]

Realtors, banking groups, trial lawyers, doctors, the Kansas Chamber of Commerce and Industry, and the Kansas National Education Association are always among the leaders in campaign contributions. In the 1984 election cycle the Kansas Realtors Association PAC contributed more than $91,000 to legislative candidates, while the second biggest contributor, the KNEA, contributed just under $69,000.

We asked legislators in our survey, "Are there any particular groups especially influential because of their PAC activity? Which ones?" Only 26 of the 86 legislators responded, listing one or more groups that they thought were particularly influential. The most-named group was the KNEA (named by 21 of the 26 respondents), followed by the Kansas Chamber of Commerce and Industry (15 mentions) and the Kansas Bankers Association (9 mentions). It should be noted that most agriculture groups do not have PACs in Kansas. Officials of the Kansas Farm Bureau have long sought to create a political action committee for the group, but the membership has yet to give its approval.

Almost all legislators have a relatively benign view of direct PAC influence on individuals, believing that money is given without strings attached ("Often I get a check and never hear from the group again.") or is in amounts too small for influence. Forty-seven percent of the legislative respondents said that PACs had done more good than harm, and another 39 percent indicated that PACs had done about "equal good and bad" in the political process. The majority felt that regulation is "effective."

Legislators are well aware of the "advantages" of PACs for incumbents; PACs make it possible for them to raise funds without tapping constituents continually. Three respondents noted that PACs allowed them (as women and/or minorities) to raise money for a successful campaign that they would not have been able to do otherwise. A number of respondents noted that PACs may contribute to legislative "professionalism" and experience by limiting turnover in office, factors that may make legislators immune to special interest pressure.

While relatively unconcerned about short-term PAC influences, some legislators have much more ambivalent feelings about the potential long-term impact of PACs on the political process. First, campaign costs, though still relatively low in Kansas compared to those of many states, have more than tripled on the average since the late 1970s, largely because of PAC money. A number of legislators expressed concern over the fact that it is difficult to raise campaign expenses without taking special interest money. Second, the increasing reliance on PACs as a source of campaign financing is seen by some as threatening legislators' ties to party and to constituents. Finally, even those legislators who are strong PAC supporters mentioned a concern that PACs are perceived by citizens as buying votes and that the image of PAC politics is an unwholesome one.

The growth of PACs in Kansas politics in the mid-1980s sparked renewed interest in both strengthening the capability of the Public Disclosure Commission to enforce campaign reform laws and limiting the role of PACs in elections. There was some support in our survey for legislation that would limit PAC contributions to no more than 50 percent of the funds raised by candidates.

Nevertheless, Kansas legislators have learned to benefit from PAC contributions and have become accustomed to living with a Public Disclosure Commission that suggests scrutiny to the public but lacks real enforcement power. In the absence of a major scandal it is unlikely that either legislators or special interest representatives will be anxious to change the system.

Conclusion

The composition of the Kansas interest group universe and the nature of special interest influence in the state have undergone major transformations since 1970. Rather than the homogeneous, rural state that is often depicted in the national news media, Kansas today is more reflective of the tensions and divisions characteristic of politics at the national level.

The number of special interests active in Kansas politics mushroomed during the 1970s and 1980s as groups quickly organized around expanding government policy initiatives, especially in the areas of education and social services. Like the nation, Kansas experienced the rapid growth of nonoccupational groups, including single-issue and public interest groups. Lobbying seems more "professional" than it was even in the early 1970s, and contract lobbyists are a much bigger part of the influence process than ever before. Grass-roots lobbying and broad-based group-coalition building seem as commonplace in Topeka as they do in Washington.

Clearly, policy making in Kansas is much more pluralistic than it was before the early 1970s. There is now much less opportunity for single-interest domination and much more opportunity for a large number of interests to have some effect on policy. Although Kansas politics are still dominated by several powerful groups, none seems as hegemonic in its policy sector as even in the early 1970s. Postindustrial social, economic, and cultural complexity now characterizes Kansas and makes it likely that domination by unchallenged interests will never again occur.

Increased interest group pluralism is not without its problems, however, especially in a state like Kansas, where the economy has had a difficult time adjusting to the weakening of agriculture and energy prices. Along with more special interest claimants and rising expectations, Kansas policy makers are confronted with a slow-growth economy, and increasing interest group conflict is the likely result. As one legislator respondent noted, "Kansas has rejoined the Union."

Notes

1. Neal R. Peirce, *The Great Plains States of America* (New York: W. W. Norton, 1973), 221–22.

2. Ex-governor John Carlin, quoted in Alan Ehrenhalt, ed., *Politics in America 1986* (Washington, D.C.: CQ Press, 1985), 559.

3. David R. Mayhew, *Placing Parties in American Politics* (Princeton, N.J.: Princeton University Press, 1986), 170–71.

4. John G. Grumm, "The Kansas Legislature: Republican Coalition," in Samuel C. Patterson, ed., *Midwestern Legislative Politics* (Iowa City: Institute of Public Affairs, University of Iowa, 1967), 51.

5. Peirce, *Great Plains States,* 238.

6. James W. Drury and James E. Titus, *Legislative Apportionment in Kansas: 1960* (Lawrence: Governmental Research Center, University of Kansas, 1960), 32.

7. Allan J. Cigler and James W. Drury, "Kansas," in Leroy Hardy, Alan Hislop, and Stuart Anderson, eds., *Reapportionment Politics: The History of Redistricting in the Fifty States* (Beverly Hills, Calif.: Sage, 1980), 121–29.

8. Manning Dauer and Robert G. Kelsay, "Unrepresentative States," *National Municipal Review* 44 (December 1955), 571–75, 587.

9. John White and Norman C. Thomas, "Urban and Rural Representation and State Legislative Apportionment," *Western Political Quarterly* 17 (December 1984), 724–41.

10. Robert S. Erikson, "The Partisan Impact of State Legislative Reapportionment," *Midwest Journal of Political Science* 15 (February 1971), 57–71.

11. Timothy G. O'Rourke, *The Impact of Reapportionment* (New Brunswick, N.J.: Transaction, 1980), esp. 27–43, 73–93.

12. Marvin Harder and Carolyn Rampey, *The Kansas Legislature: Procedures, Personalities and Problems* (Lawrence: University Press of Kansas, 1972), 131–46.

13. See, for example, D. R. Songer et al., "Voting Cues in Two State Legislatures," *Social Science Quarterly* 66 (December 1985), 983–90.

14. Marvin Harder, "Interest Groups," in Marvin Harder, ed., *Interest Groups and Lobbyists in Kansas State Government* (Lawrence: Center for Public Affairs and the Capitol Complex Center, University of Kansas, 1983), 8.

15. Ibid.

16. Harder and Rampey, *Kansas Legislature,* 233–40.

17. Information provided by the Kansas secretary of state's office, March 1987.

18. Harder and Rampey, *Kansas Legislature,* 206.

19. For a general discussion of the growth of institutions in the political process, see Robert H. Salisbury, "Interest Representation and the Dominance of Institutions," *American Political Science Review* 78 (March 1984), 64–77.

20. Marvin A. Harder and Raymond G. Davis, *The Legislature as an Organization* (Lawrence: Regents Press of Kansas, 1979), 140.

21. Harder and Rampey, *Kansas Legislature,* 205.

22. The sample population was derived from the list of registered lobbyists provided by the Kansas secretary of state's office in October 1986.

23. James W. Drury, *The Government of Kansas,* 3d ed. (Lawrence: Regents Press of Kansas, 1980), 433.

24. See, for example, Allan J. Cigler and John Mark Hansen, "Group Formation through Protest: The American Agriculture Movement," in Allan J. Cigler and Burdett A. Loomis, eds., *Interest Group Politics* (Washington, D.C.: CQ Press, 1983), 84–109; Aruna Nayyar Michie and Craig Jagger, *Why Farmers Protest* (Manhattan: Kansas State University Agriculture Experiment Station, 1980).

25. Victoria Sizemore Long, "Kansas Legislature Is Said to Favor Bill for Statewide Banking," *Kansas City Times,* January 20, 1987.

26. Some Kansas unions are affiliated only with the national AFL-CIO, others with only the state organization, and others with both.

27. Harder and Rampey, *Kansas Legislature,* 198.

28. Ibid., 233–40.

29. Dan Bearth, "Pete McGill: Legislator Turned Lobbyist Changes Politics into a Growth Industry," *Kansas Business News* 2 (September 1981), 22–26.

30. Ibid.

31. For an insider's portrait of contemporary Kansas lobbying, see Marvin Harder, ed., *Interest Groups and Lobbyists in Kansas State Government* (Lawrence: Center for Public Affairs and the Capitol Complex Center, University of Kansas, 1983).

32. John Marshall, "Money Talks in Statehouse Politics," *Garden City Telegram,* March 7, 1986.

MICHIGAN

Diversity and Professionalism in a Partisan Environment

WILLIAM P. BROWNE and

DELBERT J. RINGQUIST

The circumstances surrounding statewide diversity of interests, a strong partisan heritage, and a recently emergent professionalized government have conferred a distinctive character on the politics of organized interests in Michigan. Michigan interests show a decided tendency to assume a policy-making partner's role with state officials. That is, private organizations attempt to build ongoing relationships with state officials who, because of professionalized government, are influential and regular players within each specific issue area. A large number of full-time representatives from very diverse interests employ broadly based strategies of providing policy information, offering electoral assistance, and mobilizing constituents as demonstrations of group support, all for the specific purpose of securing and maintaining regular access to partisanly divided policy deliberations. The lobbyists for interests having common members or problems also seek regular interaction with one another, intergroup coalitions on important issues, and an avoidance of open policy conflict among themselves. These conditions make organized interests a prominent and important part of Wolverine state politics.

The Socioeconomic Environment

That some aspects of representation are new ones while others are historically important seems axiomatic of interest group politics in the American states of the 1990s. Michigan is no exception to that rule. Although the politically elitist mentality of both organized labor and automotive industrialists retains an impact on state policy making, there are now other contenders for influence because of changes in the state's policy focus. Indeed, contenders exercise their prerogatives in a policy environment that increasingly segments issues and resolves them in piecemeal fashion. These other private interests have gained their greatest advantages as the state and its multiple constituencies have struggled to survive and adjust to changing economic fortunes.

Such adjustment is not just a recent phenomenon in the face of a threatened auto industry. The Hudson Institute, in analyzing Michigan's economic potential, notes that "the state has ridden a roller coaster" of booms and busts for nearly two centuries, always returning to prosperity.[1] Michigan policy makers and business leaders now plan their responses to an internationally changing auto industry in the hope that a more diversified economy can make future economic rides less tumultuous than that familiar roller coaster that has often been so devastating to state residents. The collapse of the timber industry and the periodic sales slumps in the auto industry are examples of busts that the state no longer wishes to face. The big change is that state officials want actively to encourage, through public policy, a different economic climate. The state has diversified, but the effects, like Michigan itself, are complex. Agriculture and tourism, respectively, have become the state's second- and third-ranked industries. Both are internally diverse as well. The state produces more than fifty different cash crops and, as a result, has not suffered the same financial declines as those whose agricultural sectors are dependent on feed grains. Tourism is both a winter and summer business that overlaps regionally to bring visitors to many recreational areas throughout the year. Both these industries have been the subject of state development efforts to promote growth. So, too, have small commercial businesses and smaller-scale manufacturers, two other important contributors to the state's economy.

Yet diversity has not displaced the dominant economic importance of the auto industry. Although the current production rate is less than half of the 60 percent level of the 1930s, and down approximately 20 percent from 1978, Michigan still assembles nearly 28 percent of all U.S. autos. Even larger shares of many components, as well as tooling for the industry, are concentrated there. In addition, a large percentage of smaller industries in the state are auto-dependent, including newly emergent robotics and assorted high-tech businesses along with older firms specializing in textiles and electronics. No matter what the shape of future transitions, state officials agree, Michigan's auto industry and economic prospects are intertwined. The reasons for this tie are quite clear. None of the others, alone or in tandem, will sustain the state economy. For example, income generated by the on-farm component of agriculture yielded less than 1 percent of total personal income for the state in 1984. Tourism and its service industries accounted for only 6.8 percent of total 1984 state employment, equal to 46 percent of the personnel employed by the public sector within the state but seasonal in its opportunities for earning personal income.[2] Despite these limitations, state officials recognize that agriculture and tourism, making use as they do of Michigan's vast outstate natural resources, can be employed as a hedge against further auto manufacturing losses. This need for still other supplements to the state's economic base has also led to efforts to reestablish the lumber and timber industries.

For the same reasons, state officials have become quite protective of Michigan's other big businesses. Chemical, pharmaceutical, furniture, oil, transportation, and breakfast-cereal companies have long been established, particularly in cities apart from the southeast Michigan quadrant of auto-dependent industry. And development-conscious state officials have shown a concern for assisting such auto-dependent industries as machine tooling and robotics in penetrating nonauto manufacturing and health-care-related businesses. As a consequence, Michigan public policy questions are as preoccupied with facilitating high-tech investment as they are with returning auto production capacity. While public officials worry about auto workers' jobs, they are no less focused on such things as assistance to farmers, encouragement of tourists, and the role of educators in assisting economic growth. For Michigan, these are policy concerns that were not in evidence before 1970.

The Political Environment

The changing policy concerns of the Michigan government result as much from an evolution in state politics as they do from shifts in economic fortunes. The new state government of the 1970s, 1980s, and 1990s claims to be less willing than all its predecessors to put up with economic busts in return for intervening years of politically rewarding prosperity. This unwillingness stems partly from a basic change in the way issues come before the state legislature, a situation that certainly affects the representation of interests in Michigan. Partisanship, as Democrats and Republicans compete as champions of economic growth, is one important factor. The state began as a populist, Democratic one, and that influence has often been reinforced in its political history. Although the conversion to the Republican party was statewide after the Civil War, several of that party's governors were elected by promoting progressive policy reform. The elections of Hazen Pingree in 1890 and George Romney in 1962, 1964, and 1966 are examples. As with other progressive Republicans, Pingree and Romney were elected when factious party infighting threatened to turn the government back to the Democrats. At other times, the governing Republican party reflected a solid conservatism attributable to its active business leaders and, to a lesser extent, the attitudes of outstate Michigan residents.

The Great Depression of the 1930s was devastating to Michigan, by then economically dependent on auto manufacturing. Nonetheless, Democratic resurgence in the state was very short-lived. Though Democrats won the governorship and both legislative houses in 1932, all statewide offices and the legislature returned to Republican hands two years later. Only the auto-dominated Detroit area and the west and central Upper Peninsula did not follow outstate areas back to Republican ranks. This sectional division became a permanent fixture of the Michigan electoral arena, and stable two-party politics developed within the state and its fragmented political culture of white urban, black central city, and rural residents.[3] Union members were early Democratic supporters, but the United Auto Workers and other organized unions did not play a leadership role in the party until after 1946. From that point on, the UAW and AFL-CIO were involved in electioneering and organizing issues — predominantly from a liberal agenda — for the party. In the process, labor became the Democratic party core. Though blacks and other liberal urban residents counted as other regular supporters, Democrats gained political control only after employing an outstate strategy of adding more conservative voters to their ticket.[4]

Even as a two-party state, however, Michigan was in for more change. Labor union members, especially as they joined the middle classes, did not continue to provide consistently high rates of electoral support for the Democrats. Ticket splitting, particularly when influenced by popular personalities running for statewide office, became commonplace for both parties. Electoral campaigners of the early 1970s felt compelled to make pioneering use of public opinion polls to allow statewide candidates to address issues pertinent to specific locales within Michigan.[5] The result is a paradoxical one: a strongly competitive party situation built on traditional alliances facing a shifting electorate that is often attracted to issues and issue-directed personalities first. That mix produced a Democratic presidential primary election victory for George Wallace in 1968 and concurrent state landslides for Democratic presidents and Republican governors in the 1960s. From the perspective of organized state interests, this situation is a volatile and shifting one in which organizations have had to move from being electoral partisans to policy activists. Only direct intervention keeps interest demands in front of competitive and busy state policy makers who can easily bog down in party disputes.

The development of professionalized government is a second factor that has altered the representation of issues within Michigan. Operating under a competitive party structure, state officials found it useful to stabilize government and prevent electoral disarray. Modern management techniques were established by 1937 as civil service was brought to an administration that already practiced executive budgeting. The 1963 constitution, revised as Governor George Romney mobilized a citizens' movement to reform state government against partisan control, brought about consolidation of agencies, greater accountability to the chief executive, openness to citizens and groups, and better reporting of performance to the legislature and public.

The postconstitution legislature of 148 members and strong central leaders in each house operates nearly as a state-level equivalent to the professionalized U.S. Congress. A fully staffed Legislative Service Bureau has existed since 1941 to study issues, draft bills, and provide other policy assistance. These services have expanded gradually to include individual offices with personal aides for each legislator, additional staff and offices provided under the direction of the majority and minority leadership in both houses, research staffs for each committee, and House and Senate fiscal staffs for independent budget analysis. Legislators serve full time, are in Lansing most of the year, and are afforded incentives to stay in government by a retirement plan that vests them after eight years of service. As a result, this partisanly uncertain state is governed by a well-supported chief executive, a competently managed bureaucracy, and legislators who are constantly involved in state government. It is an environment in which both the values of the citizenry and positive knowledge about policy needs are important parts of decision making. For interest representations, it means the need to be as expertly informed and as professionally competent as those who make state policy.

Interest Representation: A Historical Perspective

Michigan, in terms of the conditions outlined earlier, has always been a special interest state, as policy makers responded to prevailing and emerging state problems. Sometimes these policy responses were sparked by social forces that were of electoral consequence, such as rural settlers or labor members, particularly during times of Populist unrest when banks, businesses, and railroads were regulatory targets. At other times, state government was adjusting to economic booms and busts. Michigan's national reputation as a labor state reflects only one of several transitional periods in its history and, unfortunately, disguises the diversity of interests that have long been represented within the state.

Attention to organized interests began as extractive industries and businesses won special favors from state government in the midnineteenth century. Trapping and fishing industries, and later timber and agriculture, benefited from the large land expanse that was turned over to those who used Michigan's natural resources. State government also facilitated railroad and shipping enterprises that linked outstate industries to Detroit, the largely commercial city that served the extractive economy. Banking, as a key to commercial development, also received strong support. Lawmakers did the same for the copper mining interests of the Upper Peninsula as they developed in the 1880s.

Even the 1847 conflict that led to the designation of midstate Lansing as the capital indicated that both commercial and outstate interests knew state government was more than a neutral arbitrator of differences.[6] Outstaters did not want the center of state government in Detroit, associated with commercial problems and aloof from those who provided the raw materials for urban growth. These differences increased after 1904, as Detroit began its first manufacturing and related immigration surge while outstate suffered as the once-explosive timber harvest ran its course.[7]

State government's cooperation with organized interests became an even more valued necessity during these years. Michigan funds, as well as some of the earliest federal grants, provided transportation assistance as lumber interests, bicycle clubs, tourism organizations, Michigan developers of Florida property, and auto industrialists escalated the demand for highways.[8] Just as the lumber industry had gained unrestricted access to timber resources, the new industrialists sought protection for their frequently criticized employment practices. So, well before the rise of labor, Michigan was a state where government was accustomed to both distributive and regulatory policy demands from organized interests. It also was a place where politicians had periodically riled citizens against the scourge of special interests when policy demands had been so abusive as to be destructive to state resources.

The large auto industries that had come to dominate state manufacturing showed an even greater concern with state government beginning in the 1930s. At first, they sought public policies that would facilitate auto sales, a strategy that pitted General Motors and Ford against one another in a contest for partisan control over state government.[9] Then, while this partisan split between the two auto giants continued, labor began its struggle for control of the Democratic party as its leaders finally recognized the importance of a protective state government.

Throughout the 1960s, Michigan politics were beset by competing policy demands from a variety of sources: autonomous auto companies, organized labor divided into two camps by the UAW and the AFL-CIO, and several outstate interests that disagreed among themselves but together disliked the attention directed to the southeastern Michigan home turf of both the auto industry and labor. In addition, the Detroit riots of 1967, along with popular concern for civil rights, directed new attention to the state's 12.9 percent black population.

The previously cited contextual factors of partisanship and professionalism in state government were no less important than economic and social ones in affecting the behavior of organized Michigan interests throughout these transitions. The politics of competing interests have always been played out within that partisan setting, especially from the Civil War through the later years of the Romney administration in the 1960s. The differences between outstate and commercial or manufacturing interests were left to be resolved within the Republican party, the partisan choice of those whom these interests represented. The Republicans' impact produced primarily laissez-faire policies and infrastructure support. Although these solutions never satisfied all Republican policy claimants within the factionalized party, they did allocate enough benefits to hold alliances together. After all, these interests were concerned first with their unrestrained flexibility in using natural resources and employees as they saw fit rather than with state-sponsored development. Thus their leaders apparently were quite content to sacrifice autonomy to partisan control if it meant that government left them alone. When the Democratic party once again attained governing status within the state, the same phenomenon occurred. Labor interests, operating within the party, opted to champion both self-protective labor policies and the progressive social welfare and conservation causes of Democratic allies as these were cultivated throughout the state.

By the time professionalized government took hold in Michigan in the late 1960s and early 1970s, a plethora of otherwise neglected organized interests was eager to deal directly with state government and bypass the parties. Governor William Milliken's bipartisan approach to issues in both electioneering and policy making only heightened this enthusiasm for pressing demands with state officials rather than party leaders. As a consequence, interest representation expanded. Outstate interests such as agriculture and local governments found administrative and legislative champions of their own where they previously felt ignored in the morass of partisan infighting. Newly organized interests, such as the aged, also identified with and turned their support to state officials. In turn, officials directed attention to their new clientele's relatively noncontroversial problems with no need for a commitment from party leaders. Other new but more conflict-oriented interests also had an advantage in that they found state officials who would listen to them, encourage their efforts, and even protect them from policy antagonists.

Environmentalists are one example of a set of contentious organizations that would never have gained agenda status under the old-style, mostly partisan state operations. Manufacturing interests, the environmentalists' favorite Michigan targets, would have kept them unrepresented by refusing Republican party recognition. Democrats would also have avoided them for two reasons of party maintenance. First, the Democratic party deferred to another antagonist of the environmentalists—the fur, fish, and game conservationists who had gained and provided support within the party. Second, support of environmental issues would have heightened conflict between labor and industry and created another set of issues that would strain already strapped political resources and threaten jobs.

The Current Structure of Michigan Lobbying

What constitutes the new and expanded universe of organized interests in Michigan can be seen by looking at lobbyists registered under Michigan's reformed Lobby Registration Act of 1978. When the law became effective in 1983, after five years of court challenge by private interests, lobbying was defined as any direct communication with a public official (administrative, judicial, boards, commissions, as well as legislative) for the intent of influencing any aspect of public policy. All individuals who make such contacts are now required to register as lobbyists with the Department of State, file yearly expenditure reports, and report personal salaries or compensation for their public affairs work.

This action, though it merely covers the conventional definition of lobbying as an encompassing act of political advocacy, was an abrupt change for the state. Under previous law, a lobbyist was more narrowly defined as anyone attempting to influence the passage of legislation by contacting legislators or legislative committees. Exemptions were allowed for those who restricted their contacts to formal appearances or written communications. Only registration was required.

The implementation of the new law saw registration increase dramatically. A 1960 study of Michigan lobbyists by DeVries found 367 registered lobbyists,[10] a number that remained relatively constant through 1983, when 355 registered agents were identified in the state. In 1984, with organization officials of all types worried about legal conformity, the number of registrants grew to more than 1,600. By 1986, as enforcement intensified and knowledge of the act spread, more than 2,100 lobbyists were registered. Of these, 44 percent represented business interests; 16 percent, health-care organizations; 2 percent, farm organizations; 1 percent, environmental and conservation causes; 2 percent, labor unions; 6 percent, citizen and civic reform concerns; 7 percent, local government; and 11 percent were themselves state officials.[11] Despite this business bias, nearly every conceivable state interest is represented by one or more agents. Even the Detroit Tigers, individual small-town hospitals, and an array of emerging industrial parks are represented by registered lobbyists.

Academics tend to think of this broad range of interests as the most descriptive way of looking at a state's agents of influence, but Michigan policy makers and lobbyists do not agree. To them, this long list of individuals is not a complete picture of interest group representation. The respondents to this study, for reasons that are explained in more detail in sections below, distinguish between those who regularly lobby (even though they may be volunteers) and those who do not. The regular lobbyists are viewed as those on whom policy makers and other private representatives depend as advocates for and experts about specific state interests. The others, as one legislative leader explained, are seen "as pretty much regular citizens, people with a gripe or a point of view that they want to air." State officials, on the other hand and despite lobbying regulations, are perceived as having a different job than private interest representatives. As another legislator explained, "They're part of the team. We can't depend on them to articulate the views of Michigan's citizenry. They, as they should, support their own programs."

Registered lobbyists, especially the numbers, are misleading from yet another perspective. Many organizations, even after the law was modified in 1986 to exclude a few commissions and boards as targets of lobbyist influence for registration purposes, continue to register anyone they think may contact—or even fish with—a policy maker. Chrysler

Corporation, after years of having 1 registrant, had 43 lobbyists in 1986. The Michigan Hospital Association, E. F. Hutton and Company, Consumers Power, and Perry Drug Stores, respectively, registered 22, 20, 16, and 13 employees as lobbyists in 1986. Most of these individuals see the state capitol more frequently as tourists than as corporate representatives.[12]

"Regular" lobbyists, or the "professionals" as respondents tend to call them, are for the most part those individuals who were registered before the law changed in 1983. In addition, respondents believe, a few more multiclient lobbyists have swelled the ranks of the professions. As a result, approximately 400 lobbyists routinely interact with state officials either as part of their jobs or, in a few instances, as part of an avocation associated with some important organization in their lives.[13] Since 1960, however, this number of full-timers has quadrupled.

Regular lobbyists, along with state party officials, are also involved in yet another regulated facet of state interest group activity, political action committees. Organized interests operate the largest number of active Michigan PACs (Table 6.1).

Table 6.1. Number of actively contributing PACs in Michigan, by category, 1984

Category	No.	%
Party committees	43	9
Professional associations	34	7
Business	162	35
Labor	131[a]	28
Governmental committees	25	5
Citizen groups	39	8
Indeterminant	28[b]	6
Total	462	98

Source: State Elections Bureau, Independent and Political Committee Statistics, (Lansing: Secretary of States Office, 1986).
Note: Percentages do not total to 100 because of combining categories and rounding.
[a]Twenty-five were teacher organizations, and 25 were Teamster organizations.
[b]Eleven were law firms.

PACs developed in Michigan under the relatively nonrestrictive Campaign Finance Act of 1976. By 1986, more than 1,200 PACs had been organized as either political or independent committees. Legal restrictions primarily govern their cash and in-kind contributions and expenditures rather than their organization and operation. Because of methods of record keeping, even the total amount of PAC money going to individual candidates is difficult to reconstruct. The intent—other than disclosure—is to ascertain that no political committee exceeds the maximum contribution level of $250 to state House candidates, $450 to state Senate candidates, and $1,700 to statewide candidates. But with only minimal reorganization, six months of operation, and contributions from twenty-five individuals, independent committees can be restructured from the political committees and are then able to donate ten times that amount to each candidate.

Many PACs are active for only one or a few years, but the number of actively contributing PACs continues to grow. In 1978, 323 committees reported expenditures. By 1982 there were 442. And in 1986, 513 contributed to candidates. Contributions also grew, but this change is at least in part a reflection of different types of elections. For example, PAC contributions, according to the Department of State, totaled $6,742,029 for the presidential and state House elections of 1984. In 1986, with both state House and Senate candidates as well as the governorship up for election, PAC contributions increased to $7,549,326.

Contributions change as issues shift as well. In 1986 only eleven of the largest twenty contributors of 1984 were still ranked in the top twenty (Table 6.2). Three newly ranked health-care committees, for example, organized or incurred expenditures for 1986 in response to medical liability issues that were then before the legislature.

Money politics has its own bias within the state, however. The largest thirty-five PACs provide approximately 40 percent of campaign contributions. Though business PACs are among the largest committees, labor—especially the UAW—is consistently the biggest spender. Not unexpectedly, given labor's historical ties, unions favor Democratic party candidates. These expenditures, according to respondents, reflect the tendency of union leaders to elect sympathetic candidates as a primary

Table 6.2. Top Twenty PAC contributors in Michigan, 1984 and 1986

Rank	1984[a]	1986[b]
1	Michigan United Auto Workers PAC ($389,028)	Michigan United Auto Workers PAC ($287,390)
2	Michigan State AFL-CIO, COPE Fund ($336,221)	United Auto Workers SEMPAC ($276,561)
3	Civic Improvement Program, General Motors ($308,905)	Right to Life of Michigan ($224,526)
4	Michigan Education Association PAC ($290,790)	Realtors PAC of Michigan ($201,485)
5	Democratic National Committee, Non-Federal ($223,500)	Michigan State AFL-CIO (254,790)
6	United Auto Workers SEMPAC ($202,614)	Region 1-D United Auto Workers ($201,420)
7	Michigan Democratic Party Policy committee ($183, 228)	Michigan Education Association PAC (180,765)
8	House Democratic Victory Fund ($152,627)	Michigan Trial Lawyers PAC ($135,910)
9	Realtors PAC of Michigan ($115,225)	Michigan Beer and Wine Wholesalers PAC ($135,866)
10	Allstate Insurance Company PAC ($113,465)	Michigan Doctors PAC ($134,290)
11	Region 1-D United Auto Workers ($112,711)	State Chamber PAC ($123,033)
12	Republican Majority Committee ($111,338)	Consumers Power PAC ($111,150)
13	House Republican Campaign Committee ($110,020)	United Auto Workers Region 1-C ($98,750)
14	Michigan Wine and Beer Wholesalers PAC ($92,924)	Lawyers PAC ($98,450)
15	United Auto Workers Greater Flint CAP Council ($88,840)	Detroit Auto Dealers PAC ($92,950)
16	Michigan Doctors PAC ($87,150)	Michigan Bankers Association ($91,505)
17	Michigan Bankers Association ($84,739)	House Democratic Victory Fund ($85,265)
18	State Chamber PAC ($82,817)	Hospital Association PAC ($78,081)
19	House Majority Committee ($76,670)	Health and People PAC of Blue Cross and Blue Shield ($77,990)
20	Ford Motor Company Civic Action Fund ($76,590)	Dental PAC of Michigan ($68,080)

[a]State House and presidential races.
[b]State House, State Senate, and gubernatorial races.

aspect of their total lobbying strategy. As can be seen by comparing Table 6.2 with the list of most powerful state interests presented below, this is not a pervasive strategy among those interests reportedly the most influential in state politics. Campaign politics is only the most public part of representing private interests in Michigan.

The Dynamics of State Lobbying

Recent research on state lobbying found that Michigan interests behave somewhat differently than their cohorts from other states.[14] Michigan lobbyists act as policy-maker partners who work with state officials to fashion and finalize the details of public policy. To do so, they routinely cooperate with legislators, bureaucrats, and other organized interests that share some stake in the pending issue.[15] Compared to Michigan lobbyists, similar interests in other states interact differently with other policy participants. They are more prone either to act as organized opponents of other policy players within the issue area or to become dependent on state officials, who raise and resolve most issues on their own.

Interviews with legislators and lobbyists for this study support that earlier finding for a large number of issue areas in which state government must repeatedly take policy action. Interest groups in Michigan are policy partners in such diverse areas as agriculture, banking, education, environmental quality, insurance, recreation, small business development, social welfare, and workers' compensation. On these and other policy questions, a number of established interests and their well-connected representatives are expected participants whose advice and proposals are thought of by policy makers as a routine part of the policy process in Michigan.

This situation has meant the development of numerous issue networks in state government and the refinement of specific expectations as to what lobbying means in state government. As Hugh Heclo described them for national government, *issue networks* are composed of the legislators, legislative staffs, administration officials, department and agency personnel, and private sector representatives who regularly meet on recurring policy matters.[16] Such networks, respondents agree, typify Michigan politics with its highly involved legislature and expert bureaucracy. Interests play the principal role of policy advocate and support mobilizer within the networks, pushing policy makers to take action. Without some well-placed private interest advocates, few policy proposals advance very far in an environment where partisan obstacles so easily arise.

For this reason, Michigan lobbying has come to mean a very specialized form of advocacy and brokering in which private interest representatives articulate what they claim to be are the strongly held preferences of their members or patrons in order to demonstrate real policy demand. State administrators may also be policy advocates, but they are necessarily more policy neutral and, as mentioned, not thought of as lobbyists. Nor are private citizens and business leaders who are in Lansing only long enough to express but not negotiate their policy preferences. Lobbyists, as viewed by policy makers, are seen as expected participants because they are valued as major contributors to state public policy. As such, these individuals lobby both legislators and administrators in the same general way and at the same time as part of their broad strategy of extensive involvement. Michigan lobbyists, active as they are in all facets of policy development and implementation, see legislative and administrative lobbying as indistinguishable components of a job whose requirements mandate getting as many parts of the relevant issue network as possible behind a mutually acceptable proposal or compromise.

These arrangements produce four important conditions that affect the policy influence — indeed the power — of Michigan's organized interests and that are explored further in the remainder of this chapter. First, Michigan has seen the emergence of a highly professionalized lobby because of the need to work regularly with a professionalized but still divided state officialdom. Second, this professional lobby has expanded in response to interests that are routinely represented in Lansing's issue networks as well as those that only infrequently demand public policy attention from an activist state government.[17] The latter interests, in need of established policy players, make extensive use of multiple-client consultant lobbyists to be represented effectively. Third, considerable intergroup tensions are inherent in the process of representing so many interests in close relationships with state policy makers. Finally, grass-roots reactions to what are perceived as professionally isolated political maneuvers produce a flurry of backlash reactions as part of interest politics in the state. Important organized grass-roots interests, removed from the professional mainstream of Michigan politics, find ways to exert considerable policy impact nonetheless.

Lobbyists as Professionals

Lobbyists, like state legislators and administrators, do not attain professional status on the basis of advanced training for their jobs or specific and accredited standards of performance. In that sense, they are quite unlike medical doctors and more like successful sales representatives, who prove themselves through their experience. Zeigler and Baer, in their study of state lobbyists, concluded that political participants become professionals as they acquire "a generalized body of skills possessed in common by members of a political elite."[18] Professionals, in summary and as seen in Michigan policy circles, are highly experienced in a specific setting, highly involved with those who participate in performing certain tasks, and judged competent in the eyes of those with whom they work. The lobbyist as professional gains that status in a policy-making setting by being a recognized player in securing the passage of legislation and by seeing to its implementation. Lobbyists, as practitioners of political manipulation, are recognized as professionals because policy makers need the advocacy they provide, not because state officials see them as personally desirable individuals with whom to work.[19]

To acquire background information on state lobbying, we conducted fifty-six in-depth interviews with various policy-making participants.[20] In addition, we sent a mail survey of mostly closed-ended questions to all state legislators and representatives of all private sector interests that lobby in the state.[21] Respondents to both sets of interviews overwhelmingly believed that Michigan lobbyists in general meet professional criteria. First, the professional label was accepted widely. Eighty-three percent of private interest representatives agreed that lobbyists are "competent professionals." Eighty-seven percent of legislators agreed. Lobbyists also were judged as generally knowing "their business." Eighty-six percent of lobbyists agreed with that assessment, as did 96 percent of legislators. Almost all dissenting legislators, to both questions, were those who had served only a short time and, presumably, had not yet learned to respect lobbyist skills.

Second, most Michigan lobbyists are experienced and involved in the policy process (Table 6.3). Sixty-seven percent of the respondents have been lobbyists for five years or more. The mean average for length of time as a lobbyist is 10.1 years. Thirty-three percent of lobbyist respondents had held other policy-making jobs in state government, in-

Table 6.3. Experience and background of Michigan lobbyists

Lobbying Experience	Lobbyists %	No.	Former Political Position	Lobbyists %	No.
3 years or fewer	28	46			
4 to 7 years	28	46	State policy maker	34	57
8 to 15 years	26	44	Political party official	28	47
16+ years	18	31			
Total	100	167			

cluding more than half of those with five or fewer years of lobbying experience. This experience level is slightly lower than that found by Zeigler and Baer for other states with a professional lobby.[22]

During the in-depth interviews both policy makers and lobbyists emphasized that their jobs meant constant contact with one another (Table 6.4). Survey respondents acknowledged the same high level of interaction. There were few private interest representatives whose jobs involved mainly organizational management or technical work. Only 17 percent of the lobbyist respondents did not report weekly contact with state legislators or their staffs, and only 10 percent did not report such regular contact with nonlegislative state officials. In contrast, 45 percent of the lobbyists reported an average of six or more contacts with legislative personnel per week. Forty-three percent reported at least the same level of contact with other state officials. In addition, from a list of fourteen lobbyist activities, lobbyist respondents ranked working with other private interest representatives as their fourth most important job. Only direct policy-maker contacts were rated higher. Quite clearly, Michigan lobbyists are at the center of a flurry of interactive policy discussions in Lansing.

Table 6.4. Frequency of contacts and perceptions of access to legislators and staff by Michigan lobbyists

Average Legislative Contacts/Week	Lobbyists %	No.	Average Staff Contacts/Week	Lobbyists %	No.
None	17	29	None	10	17
1 to 5	36	60	1 to 5	44	73
6 to 10	17	28	6 to 10	20	33
11 to 5	11	18	11 to 15	8	14
16 to 25	6	10	16 to 25	12	20
26+	11	19	26+	3	5
Total	98	164	Total	97	162

Note: Percentages do not add to 100 because of grouping of categories and rounding.

Despite the manipulative nature of lobbyists' job, Michigan legislators hold lobbyists in generally high regard in addition to viewing them as competent. Eighty-four percent of survey respondents had either "quite a bit" or "a lot" of confidence in lobbyist information. Fifty-five percent claimed that most lobbyist information was personally helpful. No legislators felt that "very little" or none of their information was helpful. Eighty-three percent agreed that "lobbyists cannot get along without having a good reputation." Ninety percent agreed that a good reputation resulted from perceptions of trustworthiness. These data suggest strongly that Michigan policy makers, much as they did in the early 1960s when a Chrysler lobbyist helped direct tax reform on the phone from a Senate office,[23] not only respect but willingly accept lobbyists as part of their policy-making circle. Lobbyists are subscribers on the legislative computer system, with access to all writing, legislative votes, and other data available to legislators.

Lobbying Strategy and Tactics

The behavior of Michigan lobbyists is very much determined by their positive reception by state policy makers. Given the expected and useful advocacy that organized interests provide, it is not surprising that lobbyists find the state capital a hospitable environment. "We're made to feel welcome," was a typical lobbyist comment. A legislator responded similarly in noting that she and her colleagues "invite as much participation as possible. It remains, to a fault, a very open-door process for those with something to say." In the closed-ended survey 90 percent of legislator respondents believed themselves to be continually accessible to lobbyists. Also in that survey 75 percent of legislators and 61 percent of lobbyists agreed that "legislators will talk to anyone who will bring them fresh information." There was additional support for the importance of providing information as the principal form of advocacy. Ninety-four percent of legislators and 66 percent of lobbyists agreed that "information is a strong source of power to lobbyists." Sixty-eight percent of legislators believed that the "legislature could not function as well as it does today without lobbyists."

Information, however, means different things to different people. Michigan policy makers apparently are no exception. Lobbyists who discussed their strategies noted that state officials need to be provided different sorts of information, depending on who they are. Administrators charged with policy operations, according to several lobbyists, primarily want positive or value-free information on how their programs are meeting prescribed goals. The governor's staff and close gubernatorial allies want the same type of information on the few major policy goals set by the chief executive. "In that office," said a veteran public affairs consultant, "you have to talk about whether or not a program is assisting the state's economic development, not whether the program is achieving its own success or whether it's good for farmers." Lobbyists agreed that more legislators also want information about their favored policy concerns rather than about the specific program under discussion. As one concluded, "[The senator] always wants to know about how downtown Detroit gains, not how many citizens are served statewide or whether employers find that the program [under consideration] improves job skills."

Value-laden but factually specific information about such things as how a program is likely to be received by the electorate in Traverse City or whether it will enrage public schoolteachers has no less importance than information about the likelihood of a policy's success in attaining its goals. Lobbyists agreed that some legislators want such information during the earliest deliberations on most bills. When a vote is near, however, "most legislators will be asking those questions." Such comments explain why 45 percent of legislators agreed that lobbyists themselves "are often helpful in providing me political information on how segments of my constituents feel on political issues." They also believed, as lobbyist advocates surely want, that the information they receive reflects grass-roots views. Seventy-four percent of respondent legislators felt that "association lobbyists are not able to press their position on issues when their members are not in common agreement." Legislators were not alone in having such needs, however. Lobbyist respondents believed that the governor wants attitudinal information, but on fewer issues. Administrative respondents with program responsibilities also wanted information about likely citizen reactions as a means of developing acceptable proposals for elected officials.

Interest representation, as a consequence of the varying weights policy makers give to different types of information, is complex in Michigan. A few established interests usually follow a relatively simple strategy with a dominant emphasis. The UAW's electoral strategy is the best example. But there are others. Traditional agricultural interests, such as the Farm Bureau, attempt to achieve most of their goals through the state Department of Agriculture and the state's land-grant university. On the other hand, the Michigan Education Association works a great deal with legislative committees and, to gain extra momentum, uses its members to make extensive contacts with state legislators. The big three auto companies still exercise their greatest influence by emphasizing to everyone in Lansing how important they are to the state's economy.

Most interests follow a more balanced multifaceted approach, however, primarily because they lack the solid policy-maker alliances or persuasively simple arguments noted above. Lobbyists, as a consequence, find themselves working a broad array of issue network participants who have some voice in the matter under consideration. Even when in the advantageous position of trying to defeat an issue, representatives of an organized interest go through a checklist of who might be most concerned with the proposal and then follow through by making their own direct contacts or by urging a coalition partner to do so. This expanded list always includes legislative committee members, legislators with heavily affected constituents, staff who serve legislative leaders, administrators from affected related agencies, officials from the extensively involved Department of Management and Budget, gubernatorial aides, and other related interests. In addition, it may often prove necessary personally to update House and Senate leaders, executive officials, and even the governor. As can be imagined, the specific individuals who constitute these issue networks vary greatly depending on the exact issue, who has jurisdiction, and who becomes concerned both in and out of Lansing. Therefore, the checklist of whom to contact provides no ready formula for seeing specific people at a certain time. Lobbying strategy, as a result, is often developed tediously and only after complicated discussions.

For example, to enact workers' compensation reforms in the mid-1980s, House and Senate leaders worked closely with committee chairs and the representatives of both labor and industry, especially the auto industry. In addition, Governor James Blanchard kept visible as a major player on that issue, prompting participants to keep negotiating. Even relatively minor issues can involve large numbers of participants in ongoing discussions. A floating tire breakwater proposed for a small Michigan marina became, not uncommonly, more than a simple request of the corporate attorney to the Department of Natural Resources (DNR) in 1987. Before the breakwater was finalized, networking players included five legislative offices, the attorney general's office, the DNR director's office, DNR divisions of fisheries and waterways, DNR legal counsel, the Michigan United Conservation Clubs, and the Michigan Boating Industry Association. Other involved parties who followed the proceedings included the Chair of the Natural Resources Commission, the Senate Majority Leader's staff, the governor's office, and the Michigan Charter Boat Association.

The tactical behavior of every organized interest in the state is structured by this complex networking between professional policy makers. Organizations that regularly make state policy demands, or otherwise are affected by those interests that do, must have a well-developed public affairs program. The several points where policy ideas may originate must be continuously monitored. A great many contacts with policy participants need to be made. In short, these regularly participating private interests work hard to secure and maintain a place for their representatives in policy making. Even General Motors, with its importance to the state economy, and the Farm Bureau, with its allies in the Department of Agriculture, must establish their presence and knowledge to interact effectively with many participants in one or more issue networks. PAC contributions, issue briefings, sponsored research results, public opinion polls, public relations campaigns, and threats of court litigation are just some of the major tactical activities used to get and keep such attention.

Other organizations that deal with state policy only on a periodic basis also must know what goes on in Lansing and how to get quickly involved with policy players on any pending issue. Without a regular public affairs presence, these interests can be at a serious disadvantage. Most are not, however. Instead, associations and firms compensate by joining alliances led by the major, more ongoing players within their issue areas. This practice leads to the commonplace peak associations that help represent and organize smaller interests and serve as an umbrella for coalition activity. The Michigan Agriculture Conference, Michigan Senior Advocates Council, Michigan Manufacturers Association, and Michigan State Chamber of Commerce are only a few examples of organizations that integrate closely related interests and bring some representatives to Lansing who would otherwise not come. As a result, charter boat operators, cherry growers, apple growers, construction subcontractors, auto part suppliers, and regional aging organizations all secure support to engage in state lobbying.

Less active organizations also compensate for their lack of an ongoing lobbying presence by using public affairs consultants. Several multiclient lobbying firms have formed to assist the entry of clients into state policy making. Three firms stand out: those identified with Jimmy Karoub, Jerry Coomes, and Bobby Crim and his partner Robert Vander-Laan. Another five consultant firms have widely recognized reputations for successful representation, and still others are emerging. Respondents from these firms individually represent an average of ten clients per year, with the largest firms representing thirty-five to nearly seventy clients. A large number of interests—ranging from smaller state colleges, to large agribusiness firms such as A. E. Staley, to small groups such as the Deputy Sheriffs Association—gain professional representation in this way even though they lack an ongoing lobbying effort within their own organizations.

Still other organizations contract with multiclient lobbyists to mount the comprehensive lobbying strategies that are needed to cover all the policy bases and generate the specific information most applicable to different network players. A firm such as Ford Motor Company or Blue Cross/Blue Shield can supplement its own public affairs representatives by contracting with consultants who market different skills. Some consultants, for example, are noted for their "old boy" ties among longstanding state House officials. Others advertise themselves as issue managers who specialize in planning strategy, putting the appropriate team together, preparing materials, and adhering to a schedule. The availability of this consultancy resource, according to respondents, has allowed several interests to retain representatives equal in organizational skills to the UAW and with the same executive talent as the auto companies. Most respondents recognize the importance of this talent. Fifty-four percent of legislators and 39 percent of lobbyists agreed that multiple-client lobbyists were more successful than counterparts from other organizations. However, 23 percent of lobbyist respondents did not disagree but believed they could not judge that strength.

This diversity and extra representational capacity, existing as it does in a setting where state officials are eager to act as problem solvers, distributes political influence quite widely. There was a consensus among survey respondents that lobbyists at least occasionally have an important impact on legislators, an agreement lacking in all four states of the Zeigler and Baer study[24]. Seventy-seven percent of legislators and 82 percent of lobbyists believed that they can occasionally or frequently get "an opposing legislator to question his or her own position on a certain bill." This finding is consistent with and even somewhat more positive than the earlier research by DeVries. In 1960 two-thirds of full-time Michigan lobbyists judged their organizations' success as either good or very good.[25] But in the mid-1980s representatives of more than four times (33 to 137) as many organizations claimed to be represented at least this effectively in state government.

The Power of Organized Interests

The Major Influences

The diversity of state interests and the importance of state lobbyists to policy deliberations make for a situation in which a large number of interests are ranked as most influential. For example, the Michigan United Conservation Clubs and Michigan Education Association are considered by many policy makers and lobbyists to be equal in influence to, but not as publicly visible as, associations of organized labor and the auto manufacturers, which Morehouse considered to be dominant in state politics.[26] These interests, it appears to participants, win most of what they want on most of the issues on which their lobbyists take a firm stand. The Michigan Manufacturers Association, with its comprehensive support from large and small industries, is thought to be comparable in influence. So, too, is the City of Detroit, with its own legislative delegation, resultant ability to negotiate regional deals, and perceived orientation to black voters.

Ranking just behind these organizations, but without such strong constituent bases as the others, is a variety of established economic interests that are seen as usually being able to win. These groups represent either perceptually important economic interests or somewhat less organized but numerous constituents. All, like the most influential interests, are regular policy participants. They include representatives of hospitals, the Chamber of Commerce, Farm Bureau, farm cooperatives, the aged, state colleges and universities, local governments, insurance firms, banking, oil businesses, public utilities, tourism, beer and wine wholesalers, and auto dealers. In short, for the most part, these interests represent precisely those businesses and service providers on which state officials base their hope for economic stability and to whom, therefore, officials are willing to listen. At the least, respondents indicated, these are organized interests that can force a compromise on nearly any issue that their representatives choose to lobby hard on, as long as policy makers perceive it to be directly affecting constituents or effective operations.

Why does the list of influential private organizations stop with those interests? Respondents, on open-ended questions and during the in-depth interviews, indicated that the list of those organizations that usually win and whose lobbyists can always force some compromise could be expanded even further. However, these other organizations are interests that are conspicuous by their usual absence in Lansing, such as medical doctors. Or they are organizations within organizations that also are overshadowed in prominence by the greater involvement and recognition of comparable interests, such as the American Federation of Teachers within the AFL-CIO. As one respondent summarily concluded, "On a given issue [these organizations] can get anything done [for their occupational members] that they want. They just don't prove it very often. We're surprised when they do. For the others, we're not surprised."

Competition and Conflict

The expansion of influence is not without problems, though. A national survey of state public administrators found Michigan to be one of the highest-ranked states in terms of perceptions of private interest conflict.[27] The extended interviews for this study supported that finding. There were three reasons.

First, with so many interests actively represented and reportedly influential, policy conflicts were unavoidable. Unlike research that found little conflict between interest groups within state government,[28] most respondents volunteered information on routine and openly expressed disagreements in many issue areas. These conflicts were more than disputes over who should get what share of limited budgetary funds. Respondents also agreed as to why there was such an unusual amount of interorganizational conflict. "If you lobby long enough and hard enough," said one, "you will get a compromise that advantages you sooner or later. Now it may take three or four years, but . . ." Or, even more directly, a private interest representative concluded: "This? It's a split-the-difference state." According to such logic, influential lobbyists eventually will succeed, so there are few incentives for competitive interests to put major differences aside and cooperate very closely.

Nevertheless, many interorganizational disagreements are set aside in favor of multiple-interest coalitions and peak association agreements. This also was true of Michigan interests in 1960.[29] Seventy-four percent of lobbyists felt that very influential interests such as the State Chamber of Commerce and the Michigan Manufacturers Association limited their policy activity because of differences between member firms that also lobbied as independent organizations. This activity, while it minimized open conflict between competitive interests on most policy decisions, was pointed to as a second reason for tensions and eventual confrontations between interests.

Sooner or later, respondents claimed, organizations that often lobby together contend for leadership of their alliances. The Michigan Milk Producers Association, with its co-op support, moved to displace the Michigan Farm Bureau as the recognized voice for state agriculture, an action that destabilized other farm group relationships during legislative debates in 1986. The question of whether commercial interests gain the same recognition as manufacturers divides the otherwise cooperative Chamber of Commerce and thc Manufacturers Association. Among interests representing the elderly, the Area Agencies Association on Aging works hard to bridge gaps between state affiliates of the nationally organized American Association of Retired Persons and the National Council of Senior Citizens. The Michigan Municipal League frequently splinters into loosely supported committees to push for legislation for select types of cities. The relationships that hold these alliances together are too informal, too dependent on voluntary cooperation, and too undisciplined to subjugate private interests to common efforts for very long. The lack of any regularly agreed-on memberships in the issue networks of state government reinforces that tendency. Interest representatives, like other policy players, feel comfortable in altering the personal dynamics of policy making—that is, disrupting the issue networks—to gain representational advantages over the other participants.

Political action committees, and monetary contributions from interests more generally, are cited as a third reason for enhanced competition and conflict among groups. A large number of private interests, according to many respondents from throughout state government, act as though their representatives and members believe they can outspend and thus outlobby one another. In 1960, in contrast, Michigan lobbyists felt that financial contributions were of next to no importance.[30] Michigan's initial PAC law did little to discourage the bewildering array of committees that developed to provide electoral assistance. It seems nearly accurate to say that every organized interest active in state government either has a PAC, or has access to one through an allied peak association, or gets many opportunities to participate through committee fundraising. Private interest donations thus play an important part in Michigan elections, a dependency that leads many lobbyists to complain about the near-constant round of fundraisers that they feel compelled to attend year in and year out. In characterizing the importance of lobbyists in raising campaign funds, 83 percent of legislators found them helpful, while 11 percent considered them indispensable. Among lobbyist respondents, 58 percent judged their assistance helpful, while 31 percent believed it to be indispensable.

All respondents who discussed political contributions agreed that monetary contributions created conflict as interests contended for influence. In the closed-ended survey 48 percent of legislators and 41 percent of lobbyists believed that PAC funds were not "a positive development for state government." Another 46 percent of legislative respondents and 29 percent of lobbyists expressed reservations (that is, they didn't know) as to whether PACs were positive developments (Table 6.5).

During the in-depth interviews many respondents were even more hostile to PACs. Respondents maintained that the reason fewer lobbyists than legislators felt information to be important was because lobbyists know that their contributions often buy cooperation. Some respondents went so far as to predict a major state scandal within the next few years over PAC contributions and associated charges of bribery. These individuals proved to be excellent forecasters, for a multiclient lobbyist, Judy

Table 6.5. Legislator and lobbyist perceptions of PACs and campaign financing in Michigan

PAC Funding Is a Positive Development			Lobbyist Seen as Important in Providing Campaign Funds		
Response	Lobbyists (%)[a]	Legislators(%)[b]	Response	Lobbyists (%)[a]	Legislators(%)[b]
Disagree	41	48	Unnecessary	7	5
Reservations	29	46	Helpful	58	83
Agree	30	6	Indispensable	31	11
Don't know	0	0	Don't know	4	1
Total	100	100	Total	100	100

[a]N=167.
[b]N=83.

Augenstein, was arrested within the year on charges of bribery of a state legislator through the use of PAC funds controlled by her firm.

Other respondents just were irritated that some interests can more easily raise larger sums of money than they. An especially frustrating concern of lobbyists was the role of multiclient lobbying firms such as Augenstein's. These firms regularly donate, for example, $100 from each client to each selected legislator's fundraising campaign. A firm with fifty-five clients, respondents worry, "buys a lot of access that others can't get." Since several association and corporate representatives claimed that they used multiclient firms only because of their reputed easy access to the governor's office and the legislative leadership, there is some basis for these worries. It appears, then, that a professionalized environment does not just foster coordination and well-informed decision making. Skilled lobbyists, in search of individual power, apparently learn other things that undermine cooperation, even between interests that have otherwise much in common.

Out, But Not Down and Out

The expansion of power and influence within the professionally directed confines of Lansing has limits, however. And, as a result of that fact, it also has a reactive counterpoint. The sensitivities of those who cling to the Populist traditions of the state—with its periodic citizen movements in support of railroad, labor, and constitutional reform leaders—have been predictably offended by the isolation of professional policy makers and lobbyists as insiders in the state capital. Potent interests, based on voter strength and the availability of referenda and recall elections, have emerged, and they regularly enter the calculus if not the chambers of state decision making.

Not surprisingly, given the impact of inflation on increasing property values and taxes as well as citizen sentiments that blame increased state spending on professional politicians and special interests, contemporary reform activity has been directed mostly toward tax reduction.[31] Taxpayer organizations were formed in many Michigan counties; and two entrepreneurs, Richard Headlee and Robert Tisch, spearheaded statewide organizations to place tax reform issues on general election ballots. These appeared in 1976, 1978, and 1980. Three of the four proposals were defeated only with intense opposition led by state officials and supported by representatives of nearly all of the state's most influential economic interests. In 1983, taxpayers successfully recalled two state legislators who had not supported reform. Many of the same activists, making the same arguments against state officials, attempted to place a proposal on the 1986 ballot to mandate a part-time legislature. The combined effect of this activity has been a greater than usual sensitivity to tax issues and grass-roots noise generated by tax reformers. When asked specifically about these loosely organized taxpayers' interests, respondents all rated them as among the very most influential lobbies in the state. They gained this recognition despite the fact that their representatives often lack political sophistication, friends in Lansing, and direct representational strategy. Nonetheless, because these interests represented large numbers of citizens and a potential for electoral power, income tax and property tax cuts with associated limits on state spending were viewed as high priorities by both the Democratic governor and Republican legislative leaders throughout the mid-1980s. Thus, other interests, as advocates of costly policy initiatives, feel the impact of taxpayers and their organizational representatives. Even in the face of potentially declining revenues, policy makers argued for tax cuts and restricted spending because of the perceived influence of these citizen reformers.

Other organized interests, in addition to and in imitation of tax protesters, have gained political prominence through the large numbers of voters associated with movement-style politics. Right-to-life proponents and aged interests, for example, attained their high ranking as influential because of activist members who were willing both to come to Lansing in support of their group's regular lobbyists and to give money to organize their movements. A Michigan Senior Power Day produced some of the largest turnouts ever seen for this national event. Right-to-lifers routinely produce similar crowds when an issue such as public funding for Medicaid abortions is on the legislative agenda. Although others—from dissident farmers to sportfishers—have used the same protest tactics, their lack of a statewide presence or a mixed lobbyist/angry voter strategy has prevented the extension of the direct influence of citizens very far into Michigan state government.

These interests and others do have one option, judicial litigation, still available to them as outsiders from state government. Minorities that have felt unrepresented frequently go to court, a threat that causes state policy makers to act responsively. The state's small Hispanic and Native American populations have made the greatest use of threats and litigation. Migrant workers secured state concessions on education programs from the legislature. In a dramatic case that created acrimonious relations between Native Americans and mostly white tourists, businesspeople, and sports enthusiasts, the American Indians of northern Michigan brought suit, won unrestricted fishing rights to the Great Lakes, and eventually negotiated a favorable settlement with the state to sustain that fishing.[32] Since that time, minority lawsuits have been carefully handled as a major priority by all state agencies. Thus, power is further distributed among Michigan's private interests.

Conclusion

Despite Morehouse's listing of Michigan as a state where interest groups have weak influence,[33] it seems more accurate to describe that influence as moderately strong. A great many organized interests do succeed in attaining many of their policy goals. Therefore, they exhibit an important degree of power. Moreover, state government appears exceptionally open to interest participation, even welcoming the advocacy of interest representatives. Even antagonistic interests, especially by cultivating constituent pressures, can become exceptionally influential in Michigan.

Yet Michigan interests are constrained by several factors: partisan influence with its demand for brokered negotiation, skilled professionals who operate state government from the perspective of their own well-defined roles, the checks that result from the high number of organizations exercising influence, and the tendency of policy makers to compromise eventually to accommodate most perceptually important interests. Michigan interests can be portrayed best as policy-making partners rather than dominant political forces. Moreover, organized interests in the state gain a great deal of what they want because they represent a wide variety of economic forces that are believed to be important to the state and its goal of economic diversification. Thus, it seems that organized interests benefit as much from willing state government cooperation as they do from any inherent ability to force accommodation. Lobbyists, as a result, appear strong in the way they adapt to the socioeconomic and political environment of Michigan, but they are still unable to control state government in any absolute way.

Things appear destined to remain this way for the foreseeable future as this divisive state struggles toward greater economic diversification and the resulting entry of even more and better-represented interests into government policy making. Organized interests will continue to be moderately strong because active state policy making requires some vehicles that can bridge the many gaps between liberals and conservatives, Republicans and Democrats, professionals and party hacks, urban and outstate residents, blacks and whites, auto manufacturers and nonauto industries, and whoever else can splinter agreement in a large and resource-rich state. In spite of partisan strength in Michigan, organized

MICHIGAN

interests best perform the task of generating policy demand among the state's officialdom.[34] Interests will probably become no stronger, however, because no one can control such a complex and divided environment.

Notes

1. Hudson Institute, *Michigan Beyond 2000* (Indianapolis: Hudson Institute, Inc., 1985).
2. *Economic Report of the Governor* (Lansing: State of Michigan, 1985), 22, 70, 134, 140.
3. John F. Bibby, Cornelius P. Cotter, James L. Gibson, and Robert J. Huckshorn, "Parties in State Politics," in Virginia Gray, Herbert Jacob, and Kenneth Vines, eds., *Politics in the American States,* 4th ed. (Boston: Little, Brown, 1983), 66.
4. This historical analysis of parties and groups is derived from Willis F. Dunbar and George S. May, *Michigan: A History of the Wolverine State* (Grand Rapids, Mich.: William B. Eerdmans, 1980); see also J. David Greenstone, *Labor in American Politics* (New York: Alfred A. Knopf, 1969).
5. Walter D. DeVries and V. Lance Tarrance, *The Ticket-Splitter: A New Force in American Politics* (Grand Rapids, Mich.: William B. Eerdmans, 1972), 101-10.
6. Ferris E. Lewis, *State and Local Government in Michigan* (Hillsdale, Mich.: Hillsdale Educational Publishers, 1968), 5.
7. Melvin C. Holli, "Part 2: Commercial to Industrial City, 1850 to 1900," in Holli, ed., *Detroit* (New York: New Viewpoints, 1976), 60.
8. Dunbar and May, *Michigan,* 568-72.
9. Holli, "The Automobile Industry Takes over Both Parties," in Holli, ed., *Detroit,* 209-18.
10. Walter D. DeVries, "The Michigan Lobbyist: A Study in the Bases and Perceptions of Effectiveness" (Ph.D. dissertation, Michigan State University, 1960), 21.
11. State Elections Bureau, *Independent and Political Committees Statistics* (Lansing: Secretary of State's Office, 1986).
12. Ibid.
13. DeVries, "Michigan Lobbyist," 21.
14. William P. Browne, "Variations in the Behavior and Style of State Lobbyists and Interest Groups," *Journal of Politics* 47 (May 1985), 450-68.
15. William P. Browne, "Policymaking in the American States: Examining Institutional Variables from a Subsystems Perspective," *American Politics Quarterly* 15 (January 1987), 47-86.
16. Hugh Heclo, "Issue Networks and the Executive Establishment," in Anthony King, ed., *The New American Political System* (Washington, D.C.: American Enterprise Institute, 1978), 113-15.
17. Harmon Zeigler, "Interest Groups in the States," in Gray, Jacob, and Vines, eds., *Politics in the American States,* 119-23.
18. L. Harmon Zeigler and Michael Baer, *Lobbying: Interaction and Influence in American State Legislatures* (Belmont, Calif.: Wadsworth, 1969), 86.
19. Ibid., 93.
20. Respondents were selected on the basis of leadership positions, longstanding involvement in state government, reputations for influence noted by other respondents, and willingness to engage in long conversations.

21. Response rates were 57 percent for legislators (83 completed and returned) and 35 percent for lobbyists (167 completed and returned). We would like to thank House and Senate leaders of both parties for assisting us in getting this good rate of return. Questions were sent to all 1982 registered lobbyists who were still registered in 1986 and new registrants who seemed to be active lobbyists. Far higher returns came from the 1982 registrants. This greater response by long-registered lobbyists leads us to believe that we had higher than the reported rates of return from those who most actively lobby state government officials.

22. Zeigler and Baer, *Lobbying,* 61.

23. DeVries, "Michigan Lobbyist," 14–16.

24. Zeigler and Baer, *Lobbying,* 155. More lobbyists in Michigan (3 to 31 percent) felt efficacious than in the other four states. More Michigan legislators ranked lobbyists as more effective, from 22 to 55 percent higher than in the other states.

25. DeVries, "Michigan Lobbyist," 37.

26. Sarah McCally Morehouse, *State Politics, Parties and Policy* (New York: Holt, Rinehart & Winston, 1981), chap. 3.

27. Glenn Abney and Thomas Lauth, "Interest Group Influence in the States: A View of Subsystems Politics" (Paper presented at the annual meeting of the American Political Science Association, Washington, D.C., 1986).

28. Charles W. Wiggins, "Interest Group Involvement and Success within a State Legislative System," in Norman B. Luttbeg, ed., *Public Opinion and Public Policy* (Itasca, Ill.: F. E. Peacock, 1981), 226–39.

29. DeVries, "Michigan Lobbyist," 150.

30. Ibid., 155.

31. Charles Press et. al., *Michigan Political Atlas* (East Lansing: Center for Cartographic Research and Spatial Analysis, Michigan State University, 1984), 52–53.

32. *U.S. v. Michigan,* May 1979, 471 Federal Supplement 192.

33. Morehouse, *State Politics,* 108–12.

34. There are no criteria for measuring the comparative power of organized interests. But we see little evidence to support Zeigler's contention that strong government and strong parties in complex economies negate strong interests. See his "Interest Groups in the States," 125–30. Rather, Michigan is very much like California. See John Syer, "California: Political Giants in a Megastate," in Ronald J. Hrebenar and Clive S. Thomas, eds., *Interest Group Politics in the American West* (Salt Lake City: University of Utah Press, 1987), 33–48.

MINNESOTA

Labor and Business in an Issue-Oriented State

CRAIG H. GRAU

In the 1988 presidential election Minnesota ranked highest among the states in voter participation. Political participation does not end with elections, however, for many Minnesotans. They have formed numerous groups trying to influence state governmental policy, as one would expect in a state with a moralistic political culture.[1] These groups are not from the private sector only, such as the Minnesota AFL-CIO and the Minnesota Association of Realtors, but are also public-sector associations such as local governments and agencies of the state government. None of these groups exists in a vacuum. For example, given the regional fear of economic decline in the midwestern and northeastern states, it is not surprising that business and labor groups both inside and outside of government are politically important. Not as obvious but also significant are groups that organize around noneconomic issues such as abortion. To understand more clearly which groups are the most prominent in Minnesota, it is important to understand the economic, social, and political environment.

Environment

Minnesota is more populous than most of the states, ranking 21st. Because of its physical size, however, it is only 34th in average density of population per square mile.[2] Although Minnesota is famous for its north woods, farm country, and 10,000 lakes, it is an urban state. Two-thirds of the state's population lived in urban areas at the time of the 1980 census, which placed it 22d among the states in metropolitan area population.[3] One of these areas, the Minneapolis–St. Paul standard metropolitan statistical area (SMSA), is particularly significant. The part of this SMSA that is in Minnesota (a section is also in western Wisconsin) contains one-half of the state's population.[4] The Twin Cities metro area is not only the largest in the state, but unlike the situation in many other states, it includes the major campus of the land-grant university, the state capitol, the state prison, the major business centers, and all of the major league sports teams. Given the prime importance of the Twin Cities, the rest of the state is often referred to as "outstate Minnesota." Many of the major business and labor leaders reside in the same metropolitan area with government officials where public policy is made and carried out.

The areas outside the Twin Cities are not uniform. Agricultural Minnesota is mainly to the south and west of the Twin Cities. Minnesota was 7th in net farm income in 1985.[5] To the northeast of the Twin Cities is the Mesabi Range, the home of the iron mining industry. The forest products industry is also important in northern Minnesota.

In addition to mining and timber, business in Minnesota includes traditional food processors and handlers such as Cargill, Pillsbury, and General Mills. Minnesota Mining and Manufacturing (3M), best known for adhesive tape, as well as Honeywell, Control Data, and other more technological firms, are also prominent, especially in the Twin Cities area. The Dayton Hudson store chain and Northwest Airlines are headquartered in the state. The Twin Cities is also a major banking center. Labor, organized into unions, is an important force in Minnesota. In 1982, 24.5 percent of Minnesotans were members of unions, compared to 21.9 percent nationwide.[6] Minnesota is also well known as a medical center. Best known is the Mayo Clinic in Rochester. The number of physicians per capita in Minnesota (1985) placed it 12th in the nation, and the number of dentists (1984), 7th.[7] Business, labor, and the professions have strong bases on which to launch lobbying efforts in the state.

The stereotype of Minnesota is a land populated by Norwegians and Swedes. According to 1980 census statistics, however, Germans are the largest group, comprising nearly one-half of the single-ancestry group and what the census refers to as the *selective multiple ancestry group*. English and Irish combined also surpass those of Swedish single ancestry.[8] The population is 96 percent white, compared to the national average of 83 percent.[9] In terms of religion, the Lutheran and Roman

Catholic churches have large numbers of adherents, although more fundamentalist sects have been active politically of late. Overall, Minnesota ranked 4th in the United States (1980) in Christian church members.[10] With this combination of social characteristics, it is not surprising that Minnesota has an active prolife movement and that racial politics are not as prominent as in some states.

In addition to social and economic characteristics, political parties influence group politics. Thinking politically of Minnesota probably brings Hubert Humphrey and Walter Mondale to mind. After the Second World War, Humphrey, Mondale, and others led a move to merge the Democratic party with a third major party in Minnesota, the Farmer-Labor party. From the mid-1950s until the late 1970s the Democratic Farmer-Labor party (DFL) seemed to have momentum on its side. For twenty years (1958–78) the DFL controlled both U.S. Senate seats. From 1962 until 1978 it controlled the governorship for all but four years. In the state legislature the early 1970s were a turning point for the DFL. From the 1910s until the early 1970s Minnesotans chose legislators without party designation. When caucusing in the state's lower and upper houses, however, legislators divided into liberal and conservative caucuses. The dominant caucus in the state Senate was the conservative one, and conservatives often dominated the state House of Representatives as well. With an increase of liberals, though, the decision was made to return to party designation for state legislative candidates. This development, coupled with the aftermath of Watergate, made the DFL clearly the dominant party after the 1974 election. It controlled all major statewide offices and both state legislative chambers. Democratic support was usually based on the traditional coalition that made it the major party in the country—labor, minorities, and central cities, generally have-nots seeking equal opportunity.

With individuals increasingly not identifying with political parties in the 1970s, the Republican party renamed itself the Independent-Republican party. With its longtime leaders gone, a DFL massacre occurred in 1978. The Independent-Republicans took both U.S. Senate seats and the governorship and forced the DFL to share control of the state's lower house. Since that time, however, the DFL has regained control of the governorship and has lost control of the state House for only two years, 1985–86, while maintaining control of the state Senate.

Republicans have stressed the need for a healthier business climate. A DFL-controlled state government makes for a friendlier environment for labor. Both parties spend a great deal of time discussing issues at their conventions.

Democrats and Republicans, though, are not always internally unified. In 1978 the DFL-endorsed candidate for the U.S. Senate was defeated in the DFL primary. Four years later the DFL-endorsed candidate for governor also lost. That same year the Independent-Republican-endorsed candidate for governor was also defeated by a challenger. In the DFL party some splits have occurred between liberals and moderates, and regional differences also exist within the party. The Independent-Republican party seems to have a split between traditional Republicans and Christian fundamentalists. A weakened party system can allow a group that does not have a majority within the major party to succeed nevertheless. Business and prolife groups are not totally ineffective, for instance, when the DFL is in control.

The very nature of state government compels certain groups to stay active no matter what the political climate happens to be at the time. For example, it is not surprising that teachers and other public employees lobby the state. Their working environment and jobs are at stake.

Interest Groups

Lobbying of the state government by interest groups is influenced by the rules of the game as set out in state law. The major lobby registration requirements were brought about by the Watergate era in the mid-1970s. Given alterations made during the 1990 state legislative session, a lobbyist is legally defined as

An individual
(1) Engaged for pay or other consideration, or authorized *to spend money* by another individual, association, *political subdivision, or public higher education system,* who spends more than five hours in any month or more than $250, not including the individual's own travel expenses and membership dues, in any year, for the purpose of attempting to influence legislative or administrative action, *or the official action of a metropolitan governmental unit,* by communicating or urging others to communicate with public *or local* officials; or
(2) Who spends more than $250, not including the individual's own traveling expenses and memberhip dues, in any year for the purpose of attempting to influence legislative or administrative action, *or the official action of a metropolitan governmental unit,* by communicating or urging others to communicate with public *or local* officials.[11]

Among those excluded are public officials and paid expert witnesses. The 1990 amendments also continue to exclude state employees, defined to include those in higher education. A nonelected local or subdivision employee is excluded as a lobbyist unless that person spends more than fifty hours a month on lobbying and related activities.[12]

When lobbyists do register, they must make reports listing certain types of receipts and expenditures, including disbursements for publication and distribution of lobby materials, telephone and telegraph, postage, fees (including allowances), entertainment, travel, and expenditures such as each honorarium gift equal to or greater than $50 to public (as well as local) officials.[13]

In 1990 amendments to the lobby disclosure law placed special regulations on individuals or associations that spend "more than $500 in the aggregate in any calendar year to engage a lobbyist, compensate a lobbyist, or authorize the expenditure by a lobbyist" or "those not included in the above that spend $50,000 lobbying." These principals must indicate which category reflects their total lobby expenses: $501–$50,000, $50,001–$150,000, $150,001–$250,000, $250,001–$500,000, and so on.[14]

For many of the years covered by this study, reports were not as thorough. The city of Minneapolis, for instance, reported spending $2,741 for lobbying in 1985, but a newspaper report stated that the city was "spending $427,960 for 10 lobbyists. (The figures are for all who work in lobbying and related functions for the city, including secretaries and part-time interns.)"[15]

Major lobby groups can be divided into categories. Business, labor, and some professions stand out in an examination of reported expenditures, but governmental units and moral-issue groups should not be forgotten.

Among the large variety of business organizations are general groups such as the Chambers of Commerce, the Business Partnership, and the National Federation of Independent Business. In Minnesota not only does the state chamber lobby but so do various city affiliates, most notably those of St. Paul, Duluth, and Minneapolis. Since 1979, the chambers have been consistently among the leaders in disclosed lobbying expenditures (Table 7.1).

The Business Partnership, similar to the Business Roundtable that operates in Washington, D.C., is a group of chief executive officers of some of the largest businesses in the state.[16] Although the Partnership has not been a major spender by itself, it has become well known as an idea generator. Meanwhile, the National Federation of Independent Business has tried to provide a voice for small businesses.

Business trade associations are numerous. Among the most prominent are transportation interests such as railroads and truckers, building associations, liquor dealers, and, especially in more recent years, bankers. Attempts to change branch banking laws have drawn bankers into

Table 7.1. Minnesota interest groups reporting the top twenty lobby expenditures for three to seven years, 1979-85

Interest Group	Years
Chamber of Commerce, St. Paul	7
Minnesota Association of Commerce and Industry	7
Minnesota Education Association	7
Minnesota Mining and Manufacturing (3M)	7
National Federation of Independent Business	7
Northern States Power	7
Minnesota State Medical Association	6
Northwestern Bell	5
Minnesota Railroads	4
Minnesota Power	3
Ashland Petroleum	3
Chamber of Commerce, Duluth	3
Minnesota Association of Realtors	3
Jobs for Minnesota	3

Source: Minnesota Ethical Practices Board, "Lobby Disbursement Summary," 1979, 1980, 1981, 1982, 1983, 1984, 1985.

the legislative process, creating division within the ranks. Two banks and two associations were highlighted for expenditures by a Minnesota newspaper in the first three months of 1986. The leading issue seemed to be legalizing interstate banking with the four border states, which was approved.[17]

Some individual companies are always evident in lobbying. Since 1979, 3M has been in the top twenty expenditure category every year. In 1986 the general public became aware of 3M's success when a bill was passed requiring new license plates for residents. 3M produces a product used in manufacturing these plates.[18] A special category of individual businesses that lobby are the utilities. Concern about rates led many to spend a relatively large amount of money on administrative lobbying compared to other groups. The utility interests included Northern States Power and Minnesota Power, electrical utilities, and the "Baby Bell" for the region, Northwestern Bell.

Labor is evident among lobby organizations, but the parent organization of many, the AFL-CIO, does not fall within the top twenty group spenders, on the basis of disclosed expenditures, in an average year. It appears that the two groups of labor most interested in lobbying are teachers and public employees.

Teachers' salaries are set by local school districts, but the amount of state aid to these districts is crucial for a healthy educational climate for teachers. In Minnesota, the AFL-CIO affiliate, the Minnesota Federation of Teachers (MFT), is active at the capitol, where it represents teachers in large, unionized communities such as Duluth and the Twin Cities. The Minnesota Education Association (MEA) represents many districts as well as some college and university faculties and also reports large lobby expenditures.

State and municipal employees are most concerned with actions in state government which affect their working lives, and the American Federation of State, County, and Municipal Employees (AFSCME) and its affiliates have a presence in St. Paul. In addition, given the large role the state plays in transportation questions, employees in the trucking industry (Teamsters) and railroads are interested in state activities.

Members of professions are also very prominent when one looks at lobby expenditures. Especially evident are doctors and realtors. Dentists, other health-care providers, and trial lawyers have been involved, as have insurance agents. The professions are not necessarily unified. Issues such as malpractice limits may divide lawyers, doctors, and insurance agents.

Farmers are less evident among the top lobby spenders, although the Minnesota Farmers Union leadership, the Minnesota Farm Bureau, and other farm groups lobby in St. Paul.

Finally, there are private groups that form for specific issues. When these issues are long-lasting, the organizations can become permanent fixtures. For ephemeral issues, groups are here today, gone tomorrow. In the former category are groups concerned with abortion. Among them are a prolife group, Minnesota Citizens Concerned for Life, and a prochoice group, the Abortion Rights Council of Minnesota. In the latter category seems to be the Triple 5 Corporation, which lobbied for state aid to build a huge mall in the city of Bloomington.

Private groups, however, do not monopolize the governmental process. Cities, especially larger ones such as Minneapolis, Duluth, and Bloomington, have been lobbying a great deal. Counties, particularly those in metropolitan areas, lobby as well. If the state decides to help counties with high welfare burdens, for instance, it will reduce local property tax rates.[19] The higher education systems also lobby for needed state funding, as do school districts. Certain agencies within state government lobby as well. The Planning Department provides technical assistance to the other agencies for legislation in which they are particularly interested.[20] Education, human services, health, and transportation agencies are active during the session; in 1987, for example, there were sixty or more bills that had implications for the Transportation Department. The Minnesota Environmental Protection Agency and the attorney general's office are also active. Governor Perpich particularly made an effort to run executive branch lobbying more directly from his office. A typical agency may have two or three people specifically assigned to liaison work during the session. The attorney general's office has had ten or more working at the capitol at various times during a session.

Interest Group Activities

The groups mentioned above and others may choose to lobby public officials directly or indirectly (their tactics are discussed later), but some groups also participate in the selection of public officials. Numerous groups outside of official political party organizations donate to political campaigns. More than three hundred such groups were listed as having made contributions to state candidates in the 1986 Ethical Practices Board report, compared to fewer than two hundred in 1978.[21] Over that eight-year period two-thirds of the top twelve donors remained basically the same: AFL-CIO, teachers (MEA-MFT), public employees, doctors, car dealers, realtors, and lawyers (Table 7.2). Two labor and two professional groups were replaced by those seeking to elect women to office, retirees in Minneapolis, the Minnesota Chamber of Commerce, and a fund to help the Majority Leader of the Senate assist in electing others of his persuasion.

Table 7.2. Top twelve nonparty political committees and funds in Minnesota, 1978 and 1986

1978	
Group	Contribution ($)
AFL-CIO	119,800
IMPACE (Minnesota Education Association)	102,598
Minnesota Real Estate Association	78,061
Committee of Automotive Retailers	64,560
Minnesota Lawyers for Incumbent Judges	62,844
Minnesota Medical Association	62,540
Teamsters	33,813
United Auto Workers	23,500
Minnesota Federation of Teachers	20,569
Minnesota Bankers Association	19,050
Minnesota Dental Association	18,939
Public Employees (PEOPLE)	18,575

1986	
Minnesota Medical Association	129,418
IMPACE (Minnesota Education Association)	127,510
AFL-CIO	117,244
Minnesota Federation of Teachers	94,150
Committee of Automotive Retailers (CAR)	87,600
Minnesota Women's Campaign Fund	75,100
TRIAL PAC	61,750
Public Employees Union	59,700
Minnesota Association of Realtors	59,036
Minnesota Chamber of Commerce	54,775
Minneapolis Municipal Retirement	43,183
Friends of the Majority Leader	42,829

Sources: Minnesota Ethical Practices Board, "Campaign Finance Summary 1978: Political Committees and Funds," St. Paul (1979); "Campaign Finance Summary 1986: Political Committees and Funds" (1987).

Many of these groups can supply campaign workers in addition to money. In a survey conducted among legislators and lobbyists, both money and workers were seen as valuable. Surveys were sent in June 1987 to 163 legislators who had served more than one term in the legislature and 5 who served one. Two hundred eighty-four selected registered lobbyists from groups that paid their lobbyists more than $500 were also surveyed.

The 71 legislators (42 percent response to the survey) and 126 lobbyists (44 percent response) were asked to rank financial contributions, endorsement, providing campaign workers, and research according to their effectiveness in aiding a candidate for public office. Legislators and lobbyists both felt that financial donations and providing campaign workers were the two most effective ways (47 percent and 38 percent, respectively, for the 66 legislators responding to the question; 45 percent and 42 percent for the 122 lobbyists responding).

In the same survey both legislators and lobbyists were asked to rank the top five most effective groups at election time. In a count of the number of times groups were noted in first and second places, three groups were mentioned the most by both lobbyists and legislators. Eighty percent of the legislators and 63 percent of the lobbyists answered the question. Thirty-one percent of legislator choices were for teacher unions (35 percent with the inclusion of education), 28 percent for the AFL-CIO or labor generally, 16 percent for the Minnesota Citizens Concerned for Life (MCCL) or prolife, and 6 percent for public employees. Lobbyists chose teacher unions 25 percent of the time (including education); AFL-CIO, labor, and unions generally, 28 percent; and the MCCL, 10 percent. The Minnesota Chamber and business were selected by 5 percent of the legislators and 6 percent of the lobbyists. No other group received more than 5 percent except political parties, which were mentioned by 7 percent of the lobbyists. The survey indicates agreement on the electoral effectiveness of labor (including teachers), the prolife groups, and to a lesser extent business.

In an election year, committees are limited to contributing $1,500 for a state Senate race and $750 for a House race. Though donations from political funds can be substantial, a typical major donation to a state representative candidate seemed to be on the order of $200 in election year 1984.[22] That amount does not seem to be enough to lead a legislator to behavior modification. One might speculate, though, that donations made early in the campaign are more important than later ones and that the contributions of interest groups are valuable "up front" money.

Incumbents have had a special advantage in soliciting interest group money. One lobbyist, quoted by the *Minneapolis Star and Tribune,* said that in 1985 he "was invited to 90 legislative fundraisers at a cost of $5,945. He attended about half of them and paid $2,827."[23] The lobbyist is in a predicament. If he or she goes, it costs. If he or she does not, will the legislator be as accessible? Fundraisers during sessions were outlawed in 1990.

Clearly, as in Congress, some legislators are strategically located in the legislative process. In 1985, which was not an election year, two of the three state senators who received the largest amount of contributions from interest group funds were the chair of the appropriations committee and the chair of the finance (tax) committee.[24] In election years some prominent legislators then donate money to fellow candidates who find it difficult to raise funds.[25]

Interest groups that donate money to candidates for public office seem to be in aggregate, as opposed to individually, as important financially as political parties. Of course, interest group funds and political party contributions are not mutually exclusive. Major donors, for example, to the state House of Representatives Independent-Republican campaign committee in 1984 included a number of interest group committees. Monetarily, 45 percent of the party's donations came from such sources, as did 60 percent of the monetary donations of the major contributors to the DFL state party central committee.[26]

Many groups have found that campaign time is also a good time to lock in support for their issues. A popular technique is to determine a legislator's stand before his or her arrival at the capitol. Some legislators receive twenty to forty polls by groups trying to determine their stands on issues before campaign donations are dispersed.[27]

Although election activities are important to certain interest groups, the ultimate goal is to influence the decisions of governmental officials. To achieve this end, groups provide information. The magnitude of the effort in Minnesota can be glimpsed by examining lobby reports.

In 1985 the Ethical Practices Board indicated that 1,074 lobbyists for 868 associations or 16 individuals had reported spending $2,494,085. Less than 25 percent spent more than $1,000 for those items that must be disclosed.[28] In 1987 those registering as lobbyists had increased to more than 1,200, yet this figure is not a true total since public officials, among others, do not register.

Public officials can be lobbied directly or indirectly through their constituents. Those groups that have a large membership, such as labor, have power, as do those that have money to purchase advertisements and hire professional lobbyists, such as businesses. Moral zeal is an impetus for sacrifice to promote one's cause and is especially evident among issue-oriented groups.

Lobby Tactics

Lobbying governmental officials is probably the best-known tactic of influencing legislators, but many interest groups also lobby indirectly. If a legislator is concerned about reelection, having constituents contact him or her about an issue may be persuasive. Certain groups have a natural advantage. There are schoolteachers in every legislative district and probably car dealers and medical personnel in a majority. When such a situation does not exist for a group, it may try to create constituencies by running advertisements or holding press conferences to get its point across to the public. Readers, listeners, or watchers may be persuaded to that point of view and take action. The amount of money spent on these types of campaigns seems to be growing in Minnesota. Business interest groups often use this strategy, but there is debate on its effectiveness. A writer for the *St. Paul Pioneer Press and Dispatch* describes business groups' advertising tactics as follows:

> By running ads that reduce complicated policy issues to slick 30-second spots or a few paragraphs of emotional text, they can unleash a flood of constituent mail. Since ad campaigns also elicit legislative backlash, their net effect is unclear.
> Nonetheless, the danger is twofold. The complex policy questions are reduced to emotional backers and few other interested parties have the money to keep up with public appeals by business.[29]

A Minnesota Chamber spokesperson commented, "Advertising works. It's been enormously successful for us." Reportedly, in the 1983–85 period the chamber spent $350,000 on ad campaigns.[30]

In 1987 another indirect lobbying campaign by the Minnesota Chamber preceded a surprising shift among DFLers in the Minnesota House. "With full-page newspaper ads and at news conferences in airports around the state, Chamber president Win Borden portrayed DFL legislators as pickpockets and robbers." Ten days later, after hearing complaints from voters, the DFL caucus voted 47–31 to cut $200 million from an earlier budget.[31] Although it is always difficult to determine cause and effect in politics, the two events seemed rather dramatically coincidental.

Many organizations still follow the tradition of sending lobbyists to lobby the legislators directly to make their case. In the 1950s "most members of that almost all-male body [the legislature] stayed in downtown hotels and spent their evenings discussing state affairs with lobbyists lined up four deep at the Gopher Grill in the Hotel St. Paul."[32] One veteran lobbyist notes how things have changed: "In the old days it was just lean, lean, lean. . . . Now lobbyists are likely to tote fat notebooks of research into committee rooms and legislators' offices."[33] Information is the new style of power.

One of the questions I asked lobbyists and legislators in the survey concerned the most effective means of conveying information. Examining six methods of presenting positions to legislators, both legislators and lobbyists (based on first and second rankings — 139 choices by legislators and 233 by lobbyists) felt that the most effective way of lobbying, given the choices, is to meet with legislators in their offices (45 percent and 47 percent, respectively). The next first and second choices went to working with staff (22 percent and 27 percent). Less effective were appearing at hearings (18 percent and 8 percent, the widest disagreement), meeting socially (4 percent and 7 percent), calling on the telephone (7 percent and 8 percent), and chance meetings (3 percent and 3 percent).

Lobbyists tend to aim their direct efforts toward the legislature, according to the survey. Roughly two-thirds (68.5 percent) of the efforts are aimed at the two legislative bodies, and one-fifth (20.2 percent) at the state agencies. The governor's office receives less than 5 percent (4.5 percent) of their attention and the judiciary less than 1 percent (0.4 percent). Respondents noted that they spend about 6 percent (6.4 percent) of their time lobbying others, such as the local and national governments. They seem to spend about 39 percent of their time lobbying public officials who are their supporters, a bit more with uncommitted officials (42 percent), but only half as much time (19 percent) with opponents.

When respondents were asked to rank in terms of importance the five types of services lobbyists provide, keeping legislators informed about pending legislation received a plurality of first- and second-place choices by legislators and lobbyists (42 percent and 34 percent of the 138 and 230 choices, respectively). Helping legislators build support for their bills was given 28 percent and 33 percent, respectively, of the legislators' and lobbyists' top two choices. Providing information about the lobbyist's organization was chosen by 21 percent and 18 percent. Keeping legislators informed about attitudes of other legislators (4 percent and 7 percent) and agencies (3 percent and 2 percent) were far behind. Lobbyists added 6 percent in "other methods," and especially noted was supplying data and research.

To communicate their message to legislators, lobbyists, as one might expect, felt that hiring a skilled lobbyist was most effective. Based on their first two rankings of five choices, using a skilled lobbyist was chosen 34 percent of the time by lobbyists but only 24 percent by legislators. Legislators, on the other hand, felt that sending organization members to the capitol to lobby personally was the most effective (36 percent), while lobbyists chose members 22 percent of the time. (First choices among legislators favored members slightly over lobbyists – 34 percent to 31 percent, while lobbyists' first choices favored lobbyists over members by a wider margin – 50 percent to 28 percent.) Supporting candidates in elections was chosen 19 percent by legislators, 12 percent by lobbyists; a letter-writing campaign, 11 percent and 12 percent; and forming coalitions with groups, 8 percent and 10 percent respectively. Surprisingly, both legislators and lobbyists thought that running advertisements in the mass media was the least effective (1 percent and 0 percent), even though its use has been growing, as noted above.

Lobbying also takes place in the executive branch.[34] Knowing that an agency is supporting a bill, a group may join forces or argue privately against it before an all-out battle takes place in the legislature. An agency, in turn, may suggest that a group activate its members to support a bill in their mutual interest or talk to the media. Once a bill is passed, one might expect groups to contact the planning department that makes recommendations to the governor on signing or vetoing legislation. This step is taken less than 10 percent of the time, however.

Lobbyists seem to be of three types. First, there are volunteers and single individuals who lobby. Second, groups may pay "in-house" lobbyists to present their case. (Their counterparts in the executive branch are people working in the agencies.) Finally, an apparently growing and very prominent group is made up of lobbyists who serve a number of associations. The Ethical Practices Board indicates that as of May 11, 1987, 69 of the more than 1,200 registered lobbyists represented more than five organizations. Two of the most prominent were North State Advisors, some of whose members listed more than 30 clients, and Ross Kramer, of the Messerli and Kramer law firm, who had 26. Three other law firms well known as lobbyists are Larkin, Hoffman, Daly, and Lindgren; O'Connor and Hannon; and Lindquist and Vennum.

Professional law-firm lobbyists are different from in-house lobbyists. Multiclient lobbyists know more legislators, given the number of associations they serve. Some firms, such as North State, have large campaign funds as well. According to records of the Ethical Practices Board, North State donated more than $40,000 to candidates in 1986.[35] When respondents were asked to name the five most effective individual lobbyists, it is not surprising that North State Advisors (which includes Doug and Tom Kelm), Ross Kramer, and another professional group,

Spanno and Lennes, were noted. Only the AFL-CIO team was indicated as many times.

Overall, the lobbyists surveyed averaged 9.5 years of service. Seventy-one percent have completed some postgraduate college work, and 90 percent were at least college graduates. Most have a liberal arts background.

When asked which groups were the most effective at lobbying during the legislative sessions, legislators named the AFL-CIO, labor generally, the teachers' unions, and public employees in 44 percent of their top two choices. These same groups accounted for 47 percent of the lobbyists' responses. Business organizations generally, especially the Minnesota Chamber, the Business Partnership, the National Association of Independent Business, banks, insurance, and utilities, were chosen by 11 percent of the legislators and 18 percent of the lobbyists. The prolife groups were noted by 18 percent of the legislators and 8 percent of the lobbyists. Many other choices were noted less often. Among legislators, these include the governor and state agencies (8 percent). Lobbyists included farmers, with 4 percent. Effectiveness may vary, depending on the issue and political climate, which at the time of this survey found the government controlled by the Democratic Farmer-Labor party.

Lobby activity seems to be increasing. Based on reported expenses, lobbying took a dramatic jump in 1985; lobby materials and media advertising have become the two largest lobby expenditure categories of those reported (Table 7.3).

Sessions during odd-numbered years, such as 1985, are longer than those held during even-numbered years and are traditionally budget years (although recently, adjustments in the budget have occurred at various times). During the 1981 session less than $1 million was reported as lobby expenses. In 1983 roughly $1.2 million was reported, and in 1985 spending shot up to $2.5 million.[36] The top twenty groups that reported spending accounted for 40 percent of lobby expenditures in

Table 7.3. Percentages of total lobbying disbursements in Minnesota, by reporting category

Category	1980	1983	1984	1985
Entertainment, food, beverages	29.5	24	20	16
Lobby materials	23.9	26	23	23
Fees & allowances	21.4	8	6	15
Postage, telephone, telegraph	10.8	10	8	12
Travel & lodging	8.7	8	10	9
Media advertising	0.5	19	16	17
Other	5.2	5	17	8
$ (in millions)		1.2	1.1	2.5

Source: Minnesota Ethical Practices Board, "Lobby Disbursement Summary," 1980, 1983, 1984, 1985.

1983. By 1984 they accounted for 60 percent, and by 1985, nearly two-thirds of all expenditures. The top seven accounted for one-half of the expenditures in 1985.[37]

It must be remembered that lobbyists' salaries and other items are not included in reported expenditures, but it is interesting to look at the top seven groups mentioned above. Northwestern Bell and Hanna Mining spent a great deal lobbying the administrative branch of government on utility rate questions. Two others, R. J. Reynolds and the Seat Belt Coalition, brought concerns to Minnesota from outside the state. Smoking regulations were a concern, and the automobile manufacturers were worried about federal regulations. A *Minneapolis Star and Tribune* report noted that the U.S. Transportation Department would require "air bags or automatic seat belt systems unless states whose combined populations amounted to two-thirds of the nation's population adopt seat belt laws."[38] An organization founded by American car manufacturers and foreign manufacturers with U.S. plants helped set up the Minnesota Seat Belt Coalition, and total contributions were around $300,000 in eighteen months.[39] A seatbelt law was passed in 1986, but without penalties. The remaining three of the seven top spenders were the Minnesota Chamber, a business coalition (Jobs for Minnesota), and a mall developer. These groups may not have been mentioned by those surveyed because of the narrowness of their scope, the less-visible lobby activity in their administrative area, or the temporariness of their causes.

Overall Interest Group Effectiveness

Survey respondents viewed overall effectiveness in lobbying the same way as they did effectiveness during the legislative session. When lobbyists made their first two rankings based on effectiveness, the AFL-CIO or labor generally received 25 percent; the Minnesota Education Association and teachers in general, 22 percent; and the Minnesota Chamber, Business Partnership, and business generally, 15 percent. The prolife groups received 5 percent. Others were scattered. Legislators gave the AFL-CIO, labor, and unions 22 percent; teachers and education, 19 percent; business, 10 percent; the governor and state agencies, 11 percent; and prolife groups, 18 percent. Interestingly, nineteen DFL legislators chose the prolife groups 33 percent of the time as their first choice. Independent Republicans chose the AFL-CIO or labor generally 48 percent of the time as their first choice. Apparently, those groups one tends to oppose seem more effective. Also, prolife groups appear more effective to legislators than to lobbyists who responded to the question.

Among noneconomic groups that have been viewed as influential is the Minnesota Citizens Concerned for Life (MCCL). In 1986 one writer noted that 37,000 households are on this prolife group's mailing list. It was felt that they had 40 to 41 of the 67 votes in the state Senate and 85 of the 134 in the House. When MCCL asked legislators if they would support Right-to-Life candidates for legislative leadership posts, however, the group was chastised.[40] Since the summer of 1989, prochoice forces have become more active, and polls indicate that the voters are closely split, even among Independent Republicans.[41]

By most of the gauges used to determine effectiveness, labor and business keep appearing. How successful has business been relative to labor in Minnesota? In 1986 Lynda McDonnell wrote in the *St. Paul Pioneer Press and Dispatch:* "Unlike the 1960s when business and the Conservatives ran the Capitol, unlike the 1970s when the DFL and labor unions reigned over legislative corridors, this decade's balance of power is a tennis match. Advantage to business on workers comp., taxes and Superfund. Point to labor on unemployment comp."[42]

It must be stressed that effectiveness is difficult to gauge. Passing a bill, one veteran lobbyist said, is ten times more difficult than killing one.[43] The survey indicated effectiveness by groups with issues that tend to touch a large number of people. Individual companies can, however, be effective in narrow, quiet ways. Occasionally, though, one is highlighted, and its effectiveness is noticed by more than just a few legislators and lobbyists dealing with the issue in committee. Such was the case with Dayton Hudson in the summer of 1987. For years Dayton had been viewed as a good corporate citizen in Minnesota, donating large amounts of money to charitable causes. When the corporation appeared to be a candidate for a hostile takeover, it approached the DFL governor. A special session was called in seven days to pass the antitakeover legislation Dayton favored.

The mobilization of support was impressive. A newspaper reporter noted, "By any yardstick it was a boggling show of clout."[44] A team of company lawyers drafted the legislation. Dayton officials visited mass media outlets around the state. Employees wrote to legislators. Lobbyists were hired to add to the normal corps. Those added were North State Advisors; Messerli and Kramer; Larken, Hoffman, Daley and Lindgren; and O'Connor and Hannon. Two independent lobbyists, Larry Redmond and Ron Pratt, were also hired. The AFL-CIO has long been against takeovers by corporate raiders, so even though Dayton Hudson is largely nonunion, labor also helped. The DFL, stung by attacks that it was antibusiness, was happy to show that it was not. Only five legislators voted against the measure, which passed in the one-day session. Shortly thereafter, a full-page Dayton Hudson newspaper ad appeared that simply said, "There's no place like home. Thanks, Minnesota."[45]

Conclusion

In her book *State Politics, Parties and Policy,* Sarah McCally Morehouse categorizes Minnesota as a state in which pressure groups are weak. She also notes that Minnesota's parties are strong and that most of the weak interest group states have strong parties.[46]

Morehouse measures party strength by averaging the governor's percentage in his or her primaries from 1956 to 1978. Since then, however, Minnesota has had two gubernatorial primaries in which the governor-to-be won by percentages that would categorize Minnesota as a weak party state. One cannot base a conclusion on the last two elections, but they may indicate a trend. If parties are weaker, might groups be increasing in power?

It appears that since 1975 interest group influence has increased. Legislators polled in the study believed so, and more of those who served longer saw an increase. Of the legislators who had served one to five years, 48 percent said they saw an increase of influence. Of those who served six to nine years, 65 percent noted the increase, and for those who had been a legislator for ten or more years, 95 percent saw an increase of influence. These findings coupled with increases in lobby expenditures, seem to indicate a strengthening of interest groups in Minnesota.

In general, labor (especially teachers) is regarded as effective. Labor may be decreasing as a percentage of the workforce, but some sectors, such as teachers and other public employees, find lobby activity intensely important to their lives. A DFL-controlled state government may have made this trend more evident during the 1987 session. General business groups are also very evident and have been using indirect lobbying to increase support for their positions. The flight of business to other regions of the nation and world makes the arguments for a better business climate compelling. The issue orientation for which Minnesota is known is evident in the prominent place of the prolife lobby in the state. Legislators noted the effectiveness of the governor and state agencies as well. Legislators surveyed indicated that lobbyists representing local government and state agencies, as well as the governor, took up almost as much of legislators' time (46 percent) as did private groups and individuals representing themselves (51 percent). On specific issues individual companies such as 3M and Dayton Hudson or trade associations such as bankers can be very persuasive. To increase their effectiveness, companies and associations can broaden their contacts and expenditures by hiring professional firms, some of which are now engaged in a year-round profession. It should be emphasized, however, that in a state with hundreds of laws passed every two years, there are victories and defeats by probably hundreds of groups. As one lobbyist wrote on the questionnaire, "Against the odds, [there are] surprise victories."

Just as national events such as abortion decisions by the Supreme Court affect the success of groups on the state level, national issues are making it imperative that groups and companies have a presence in states throughout the country. The use of seatbelts and the attack on cigarette smoke are examples. States seem to be increasing in importance as arenas of public policy for these groups. Minnesota is moving toward a full-time government, and those seeking to influence it may find a full-time presence necessary. The effectiveness of labor, business, and certain issue groups is testimony to this fact. As a professional lobbyist remarked, "The world is run by those who show up."[47]

Notes

The author wishes to thank Rhona Dorgan for helping to tabulate the questionnaire results and Laurel Wheat for gathering background articles.

1. "Those Who Chose to Vote," *New York Times,* November 10, 1968, p. B6 (table based on CBS estimate of presidential vote as a percentage of the voting age population); Daniel J. Elazar, *American Federalism: View from the States,* 2d ed. (New York: Thomas Y. Crowell, 1972), 97.

2. Edith R. Hornor, ed., *Almanac of the Fifty States,* 1989 ed. (Palo Alto, Calif.: Information Publications, 1989), 422, 426.

3. Ibid., 425.

4. U.S. Department of Commerce, Bureau of the Census, *1980 Census of Population,* vol. 1, chap. B, part 25, p. 13.

5. "Net Farm Income Varies Widely around Nation," *News-Tribune and Herald* (Duluth), January 17, 1987, p. 5A.

6. U.S. Department of Commerce, Bureau of the Census, *Statistical Abstract of the United States, 1987* (1986), no. 692, p. 408.

7. Hornor, ed., *Almanac,* 428 and 429.

8. Bureau of the Census, *Census of Population,* chap. C, part 25, p. 46.

9. Ibid., chap. B, part 25, p. 13, and part 1, p. 12.

10. Bureau of the Census, *Statistical Abstract,* no. 77, p. 53.

11. *Minnesota Sessions Law Service 1990: Chapters 570–612* (St. Paul, Minn.: West Publishing, 1990), 1638–39.

12. Ibid., 1639.

13. Ibid., 1640–41.

14. Ibid., 1640 (first sentence, underlining removed); 1641.

15. Martha S. Allen, "Hoyt Says City Spends Too Much on Lobbying," *Minneapolis Star and Tribune,* February 8, 1985, p. 16B.

16. Joe Rigert, "Executives' Personal Touch Helped Business Lobbying Effort," *Minneapolis Star and Tribune,* April 22, 1984, p. 1A.

17. Joe Blade, "Bank Lobbyists Spent Heavily This Year," *Minneapolis Star and Tribune,* April 22, 1986, p. 16B.

18. Jack Coffman, "License Plate Question Is Leading Back to Court," *Minneapolis Star and Tribune,* June 22, 1987, p. 7A.

19. Janet Pinkston, "St. Louis County to Push State to Pay for Welfare," *News-Tribune and Herald* (Duluth), December 29, 1986, p. 1A.

20. Information is based on interviews with staff of the planning, transportation, and health departments, as well as the attorney general's office, St. Paul, Minnesota, July 21, 24, 27, and 28, 1987.

21. Minnesota Ethical Practices Board, "Campaign Finance Summary, 1978: Political Committees and Funds," St. Paul (1979), and "Campaign Finance Summary, 1986: Political Committees and Funds" (1987).

22. Minnesota Ethical Practices Board, "Candidate and Principal Campaign Committee Handbook" (1986), 5, and "Campaign Finance Summary, 1984: Principal Campaign Committees of Candidates for State Office" (July 1985).

23. Bill Salisbury, "Lobbyists' Cold Cash Gets Warm Reception," *Minneapolis Star and Tribune,* February 5, 1986, sec. 5, p. 10.

24. Minnesota Ethical Practices Board, "Campaign Finance Summary, 1985: State Officeholders," St. Paul (May 1986).

25. Minnesota Ethical Practices Board, "Campaign Finance Summary, 1986: Political Committees and Funds," 12, for instance.

26. Minnesota Ethical Practices Board, "Campaign Finance Summary, 1984: Political Committees and Political Funds," 21, 29–30.

27. "Lobbying by 'Q,' 'A,' " Editorial, *Mankato Free Press,* September 9, 1986, p. 4.

28. Minnesota Ethical Practices Board, "Lobby Disbursement Summary, 1985" (March 1986), 2, 14–32.

29. Lynda McDonnell, "Ads Help Business Exercise New Lobbying Clout," *St. Paul Pioneer Press and Dispatch,* April 7, 1986, p. 2.

30. "Advertising Outlay Increases – Lobbyists Focus on Taxes, Megamall," *Red Wing Republican,* March 27, 1986, p. 3.

31. Dave Smith, "DFL Party Has a New Fiscal Conservatism," *Minneapolis Star and Tribune,* April 24, 1987, p. 11A.

32. Bill Salisbury, "Gordon Forbes Leaving Lobby after 30 Years," *St. Paul Pioneer Press and Dispatch,* September 11, 1985, p. 3C.

33. McDonnell, "Ads Help Business," 2.

34. The following information is from the interviews described in note 17.

35. "Campaign Finance Summary, 1986: Political Committees and Funds," 16.

36. Kate Parry, "Lobbying Costs in State Double in One Year," *Minneapolis Star and Tribune,* March 27, 1986, p. 4B.

37. Minnesota Ethical Practices Board, "Lobby Disbursements Summary, St. Paul" (1983, 1984, 1985).

38. "Car Makers Help Finance Drive for Seat-belt Law," *Minneapolis Star and Tribune,* April 25, 1986, p. 1B.

39. Ibid.

40. Linda Kohl, "Abortion Opponents Keep Legislators in Line," *St. Paul Pioneer Press and Dispatch,* April 6, 1986, p. 1.

41. "Poll: Pro-Choice Candidates Have Edge," *Duluth News-Tribune and Herald,* (Duluth), December 28, 1989, p. 3A.

42. McDonnell, "Ads Help Business," p. 2.

43. Interview with Ross Kramer, St. Paul, July 30, 1987.

44. Jack Coffman, "Anti-Takeover Bill Becomes Law: Dayton Hudson Shows Its Clout in Minnesota," *St. Paul Pioneer Press and Dispatch,* June 20, 1987, p. 1.

45. Dayton Hudson advertisement, *News-Tribune and Herald* (Duluth), June 30, 1987, p. 3A.

46. Sarah McCally Morehouse, *State Politics, Parties and Policy* (New York: Holt, Rinehart & Winston, 1981).

47. Interview with Ross Kramer.

MISSOURI:

From Establishment Elite to Classic Pluralism

GREGORY CASEY and JAMES D. KING

Missouri is often described as a microcosm of the
United States, its people characteristic of the national population. In 1973 Neal R. Peirce noted
that although Missouri "is perhaps less typical of
the whole U.S.A. than [at mid-century] . . . it is still about the best
microcosm there is in our country."[1] The 1980 census figures bear out
Peirce's assessment, as the state continues to fall near the national medi-
ans for levels of education, income, urbanization, and minority population while maintaining a diverse economy.[2] Missouri is something of a
geographic microcosm as well, for within its boundaries are the fertile
farmlands of the Great Plains, the rich flatlands of the Mississippi River
delta, rugged Appalachian-like mountains, and two major metropolitan
areas. But if the state's people and land are typical, its politics are not.

The Political Climate

Missouri's political system has changed substantially between the
mid-1960s, when a strong Democratic party dominated state government, and the present time, when two weak parties are eclipsed by a
multiplicity of interest groups. In 1962, elitist interpretations of Missouri
might have held partial validity. At that time the Democratic state party
played a key role in candidate selection through its domination of pri-

mary elections (using anticipatory and subsequent dispensation of spoils) and in the policy decisions that ensued (although the actual policy decisions tended to be of lesser consequence than the struggle over jobs). With the government seated in Jefferson City, a small river town in the center of the state, while the majority of the state's population is clustered in the St. Louis and Kansas City metropolitan areas, and with the stagnancy of state government common in that era, a low-key atmosphere prevailed in which the stakes were perceived as insignificant. Much political striving went on in St. Louis and Kansas City but was not directed toward state government, which was left to an outstate crowd of in-group cronies.

The Establishment's Loss of Influence

Some observers considered this earlier era the heyday of an elite of sorts, consisting of an alliance between the Democratic state party and the Central Missouri Trust Company of Jefferson City, the main bank receiving state funds in noninterest-bearing accounts. John Fenton classified this group as having been fairly cohesive and consensual on candidate selection in the Democratic primary elections.[3] Influencing nominations for statewide offices such as governor, lieutenant governor, and the state treasurer (who actually controlled the state monies) was this loose cabal's main objective. The party primary election, set in early August by state law, attracted few voters; controlling outcomes was relatively easy. In the counties, courthouse crowds had power over sufficient jobs to manipulate election results; in the two large cities, ward organizations served the same functions; and at the state level, the party organization and the bank could dissuade serious candidates from running against their choice.

This postwar political system began raveling in 1964 when Secretary of State Warren Hearnes successfully contested the Democratic gubernatorial primary after the party establishment had decided to award the nomination to Hilary Bush, the incumbent lieutenant governor. Following Hearnes's victory, the constitution was amended to permit the governor to succeed himself. Governor Hearnes proved immensely popular in his first four-year term, so the precedent of challenging the party choice did not immediately affect the governorship, but it did infect several statewide races in 1968. Its hold broken, the Establishment could no longer use the power of dissuasion to control primary outcomes. Hearnes's second four-year term was followed by a blistering Democratic primary race in 1972 featuring five major contenders who fragmented the majority party vote, throwing the election to the Republican candidate. Four years later an insurgent Democrat—"Walking" Joe Teasdale—won another contested primary and in the general election of 1976 beat incumbent Republican governor Christopher "Kit" Bond. Teasdale proved an embarrassment to the remnants of the Democratic party organization, and although victorious in a heavily contested primary in 1980, he was defeated by Bond.

While the Democratic party showed signs of deterioration, the Republican party was on the rise. Its first breakthrough came in 1968, when charismatic Republican John C. Danforth won the attorney generalship. This success was a forerunner to a series of victories in statewide contests by, among others, Danforth (attorney general, 1968 and 1972; U.S. senator, 1976 and 1982), Bond (governor, 1972 and 1980; U.S. senator, 1986), William C. Phelps (lieutenant governor, 1972 and 1976), and John D. Ashcroft (attorney general, 1976 and 1980; governor, 1984 and 1988). The demise of the statewide Democratic party is evident from a comparison of the 1964 and 1988 election results. In the mid-1960s, Democrats held all six elective state executive offices, both U.S. Senate seats, and eight of ten congressional seats. In 1988, only the lieutenant governorship and five of nine congressional seats were in Democratic hands. After years of contested primaries Democrats are now seriously discussing banding together behind one candidate, but without an Establishment to provide impetus for unity, this hope remains elusive and pinned on unrealistic planning.[4] Despite their virtual disappearance from the state's executive branch, Democrats still maintain their majorities of roughly two-thirds in each chamber of the General Assembly, and both chambers are run by their majority party leadership (especially important in the more numerous House of Representatives).

The other key element of the Establishment until the mid-1960s, the Central Missouri Trust Company, has also suffered diminished influence in recent years. In certain respects, this change resulted from the decline in the Democratic party's ability to control nominations to key state offices. A reform-oriented Democratic state treasurer initiated a policy of placing public funds in banks throughout the state so the money would benefit economic development. Later, as interest rates rose, state monies were put out to the highest bidder, which eventually came to be out-of-state financial institutions. Central Missouri Trust Company was eventually left with less incentive to dominate state politics, and it no longer serves as the state's depository.

Show-Me Conservatism

Despite the waning of Establishment influence, Missouri has remained among the nation's most conservative states. Its conservatism is both social and fiscal. The political culture views government and political innovation skeptically, prefers low taxes and modest services, and sets a premium on local government autonomy in establishing and funding programs.[5] Moreover, the "outstate" (nonurban) background of most political leaders has inclined them to traditionalism and social stand-pattism, a preference for keeping society as it has been, and a suspicion that avant-garde developments emanating from the coasts are unsuitable for Missouri. More recently, metropolitan area legislators have come into more leadership positions; yet most of them, especially in the St. Louis area delegation, are also socially conservative. Hence, the change in the legislative leadership has refreshed the state's conservatism even while giving it a new twist. This environment necessarily conditions interest groups and lobbyists as they consider which of their goals can reasonably be achieved and how to best maneuver toward these goals.

Social conservatism has endured in Missouri, surviving many shifts in the issues. Traditional conflict over social issues pitted nonurban political leaders, more dominant in state politics, in symbolic and rhetorical battles against the decadent ways of life in the state's big cities. Conservatively oriented religious groups such as the Baptists and fundamentalist and evangelical Protestants churches have had high profiles in the outstate area, while in the two large cities the religious denominations with greatest influence are the mainstream Protestants and the Catholic church. Outstate Protestants and urban Catholics are socially conservative, but on different issues and with different emphases. Traditionally, outstate Protestant denominations opposed liquor and gambling, while support for legal drinking concentrated in the metropolitan arcas and in the German counties south of the Missouri River. Gambling, too, has found support in the metropolitan areas, where Catholic churches have frequently run weekly bingo games and where support for the state lottery and pari-mutuel betting has been strong.

In recent years liquor has become politically irrelevant as a status issue, and even gambling has come to be accepted, much to the chagrin of fundamentalist Protestants (the Missouri Baptist Convention led the most resistance to measures progressively legalizing gambling since the mid-1970s). The issue that currently rallies social conservatives is abortion. The Missouri Catholic Conference and Missouri Citizens for Life took the initial lead on this issue, and although it was a "Catholic" issue in early stages (1973 through the late 1970s), outstate social conservatives eventually joined in lobbying for the strictest possible abortion regulations. Since 1975 these prolife groups have succeeded in winning legislative approval for statutes restricting access to abortions and reducing public funding for prochoice organizations such as Planned Parenthood.

The state's fiscal conservatism is evident from revenue and spending patterns. Missouri has been a low-tax and low-service state in the post–World War II period.[6] In 1965 the state ranked 36th in per capita state and local revenue and 38th in per capita expenditures. Missouri's position at the time state government entered into its era of renascence was thus among the thriftiest of the nonsouthern and midwestern states. Nine of those ranking below Missouri in per capita state and local revenue and expenditures were southern states; of midwestern states, only Ohio took in less money than did Missouri, and none spent less. Eventually, the other states enacted new taxes and found new revenue sources, but Missouri continued its impecunious ways and ended up at the bottom of the states in per capita revenues and expenditures by the mid-1980s. In 1984 Missouri was ahead of only Arkansas in per capita state and local revenue and expenditures.[7]

The state's fall in per capita expenditure and revenue rankings results from a near-phobia concerning tax increases. In 1969 Governor Hearnes, at the peak of his popularity, advanced the idea of tax reform to maintain progressivity in the personal income tax. While supporters defended the proposal as revenue-neutral, opposition termed it a "tax increase" and mounted an initiative campaign that ended in the defeat of tax reform at the polls. Besides beginning a long slide in Warren Hearnes's popularity, this outcome made most political actors in the state wary of any measure that might look at all like a tax increase. Further evidence of the public's disapproval of tax increases is seen in the narrow passage of a sales tax increase of one-eighth cent earmarked for conservation in 1976, the resounding defeat (88 percent disapproval!) of a proposed three-cents-per-gallon increase in the motor fuel tax backed by supporters of better roads in 1978, and the adoption of a constitutional amendment—known as the Hancock Amendment—limiting state revenues in 1980.[8] These developments have fostered a conventional political wisdom among political leaders that dictates avoidance of any tax increase; tax increases have come to seem almost taboo. Since adoption of the Hancock Amendment, only one serious gubernatorial proposal and one legislative leadership plan for increasing general, nonearmarked taxation have seen the light of day; neither passed.

With political leaders unwilling to voice the need for raising taxes, no interest group thinks openly about a general tax increase to raise revenues that could then be appropriated for various purposes. Few groups believe that such a tax increase would be possible, and fewer still would be willing to push for it. Instead, interest groups try to identify new tax sources to pay for the particular program(s) or service(s) they want expanded or established.

Distressed at low state funding for education, the Missouri State Teachers Association (MSTA) sponsored an initiative drive for a sales tax increase of one cent, half for education and half for property tax relief; the other teachers' associations, the Missouri National Education Association and the American Federation of Teachers, strong in the two urban centers, lent support, and signatures were gathered inexpensively through saturation of PTA meetings throughout the state. Voter approval followed in 1982. Two years later voters approved by the thinnest of margins a one-tenth cent sales tax for soil conservation, also put on the ballot by initiative petition. A recent example of an interested party identifying a revenue source for its program is the Department of Higher Education, whose commissioner called in late 1986 for a one-year elimination of all sales tax exemptions (e.g., farm machinery and prescription drugs) to develop a fund to increase salaries at the public universities and colleges. Although nothing came of this idea, the higher education interest group was concurrently flirting with setting up an alliance with the MSTA.[9]

Fiscal Conservatism and the Paralysis of Leadership

Interest group focus on earmarked tax resources has become endemic in current Missouri politics. Also endemic is interest group use of initiative petitions, a symptom of the paralysis of political leadership. The chief political actors go out on a limb only when consensus is reached, which happens only if a crisis arises, and then they venture forth hesitantly together. For example, in 1987 the governor and legislative leadership, with support from groups across the political spectrum (e.g., the Missouri Chamber of Commerce, State Labor Council, Farm Bureau, AAA-Auto Club of Missouri), placed before the electorate a referendum increasing the state's gasoline tax. This move was taken only after it was evident that the General Assembly would have to appropriate monies from the general fund or face the loss of federal matching funds because of the disrepair of state highways. Though successful, the necessary leadership was provided only when a crisis was perceived by most.[10]

Groups fragment because they feel obliged to identify their own earmarked revenue source(s). The common interest in adequate state revenues is eclipsed as groups scramble to find monies to support their own needs. This has left the state with little ability to focus on overall services. Political figures who have dared to center attention on the level of services desired are left in the dust by candidates who spew rhetoric about tax cuts and holding the line against tax increases.[11] Thus, no one takes the lead in proposing general increases in taxes and services. A further problem is that some groups' programs are unpopular and therefore unlikely to compete effectively if an initiative petition drive is the most direct route to increased revenues; nor are such groups likely to win a public vote. Corrections, mental health, and state administration programs depend on political leaders to appreciate their value, but the political leaders' alternatives are limited because they are frozen in place by the taboo that has settled over tax increases. Thus, these groups must beg, scrape, protest, and remain vigilant to try to resist further cuts in their services.

Evolution of Missouri Pluralism

This brief review of Missouri's conservatism and leadership paralysis sets the stage for understanding the evolution of interest groups in the Show-Me state. When a party was strong, interest groups were considered fairly weak. Some groups did flex muscle in Jefferson City during the era of Central Missouri Trust Company dominance (especially the Missouri State Teachers Association), but most did not even maintain offices there. Cooperation among groups was virtually nonexistent; rather than engaging in logrolling, groups preferred to conserve their political resources for protecting their key interests.[12] State politics were lax and not oriented toward policy; the targets of interest groups seeking boons were few and simple. The governor, lieutenant governor (often a governor-in-waiting), the party leadership in the legislature, and the Democratic State Committee were the contact points. Central Missouri Trust Company targeted the governor and state treasurer in particular for efforts at control. This system's breakup coincided roughly with the state government revitalization that began in the late 1960s; with no elite controlling the gates to state government, interest groups moved into the vacuum of power left when party waned. A steady stream of groups either moved their headquarters to Jefferson City or opened offices there. The counts both of organizations and of lobbyists indicate expansion. Robert Karsch noted listings for 20 associations in the telephone directory in 1971.[13] But by 1986 at least 100 groups had listings in the Jefferson City telephone directory, with 20 other organizations maintaining offices in other central state locations within commuting distance. In addition, numerous other associations not having listings were represented by contract lobbyists. The lobbyist count is consistent with these estimates; in 1982 State Representative R. B. Grisham began publishing a directory of lobbyists with photographs; the 1985 edition portrayed 102 lobbyists, but Grisham notes that his compilation is not exhaustive.[14]

The largest increase in number of groups represented seems to have occurred in the early 1970s. John Britton, dean of Jefferson City lobbyists, identifies 1972–73 as a watershed in lobbying conditions in the state's capital. Britton, who came to Jefferson City in the 1950s, describes the lobbying atmosphere of the earlier period in terms similar to those used by Robert Salisbury in his study of the MSTA in the late 1950s. The system was slack and afforded many opportunities for changes in legislation; lobbyists often worked for amendments to update and broaden statutes, seldom encountered any opposition in doing so, and rarely had to oppose anything themselves. Compromises were possible and frequent; if legislation sponsored by a legislator was offensive in some regard, a lobbyist could approach the legislator and obtain an accommodation. But beginning in the 1970s, this loose system has tightened up. The legislative agenda has become cluttered as bills unsuccessful in earlier sessions are reintroduced; Britton estimates the percentage of new bills at 15 percent of the legislation. In the present era, lobbyists must frequently oppose proposed legislation and in doing so have become more confrontational in style. Instead of approaching the sponsor of legislation to explain an offensive feature or clause, the lobbyist must struggle. Economic lobbyists (such as Britton) now are "painted with the brush of the private interest" and must overcome what is now a liability with other assets, such as being armed to the teeth with every conceivable argument when appearing before committees. In Britton's words, "light-hearted contact has yielded to war," and the pressures that lobbyists must mount have increased, now including the use of PAC monies and direct constituent pressures. The old soft-sell tactics dictated that a lobbyist leave the legislators alone when they were home; now constituents aligned with a lobby are commonly instructed to pounce on the legislators with calls as soon as they arrive home from the General Assembly's adjournment for the weekend.[15]

Economic interests—principally business interests—tend to dominate most state political systems.[16] This pattern holds true in Missouri (Table 8.1). In 1982 four of five registered interests were associated with economic concerns. Individual businesses and business associations accounted for three-fourths of the economic interests and three-fifths of all registrants.[17] In contrast with the situation in other states, government agencies and associations are quite likely overrepresented in lists of

Table 8.1. Classification of Missouri Interest Groups, 1982

Type of Group	No.	%
Economic interests	317	79
Individual businesses	143	36
Business associations	102	26
Professional associations	34	8
Labor organizations	32	8
Agricultural organizations	6	1
Political-social groups	54	14
Government agencies & associations	29	7
Total	400	100

Source: James D. King, "Interest Groups in Missouri Politics," in Richard J. Hardy and Richard Dohm, eds., Missouri Government and Politics (Columbia: University of Missouri Press, 1985), 27.

Missouri lobbyists. This is because of the state's lobbyist registration law, which requires state executive agencies to register with the General Assembly in the same manner as private sector institutions.

The current political environment features great fragmentation of groups and a variety of access points to state government. The banking industry illustrates the inaccuracy of any elitist interpretation of Missouri's contemporary political system. Probably the most closely regulated industry in the state, it would under almost any circumstances have an interest in influencing state government. However, the stability of banking attenuated this need slightly. Bankers did not feel compelled to lobby for legislation to permit change until federal deregulation of financial institutions let loose a spirit of innovation and competition among bankers. Changes in state law eventually favored the formation of bank holding companies, or banks that own other banks; Central Missouri Trust Company became a large holding company, as did many banks in St. Louis and Kansas City. Although state law limits holding companies to a certain percentage of the deposits of the state, these companies run quite profitable operations providing correspondence services for smaller banks (local clearinghouses, data entry, etc.).

Formation of the holding companies gave potentially greater influence to the banking industry in the state but also posed difficulties for the Missouri Bankers Association (MBA), heretofore the industry's principal representative in Jefferson City. Holding companies began retaining their own lobbyists in Jefferson City for potential gain on issues on which the MBA could not speak up, lest it offend some of its members. And although nearly all banks are members of the MBA, some smaller banks formed the Missouri Independent Bankers Association (MIBA) to offer protection against holding companies, which smaller banks tend to view as predators. In this fragmented situation the MBA, in an earlier era linked to the elite, which ran the state through Central Missouri Trust Company, must perform a balancing act, taking great care to represent all its members, not tilting too much toward the holding companies nor leaning too much toward the independents, who are represented by their own organization.

Moreover, the MBA has neither automatic nor immediate influence over state government. In the fall of 1984 the MBA wrote a new banking bill that would accomplish a number of goals on its agenda, including permitting interstate banking with adjacent states that allowed Missouri banks to enter, a loosening of control over branch banking in the metropolitan areas, and an adjustment in control over branching in the outstate area. Although the association was fairly united behind the bill, it went nowhere in the 1985 legislative session. The MIBA's lobbyist expressed reservations about the change in regulation; faced with something less than the appearance of consensus, the General Assembly did nothing. The Establishment banking community simply could not have its way with ease. Reappraisals among MBA staff led to the conclusion that nothing was wrong with the lobbying effort except that the banking industry throughout the state had left all the work to the association. But the MBA's large entertainment budget and lavish PAC contributions to many legislators' campaign organizations were unavailing because the legislators felt that most bankers were lukewarm and knew that some were opposed (because of the MIBA's activities). In the 1986 session the MBA activated its grass roots; bankers from across the state supplemented the association's lobbying efforts by visiting and calling their legislators. This change in tactics brought success; the 1986 session saw passage of the interstate banking bill intact.

Most of the MBA's work is defensive and involves keeping alert for threats to the favorable state tax position of the banks and maintaining the contacts necessary to quash the resentment and jealousies that could arise against bankers easily if political leaders were to create an adverse climate of opinion. In this task it is well armed; it has many allies in the General Assembly and in the executive department. But when it desires a change in law, it must, like every other interest group in the pluralistic setting, find and activate resources suitable to the particular battle. From being part of the Establishment to confronting this harsh fact of life in the new reality of an expanded pluralism in Missouri, this one group attests to the highly competitive and pluralistic nature of interest groups in Missouri.

Another example of the workings of pluralism is seen in how the state began to cope with rising malpractice insurance rates that threatened to curb availability of medical services in certain specialties (such as obstetrics), especially in rural areas. With a crisis seemingly imminent, concerned interest groups approached legislative leaders, who told them to negotiate with one another until they agreed on a reform package. In 1986 the Missouri Hospital Association, the Missouri Medical Association, the Missouri Association of Osteopathic Physicians and Surgeons, the Association of Malpractice Insurance Companies, and the Missouri Association of Trial Attorneys together drafted a tort reform act that capped jury awards for pain and suffering at $350,000 but put no cap on awards for economic losses, and that eliminated joint and several liability in favor of proportionate liability. A classic logroll, the bill contained concessions for each group; it sped through the General Assembly and was signed by the governor thirteen days after its introduction.[18]

Not all groups can achieve internal agreement and the outward appearance of policy area consensus. In the absence of unity, they must find other means to achieve their aims. In 1978 the state's AFL-CIO affiliate faced an initiative proposal on the ballot that would legislate "right-to-work," doing away with union and closed shops. Industry supported the measure, had provided the essential backing to get the initiative petition drive going, and funded an extensive media advertising campaign. Labor fought back successfully with a new campaign ploy masterminded by Matt Reese which sidestepped public advertising in favor of mailings and telephone banks; the proposal was repudiated at the polls. In early 1986 a business group succeeding to the organization that sponsored the original petition drive started a rumor in the capital city gossip mill that the time was ripe to reconsider right-to-work legislation. In response, Duke McVey, chief lobbyist for the AFL-CIO, called for a public demonstration in Jefferson City against the suggestion. Huge numbers of labor supporters turned out for the rally on the capitol steps, and the show of force was sufficient to reaffirm the electorate's judgment that right-to-work was unacceptable. Teachers have also demonstrated on the capitol steps against budget cuts in education, as have mental health workers and families of handicapped children against budget cuts in their programs. The mere fact of these demonstrations shows that Jefferson City has come of age but is also emblematic of the versatility in tactics that interest groups must maintain to keep the edge.

Lobbying Practices

Although lobbyists and organizational leadership must be ready for nearly any tactical move, most practice classical lobbying techniques.

The Missouri state code defines a lobbyist as any individual, except members of the legislature and elected state officers, who seeks to influence any action of the General Assembly.[19] This definition is so broad that it includes employees of state agencies who appear before legislative committees or contact members on legislative business. Thus, more than one-half of all registered lobbyists—most of whom report no expenditures—represent state agencies. Local government officials who visit the capitol seeking favorable legislation, such as city mayors and council members, must also register. Despite the law, common usage does not regard representatives of state agencies as lobbyists, although the term *lobbyist* is increasingly heard in describing the activities of local government representatives. One highly reputed lobbyist, Tom Simon, is clerk of the state Supreme Court and represents it and the state court system before the General Assembly; yet lobbyists who represent private interests and who clearly respect his influence include Simon as one of their number only as an afterthought; his affiliation with the third branch of government puts him *hors concours* to them.

Contract Lobbyists

Although older interest groups usually retain lobbyists on staff, some of the recent proliferation in lobbyists has been in contract lobbyists, who represent groups either too new or too small to have a staff and/or office in Jefferson City. Several organizations have sent volunteer members to represent them before the legislature; the League of Women Voters is the best example of this mode of lobbying because its approach to government stresses involvement by its members, although many capital city observers rate its effectiveness minimal because of amateurishness. The Missouri Library Association first began to realize that it needed a lobbyist to represent its interests when the Reagan cutbacks were imposed in 1981; before, it had always lobbied through the parent agency of the State Library, the Department of Higher Education. After vacillating between an accomplished librarian and a contract lobbyist as its representative, the association chose a contract lobbyist. The League of Women Voters also retains a contract lobbyist outside the organization. The first contract lobbyist was John Britton, who began in the 1950s with the gigantic brewery, Anheuser-Busch of St. Louis, as his principal client. Britton now represents many clients (he registered nineteen during the 1986 session), and other lobbyists (many of them graduates of Britton's firm) representing multiple clients have set up shop as well. During the 1986 session nearly one-fourth of the lobbyists representing economic organizations registered more than one client.

The early 1980s saw a new upsurge in such contract lobbyists. Young men and women recruited clients more aggressively and offered a more outspoken style of representation. Whereas Britton is famous for his behind-the-scenes approach to legislators (he is considered legendary in his abilities, and an aura of mystique surrounds his operations), the new breed tends to be more front stage in style, particularly well-spoken in public, and more willing to advise clients to litigate. For instance, Pam Rich, of Rich and Associates, represents "liberal" groups (including the League of Women Voters and Impact, a coalition of mainline Protestant churches). One of her clients is the Association for the Education of Young Children, an organization seeking full licensing of day care facilities in the state. Currently, day care facilities on church premises are fully exempt from regulation, and fundamentalist churches oppose the licensing bill. Rich works for licensing in the legislative setting and has also sent her client to the judiciary because she sees litigation as an alternate and parallel strategy. The coming of age of contract lobbyists in Jefferson City may indicate a greater professionalization of the state's lobbyist corps similar to the pattern Scholzman and Tierney discovered in the nation's capital.[20] Though some of the new breed do much of the classic contacting via entertainment, others, especially those with ideological leanings, spend relatively little on entertainment.

No large law firms currently involve themselves in lobbying in Jefferson City; the city is too small to support them, and only one is located there. Large legal firms in the state's other cities are inactive in lobbying activities. Probably the largest lobbying firm is John Britton and Associates. Professional campaign consultants from out of state are not ordinarily a presence in lobbying activities; when active, these firms work on campaigns for office or on the public votes on issues that have become so frequent in Missouri; generally, it is considered de rigueur to send in someone with a Missouri connection. The Matt Reese organization, for example, was active in the opposition to the right-to-work initiative in 1978.

Access Points

Among the most important contact points for lobbyists are the leadership offices of the two chambers of the legislature, identified by members as the centers of decision making in the General Assembly.[21] The key person in the House of Representatives is the Speaker, who has been Democratic ever since 1955. The House has centralized power in the hands of the Speaker, who appoints all members of each committee (both majority and minority party members) and designates committee chairpersons without regard to any principle such as seniority. With vast resources at his beck and call, the Speaker can squelch legislation he opposes and advance proposals he favors, and on matters of high priority backbenchers usually dare not oppose him because he can punish those who demur.

Illustrative of the importance of getting the Speaker on one's side was the struggle over "big trucks." The Missouri Bus and Truck Association (MBTA), speaking for the truck lobby, sought legislation to increase the permissible length and weight of trucks on Missouri highways for years but was stymied by two successive Speakers of the House who opposed the measure. Under new Speaker Bob Griffin (succeeding Kenneth Rothman, who had been elected lieutenant governor after serving four years as Speaker) and with the concurrence of the Senate leadership, which was already persuaded of the merits of raising the limits, the bill passed in 1981. The railroads, the Automobile Club of Missouri, and the consumer-oriented group PATH (People Associated for Tomorrow's Highways) opposed the change; after the legislature passed the bill, these interests rebounded by sponsoring an initiative petition drive to refer the measure to popular decision. The Big Truck bill was defeated in a referendum in the spring of 1982, with the metropolitan counties voting against the change and the outstate area voting in favor. Since the legislative leaders in both chambers were at this time from the outstate area, they simply had the General Assembly pass the bill again to demonstrate to urban voters who was boss. But the governor vetoed the bill. Later that year Congress made the increase of permissible limits a precondition for receipt of federal highway aid, providing the MBTA with the victory it sought.[22]

Senate party leadership is a little more diffuse but still dominant. Only thirty-four senators comprise the upper chamber, and the effective legislative leader is the President Pro Tempore, always of the majority party. Yet the minority party makes its own committee appointments in the Senate, enabling it to concentrate its key members on more significant committees. Party means less in the Senate, and the senator considered most influential in the chamber is actually a Republican. Nonetheless, contact with the leadership is important for getting bills passed in the Senate also, and lobbyists must cultivate the leaders and their trusted confederates, the committee chairs.

Several points should be made before we proceed. First, the legislative party leadership's power probably is the basis for comparative state rankings that see Missouri's political parties as strong. Despite the strength of the party-in-the-legislature, however, the parties-as-organizations are in disarray and the parties-in-the-electorate are, as elsewhere, in great flux. Second, the strength of party leadership in the General Assembly does not make these officials absolute rulers. They are susceptible to influence and even anxious to please the legislators whom they lead; they entertain new ideas and are open on many issues. Their power is not inconsistent with democracy, but they do possess enough authority to head off proposals with which they heartily disagree. Even when interest groups attain a favorable hearing with the leadership, they do not stop there but proceed to cultivate legislators not in leadership positions and staffers.

In comparison with other states, in Missouri the committees are central to the General Assembly's activities and, in the minds of the legislators themselves, second only to the leadership in the decision-making process.[23] Thus the incentive to establish contacts with legislators who are not part of the leadership is strong. Lobbyists begin with friendly legislators, their friendship often won by PAC contributions to election campaign funds and entertainment provided by lobbyists (lunches, dinners, catered parties, and drinks in bars in Jefferson City, where evenings tend to be boring and lonely). Not all groups maintain entertainment budgets; primarily, economic interest groups use this tactic. In the 1986 session, lobbyists representing economic interests expended nearly three-fifths of their funds on entertainment, while lobbyists for other interests devoted between a third and two-fifths of their money to that purpose (Table 8.2). However, it should be noted that money alone is not sufficient to win the day. Lobbyists also work the legislators during the day in the capitol building.

An access point often overlooked by the general public, but not by veteran lobbyists, is the legislative staff. Each senator has a secretary,

Table 8.2. Lobbyist Registration and Expenditures in Missouri, 1986

	Economic Organizations	Social Organizations	Local Governments	State Agencies
No. of lobbyists	323	46	41	534
No. of lobbyists with multiple clients	74 (25%)	7 (15%)	1 (2%)	33 (6%)
No. of lobbyists incurring expenditures	183 (57%)	20 (43%)	18 (44%)	22 (4%)
Total expenditures	$708,017.22	$22,787.07	$31,507.71	$40,814.57
Mean expenditures of those incurring expenditures	$3,868.95	$1,289.35	$1,750.42	$1,855.21
Total expenditures by function (%)				
Entertainment	57	40	38	36
Travel	15	18	24	37
Printing	12	24	4	18
Honoraria	2	0	3	3
Other (not specified)	14	19	31	5

Source: Clerk of the Missouri House of Representatives.

although some representatives must share. These staff members are quite important to lobbyists, who take care to maintain cordial relationships with them. With staff acquiescence, the lobbyist can visit the legislator with the legislator's secretary merely announcing his or her arrival rather than checking with the legislator to see if he or she can meet with the lobbyist now. Some lobbyists actually use legislators' offices as their personal offices, storing coats there and placing and receiving telephone calls; achieving this sort of welcome obviously presumes consistent friendliness with staff. Being freely admitted to legislators' offices projects the impression that the particular lobbyist accorded these privileges is powerful and thus boosts political image as well as providing the potential for influence.

Similarly important are staffers of the research division of the Committee on Legislative Research. Each staff member serves several substantive committees, and the lobbyist who knows these individuals can notify them that Representative X has authorized a certain change in the wording in a particular bill. Getting the change made without the legislator's issuing the command personally can make the difference between passage and failure in the intense legislative session, especially in the chaos toward the end of the session. The oversight division of the Committee on Legislative Research is in charge of writing the fiscal note required for each bill. In Missouri's political culture anything that costs is almost ipso facto undesirable, and the more so the more it costs. When the Associated Students of the University of Missouri were lobbying for appointment of a student member to the university's governing board (the Board of Curators), the university's lobbyist opposed the measure and managed to stop it by having attached to it a fiscal note that increased the price substantially. The only costs invoked were to remunerate the student board member for travel and would have been minimal, but a grossly exaggerated fiscal note nonetheless spelled doom for the proposal. In the next session the student association dropped the travel costs compensation feature of the bill and got it through, defeating the university. Now that several more sessions have passed, the student organization is seeking to have the law amended to authorize remuneration for the student board member.

Another set of access points is in the executive branch. Like the legislative research staffers, executive staff members have a considerable degree of professionalization and expertise that can be tapped by lobbyists.[24] Some of these staffers are in the governor's office, and lobbyists attempt to achieve contact with them even if direct contact with the governor proves elusive. The Division of Budget and Planning prepares legislation for the governor's consideration, and lobbyists make contacts here so that the Budget Division staffer will call them to ask for their last-ditch justification for the bill—a large hint that a veto may be in the works (but possibly can be staved off by effective persuasion). Missouri's governor enjoys the item veto in appropriations legislation and also has the constitutional power to reduce appropriations passed and signed to keep the state within its means. The budget staffers are chief protagonists in these actions, and being acquainted with them can help a lobbyist make a plea or at least find someone to hear him or her out.

Only a few groups practice confrontational tactics with the legislature or governor. One notable group is Missouri Citizens for Life (MCL), a prolife organization with chapters and allies in most areas of the state which is unafraid to buttonhole and threaten legislators who oppose its agenda. Missouri's social conservatism makes it unnecessary for MCL to use such tactics extensively, but this group and its allies do not hesitate to engage more or less openly in electoral reprisals against political figures who speak out for abortion rights. Among the notches in its holster are former U.S. Congressman James Symington, who finished third in the 1976 Democratic senatorial primary to succeed his father (former U.S. Senator Stuart Symington), in large part because Right to Lifers swung their votes to a more conservative candidate; and Harriett Woods, the incumbent lieutenant governor, whose run for the U.S. Senate in 1986 was adversely affected by her call for preserving abortion rights. The Missouri Public Interest Research Group (Mo-PIRG) does not quail at confrontational tactics either. Similarly, the AFL-CIO publicly took on business organizations calling for right-to-work legislation, but most groups shy away from such public controversy and seek to avoid clashes with other interest groups.

Economic lobbying is considered more challenging—more "hard core," in the words of one lobbyist. Even though lobbyists discount their possibilities of prevailing on any given issue, they talk in terms of trying to increase their batting averages, of fighting the odds. Some groups are not involved in economic lobbying, and their agendas can be easier to advance. For instance, the Missouri Bar Association has frequently proposed various reforms of the judiciary and prosecutors' offices; by putting these ideas forward only when agreement within the bar has been forged, this association can report consensus to the General Assembly on its measure. Moreover, the proposals themselves carry minimal cost and often promise considerable cost savings over time by increasing efficiency in the administration of justice. Legislators can support such good government bills almost without detriment altogether, and lobbying for them is consequently substantially easier than putting pressure on legislators in an economic policy area.

Nonlobbying Activities

The growth in active interests is evident in the electoral arena as well as at the capitol. Both national and state political systems have witnessed the explosive growth in the number of political action committees seeking to influence election outcomes and, as a consequence, improve their chances of securing their policy objectives.[25] In contrast to the national level, where both the number of PACs and the amount of PAC expenditures have increased dramatically, the most startling change in Missouri has been in the increase in the amount of PAC receipts and direct expenditures (Table 8.3).[26] The number of PACs in Missouri increased 48 percent from 1978 to 1984, while PACs' direct contributions grew nearly 500 percent. Although the bulk of this growth occurred between 1978 and 1980, the pattern of growth in expenditures is unbroken over the period of four elections. The 1986 elections witnessed a slight decline in both the number of registered PACs and PAC contributions, almost certainly due to the absence of a gubernatorial contest, but their numbers remain significantly greater than a decade before.

Although the evidence is slim, Missouri appears typical of midwestern states in that state candidates receive roughly one-third of their campaign funds from political action committees.[27] The shares of contributions coming from PACs in recent state executive and legislative races has ranged from 28 percent (1984 attorney general contest) to 39 percent (1984 state treasurer contest) (Table 8.4). The 1985 lieutenant governor's race is the only significant exception to the "one-third" generalization; collectively, the seven candidates for this post received only 14 percent of their funds from PACs.

Missouri election laws permit direct contributions from corporations and labor unions, rather than requiring the creation of political action committees, and do not limit contributions. As a result, corpora-

Table 8.3. PAC Activity in Missouri, 1978-86

Year	No. of PACs	% Change from Previous Election	Total Direct Contributions ($)	% Change from Previous Election
1978	256		452,839	
1980	305	+19	1,427,051	+215
1982	311	+2	1,606,148	+13
1984	380	+22	2,591,533	+61
1986	344	-9	2,295,950	-11
Total change, 1978-84	+124	+48	+2,138,694	+472
Total change, 1978-86	+88	+34	+1,843,111	+407

Source: Roy D. Blount, Secretary of State, 1986 Missouri Annual Campaign Finance Report (May 1987), 334.

Table 8.4. PAC Contributions to State Government Candidates in Missouri, 1984 and 1986

Office	Year	No. of Candidates	Total PAC Contributions ($)	Share of Total (%)[a]
Governor	1984	7	2,448,815	34
Lt. governor	1984	7	149,247	14
Secretary of state	1984	5	201,071	29
State treasurer	1984	3	276,909	39
Attorney general	1984	3	200,796	28
State auditor	1986	3	441,416	30
State Senate	1984	36	600,599	37
	1986	35	657,448	33
State House	1984	277	979,629	36
	1986	268	1,459,414	36

Sources: Roy D. Blount, Secretary of State, 1984 Missouri Annual Campaign Finance Report (August 1985), 248; Roy D. Blount, Secretary of State, 1986 Missouri Annual Campaign Finance Report (May 1986), 328.

[a]PAC contributions as a percentage of total contributions to all candidates seeking that office.

tions and business associations contribute more than do other PACs (Table 8.5). In 1984, corporations and business associations contributed more than $2 million to candidates for governor, state executive positions, and the General Assembly. This figure represented more than half of total PAC contributions. Corporations and business associations spent another $4 million on ballot proposals, more than four-fifths directed at a proposal concerning nuclear power plant cost and operation. With only a state auditor's race and legislative races in 1986, trade and professional association PACs outspent corporations and business associations. The relatively low level of activity by labor unions and their PACs is a consequence more of large corporate contributions than of lack of labor interest or resources. They simply are not in a position to spend dollar for dollar with corporations and are therefore more cautious with their funds, reserving a portion to fight or push certain ballot proposals.

The electorate provides a second access point for interest groups in Missouri not available to groups in some other states. Under provisions of the state's constitution, proposed constitutional amendments and statutes may be placed before the voters for their approval by either legislative referral or initiative petition. Of the two, the latter is most important to interest groups, as it provides the means for bypassing the General Assembly if efforts to influence that body prove futile. The previously mentioned public votes rejecting the antilabor right-to-work constitutional amendment and overturning the statute permitting larger trucks on the state's highways are cases in point. Missouri's procedures for reaching the ballot via an initiative petition are among the most rigorous in the nation. Nonetheless, the use of public votes to settle policy ques-

Table 8.5. PAC contributions in Missouri, by source, 1984 and 1986

Groups Making Contributions to Candidates	1984		1986	
	Amount ($)	%	Amount ($)	%
Corporations, businesses, and business associations	2,266,202	55	582,505	23
Labor organizations	106,260	3	60,802	3
Labor PACs	181,011	4	287,567	12
Corporate, trade, and professional association PACs	1,073,001	26	1,200,358	48
Other committees	469,938	12	352,401	14
Total	4,096,412	100	2,483,633	100

Groups Making Contributions on Ballot Measures	1984		1986	
	Amount ($)	%	Amount ($)	%
Corporations, businesses, and business associations	4,209,504	99	179,986	68
Labor organizations	11,276	a	68,000	25
Labor PACs	0	0	0	0
Corporate, trade, and professional association PACs	7,000	a	16,000	6
Other committees	630	a	0	0
Total	4,228,410	100	263,986	100

Sources: Roy D. Blount, Secretary of State, 1984 Missouri Annual Campaign Finance Report (August 1985), 248; Roy D. Blount, Secretary of State, 1986 Missouri Annual Campaign Finance Report (May 1986), 328.
aLess than 1 percent.

tions has increased in recent years, as various interests find themselves stymied by the General Assembly's unwillingness to consider tax increases or more liberal social legislation.[28]

The courts provide yet another access point for interest groups, as they do in other states. For the most part, litigation has been a tactic of last resort, although the newer breed of lobbyists counsels it more readily. Groups failing in the legislative or electoral arenas frequently turn to the courts for assistance. The successful petition drives that placed the Right-to-Work bill, the Hancock Amendment, and the Big Trucks bill on the ballot were challenged on the grounds that signatures were improperly gathered or that constitutional provisions for regulating the adoption of constitutional amendments were violated. The Missouri Baptist Convention has fought in the courts nearly every proposal to legalize forms of gambling, always unsuccessfully. In the fall of 1987 this group decided to litigate against Missouri's joining a multistate lottery, despite an opinion from the state attorney general that the state constitutional amendment permitting the lottery also gave leeway for participation in lotteries outside the state boundaries. Generally, state courts decline to intervene.[29] Perhaps most successful in litigation have been prochoice and civil rights groups, which have found the federal courts willing to overturn state statutes restricting access to abortions and to impose court-ordered desegregation plans on school districts in the St. Louis and Kansas City areas, mandating state appropriations and even imposing new taxation in the affected localities in the process.

Group Power in Missouri

Historically, interest groups in the Show-Me state have been considered less influential than those in other states. The 1950 American Political Science Association study of state political systems classified Missouri's interest group system as "weak," but subsequent studies have placed it near the national median or typed it as "moderately strong." That these conclusions were reached is understandable, as the studies tended to be conducted during or just after the heyday of the Establishment.[30] What these studies fail to consider is that though no single group or cadre of groups dominates state politics, interest groups are nonetheless significant and highly influential actors in the Missouri political system. The void created by the demise of the elite made up of the Democratic party leadership and Central Missouri Trust Company has been amply filled by a variety of groups. The elitism of the 1950s and 1960s was replaced by a strong pluralism in the 1970s and 1980s.

Despite the evolution of pluralism, certain groups have higher profiles and are generally successful when they muster their resources. Interestingly, the groups that were identified as the most influential in the 1960s have maintained their positions of status. Drawing on a number of sources, Sarah McCally Morehouse developed a list of a half dozen groups deemed to be most influential in the state.[31] Of those identified by Morehouse as "powerful," only the Missouri Farmers Association (MFA) has weakened significantly in recent years. This organization, representing small farmers, lost its political base during the farm crisis (as many small farmers folded), and the Missouri Farm Bureau Federation (MFBF), representing larger agricultural interests, filled the void. The MFBF's ability to generate support was demonstrated in 1980 when it used its extension personnel in the counties to gather the signatures to place the Hancock tax limitation proposal on the ballot.

Two influential Missouri groups with checkered pasts still rate as among the more influential in the state. The Missouri Bus and Truck Association failed to win legislative approval for its Big Truck bill (its major policy initiative) during the late 1970s because of opposition from two Speakers of the House, but the group rebounded to push the bill through the legislature twice, the second time after the voters had rejected it on an initiated referendum. The Missouri State Teachers Association (MSTA) saw its influence wane during the later 1970s (losing position to the Missouri Education Association and Missouri Federation of Teachers) but demonstrated its strength in the successful initiative petition drive to increase the sales tax for education in 1982. Like the MFBF, the MSTA gained influence when it moved beyond its own substantive policy area into the broader issue of taxation.

Two organizations rose in stature in the 1980s to the point of rating among the state's most powerful: the Missouri Bankers Association (MBA) and Missouri Citizens for Life (MCL). As noted earlier, the MBA dominates banking legislation in the state, and its ascendancy is based on its taking the torch passed on to it by the Central Missouri Trust Company as that institution lost influence. MBA's failure to succeed with banking reform in 1985 resulted from a strategic error, not lack of influence. Once an appropriate strategy was adopted, the organization's legislation won approval with ease.

As the state's leading prolife organization, MCL has a strong record of winning approval for legislation restricting access to abortion. MCL and the Catholic Conference began lobbying for the strictest abortion regulations possible after the federal courts issued their opinion in *Roe v. Wade* (1973), effectively legalizing abortion. The General Assembly was receptive to this point of view and enacted fairly strict abortion laws, which were overturned in 1976 and 1983 after being challenged in federal courts by prochoice organizations.[32] Missouri's General Assembly also became one of several state legislatures to petition Congress for a constitutional convention to overturn *Roe*. Under pressure from MCL and its allies, in the 1986 session the legislature passed a new bill restricting abortions, with provisions prohibiting the use of public employees and facilities for performing or even counseling nontherapeutic abortions; the governor swiftly signed the bill into law. As before, the only recourse for MCL's opponents was the federal courts. The result was the U.S. Supreme Court's decision in *Webster v. Reproductive Health Services* (1989), which opened the door to increased state regulation of abortions and provided prolife forces with hope for overturning *Roe*.[33] In turn, *Webster* and the prospect for greater state restrictions on abortion supplied the impetus for prochoice forces in Missouri to organize in preparation for the 1990 legislative session, in which they were able to neutralize their prolife opponents.

Perhaps the key to understanding contemporary interest group politics in Missouri is the axiom that groups generally restrict their involvement to specific issues, rarely seeking to expand into new vistas. As a consequence, no single organization consistently dominates the political scene, regardless of the issues. In a classic example of pluralism the groups involved change as the issues change.

In the Future

No dramatic changes in interest group politics in Missouri appear on the horizon; neither resurrection of the Establishment nor restoration of the political parties is in sight. Instead, pluralism is well entrenched. Individual interest groups will continue playing significant roles in the formulation of public policy, each operating more or less independently, cooperating with other organizations only on specific issues at specific times. Their activities will be conditioned by the enduring conservative political climate.

A development that might upset the status quo is the federal tax reform of 1986; since the Missouri tax return is pegged to the federal tax return, as people's federal tax liability declines, their state tax liability rises. Hence collections are expected to increase by some yet-unknown amount (called the "windfall"). Governor Ashcroft initially called for a tax cut to hand the difference back to the taxpayers, but the legislative leadership did not support such a move. By January 1987 Ashcroft had turned around and proposed a budget that would spend nearly all the windfall tax revenues that the Hancock Amendment would permit. (Under provisions of the Hancock Amendment, if the state exceeds the ratio between personal income and state revenues set by the amendment, a tax refund on the basis of income tax collections must take place, and Ashcroft's original budget would have to have stayed under that figure to avoid the necessity for a refund.) To outmaneuver the governor, the Democratic leadership of the House set a June referendum on whether or not the state should keep the windfall; however, the Senate jettisoned that idea. The idea of a referendum went nowhere, the idea of refunding part of the windfall went nowhere, and the legislative session ended in a stalemate on the issue.

Atypically, in this case legislative paralysis automatically increases state tax collections. If this process engages the refund provisions of the tax limitation amendment, the more's the better in the view of interests wanting more state funding, such as the teachers' groups, the mental health groups, and the advocates of improvements in corrections facilities. Such groups hope that the state Supreme Court will invalidate the refund provision of Hancock on state constitutional grounds (giving back public monies in proportion to taxpayers' income tax liability when the majority of the taxes are collected through sales and excise taxes).

However, the state Supreme Court has tended to dodge the fiscal problems caused by the Hancock Amendment, so it might decline to intervene. Possibly, increased state collections may dissipate the taboo that has discouraged state tax increases, lightening the struggle for funding and relaxing tensions among the multiplicity of groups.

Or the struggle may intensify, and the task may get harder. In 1987 another group, the Missouri Taxpayers Watchdog Association, announced plans for a petition drive to limit taxes in the state; three constitutional amendments were proposed, together with an initiative statute. The constitutional amendments would require a two-thirds majority for all new sales taxes, require computing revenue currently outside the Hancock ratio (because adopted by public vote later than the Hancock ratio) to be included within the ratio, and require that any increase in property tax be approved not just in a public vote but by a two-thirds majority.[34] Needless to say, these proposals are radical and would paralyze political leadership even further. Without sponsorship by a larger interest, this group's proposals failed to get the required number of signatures. Despite this defeat, the effort gives some idea of the legitimacy in the state of antitax fever and of expression of any idea by any group.

With the stakes of outcomes in state government higher than before, Missouri interest groups have created a tauter, more pluralistic, more densely organized pattern of behavior for themselves. If anything, the prevailing conservatism heightens the need for organization: new groups keep awakening, and the progression of organization advances. Yet Missouri may be on the cusp of change. National preoccupation with tax limitation may evaporate with the passing of the Reagan administration, and the state mood would be affected by new national political values. We have already seen the governor and General Assembly work out a much-needed increase in gasoline taxation (spring 1987). But even if Missouri's irredentist fiscal conservatism ebbs, the pluralism of interest groups will remain. If higher revenues become possible, group appetites will be whetted for more, and groups now lying low out of hopelessness will activate themselves and press for yet more. We foresee a continued upward curve in group activities and pressure on the state government.

Notes

The authors express their gratitude to John Ballard of the Governmental Affairs Institute of the University of Missouri Extension Services for his careful reading of and sound advice on this chapter.

1. Neal R. Peirce, *The Great Plains States of America* (New York: W. W. Norton, 1973), 30.

2. Richard R. Dohm, "Political Culture in Missouri," in Richard J. Hardy and Richard R. Dohm, eds., *Missouri Government and Politics* (Columbia: University of Missouri Press, 1985), 14–15.

3. John Fenton, *Politics in the Border States* (New Orleans: Hauser Press, 1957), 141.

4. Fred W. Lindecke, "State's Democrats Groping for Way Out of Wilderness," *St. Louis Post-Dispatch,* July 26, 1987.

5. Dohm, "Political Culture in Missouri," 17–24.

6. Peirce attributes this condition to "the superior political skill of rural and small-city legislators and politicians." This suggestion that but a few legislators have determined state fiscal policies without regard for the popular will overlooks the dominant political culture of the state plus the fact that members of the General Assembly have generally identified taxation and economic issues as the state's most important problems. See Peirce, *The Great Plains States,* 39; Wayne L. Francis, *Legislative Issues in the Fifty States* (Chicago: Rand McNally, 1967), 122–25; and Wayne L. Francis, James D. King, and James W. Riddlesperger, Jr., "Problems in the Communication of Evaluation Research to Policy Makers," *Policy Studies Journal* 8 (special issue 3, 1980), 1187–88.

7. U.S. Bureau of the Census, *Government Finances in 1964–65* (Washington, D.C.: Government Printing Office, 1967), Table 22; U.S. Bureau of the Census, *Government Finances in 1983–84* (Washington, D.C.: Government Printing Office, 1985), Table 24.

8. Modeled after California's Proposition 13 and known for the Springfield businessman who brought it to life, the Hancock Amendment created a ratio between the state's revenue and total personal income that cannot be exceeded unless the General Assembly declares an emergency or direct voter approval is given. For instance, the amendment did not limit local government revenues and expenditures, except that public votes were required for all increases in taxes, licenses, and fees. When the state Supreme Court maintained its narrow construction of the constitutional amendment, the public-vote provision came to mean that local governments providing softball and baseball diamonds through their parks and recreation programs could not raise team fees without a public vote. Since any statewide tax adopted by a public vote is exempt from the ratio, it has also impelled interest groups to seek public approval for new taxes earmarked for their programs.

9. Mike Reilly, "Higher Ed Left Behind in Tax Move," *Columbia Tribune,* August 24, 1987; Rudi Keller, "MSTA Chief: UMC Could Benefit from Tax Hike," *Columbia Tribune,* August 31, 1987.

10. Mike Reilly, "Tax Issues Unmask Best and Worst of First-term Governor," *Columbia Tribune,* June 21, 1987.

11. The state treasurer, Mel Carnahan, ran in the Democratic gubernatorial primary in 1984, raising this theme; unable to attract sufficient funding, he came in second. Many observers attribute his difficulties in fundraising to his having mentioned the idea that better services might require higher taxes.

12. Nicholas A. Masters, Robert H. Salisbury, and Thomas H. Eliot, *State Politics and the Public Schools: An Exploratory Analysis* (New York: Alfred A. Knopf, 1964), 36–38.

13. Robert F. Karsch, *The Government of Missouri,* 11th ed. (Columbia, Mo.: Lucas Brothers, 1971), 54.

14. R. B. Grisham, *Missouri Lobbyist Directory,* 83d General Assembly (West Plains, Mo.: Quill Print).

15. It should be noted that the period of change Britton identifies coincides with several other political watersheds: 1972 saw the election of Kit Bond, the first Republican governor of the postwar period, who appointed a number of young out-of-state brain-trusters to key positions in patronage agencies and who also oversaw administrative reorganization of the executive branch. These political and bureaucratic changes each rendered less secure the formerly dominant forces (the Democratic party, older public servants in patronage agencies, all employees of restructured agencies), shaking loose state government from its lax situation. Moreover, another important development in public life occurred in 1970, when the electorate voted repeal of Governor Hearnes's tax reform, effectively imposing a taboo on discussion of tax increases. Before this time the state ran annual surpluses, but the surpluses disappeared in the 1970s as competition for program dollars intensified. Britton outlined these changes in remarks on February 7, 1987, in an Associated Students of the University of Missouri conference.

16. Wayne L. Francis, "A Profile of Legislator Perceptions of Interest Group Behavior Relating to Legislative Issues in the States," *Western Political Quarterly* 14 (December 1971), 703–5; L. Harmon Zeigler, "Interest Groups in the States," in Virginia Gray, Herbert Jacob, and Kenneth N. Vines, eds., *Politics in the American States,* 4th ed. (Boston: Little, Brown, 1983), 103.

17. James D. King, "Interest Group Politics in Missouri," in Hardy and Dohm, eds., *Missouri Government and Politics,* 27.

18. Nancy Bazzano, "Malpractice Crisis," unpublished paper, 1986.

19. Section 105.470 RsMo 1982.

20. Kay Lehman Scholzman and John T. Tierney, "More of the Same: Washington Pressure Group Activity in a Decade of Change," *Journal of Politics* 45 (May 1983), 351–77.

21. Wayne L. Francis and David Valentine, "The Missouri General Assembly," in Hardy and Dohm, eds., *Missouri Government and Politics,* 68–72.

22. King, "Interest Group Politics in Missouri," 37–39.

23. Francis and Valentine, "Missouri General Assembly," 71–72. That members of the legislature do not consider their party caucuses important is another indication of the demise of political parties in the state.

24. Jefferson City lobbyists define *lobbying* as an activity before the legislature, and the term *administrative lobbying* brings to their minds not the activities involved in colonizing bureaucracies but rather those of state agency employees who are registered lobbyists because they have testified before the legislature or engaged in legislative contacts.

25. Larry J. Sabato, *PAC Power: Inside the World of Political Action Committees* (New York: W. W. Norton, 1985), 10–16; Ruth S. Jones, "Financing State Elections," in Michael J. Malbin, ed., *Money and Politics in the United States: Financing Elections in the 1980s* (Chatham, N.J.: Chatham House, 1984), 186–93; Zeigler, "Interest Groups in the States," 117.

26. The data in Tables 8.3–8.5 are for what the Missouri State Code defines as "continuing committees." A continuing committee is "a committee of continuing existence whose primary or incidental purpose is to receive contributions or make expenditures to influence or attempt to influence the action of voters" (Section 130.011 RSMo 1982). Included are traditional PACs and other political organizations but not political party committees. These continuing committees were not required to report their transactions before 1978.

27. Jones, "Financing State Elections," 183.

28. David A. Leuthold and Tamera Fine-Trail, "The Initiative, Referendum, and

MISSOURI

Other Public-Issue Votes," in Hardy and Dohm, eds., *Missouri Government and Politics,* 51–52.

29. King, "Interest Group Politics in Missouri," 35, 37–38; Jim Mosley, "Opinion May Free Missouri to Join Multistate Lottery," *St. Louis Post-Dispatch,* September 25, 1987.

30. Belle Zeller, ed., *American State Legislatures* (New York: Thomas Y. Crowell, 1954), 190–91; Francis, *Legislative Issues in the Fifty States,* 40–45; Sarah McCally Morehouse, *State Politics, Parties and Policy* (New York: Holt, Rinehart & Winston, 1981), pp. 108–12. Morehouse's typology of state interest group systems is more current but is based on the older literature.

31. Morehouse, *State Politics,* 110.

32. *Planned Parenthood of Central Missouri v. Danforth* 428 U.S. 52 (1976); *Planned Parenthood of Kansas City v. Ashcroft* 462 U.S. 476 (1983).

33. *Webster v. Reproductive Health Services* 109 S.Ct. 3040 (1989).

34. "Group's Petition Drive Aims to Limit State Taxing Power: Plans More Restricting than Hancock Bill," *Columbia Tribune,* August 31, 1987; see also "The Tax Revolt: Still Alive in Missouri?" *Columbia Tribune,* September 18, 1987.

NEBRASKA
Almost Heaven

JOHN C. COMER

Nebraska has been labeled a strong interest group state.[1] In examining this assertion and exploring the role and influence of interest groups in the state's politics, we can begin by asking, as E. E. Schattschneider did in 1960, "Whose game do we play?"[2] When the game of politics is limited to organized interests or groups with an immediate stake in an issue, the outcome can often be controlled, that is, resolved to the benefit of those directly involved. When the game expands to include larger numbers, however, the outcome can no longer be ensured. In this case the original participants often lose control as other elements come into play with new and different resources to influence the outcome. Thus, the scope of conflict bears on who wins and who loses in politics. Organized interest groups have a stake in limiting the scope of conflict. By doing so, Schattschneider argued, they can determine the outcome.

Where conditions inhibit the expansion of conflict, we can expect interest groups to be influential. Nebraska is a strong interest group state because several conditions limit the scope of political conflict. First, the citizenry is relatively homogeneous in social and economic characteristics and political outlook. With little to disagree about, they are not easily drawn into political issues and conflicts. Second, the activities of state government are not particularly salient to many Nebraskans. Lack of interest and involvement means that policy makers are free to respond to organized groups that articulate demands. Third, political parties in Nebraska are very weak. Where political parties are weak, interest groups tend to be strong.[3] Nonpartisanship is strongly rooted in the state, evident in the state's nonpartisan legislature, and influential in the state's politics.[4] Weak political parties may also explain lack of citizen interest and involvement and the absence of political conflict. Competitive parties seek to mobilize citizens and often do so by exploiting conflicts among them. These conditions create an environment, as we shall see, that is conducive to strong interest groups in the state.

The Political Environment

The story of Nebraska politics begins with the people and the land. Like many states west of the Mississippi River, the land and drawing sustenance from it have shaped the attitudes of Nebraskans, which in turn have shaped the politics of the state.

Nebraska is a large state, 77,227 square miles. It is 415 miles east to west and 205 miles north and south. The state rises in a series of plateaus from an elevation of about 800 feet in the southeast to 5,400 feet on the western border. Omaha, the state's largest city, with a population of 334,000, is located on the eastern border. Initially a jumping-off point for pioneers on their way west in the late 1850s, today it is a railroad, meatpacking, and manufacturing center serving eastern Nebraska and western Iowa. West of Omaha, the Missouri River bluffs on which the city is built give way to gently rolling countryside. Fifty miles southwest is the city of Lincoln, the second largest city (pop. 180,000) and the state capital. One-third of the state's population resides in these two communities. Farther west begins the flat prairie grasslands of the Great Plains, which extend into Colorado and Wyoming.

The hot, dry, treeless plains led early pioneers to bypass Nebraska in favor of more promising conditions in California and Oregon. Army expeditions in the early 1800s characterized the region as the "Great American Desert." Major Stephen Long described the Platte River valley, which extends across the state, as "almost wholly unfit for farming."[5] Only after other, more desirable lands were settled did pioneers in search of a new life turn to Nebraska.

The Homestead Act, passed by Congress in 1862, attracted settlers to the region. From 1880 to 1890 the state's population doubled, from slightly less than a half million to just above a million. Today, the population numbers only 1.6 million. Conditions on the plains demanded that the early settlers be strong and hardy as well as adaptable. Limited rainfall and drought made farming difficult. The development of the state as a leading producer of beef, hogs, corn, and wheat suggests a "can do" spirit among Nebraskans. Nebraskans have learned to adapt to the land and, in some respects, to control it.

Perhaps influenced by the hard times on the plains, early settlers shared some important attitudes. Nebraskans were, for example, a frugal lot, particularly when it came to government spending. Nebraska joined the Union in 1867, but the move was not supported by everyone. Several earlier votes had rejected the idea. The nay-sayers were concerned that statehood would increase the financial burden on the state's residents.[6] The potential for savings was one argument that moved many Nebraskans to support the nonpartisan, unicameral legislature adopted in a statewide vote in 1934.[7] One house would be cheaper than two. A concern for cost of government also keeps state legislative salaries among the lowest in the nation. Although the demands of the job are considerable, voters in several elections have chosen to keep the salary at $4,800 a year.

Conservatism is another attitude strongly rooted in Nebraska's past. Nebraskans are resistant to change and oppose government initiatives, particularly those that cost money. Frugality combined with support for the status quo have put the state in the Republican column in most presidential elections since the state's founding. In the close elections of 1960, 1968, and 1976 the Republican candidates carried both Omaha and Lincoln and all except four of the state's ninety-three counties. In 1984 Nebraska was Reagan's fourth-best state, his second-best in 1980. The state is also represented by three Republicans in the U.S. House and one in the U.S. Senate. Republicans usually win state-level offices as well.

Nebraskans are also fiercely independent. Liberal George Norris, who represented the state in the U.S. House from 1909 to 1913 and the U.S. Senate from 1913 to 1943, won the support of Nebraskans with his free and independent spirit.[8] Similarly, U.S. Senator Ed Zorinsky, a Republican turned Democrat who served from 1976 to 1987, made a career out of being independent. The conservatism and independence of Nebraskans have made it difficult to organize the state for political purposes. Historically, political parties have been very weak institutions in the state. The only nonpartisan legislature in the nation is one indication. Another is the frequency with which candidates change parties if prospects for nomination and election appear better elsewhere. The voters often reward such behavior with a victory. Zorinsky was a registered Republican shortly before winning the Democratic nomination in 1976. Terry Carpenter, a powerful force in state politics for many years and winner of the Democratic nominations for U.S. congressman and senator and Nebraska governor between 1934 and 1972, ran and was elected delegate to the Republican National Convention in 1956. He achieved notoriety by nominating "Joe Smith" for vice-president as an alternative to Richard Nixon.

Nebraskans also tend to be passive toward government. The political culture of the state, reflected in citizens' orientations toward state government, can be described, in Almond and Verba's terms, as a *subject political culture.*[9] Citizens are aware of state government and able to evaluate its performance, but they are insensitive to their role in shaping government policy as participants. In surveys, for example, only a small minority responds that state government is important and that they pay much attention to it.[10] Knowledge of state government is not particularly high either. Although Nebraskans support the institutions of state government, they are not involved with them.

Thus, Nebraskans are, in general, resistant to change and relatively passive with respect to state government. On the one issue that seems to activate them, state spending, there is widespread agreement: spending should be minimal. Indeed, few major issues divide the citizenry. The absence of conflict makes it difficult to organize the state. Political parties have little to work with, and Nebraskans' penchant for independence is an obstacle to organizing under any circumstances. Thus, Nebraskans are rarely drawn into political conflicts of much significance, and issues are typically resolved in the state legislature with the involvement of only those interests directly affected. In such an environment one would expect interest groups to be active and successful.

Once the backbone of the state's economy, farming has declined in importance in recent decades. In 1960, 26 percent of all jobs were on the farm; in 1985, only 10 percent.[11] In 1960, farming accounted for 16 percent of the gross state product (the market value of all final goods and services produced in the state). By 1984 the figure was 12 percent. Although farming remains important and much of the state's economy is linked to it, other sectors have gained in significance since the 1960s. They include banking and finance, transportation and communication, trade, services, and government. Of course, some of the growth in these areas is tied to farming, and when the farm economy declines, as it did in the early 1980s, these sectors are affected (Table 9.1).

Financial interests represent a major component of the state's economy. Four hundred seventy-two banks are chartered in the state, with assets totaling $16 billion. Thirty-three life insurance companies are headquartered in Nebraska, and another 611 are licensed to do business. In 1987 the Nebraska insurance firms had $115 billion of insurance in force. Following the national trend, the service economy of the state has grown substantially. Between 1975 and 1987 the number of people em-

Table 9.1. Nebraska gross state product, by sector, 1960 and 1985

Sector	1960 (%)	1985(%)	Difference(%)
Agricultural services	0.3	0.3	0
Construction	5.4	3.3	-2.4
Farm	16.1	11.9	-4.2
Finance, insurance, real estate	15.1	16.9	+1.8
Government	11.0	12.3	+1.3
Manufacturing	14.4	14.4	0
Mining	1.1	0.7	-0.4
Services	8.0	11.6	+3.6
Transportation, communication, utilities	11.2	12.3	+1.1
Trade	17.3	16.4	-0.9

Source: Bureau of Business Research, University of Nebraska-Lincoln.

ployed in services increased 33 percent. Railroads are a significant part of the transportation industry, with nearly 5,000 miles of main track and $1.2 billion of business in 1985.

Government is another major industry. In addition to state government, there are 3,324 local governments. This figure includes 93 counties, 534 municipalities, 471 townships, 1,195 school districts, and 1,192 special districts. Nebraska ranks 8th in the nation in the number of local units and on a per capita basis ranks 1st. Local government employs 84,200 people and spends nearly $4 billion a year. The state adds another 34,200 employees and spends nearly $2.2 billion a year.

Apart from the state's nonpartisan, unicameral legislature, called the Unicameral, the structure of government is much like that in other states. There are three branches of government. The governor is considered a strong executive in terms of formal powers, with authority to prepare and submit a state budget, appoint and remove executive personnel, and veto legislation, including specific items (item veto) from appropriations bills. In practice, however, Nebraska governors have tended to be weak in terms of using political power to shape the policy direction of the state.[12] The state has a Supreme Court, with justices appointed through a screening process involving citizen committees, the state bar association, and the governor. Judges must run for re-election by having the voters decide whether a judge should be retained, the so-called Missouri Plan. As in other states, the Supreme Court has the power of judicial review; however, it takes a five-person majority on the seven-member court to declare an act of the legislature unconstitutional.[13]

The Nebraska Legislature is the only unicameral body in the fifty states, and it is the only nonpartisan legislature. As reforms go, it is unclear whether the adoption of the nonpartisan, one-house legislature was a step forward or backward. A number of factors account for its adoption in Nebraska in 1934. First, the proposal had the support of some influential Nebraskans. George Norris argued that a unicameral legislature would serve the people better by eliminating the need for conference committees.[14] When the two chambers of a bicameral legislature pass different versions of a bill, Norris maintained, the conference committee, composed of five or six legislators from both chambers working in secret to resolve differences, subverts the public interest. He argued that it is easier for an interest group in pursuit of selfish interests to influence a half dozen legislators than to influence the entire body. Compromises struck in conference committee, Norris felt, often undo the work of both legislative chambers. A one-house legislature would have no need for conference committees, and all the work, Norris reasoned, would be out in the open. Norris also felt that partisanship, though appropriate to national affairs, had no place in the conduct of the state's business. Although nonpartisanship in this instance meant only that state legislators would be elected without party labels on the ballot, Norris campaigned tirelessly for the adoption of an amendment to the Nebraska Constitution that would establish both a one-house state legislature and election to it on a nonpartisan ballot.

The depression and drought of the 1930s also were important in the adoption of a nonpartisan, one-house legislature.[15] The prospect of reducing the cost of state government during hard times was attractive to many people. The specific amendment fixed the maximum size of the Unicameral at 49, compared to the 133 who served in the bicameral legislature. Savings from salaries alone would be substantial.

Assessing the impact of the change is difficult. Has it, as Norris maintained, made the legislature more responsive to public needs? Has it reduced the influence of special interests? Some argue that the reduced size of the legislature has enhanced the influence of interest groups, as there are fewer legislators to persuade. Some also maintain that the elimination of political parties in the organization of the legislature allows interest groups a greater role in the legislative process. Certainly, the absence of parties has changed the legislature. There are no party leaders. Committee chairs are elected by the entire body. A small body, 49, means that friendship and personal relations are important. Coalitions are rarely based on party, although in 1987 all but one legislator identified with a party. Nor is ideology important. Coalitions appear to be carved out anew with each issue. Occasionally, Omaha aligns against Lincoln, and urban against rural, but more typically alignments seem random.[16] We cannot assess whether the change to a nonpartisan legislature has enhanced the role of interest groups, but we can evaluate how interest groups fare, in general, in Nebraska politics. We begin by examining the laws that govern interest group activity in the state and the attitudes and opinions of lawmakers toward interest groups.

The Interest Group Environment

In the mid-1970s the Watergate scandal brought calls for campaign finance reform. In Nebraska a coalition of sixteen groups called the Common Cause Coalition for Open Government sought to put an initiative on the ballot requiring disclosure of campaign contributions. Before the initiative was voted on, however, the legislature passed the Nebraska Political Accountability and Disclosure Act (PADA), which dealt not only with disclosure but with conflict of interest and lobbying. Before PADA, lobbyists were required to register with the clerk of the legislature. Under PADA, lobbyists are required to register and to file monthly and year-end reports.

Lobbying is defined as the practice of promoting or opposing the introduction or enactment of legislation before members of the legislature or executive agencies. All who engage in lobbying are required to register at the start of each new legislative session and to pay a $35 fee. Separate registrations must be filed for each individual or group, labeled *principals* in the law, a lobbyist represents. Inclusion of executive branch lobbying means most lobbying activity is covered; however, public officials (except at the University of Nebraska), the press, and private citizens who limit their activities to testifying at legislative hearings are exempt.

Registration also requires identification of the specific individual to whom the lobbyist is responsible, of compensation paid to the lobbyist, and of matters on which the lobbyist expects to lobby. Monthly reports required of both lobbyists and principals must itemize receipts and expenditures associated with lobbying activities, and year-end reports must identify all legislation lobbied for during the session as well as one's opposition or support. Enforcement is left to the Nebraska Accountability and Disclosure Commission (NADC), which is to summarize and publish information and investigate and prosecute violations. To date, most matters to come before the commission have dealt with conflict of interest and campaign finance. As lobby laws go, Nebraska's seems comprehensive and effective in terms of documenting who does what for whom. However, it does not check or even balance the influence of interest groups in the political process. Indeed, no law, short of denying interest groups their constitutional rights, can.

The most effective constraints placed on interest groups are, of course, the attitudes and values of policy makers themselves. How do they view the activities of interest groups? Though most who have been involved in politics for any length of time recognize the value of interest groups, we might expect some variation from one state to another. Wahlke and his colleagues, for example, found some variation across four states in legislators' knowledge of interest group activity and their feelings toward such activity.[17] In Tennessee 23 percent of the state's legislators, termed *facilitators* by the investigators, were informed about interest group activity and were positive toward it. In Ohio the number was 43 percent. Forty percent of the Tennessee legislators, termed *resisters,* were knowledgeable and negative. Twenty percent of the Ohio legislators were resisters. A similar study by Johnson of Nebraska legislators in 1968 found 60 percent facilitators and only 2 percent resisters.[18] Kolasa, similarly, notes that the attitudes of Nebraska legislators toward lobbyists are positive. He concludes that "few lobbyists are looked upon as outsiders; rather they are viewed as an asset and integral part of the legislative struggle." This positive response, Kolasa observes, is based on lobbyists' usefulness as a source of information and research.[19]

The positive feelings of legislators toward interest groups were confirmed in a survey of Nebraska legislators and lobbyists in the fall of 1986.[20] Legislators were asked whether the activities of interest groups are often contrary to the public interest. Fifty-two percent disagreed with the statement (Table 9.2). Thirty-seven percent agreed, and 11 percent strongly agreed. Legislators were also asked whether they agreed that lobbyists' activities were a form of improper pressure. Ninety-six percent disagreed. Legislators were next asked their feelings regarding lobby registration and financial disclosure requirements. Fifteen percent felt that the Nebraska law was too strict. Seventy percent thought it was fair, and 11 percent felt that stricter controls were necessary.

Legislators were also asked to rank a series of statements focusing on the impact of interest groups on the political system. Responses (averaged over all legislators) are shown in Table 9.2.

Using these data, we can argue that Nebraska legislators see interest groups as necessary and valuable, providing useful services that might not be available if interest groups did not exist. Legislators reject the idea that interest groups are ineffectual and unnecessary. Although some sentiment is expressed that interest groups will act contrary to the public interest, it is apparent, consistent with Johnson's and Kolasa's findings, that the environment in which interest groups operate is positive and facilitating. Lobbyists are seen as contributing something useful and necessary to policy making. These data support the view that Nebraska is a strong interest group state. Interest groups may not, however, always

Table 9.2. Nebraska legislators' evaluations of the role of interest groups in the political system

Statement	% Disagreeing
Activities of interest groups are often contrary to the public interest.	52
Activities of lobbyists are a form of improper pressure.	96
Nebraska's lobby and disclosure law is far too strict.	70

	Average Response[a]
Interest groups are necessary and valuable.	1.7
Interest groups are useful in providing information and services otherwise unattainable.	1.7
Interest groups reduce the rationality of the legislative process.	3.0
Interest groups are ineffectual and probably unnecessary.	4.3
Interest groups often act contrary to the public interest.	3.3

[a]Responses were ranked from 1 through 5, with 1 representing the statement that most closely reflects the legislator's judgment regarding the role of interest groups in the political process.

contribute to what legislators perceive as the public interest. This may reflect an imbalance in what we might label the state's pressure system, which may favor some interests over others, a subject we turn to next.

The Pressure System

The term *pressure system* refers to all organized interests active in the state. One measure of it, albeit incomplete, is the list of groups that register as lobby groups with the state. Though such an enumeration excludes public agencies and legislators themselves, registrations provide a fairly complete picture, and by examining them, we can get some idea of the system's size as well as balance.

In 1986, 722 groups and organizations were registered with the state, almost double the number of 1974 (Table 9.3). Of course, the number of groups does not address the issue of balance. To evaluate this matter, we need to look at the content of the pressure system. What types of groups are represented? Table 9.4 identifies registered groups for the

Table 9.3. Number of lobbyists and groups registered in Nebraska, 1973-74 to 1985-86

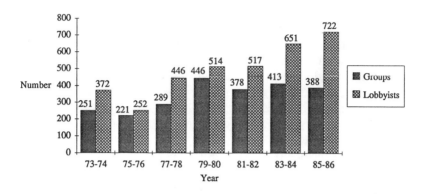

years 1971 and 1986. Although the Nebraska pressure system seems fairly broad in terms of the groups represented, it shows the same business bias found in many other states as well as at the national level.[21] Business is overrepresented, with 35 percent of all groups of this type. A more liberal classification would find 42 percent of all groups falling into this category. The system is fairly broad and diverse, but it is biased. This bias may underlie some legislators' responses, reported earlier, that interest group activities are often contrary to the public interest.

Table 9.4. Types of lobby groups registered with the state of Nebraska, 1971 and 1986

Type	1971(%)	1986(%)
General business groups	10	11
Trade associations	15	13
Financial interests	10	11
Public utilities	3	1
Private utilities	2	1
Communication	2	3
Local governments	9	4
Associations of governments	2	1
Labor unions	6	4
Professional associations	7	6
Civic organizations	2	3
Educational organizations	9	8
Transportation	1	2
Political groups	1	2
Religious groups	0	0
Cause groups	5	11
Handicapped, women's, veterans', and elderly groups	3	3
Agriculture groups	2	2
Commodity groups	2	2
Health groups	3	7
Other	6	4
Total	100	99

Source: Clerk of the Nebraska Legislature

The pressure system has grown since the mid-1970s, but the shape of the system has not changed a great deal. Although more groups were represented in 1986, the pressure system looked much like it did in 1971. General business, trade, and financial interests still represented about 35 percent of all groups. The number of local governments chosing to register was somewhat smaller in 1986, but the number of cause and health groups increased. The latter development no doubt reflects the pattern nationwide, in which large numbers of public and single-issue interest groups formed during the 1970s and 1980s when health care and health-related issues emerged as major concerns not only for consumers but for practitioners as well.

We can conclude that the Nebraska pressure system is fairly broad and perhaps large compared to the size of the state; however, business dominates the system in terms of numbers. One might expect a wide variety of interests to form interest groups where group activity is an effective instrument for influencing government, and though a pressure system with a variety of different types of groups can lead to competition among them and a lessening of group influence generally, this is likely to be the case only where there are fundamental disagreements among major elements of the pressure system. In Nebraska, where agriculture, business, and the state's economic well-being are intimately related, such disagreements do not exist.

The Lobbyists

The number of lobbyists, reflected in registrations, has increased since the mid-1970s but has leveled off or even declined slightly from a high of 446 in 1980 (see Table 9.3). Part or all of the increase may be explained by Watergate and related events, which led to a change in the law in 1976 that made the registration requirement somewhat more explicit. Lobbyists also may have taken the law a bit more seriously after the Watergate period. It is also plausible to assume that some of the increase reflects the corresponding increase in the size of the pressure system.

Although our sample of lobbyists (Table 9.5) does not allow us to assess the percentage of those registered who are independent or contract lobbyists as opposed to association or "in-house" lobbyists, among those interviewed, 24 (69 percent) identified themselves as in-house and 11 as independent (31 percent). We do not know if in-house lobbyists are more typical of Nebraska than independent lobbyists or if the pattern is changing in some way. However, in-house lobbyists, again those in our

Table 9.5. Selected characteristics of Nebraska lobbyists (in percent)

| Characteristic | Total | Lobbyists | |
		In-House	Independent
	(N=35)	(N=24)	(N=11)
Years of lobby experience	100	69	31
0 to 5	34	33	36
6 to 10	23	21	27
11 to 15	14	17	9
16+	29	29	27
	100	100	99
Lobby in other states			
Yes	29	38	9
No	71	63	91
	100	100	100
Education			
High school	6	8	--
Some college	17	25	--
B.A.	20	21	18
Graduate work	9	8	9
Graduate or law degree	49	38	73
	100	100	100
Major in college			
Economics	10	5	18
Political science	43	37	56
English	13	21	--
Journalism	10	11	9
Other	24	26	17
	100	100	100
Occupation[a]			
Attorney	21	8	41
Teacher	12	15	6
Reporter	7	8	6
Legislative staffer	14	8	24
Other	46	61	23
	100	100	100
Born in Nebraska			
Yes	60	70	45
No	40	30	55
	100	100	100
Years lived in Nebraska			
10 or fewer	14	17	9
More than 10	86	83	91
Total	100	100	100

[a]Because more than one occupation was mentioned by some, the N here is 43.

sample, have been at it longer than the independents, which suggests that Nebraska may be moving toward the full-time professional lobbyist.

Not unexpectedly, lobbyists in Nebraska are highly educated and come from occupations that are related to politics or provide skills useful in lobbying. Most have their roots in Nebraska or have lived in the state for some time. Most of their lobbying experience is limited to Nebraska. They are an elite group in terms of education and occupation but are firmly grounded in the state. In-house lobbyists have been at it a bit longer than independents and are more likely to have lobbying experience outside the state. As a group, in-house lobbyists are less educated than independents and less likely to have practiced law before becoming a lobbyist. As in many states, what we might call the full-time, professional lobbyist with many clients may be replacing the lobbyist employed by a single organization and with duties in addition to lobbying. However, this survey's professionals are not exclusively the law firm or public relations firm types. Employed full time, with several clients, they are primarily single individuals who have established themselves as effective lobbyists and are sought out because of their experience. Many are former legislators.

The Tactics of Interest Groups

Interest groups can employ two types of tactics: those designed to elect public officials who are sympathetic to a particular point of view and those designed to persuade elected or appointed officials of the merit of a particular point of view.

Let's look first at how interest groups in Nebraska are involved in state elections. Legislators were asked how interest groups helped them in the last election. All but one respondent indicated that they received campaign contributions. Three-fourths answered that some interest groups had endorsed their candidacy. Slightly more than 40 percent indicated that groups supplied their campaigns with workers, and about one-third reported that groups assisted in developing a campaign strategy. These data indicate substantial group involvement in legislative elections, but the findings are difficult to evaluate. Perspective can be gained by comparing interest groups to political parties. In the late 1960s Kolasa found that party activity in legislative elections did not meet what he defined as a minimal standard. On the other hand, interest group activity was substantial. He concluded that "the difference [in party and interest group activity] in legislative elections is so substantial that the dominance of nonparty group activity clearly stands out vis-à-vis party activity."[22]

Groups mentioned as particularly helpful at election time were the Nebraska State Education Association (NSEA), the AFL-CIO, the Nebraska Association of Public Employees, bankers, realtors, and business in general. A smaller number identified the telephone industry and agriculture groups. The unions and professional associations have both large memberships and financial resources. They can supply campaign workers as well as campaign funds. The banks, realtors, and businesses are primarily sources of campaign funds.

Although groups and organizations, including unions, can make unlimited contributions directly to political campaigns, the chief mechanism for channeling money is the political action committee. Such committees can be established by filing a statement of organization with the PADC and setting up the appropriate bank accounts. Beyond that, PACs are required to file reports relevant to each campaign to which they contribute, as well as an annual report.

Campaign expenditures in state legislative elections have nearly tripled since 1978. One candidate set a record by spending $92,000 to win election in 1982. Along with campaign expenditures, the number of PACs and PAC contributions to candidates have also increased (Table 9.6). The number of PACs rose from 43 in 1979 to 111 in 1987, and PAC spending nearly doubled during this period.

Table 9.6. PAC spending in Nebraska, 1978-84

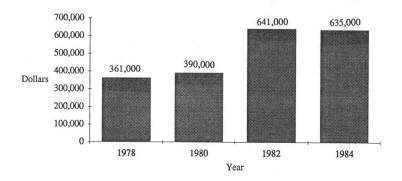

In 1984, contributions to legislative candidates totaled $954,139. Thirty-four percent came from PACs. Business and labor groups contributed 11 percent; individuals, 9 percent; and political party committees, 2 percent. The remaining 44 percent came from different sources in contributions of less than $100.[23] Total PAC contributions to all candidates came to $635,000 (Table 9.7). It is clear that interest groups, especially PACs, are heavily involved in state elections, contributing roughly 45 percent of each campaign dollar. This figure, along with in-kind contributions, means that interest groups contribute well over 50 percent of total campaign resources.

Among the largest PAC contributors in 1984 were the NSEA, Mutual of Omaha, trial attorneys, the Nebraska Medical Association, bankers, and realtors. Among the largest business and union contributors were the United Transportation Workers Union, Union Pacific Railroad,

Omaha National Corporation (a bank), and Peter Kiewit Construction (an Omaha construction firm). The modest, or nonexistent, role of political parties means that dependency on interest groups is likely to increase in the future as candidates require greater and greater resources to wage an effective campaign and have no place to turn except interest groups.

The increasing reliance of candidates on PACs and groups to finance political campaigns raises another issue. Consistent with nationwide trends, the growth of PACs had largely been among business groups. Twenty-six of the 61 PACs registered in 1984 represented banking and finance (12), trade (11), and general business (3). Only 3 represented labor. There were 8 cause PACs and 7 health PACs. Business PACs led all others in total campaign contributions. Although small donations of less than $100 make up the largest percentage of campaign contributions, the concern is whether PAC dollars and contributions from groups give business interests greater access and influence in state policy making. The answer is probably yes, although this likely has always been the case.

Table 9.7. Number of PACs and PAC contributions in Nebraska, by type, 1984

PAC Type	No.	Total Contributions ($)
Business[a]	26	260,100
Private Utility	2	28,300
Government	1	7,000
Union	3	8,800
Professional	2	51,500
Education	4	85,000
Cause	8	18,600
Commodity	1	12,100
Health	7	72,300
Energy	5	53,600
Other	2	37,700
Total	61	635,000

Source: Nebraska Accountability and Disclosure Commission, A Summary of Political Campaign Financing, 1984 (Lincoln, 1985).
[a]Includes banking, insurance, real estate, trade, and general business PACs.

In addition to trying to elect public officials sympathetic to a particular point of view, interest groups seek to persuade public officials of the merits of a particular policy. In doing so, groups rely on a number of tactics. Before identifying them, however, it is helpful to identify the arena in which most lobbying takes place and the amount of lobbying that goes on. Lobbyists in the 1986 survey were asked what percentage of the time they spent lobbying the legislature, executive agencies, and courts. Not surprisingly, the legislature was identified as the arena in which lobbyists spend most of their time—79 percent (on average), comparied to 17 percent for executive agencies and 4 percent for the courts. Independent lobbyists reported spending 82 percent of their time lobbying the legislature, and in-house lobbyists reported 77 percent. In-house lobbyists spent, on average, 18 percent of their time lobbying the executive and 4 percent lobbying the courts. Independents spent 9 percent of their time lobbying the executive, and no time lobbying the courts. Several of the in-house lobbyists and one independent indicated that in addition to lobbying the three branches of government, some time, in some instances a great deal, is spent lobbying clients and/or the organization. It appears that at least some lobbyists must direct their efforts in two directions, toward policy makers in an effort to persuade them, but also toward the clients' parent organizations in an effort to win their support.[24]

Sixty percent of the lobbyists surveyed indicated that they lobby five or more days a week when the legislature is in session. All but one (97 percent) indicated that they lobby between sessions. There is little difference here between in-house and independent lobbyists. Thus, the end of the session, alternately ninety and sixty legislative days long, doesn't necessarily mean an end to lobbying. It is however, less visible.

In terms of the tactics groups employ, we can distinguish between those that are used simply to gain access and those that are used to persuade. Table 9.8 identifies tactics reported by lobbyists to be effective in gaining access to legislators; Table 9.9 lists tactics reported to be effective in achieving group goals. With respect to gaining access, both in-house and independent lobbyists ranked old-fashioned one-on-one contact in a legislator's office as most effective. Of course, the lobbyists interviewed here are likely to be well known and to have little difficulty gaining a personal hearing. However, midwestern hospitality probably goes a long way to opening up doors for even an unknown. Working through legislative aides is another effective strategy for gaining access.

Table 9.8. Methods of gaining access to legislators, as ranked by Nebraska lobbyists

Tactic	All	In-House	Independent
	Average Ranking[a]		
Meeting with legislators in office	1.5	1.7	1.1
Working through aides	3.8	4.0	3.6
Meeting with legislators socially	4.1	3.9	4.8
Meetings with several legislators	4.3	4.0	5.1
Giving testimony	4.8	4.4	5.6
Working through other legislators/groups	5.0	4.7	5.9
Telephone calls	5.1	5.1	5.4
Formal submissions (reports, etc.)	5.5	5.0	6.7
Chance meetings with legislators	6.0	5.9	6.3

[a]Range is from 1 (most effective) to 9 (least effective).

Table 9.9. Tactics for achieving group goals, as ranked by Nebraska lobbyists

Tactic	All	In-House	Independent
		Average Ranking[a]	
Personal contact with legislators	2.0	2.1	1.7
Using group members and/or clients	4.1	4.3	3.8
Joint lobbying with other groups	4.3	3.8	5.3
Personal contact with executives	4.6	4.0	5.9
Appearing before committees	4.7	4.5	5.2
Personal contact at social events	4.7	4.3	5.4
Mobilizing public opinion	5.1	5.0	5.4
Working with legislative aides	5.3	4.9	6.4
Letter-writing campaigns	6.5	6.0	7.6

[a]Range is from 1 (most effective) to 9 (least effective).

Less successful are formal hearings, social encounters, joint sessions with several legislators, and working through other groups and legislators. Some responded to an open-ended query that just being around helps. Again, being available may apply only to those who are well known. Friendship ties are also a factor. Although more than 380 lobbyists were registered for the 1985–86 session, a much smaller number are regularly available. In a legislative body of only 49, friendships develop that facilitate access.

Gaining access is much simpler task than being persuasive. It is one thing to get through the door; it is another to win a vote. Lobbyists were asked to rank a number of tactics in terms of their effectiveness in achieving their groups' goals (Table 9.9).

Here again personal contacts rank the highest for both in-house lobbyists and independents. Preferences for personal contacts as a lobbying strategy should not come as much of a surprise. Milbraith finds, in his study of Washington lobbyists, that they considered the personal encounter most effective.[25] Similarly, Zeigler and Baer, in their examination of lobbyists in four states, conclude that face-to-face lobbying is more effective than other techniques.[26] Schlozman and Tierney also find direct contact to be the most frequently used technique by Washington lobbyists.[27] One value of personal encounters, from the lobbyist's point of view, is that he or she is in control. He or she can structure the content of the message and respond to any questions that may come up. The low rank given to contacts with executive personnel and civil servants confirms data presented earlier that the legislature is the arena where most lobbying takes place.

Before turning from this subject, let us address briefly the topic of lobbying by state agencies and executive personnel; these lobbyists are a part of the pressure system, too. For those agencies under the governor's authority—about thirty so-called code agencies—all lobbying is cleared through the governor's Policy Research Office (PRO). Each agency has a legislative liaison and meets as a group with the PRO once a week during the session and once a month after the session. Here issues are raised and discussed, and decisions are made as to whether the governor or an agency should support a bill. Agency support does not necessarily mean gubernatorial support.

Liaisons have the task of monitoring legislative developments in their areas and keeping in touch with legislators and staff. During a busy session, as few as two or three hours a day or as many as eight to ten might be spent on lobbying activities. In addition to reading and evaluating legislation, liaisons provide testimony at legislative hearings, meet with legislators in their offices, and, in general, make themselves available to answer questions. They also work with lobbyists and groups in drafting legislation and lining up opposition or support. Lobbying by agency personnel, even on behalf of the governor, can be a sensitive matter with some legislators. Terry Carpenter often chastised state agency personnel and complained that if the governor had something to say, he should come to the legislature and say it himself. Agencies independent of the governor operate in similar fashion but need not clear their activities with the PRO.

The Influence of Interest Groups

A final and perhaps the most important concern is the influence of interest groups in state politics. Legislators were asked to rate the influence of interest groups on public policy. Fifteen percent responded that their influence is crucial; 52 percent, very important; and 4 percent, unimportant. Seventeen percent of the lobbyists who responded to the survey indicated that the influence of interest groups is crucial; 60 percent, very important; and none, unimportant. Lobbyists were asked to rank the influence of interest groups in comparison to other institutions in the state, including the legislature and governor (Table 9.10). The legislature received the highest average ranking, and interest groups were ranked third, only slightly less than the rank given the governor. Though

Table 9.10. Nebraska institutions with influence in policy making, as ranked by lobbyists

Institution	Average Ranking[a]
Legislature	2.0
Governor and staff	2.7
Interest groups	2.8
Press	3.7
State departments and agencies	4.2
Courts	4.9

[a]Range is from 1 (most influence) to 6 (least influence).

perception of influence is not quite the same thing as influence itself, we expect perceptions to correlate reasonably well with actual influence. Moreover, these findings are consistent with assessments made by others. The data suggest that interest groups have substantial influence in policy making.

We cannot, however, assume that all interest groups are equally successful in influencing policy making. Morehouse, in her examination of interest groups in the states, observes that the following are strong in Nebraska: the Farm Bureau, Omaha National Bank, Northern Natural Gas, Union Pacific Railroad, Northwest Bell Telephone, and the education lobby.[28] Kolasa identifies the Nebraska and Omaha Education associations, the City of Omaha, the Nebraska League of Municipalities, and liquor and public power interests.[29] Legislators and lobbyists in the present study were asked to identify the five most effective interest groups in the state during elections and during the session (Table 9.11).

With respect to effectiveness in elections, both the Nebraska Education Association (NSEA) and the Nebraska bankers received high marks. Of all the groups noted, 22 percent of the mentions by state legislators identified Nebraska bankers as the most effective in elections; 18 percent of the mentions identified the NSEA. A smaller percentage mentioned business groups, the University of Nebraska, labor groups, and the Republican party. Mention of the Republican party may surprise some who feel that the parties play little, if any, role in recruiting candidates to run for the legislature or in providing candidates with campaign resources. Perhaps the party, following the lead of the national Republican party, has become more active in recent years. It is also curious what role the University of Nebraska might play in elections. The university actively lobbies the state legislature, but it has no resources to contribute to candidates in elections. Nor are university employees typically involved in campaigns in an orchestrated way. The NSEA received the most mentions by lobbyists, with the Bankers Association second. Business, labor, and the Republican party received several mentions here, too, along with farm organizations, the press, agribusiness, and abortion groups.

Although there is some reason to expect that the groups most effective during elections are also the most effective during the session, the resources necessary for one are not the same as those necessary for the other. However, with one or two exceptions, the groups identified as effective in elections are also those mentioned as most effective during the session. The Bankers Association is most frequently mentioned by both legislators and lobbyists. The NSEA is the second most frequently identified group among lobbyists, and it comes in third among legisla-

Table 9.11. Most effective interest groups, identified by Nebraska legislators and lobbyists

Legislators' Choices	In Elections (%)
Nebraska Bankers Association	22
Nebraska Education Association	18
Business, Chamber of Commerce, Nebraska Association of Commerce and Industry (NACI)	10
Republican party	8
AFL-CIO	5
University of Nebraska	4
Total mentions: 103	

Lobbyists' Choices	
Nebraska Education Association	21
Nebraska Bankers Association	16
Business, Chamber of Commerce, NACI	11
Republican party	10
AFL-CIO, labor	7
Farm organizations	5
Press	5
Agribusiness	4
Abortion groups	4
Total mentions: 99	

Legislators' Choices	In Session (%)
Nebraska Bankers Association	20
University of Nebraska	11
Nebraska Education Association	9
Nebraska State School Board Association	6
Nebraska Association for Retarded Citizens	5
Business, Chamber of Commerce, NACI	5
Legal profession	4
Total Mentions: 95	

Lobbyists' Choices	
Nebraska Bankers Association	19
Nebraska Education Association	15
Farm organizations	6
Business, Chamber of Commerce, NACI	5
AFL-CIO	5
University of Nebraska	5
Nebraska League of Municipalities and Association of County Officials	5
Professional associations (doctors and lawyers)	5
Total mentions: 129	

tors. Other groups receiving several mentions by legislators are the Nebraska Association for Retarded Citizens, the Nebraska State School Board Association, and the legal profession. Several lobbyists also mentioned the University of Nebraska, the Nebraska League of Municipalities, the Association of County Officials, farm groups, and professional associations.

The most effective lobbies, then, whether in elections or during the session, are linked to legislators' constituents. The NSEA has teachers in every legislative district and most small towns have a bank. Though teachers have been an active political force for some time, activity on the part of bankers has been less or at least less visible. Recent activity may reflect a concern with issues related to deregulation and the declining agricultural economy, which has made rural and small-town banks particularly vulnerable. Apart from lobbying activities, there may also be the pull of the local community here. Nebraskans have a strong commitment to the state's small towns and rural areas. Support for the local schools and banks may reflect this commitment. The issue of whether out-of-state banks should be licensed in Nebraska has been a major concern of large banks.

Labor has never been particularly important in Nebraska politics, although the United Transportation Workers Union has been an effective agent in representing its members' interests. Several mentions identifying the University of Nebraska as an effective lobby may surprise university faculty and employees, who have expressed the need for the university to do a better job lobbying the state. To be an effective lobby doesn't necessarily mean winning or winning big. It may also mean protecting what one has.

One might have expected business and farm organizations to be mentioned more frequently; however, the favorable climate of opinion that exists in Nebraska among elites as well as the general population toward both may mean that these interests do not need an extremely active lobby group. On the other hand, if we include mentions of banking, insurance, and agribusiness interests, business clearly dominates. To lump all of these together, however, suggests a cohesiveness that may not actually exist among business groups.

More than fifty groups were mentioned in all. It is clear that many groups are seen as effective, reflecting each legislator's or lobbyist's unique experience. It is also clear that even in a homogeneous state like Nebraska the pressure system is complex.

Finally, there are few major differences between the groups identified in Table 9.11 and those mentioned by Morehouse and Kolasa. Kolasa mentions the NSEA and the Omaha Education Association, and Morehouse refers to the education lobby, which includes the NSEA and local associations, as well as local associations of school boards and school administrators. Consistent with the findings here, Morehouse refers to the Farm Bureau and the Omaha National Bank. Some in the present survey mentioned the League of Municipalities and Association of County Officials, referred to by Kolasa, and some mentioned the railroads and telephone companies, identified by Morehouse. Since the publication of Morehouse's work, Northern Natural Gas, another group identified there, has removed its headquarters to another state. Neither Kolasa nor Morehouse identifies the University of Nebraska, labor, or the Republican party. Nor do they mention abortion groups or the professions. These differences, no doubt, reflect the particular issues that define different sessions of the legislature. Issues related to banking, for example, have been on the legislative agenda in recent years. Public power issues, an interest identified by Kolasa, have been less a topic of discussion.

Conclusion

Political scientists have identified several states with strong pressure systems, that is, states where interest groups have a sizable influence in the political process. Nebraska is one. From the perspective of lobbyists and interest groups, these states are almost heaven. In Nebraska, attitudes toward interest groups, at least among state legislators, probably where it counts the most, are quite positive. Legal restrictions on interest groups are not severe, nor are they limiting. Lobbyists and interest groups are required to register and file financial statements. There are no limits on what interest groups can spend in lobbying or on contributions to political campaigns. With the rising costs of campaigns, groups and PACs have increasingly come to play a major role, and there is every indication that they will become still more important in the future. It is unclear whether this trend represents a significant change from the past, that is, before laws were passed requiring financial disclosure. The biggest part of the campaign dollar channeled through PACs and groups comes from business, broadly defined. Consumer, labor, and public interest groups are conspicuous by their absence.

Interest groups are also quite influential in policy making. This fact, however, doesn't necessarily mean that public policy is bad. Legislators did express some concern, though, that the public interest, as they define it, sometimes suffers. Among the influential groups, the NSEA stands out as does the Nebraska Bankers Association. To a certain extent, the list of those interest groups identified by legislators and lobbyists as the most effective are influenced by the legislative agenda. With respect to tactics, interest groups and lobbyists rely heavily on interpersonal contact. Most lobbying is directed toward the state legislature, as opposed to administrative agencies and the courts, and occurs year-round even though the legislature is in session only part of the year.

At least three factors contribute to the strong pressure group system in the state. First, there is an absence of social and economic cleavages among the state's population. Nebraskans are a homogeneous lot. This characteristic tends to limit the scope of conflict with respect to public issues and minimizes popular involvement in politics. Second, Nebraskans are conservative. That means, among other things, that they are supportive of the status quo. Support for the status quo gives certain interests — namely, agriculture and business — an unchallenged legitimacy. Third, political parties in Nebraska are weak, symbolized best in the state's nonpartisan, unicameral legislature. No instrument exists for organizing any kind of policy-based opposition on a continuing basis. The strong pressure system found in Nebraska supports the contention that diversity and a strong party system act as a check on the influence of interest groups.

Notes

1. Harmon Zeigler, "Interest Groups in the States," in Virginia Gray, Herbert Jacob, and Kenneth Vines, eds., *Politics in the American States,* 4th ed. (Boston: Little, Brown, 1983), 97–131; also Sarah McCally Morehouse, *State Politics, Parties and Policy* (New York: Holt, Rinehart & Winston, 1981), 109.

2. E. E. Schattschneider, *The Semisovereign People* (New York: Holt, Rinehart & Winston, 1960), 20–60.

3. Zeigler, "Interest Groups in the States," 115–16.

4. Bernard D. Kolasa, "The Nebraska Political System: A Study in Apartisan Politics" (Ph.D. dissertation, University of Nebraska, 1966).

5. James C. Olson, *History of Nebraska* (Lincoln: University of Nebraska Press, 1955), 21. The early history of Nebraska is reviewed in Olson and also in Dorothy Weyer Creigh, *Nebraska: A Bicentennial History* (New York: W. W. Norton, 1977).

6. Adam C. Breckenridge, "Innovation in State Government: Origin and Development of Nebraska's Nonpartisan Unicameral Legislature," *Nebraska History* 59 (1978), 31–46.

7. A. B. Winter, "The State Constitution," in Robert D. Miewald, ed., *Nebraska Government and Politics* (Lincoln: University of Nebraska Press, 1984), 11–34.

8. George Norris, *Fighting Liberal* (New York: Macmillan, 1947); also Norman Zucker, *George W. Norris: Gentle Knight of American Democracy* (Urbana: University of Illinois Press, 1966).

9. Gabriel Almond and Sidney Verba, *Civic Culture* (Boston: Little, Brown, 1965), 17–18.

10. John Comer, "Citizens: Attitudes and Behavior," in Miewald, ed., *Nebraska Government and Politics,* 125–46.

11. Economic statistics come from *Nebraska Statistical Handbook, 1986–1987* (Lincoln: Nebraska Department of Economic Development, 1986), 45–77.

12. Susan Welch, "The Governor and Other Elected Executives," in Miewald, ed., *Nebraska Government and Politics,* 35–56.

13. Robert Sittig, "The Judiciary," in Miewald, ed., *Nebraska Government and Politics,* 87–103.

14. Adam C. Breckenridge, "The Origin and Development of the Nonpartisan Unicameral Legislature," in John Comer and James Johnson, eds., *Nonpartisanship in the Legislative Process: Essays on the Nebraska Legislature* (Washington, D.C.: University Press of America, 1978), 14.

15. Ibid., 17.

16. Susan Welch, "The Impact of Party Voting Behavior in the Nebraska Legislature," in Comer and Johnson, eds., *Nebraska Legislature,* 101–15.

17. John C. Wahlke, Heinz Eulau, James Buchanan, and LeRoy Ferguson, *The Legislative System* (New York: John Wiley and Sons, 1962), 311–42.

18. James B. Johnson, "Representational Orientations and Nonpartisanship," in Comer and Johnson, eds., *Nebraska Legislature,* 84.

19. Kolasa, "Nebraska Political System," 369–71.

20. Questionnaires were sent out to all 49 of Nebraska's state legislators, and 27 were returned. Questionnaires were also sent to 95 lobbyists registered with the clerk of the legislature and identified by colleagues and journalists who cover state politics as the more effective and influential. Thirty-five surveys were returned. Twenty-four of the lobbyists were in-house lobbyists, i.e., they were employed by a single organization and lobbied exclusively for the organization. Eleven were contract lobbyists or independent, i.e., they were self-employed and represented one or more clients.

21. Kay Lehman Schlozman and John T. Tierney, *Organized Interests and American Democracy* (New York: Harper & Row, 1986), 65–74.

22. Bernard D. Kolasa, "Party Recruitment in Nonpartisan Nebraska," in Comer and Johnson, eds., *Nebraska Legislature,* 40.

23. Nebraska Accountability and Disclosure Commission, *A Summary of Political Campaign Financing* (Lincoln, 1984), 3.

24. Lester Milbraith makes this point in *The Washington Lobbyist* (Chicago: Rand McNally, 1963), 202–6.

25. Ibid., 212.

26. Harmon Zeigler and Michael Baer, *Lobbying: Interaction and Influence in American State Legislatures* (Belmont, Calif.: Wadsworth, 1969), 174.

27. Schlozman and Tierney, *Organized Interests,* 150.

28. Morehouse, *State Politics,* 109.

29. Kolasa, "Nebraska Political System," 288–91.

NORTH DAKOTA

Constituency Coupling in a Moralistic Political Culture

THEODORE B. PEDELISKI

North Dakota offers a unique opportunity to study pluralistic politics in one of the most rural states in the Union.[1] It is a state in which thirty-four counties out of fifty-three are 100 percent rural (having no centers greater than 2,500 in population). It has no cities over 100,000 and only four cities over 20,000 population. Agriculture dominates the state's economic profile. The deference to agriculture and rural concerns is underscored by a legislature that has the highest representation of members with farm interests in the nation.[2] The rural character of the state also affects the political issues on its agenda, whether they concern education, taxation, health care, or morality.

Though agriculture is a dominant presence, the labor force reflects a range of interests. In fact, farm and ranch operators constitute only 11 percent of the labor force of 336,000. Blue collar and trades are 15.4 percent of the labor force. The largest employer is the business section (wholesale, retail, financial, and services), which accounts for 38 percent of the labor force. Government, with some 63,000 employees, represents 18.7 percent of that same force.[3]

Major elements of this chapter are also published in Theodore B. Pedeliski, *North Dakota Politics and Government: Moralistic Political Culture on the Great Plains* (Lincoln: University of Nebraska Press, 1992).

The groups that are most active in the state's political processes include the agricultural associations (both general and specialty), the corporations and cooperatives involved in energy, and the different business interests. There is substantial representation of public institutions and employees, especially of educational interests. Most political activity revolves around economic questions, and very little reflects social issues or interests. Some 28,000 American Indians reside in the state, but there has been little interest group activity on their behalf.

The state's politics are also affected by its economic and geographic characteristics. Elwyn Robinson, the state's eminent historian, noted that isolation, dependence, and economic disadvantage are themes strongly affecting North Dakota's history.[4] Remoteness is all too evident in the state's distance from its markets, high population areas, and financial, corporate, and political centers. Several studies also indicate a political isolation that results in a lag in policy innovation behind other states.[5]

Dependence is a historical condition that continues to this day.[6] In the early years of the state, the railroads, millers, grain exchanges, and banks in Minneapolis controlled the economy and to some extent the politics of North Dakota. A common saying was that while North Dakota was drained in the west by the Missouri River, it was drained in the east by Minneapolis and St. Paul. Today the state's economy remains largely extractive and exportive, with its most vital markets (grain, livestock, petroleum) controlled by corporations headquartered out of state. The largest industrial enterprises in the state are twelve giant electricity generating plants (coal fired) and the nation's only coal gasification plant — all of which export most of their product out of state.

Heavy reliance on the staple economies of agriculture and energy extraction has led politics to be generally conducted under fear of economic distress. The state experienced a protracted agricultural depression in the 1930s and cycles of prosperity and recession since then.[7] An old saying is that the state suffers from six plagues: drought, low prices, overproduction, high interest rates, pests, and politicians. These "depression" perceptions have led the state's politicians to practice frugality with dedication. Even when times are bountiful, North Dakotans tend to fall back on a "root cellar mentality" in which there is a reluctance to increase state spending.[8]

Politically, North Dakota was a predominantly one-party Republican state for decades.[9] The fusion of the Nonpartisan League (once the Populist Republican faction) with the Democrats in 1956 provided for evolution into a two-party system.[10] The Democrats have been able to control the governorship for twenty-six of the past thirty years since

1960, to dominate the state congressional delegation, to hold the majority of state executive offices, and to control at least one house of the legislature in the last four sessions. Polls indicate that a plurality of North Dakotans now identify themselves as independents.[11] Growing party competition has not changed the fact that partisanship does not dominate issue cleavages. During legislative sessions partisan divisions are limited to a handful of issues, although they tend to be omnibus issues like tax measures or budget balancing. Issues in recent years have shown more urban-rural divisions and increasingly, east-west divisions.[12]

In any case, legislators put constituency interests above party loyalties. Following John Kingdon's model,[13] legislators reflect the common callings of their constituencies. They are citizen legislators, and their attitudes mirror those of their constituents. Legislators are responsive to constituent contacts (personal, mail, and phone) and engage in "reality checks" with interests located in their districts. Special interests find their effectiveness is increased if they can demonstrate constituency coupling. Constituency coupling for an interest group involves identification with a significant segment of the state's citizenry, identification with constituents geographically distributed throughout the state (ideally, in all districts), and linkage with a vital state economic interest.

The strong relationship between constituents and politicians is simply a reflection of the state's small population and its moralistic political culture. Daniel Elazar identified the state's political culture as moralistic with some individualistic elements.[14] A number of elements of the moralistic model have particular relevance for interest group activity.

Public service as a sacrifice is a tenet taken seriously by elected officials, public servants, and the electorate alike. It is manifest in a disapproval of any public behaviors that might involve personal enrichment from public service. Bribery or personal benefit are rare in the state's politics. There is also a rejection of the quid pro quo element of the individualistic political culture. Although a special interest or lobbyist may politically support a legislator or provide hospitality or legislative services, these acts are not to be seen as incurring any reciprocal obligation on the part of the legislator. Legislators like to maintain their independence of action. If lobbyists receive anything out of the interactions, it is the continuation of their credibility, good faith, and reputation of fairness, all essential to maintaining accessibility for future encounters. Lobbyists are considered a species of public servant that is expected to provide information, analysis, and registry of constituent reactions and opinions.

The citizen legislature, which meets only once every two years for a period of seventy to eighty days, has particular need of the services of lobbyists. Within the short period of the session the legislature must process some 1,000 House and 700 Senate bills. Legislative Council bills carry great weight because of the participation of legislators and legislative staff members in research and preparation, but for the bulk of bills, which are introduced at the request of constituents or special interests, rank-and-file legislators need cues, given by lobbyists in both formal and informal participation. Lobbyists scc the committee hearing as vital to "educating" the rank and file. Those special interests that have research bureau capabilities are held in particularly high regard by legislators. A registry of grass-roots sentiment is also important, and reinforcement of positions with a parade of local witnesses is critical for ensuring that the interest groups reflect their constituents.

North Dakota legislative procedures dictate that every bill be reported to the floor with recommendations. Legislators thus vote on every measure, and special interests have opportunity to lobby individual members in overriding committee or party direction. The independence of the floor introduces a volatility into legislative decision making that promotes lobbyist contact in regard to floor action.

A moralistic political culture also puts the ultimate check and balance on political institutions into the hands of the electorate. Easy reliance on the initiative and referendum often exerts a chilling effect on the legislature as it anticipates and attempts to accommodate referral threats. This process provides interest groups with another avenue for achieving political goals. Interest groups can bypass the legislature, and directly mobilize the electorate on issues like blue laws.[15]

In 1986 Glen Abney and Thomas Lauth, in a comparative study of interest group influence in all states, rated North Dakota first in group influence on the legislature.[16] Factors that support this finding are reliance on a part-time citizen legislature, the appetite of the legislature for expertise, procedures that involve the full chamber on every measure, the generally weak level of party discipline, nonpartisan dimensions of many important issues, and a governor with weak formal powers. Yet cultural norms strongly affirm both an independent and aloof (proper arm's length) attitude for legislators in dealing with interest group representatives.

Interest Groups Prominent in North Dakota

Outside Interests

In the early history of the state outside interests had a strong influence. Since the Northern Pacific Railroad owned 20 percent of North

Dakota's land area and had a direct interest in the establishment of hundreds of communities across the state, it is not surprising that it and other railroads involved themselves in the political process to protect their extensive interests. From 1883 to 1916 the Republican political machine, led by Alexander McKenzie, championed the cause not only of railroad companies but also of milling, banking, and elevator companies in Minneapolis-St. Paul, where the affairs of the state were conducted.[17] The control of the railroads diminished with the growth of reform groups after 1906, the introduction of the primary system, the direct election of senators, and the rise of the Nonpartisan League.

From 1920 to 1950 the railroads were still influential. They helped to establish such groups as the Tri-State Livestock and Grain Growers Association, the Northwest Farm Managers Association, and the Greater North Dakota Association. They were also instrumental in establishing and in funding the lion's share of the budget of the North Dakota Taxpayers Union.[18] The Taxpayers Union, which existed from 1931 to 1955, embraced corporation interests, tax reformers, tax resisters, and progressive reform types. Working with legislative leadership people, the group sponsored a great deal of legislation that modernized the fiscal machinery of the state and also served to protect property interests of railroads. The railroads also served informally as a research arm of the legislature. As one former legislator and present railroad lobbyist indicated to me, "The railroads filled a void. There was no legislative research council, no legislative library, no retrieval system, no legislative staff, no economic projections from Chase-Econometrics. They had the best economic information in town." In performing this public service the railroads gained an understanding that they would get fair consideration when transportation issues came before the legislature.

In the 1970s and 1980s the railroads have faded away as principal players in the political arena. The North Dakota Railways Association disbanded in 1983, and a single lobbyist looks out for the few state interests of railroads.

Agriculture Interests

Agricultural groups are expected to be one of the more active political groups in the state. The more "populist" group is the North Dakota Farmers Union (NDFU), which organized among the small and desperate farmers of the state in 1926 and grew in strength during the depression.[19] It supported New Deal farm legislation and developed connections with the Department of Agriculture in Washington.[20] It also worked for the establishment of a network of producer and consumer cooperatives throughout the state. It became instrumental in endorsing a slate of candidates in the state's elections in 1948 through the Progressive Alliance and in encouraging a merger of the Democratic party with the Nonpartisan League in 1956.[21] The NDFU was strongest in the period from 1958 to 1980. It was said that the Farmers Union was an eight-hundred-pound gorilla that no legislator could ignore. Since 1980 the organization has gone into a decline, losing financial support of cooperative auxiliaries, losing membership, and cutting staffs and lobbyist activities.[22] It is still the state's largest farm organization, with more than 31,000 families and a voting membership of more than 53,000 in 1989.[23]

Competing with the NDFU is the North Dakota Farm Bureau (NDFB), which dates its organization in the state to 1942.[24] In contrast to the NDFU, which champions to the interests of the family farm, the NDFB prefers a free-market farm economy and supports an agribusiness and promotional approach to improvement of the farm economy. During its early years it was a solidly Republican organization. In 1978 it changed its tactics. It adopted a bipartisan approach, hired a former Democratic legislator as a lobbyist, and established a grass-roots network. In 1983 it helped bring a wide range of agricultural specialty organizations (e.g., North Dakota Sunflower Growers, Red River Potato Growers, Red River Valley Beet Growers, and the N.D. Stockmen's Association) into a new group called the Agricultural Coalition. This organization served as a logrolling group on agricultural issues and also worked to strengthen the co-optive relationships that exist between the specialty farmers and the many state agricultural boards that serve commodity and livestock interests.

In recent years the farm debt crisis has given an impetus for the organization of protest groups. The National Farmers Organization has a small foothold in the state, especially in its southeast counties. A dedicated organization that began as an indigenous environmental group, the Dakota Resource Council took up farm debtor issues, but it, too, remained a small group with a constituency localized in the western counties. Organizations such as the American Agriculture Movement, the Dakota Farm Survival League, and Groundswell made attempts to organize in the mid-1980s. Radical in character, poorly organized, and strident in making demands, they attracted few followers. Individual members involved in litigation did win major gains in cases against the Farmers Home Administration (FmHA), the major target of these groups' activities.[25] Although considerable philosophic differences exist among the various agricultural interests, the influence of these organizations on the legislature when they serve common objectives is overwhelming. When the NDFU, the NDFB, the Ag Coalition, and the soil conservationists and water users unite behind a policy, the pressure is irresistible. Long-term effects of this strength can be seen in policies adopted over several decades which have achieved and maintained significant advantages for agricultural interests in tax policies exempting much agricultural activity and property, revenue sharing for counties, and legislation benefiting cooperatives.

Rural Electric and Telephone Cooperatives

Agricultural interests have a close association with the rural electric cooperatives. These cooperatives serve more than 72,000 consumers, chiefly farmers and petroleum producers. They pursue a public policy agenda that embraces concerns of agriculture, cooperatives, and energy development. They maintain one of the largest lobbyist delegations during legislative sessions and use an extensive grass-roots network to pursue programs that are often congruent with those of the North Dakota Farmers Union. Many legislators happen to be directors of their district co-ops. The electric co-op lobbyists are matched in numbers with those representing telephone co-ops.

Labor Interests

Labor interests have always played a minor role in North Dakota politics.[26] Only 14 percent of the state's nonagricultural workforce is organized. Unless the federal government is involved in large construction projects in the state, labor has a minimal membership. It is not, however, totally ineffective in this "right to work" state. It found a receptive ear, first with the Nonpartisan League and later with the Democratic party. With Democratic control of the governorship and one or both houses of the legislature, it can protect itself in the political arena.

Another development in labor politics is the emergence of the public employees' labor organizations. These groups cannot be called unions because state law does not allow for collective bargaining or compulsory arbitration. The North Dakota Association of Public Employees organized in 1964 and has been followed by more specialized public employee groups.[27] They have become more visible on the legislative scene, bargaining every two years with the legislature for a two-year contract on salaries and benefits. They operate at a tremendous disadvantage in a state where public servants are expected to serve dutifully and at a sacrifice. They do mobilize the legislative delegations in districts where state institutions are located, for they constitute a significant workforce and constituency in those cities.[28]

Education

At various times both legislators and lobbyists have indicated that the education lobby is the most influential in the state.[29] This informal coalition consists of the North Dakota Education Association (NDEA), the N.D. School Boards Association, the N.D. Council of School Administrators, the N.D. Congress of Parents and Teachers, and a state agency, the Department of Public Instruction. The NDEA is the flagship organization of this informal coalition, with 7,500 members distributed across the state. In 1971 the state began to assume a significant portion of local education costs. Since then, the NDEA has joined with the N.D. School Boards Association and the N.D. Association of Counties to maximize state "foundation aid" payments and transportation payments. The coalition wins on funding issues but divides on such issues as teachers' rights, collective bargaining, and arbitration. In these three areas the NDEA has not been legislatively successful.[30]

The NDEA has developed an effective grass-roots network, with teachers maintaining frequent contact with legislators. The NDEA was a pioneer organization in using a PAC to monitor legislative stances and distribute monies broadly across the state to both statewide and legislative candidates.

One educational association that became an intense lobbying instrument was the Home School Association. Led by religious fundamentalists, after two sessions this vocal group was finally able in 1989 to get legislation permitting parents to educate their children at home with minimal requirements.

Legislators also regard higher education interests as a very active and influential body. Not registering as lobbyists, representatives of the state Board of Higher Education and its institutions defend budgets and lobby legislators.[32]

Business Interests

Before 1920, out-of-state interests (the Minnesota Commerce and Industry Association and the Minnesota Employers Association) quietly lobbied the legislature. In 1924, local chambers of commerce and booster and road associations began to organize the Greater North Dakota Association (GNDA). It has concentrated in recent years on the promotion of economic development in the state, tourism, and creation of what are regarded as favorable tax and business climates. Representing some 2,500 business interests, the GNDA acts as a clearinghouse for economic data gathered from retail associations, government agencies, and university research bureaus. It also is served by a large board of directors (100) of community notables that are used effectively as legislator contacts. As for specific business areas, the banking industry, the North Dakota Retail Association, the North Dakota Hospitality Association, and the North Dakota Beverage Dealers are most active. The banking associations, of which there are several, and bank corporations have a large presence in the lobbyist corps (30 lobbyists in the 1989 session).

Lobbyists for business interests have also formed their own social and professional organization, the North Dakota Council of Executives. During legislative sessions the group meets once a week to discuss strategies on common issues and to exchange legislative intelligence. It is, in effect, a closed caucus of interests oriented toward probusiness policies in general.

Energy Interests

Energy production interests are also active in the political process. In 1951 North Dakota became an oil-producing state. The emergence of oil producers as political interests is reported by Robert Engler and Ross Talbot.[33] Although oil producers were subjected to reasonably strong conservationist measures, they were allowed to carry a very modest tax burden for the next thirty years. The state experienced a second oil boom between 1976 and 1982. This second boom saw the emergence of a whole series of opposing interests. Indigenous groups of landowners raised questions of environmental degradation, health, safety, and compensation for damages. Royalty owners' groups raised issues of short payments and proper accounting. Political subdivisions raised issues of impacts on community services. The oil industry generally accommodated itself to more stringent regulation of its activities. It was powerless to prevent the passage by the electorate of Initiated Measure #6 in 1980, which imposed additional extraction taxes on the industry and provided a windfall of revenues for the state. As the oil industry went into a depression in 1985, it was able in both 1985 and 1987 to get a majority in the legislature to vote it some tax relief.

The principal voice for the petroleum industry in the state is the North Dakota Petroleum Council. The Rocky Mountain Oil and Gas Association and lobbyists from the major oil producers tend to work very quietly. In addition, the Petroleum Council has a network of petroleum marketers and local oil service companies to provide constituent contacts. The lobby obtains support from the GNDA and also enlists the backing of labor unions.

Also part of the energy lobby is the Lignite Council, which represents seven lignite mining companies and the energy conversion companies, including three electric production cooperatives and three private utilities that maintain their own lobbying staffs. Basin Electric, a cooperative which operates the Great Plains Coal Gasification plant, is now the largest industrial enterprise in the state, and it is a highly regarded interest in its position as a "native" industry of giant proportions. Both lobbyists and legislators regard the energy group lobbyists as both effective and useful. Energy interests serve as an informal research arm for the legislature, particularly in regard to developmental and environmental impact studies. But though they are rated as effective, the energy companies do not win blind deference from the legislature. From 1965 to 1980, bitter battles were fought over reclamation issues and coal severance and energy conversion taxes. A balance was struck that allowed further development if more stringent environmental policies were be followed by the energy companies.[34]

Those environmental concerns were raised by indigenous groups of local landowners who in 1977 formed an organization called the Dakota Resource Council. The group took on every environmental issue, from the Garrison Diversion irrigation project, to large-scale lignite strip mining, to oil development, to clean air. Its mode of operation was to use intense and personal contacts by its farmer members. It tended to irritate politicians more than to sway them because it tread on too many interests held as vital to the state's development.

Medical Interests

The medical interests have emerged as significant players on the political scene. The three most powerful are the N. D. Medical Association, the North Dakota Hospital Association, and Blue Cross/Blue Shield. Different medical specialties now have their own active political associations. For example, the Long Term Care Association, the Nursing Home Association, Home Health Services, and scores of individual nursing homes have taken to lobbying at the legislature. This expanded lobbying activity reflects the fact that medical and nursing care issues have become salient, particularly so in a state where there is a growing elderly population and where adequate health care has been difficult to provide in isolated areas. Health care also has become a half-billion dollar industry, and even small changes in regulatory, pricing, or compensatory policies can involve millions of dollars.

Activists

North Dakota's politics have also seen increased activity on the part of other interests. The proliferation of sportsmen's groups demonstrates the continuing commitment of these groups to write their own sporting regulations and control the appointment of fish and wildlife officials.[35] The North Dakota Association of Counties is another group with strong constituency coupling that has been active in preserving local power. The 1980s have also seen a marked increase in the activity of public interest organizations that champion the causes of once voiceless groups. The elderly, speaking through the Aging Network, the Silverhaired Legislature, the American Association of Retired Persons, and the North Dakota Retired Teachers, inundate the capital when issues of retirement and medical care arise. The North Dakota Council of Abused Women Services and various child welfare associations have also become more visible. The most successful public interest group has been the Association of Retarded Citizens, which was instrumental in effecting an entire policy revolution in regard to the developmentally disabled.

Popular Democracy

Finally, the referral and popular initiative forces must be included in the lineup of influential political groups. Generally, these groups bypass the legislative arena, preferring to go directly to state residents in their political action campaigns. These groups often protest taxes or become involved in public morality issues. The antitax groups are the most ephemeral. While eschewing lobbying efforts, for example, the Nonpartisan Political Coalition, which appeared on the scene in 1989, held formal meetings and press conferences during the legislative session to convey its antitax message and threat of referral action to the legislature. Indigenous, spontaneous, and usually led by people with little previous political experience, these groups mobilize public sentiment with remarkable effectiveness. With little organization or continuity and operating on shoestring or nonexistent budgets, they picture themselves as Davids matched against the Goliaths of governmental and private interests. If opponents mount media campaigns to beat back referral efforts, the antitax people simply charge that well-financed interests are trying to buy the election.[36] In a changing environment of sophisticated public relations and media techniques they prove that popular movements working largely by word of mouth can be highly effective simply by invoking the right rhetoric and symbols.

The 1980s have seen a host of issues put on the ballot or referred by special interests seeking either relaxation or tightening of the state's blue laws in regard to permitted gaming activities or Sunday openings. The general pattern has been for a group to emerge to initiate an effort to change the status quo, immediately precipitating the mobilization of opposition. Groups emerging to promote liberalization of the laws include the North Dakota Committee for Tax Relief, the Coalition for Sunday Shopping, the Right to Shop Committee, the Fundraiser Ticket Association, and the Committee of Honest Gaming and Economic Development. Some operated as fronts for retail associations or gambling industry interests. They were opposed by such groups as Citizens for Sunday Closing, the Family Way of Life Committee, and the Council on Gambling Problems. Business groups such as the GNDA or the North Dakota Retail Association are then caught in the issue. These hotly contested matters at present provide the basis for most citizen activism on social issues.

Legal and Cultural Environment

North Dakota is a rural state with a small population and with a limited political and economic elite. It is no exaggeration to say that a personal acquaintanceship exists not only between all legislators and top state officials but also between legislators and most lobbyists and community notables. The personal equation operates in interest group politics. Lobbyists have remarked that effectiveness of lobby efforts is based not on information, size of the interest group, or support the interest group might provide a legislator, but on the personal style of the lobbyist. To maintain credibility, interests must have the "correct people" on the scene, people who have reputations developed over many sessions.

Lobbyist behavior is also conditioned by the political culture of the state. From the earliest days of statehood there was a strong suspicion of lobby activities. It was reflected in statutes that in effect banned personal lobbying and restricted lobbyists' activities to formal appearances before committees or submission of printed statements and public briefs.[37] These laws with their unrealistic expectations were finally superseded by statutes that legitimated lobbying while placing it under regulations requiring lobbyists to register, to identify sponsors, and log all pieces of legislation which they intended to influence, promote, or oppose. Exchange of money or anything of value between lobbyist and legislator was made a misdemeanor offense.[38] Under 1975 amendments, logging provisions were eliminated and lobbyists were required to wear badges and submit reports at the end of the session listing expenditures (for hospitality) of more than $25 on any legislator.[39] In the 1981 session the legislature provided for recognition of political action committees and provided for reporting of PAC contributions and disbursements (of $100 or more).[40] Regulation of lobbying is used only to provide some basic statistics about the process (for example, the total number of lobbyists involved in each session). There has been no oversight of the process or special investigations. The common perception is that there is really no abuse in the system.

Institutional norms and mores of the moralistic political culture operate to delineate the parameters of proper behavior for interests and their lobbyist representatives. For example, norms still support the extension of hospitality to legislators by lobbyists, but the norm is to extend any hospitality on an open basis for the entire legislature. A few interests (energy and public utilities) have maintained hospitality suites, but most have resorted to banquets hosting the entire legislature and spouses. The legislature's social calendar schedules these affairs for almost every working day of the session. They are conducted in a nonpartisan atmosphere and express the basic "personalism" of the state's politics. Scrupulous legislators can request the cost of the meal and pay their own shares.[41]

Traditional norms reject deals or gifts, however trivial, or personal favors from special interests. Activities perceived here as improper would ordinarily be acceptable in another political culture. A 1973 survey noted that actions considered unethical included lavish entertaining (a particular complaint of small groups not able to afford banquets for the whole legislature) or lobbying right behind the rail. Even legal activities such as contributing to legislators' campaigns, lobbying by state officials, or bringing in delegations ("mob" lobbying) were regarded as improper.[42]

Traditional norms support high standards of honesty and integrity. Legislators prefer lobbyists to use low-key approaches and to respect legislators' personal judgments. Nothing is more detested than pressure from a lobbyist (Table 10.1).[43] Pressure can be interpreted in different ways. It can appear as intimidation, as threats to campaign for opponents or giving a legislator a bad name with constituents, as persistence and stridency of demands, or as the making of excessive or untimely demands. State employees' demands are often seen in this light. Dishonesty, undependability, and arrogance also tend to make legislators react negatively. As one legislator noted, some interests are their own worst enemies. Some of the interests that evoked negative comments were the environmental groups, the Right-to-Life people, the home school advocates, and the sportsmen's organizations. In spite of their annoying ap-

Table 10.1. Lobbyists' attributes, as indicated by North Dakota legislators, 1985 session (N = 129)

Most Valued	No.	%	Least Valued	No.	%
Honesty, integrity	99	76.7	Pressure	50	38.8
Reliable information	20	15.5	Dishonesty	24	18.6
Ability to communicate	4	3.1	Unreliability	12	9.3
Friendliness	2	1.5	Narrow-mindedness	10	7.8
Respect for decisions	1	.8	Arrogance	8	6.2
No pressure	1	.8	One-sidedness	3	2.3
No response	2	1.5	Condescension	2	1.6
			Threatening	2	1.6
			No response	18	13.1

Source: Bureau of Governmental Affairs poll for North Dakota Farm Bureau, March 1985.

proaches, these groups were often successful in their legislative goals since legislators often voted in their favor just to get them out of the way and their issues off the agenda. The most highly regarded lobbyists were veteran lobbyists, some of whom had been on the scene for 20 years or more and who were noted for their courtly manners, their low-key approach, and their efforts to be helpful.

Given the low frequency of perceived improprieties, there is little impetus to impose stricter regulation of lobbyist activities. In a 1985 survey of 119 legislators, 85.3 percent felt that no more regulations were needed.[44]

Scope and Profile of Lobbying Activity

Lobbyists are a visible group during legislative sessions. Until 1975 some 250 lobbyists were registered for the typical session. With energy issues reaching the legislature, this number rose to a high of 562 and has since settled down to a figure of about 400 per session.[45] Lobbyists thus outnumber legislators by more than two to one. Table 10.2 lists the interest groups and the number of lobbyists registered for the 1989 session.

The vast majority of the registered lobbyists (80 percent plus) can be considered in-house lobbyists: executives and public relations officers whose job descriptions include legislative affairs in addition to their regular corporate duties. The cost of this lobbying activity is computed as a pro rata portion of their regular salaries. Almost all of these lobbyists are headquartered and reside in Bismarck or in the state's other major cities, and North Dakota can claim that it has citizen lobbyists as well as citizen legislators.

In numbers the second largest category of lobbyist is the volunteer citizen lobbyist. Organizations such as the rural electric cooperatives, the

Table 10.2. Lobbyists registered for the 1989 North Dakota legislative session
(N = 399)

Interest	No. of Groups	No. of Lobbyists
Agricultural	12	24
Rural co-ops (elec., tel.)	13	29
Business	21	56
Financial, insurance	15	42
Energy	15	21
Public utilities	8	22
Transportation	6	6
Medical care	24	54
Professionals	8	12
Labor, public employees	20	41
Education	8	17
Political Subdivision Public Boards	12	21
Natural resources	5	15
Fraternal	2	12
Public interest	10	15
Other, self	12	20
Onmibus[a]		5

Source: North Dakota Secretary of State's Office, 1989.
[a]Contract lobbyists representing 5 to 20 different interests.

Dakota Resource Council, the farm credit agencies, the veterans' groups, the banking associations, and even the nurses' associations have enlisted squads of member-lobbyists to blanket the legislature just before critical votes. This strategy multiplies the number of contacts and also demonstrates constituency coupling.

An important category of lobbyist is the contract lobbyist, who is almost always an attorney, usually from one of the larger Bismarck law firms. There are some twenty such lobbyists, and they represent many of the major associations and corporations represented at the legislature. Some half dozen represent five to as many as twenty clients. Professional, full-time lobbyists generally represent out-of-state corporations such as oil companies and communications companies or assist public employee groups; only thirteen such lobbyists were registered for the 1989 session. These figures do not include "lobbyists" who are not required to register. State agencies provide legislative liaisons, not only to testify but also to explain legislation or answer questions. A large department like that of human services may have up to fifteen specialists available to provide testimony. Higher education, already mentioned, has a sizable presence. Also unregistered are members of the American Indian community, who voice their interests through members of the Indian Affairs Commission or through invited tribal officials. Women's issues are promoted through a women legislators' caucus.

Strategy and Tactics

The increase of lobbyists and their activity has been associated with the development of new and more sophisticated tactics. In the 1980s, special interests concentrated on better public relations, PAC organization, bipartisan targeting, grass-roots organization and "networking," and coalition building. In terms of public imaging, all the larger and better-financed organizations expanded and upgraded their publications and magazines, some of which are distributed to broad constituencies in the state. Some of the wealthier interests, such as the banking associations, produced television spots that attractively presented their interests as promoting North Dakota.

PAC organization has proceeded slowly. As late as 1973, 48 percent of legislators thought that contributions to legislative election campaigns by special interests were improper. PAC activity increased after the authorizing legislation of 1981. From an initial twelve PACs that made contributions to statewide and legislative candidates in the 1983 elections, thirty-eight registered in 1988.[46] Table 10.3 lists the ten most active PACs operating in state elections for 1988. PAC contributions vary with the importance of the office. A gubernatorial candidate might receive as much as $1,000 from a PAC, and lesser officers such as the attorney general or agriculture commissioner, $500, but state legislative candidates obtain for the most part nominal contributions, no more than $300 from any one PAC and not more than $1,100 totally. By comparison with amounts in other states, PAC contributions in North Dakota are modest if not parsimonious.

All of the major interest groups have organized grass-roots networks. Local committees, legislative district contact people, action

Table 10.3. Top ten PAC contributors in North Dakota, 1988

PAC	Total Contributed ($)	Candidates Assisted	Average Payment ($)
U.S. West North Dakota	23,930	129	181
N.D. Oil	19,740	97	203
N.D. Education Association	24,335	81	300
Burlington Northern Employees for Good Government	7,000	65	186
Electrical Workers 714	4,850	37	131
Mon-Dak Utilities	10,175	32	270
Tenneco Employee Good Government	5,900	21	281
Phillips Petroleum	3,511	17	207
N.D. Beer Wholesalers	6,300	12	525
Texaco Political Involvement	2,250	9	250

Source: M. Douglas Johnson, "Political Action Committee Contributions in North Dakota, 1988" (unpublished research, Department of Political Science, University of North Dakota, 1989).

alerts, and phone trees now provide new channels of constituent access. The old days, when two or three postcards were interpreted as a tidal wave of opinion, have been superseded by a new atmosphere of partici- patory politics. In the 1989 legislature more than 114,000 phone calls were logged in from constituents on toll-free numbers, a figure equal to one-sixth of the state's population.[47] All this activity reinforces constitu- ency coupling. A state legislator is made to realize that membership of the group is statewide, is well represented in his or her district, and supports a vital state interest.

Bipartisan targeting is evident in the activities of the Farm Bureau and NDEA. U.S. West (formerly Northwestern Bell) has also been bipar- tisan in its PAC contributions. But most business interests continue to contribute to probusiness candidates who happen to be Republican.

Finally, more interests have taken to establishing coalitions. These coalitions vary in terms of formality of organizational structure. The Ag Coalition and Veterans Coordinating Council have formal structures. In 1989 some twenty different groups involved with hunting and fishing met to create the North Dakota Outdoors Council. The GNDA is also an umbrella organization. Informal coalitions abound. These include the "education group" (NDEA, NDASB, NDASA), the "energy group," the "medical group," and the North Dakota Council of Executives. Intersec- tor alliances have been forged to deal with specific issues.[48] The Farmers Union and labor groups have worked together, and the Farmers Union, education groups, and county organizations joined in an initiative peti- tion drive (the Measure #6 drive of 1980).

In terms of specific approaches and tactics, lobbyists find that con- tact with committee chairs and rank-and-file members is still their most important targeting strategy, in spite of the fact that party leadership people are the most critical in the legislative process. This is because much of the legislation of concern to interest groups is basically regula- tory or antiregulatory and generally of secondary or tertiary importance to the agendas of the majority and minority leaders. Majority and mi- nority leaders are also practically and politically less accessible to lobby- ists. Table 10.4 ranks the importance of different lobbying approaches.

Interest groups find greater success in opposing legislation than in promoting it. This finding was suggested in a 1977 study that attempted to measure the relative success of interest groups during the 1977 legisla- ture.[49] Of the eight groups surveyed, the success rate for proposals (48 bills) was 58.3 percent; but in regard to legislation opposed (31 bills), the success rate was 96.5 percent. Governors' proposals are particularly vul- nerable to interest group ambushes. In recent sessions proposals for school district reorganization and restructuring of the executive branch

Table 10.4. North Dakota lobbyists' rankings of lobbying tactics

	Average Ranking[a]
1. Contact with committee chairs	2.6
2. Contact with legislative rank and file	2.7
3. Committee hearings	3.3
4. Contact with party leadership people	4.3
5. Enlistment of constituents	4.8
6. Coordinated efforts with other groups	4.9
7. Contact with governor, governor's staff	5.2
8. Contact with Legislative Council	6.4

Source: Interviews by the author with twenty-four lobbyists of salient interest groups in 1988.

[a]Range is from 1 (most important) to 8 (least important).

lost all chance of success once interest group opposition vocalized.

The general conclusion of legislators is that lobbyists help the legislative process. Legislators almost unanimously agree on this point (96.1 percent). The single most important service provided by lobbyists as perceived by legislators is testimony, followed by assistance in helping the legislator to understand issues.[50] The public's views of lobbyists are also positive. A March 1987 poll of the state's residents found that 56.1 percent of respondents felt that lobbyists helped the process, while 26.1 percent thought they hindered the process and 8.2 percent felt that it made no difference.[51] The poll also asked respondents to rate the influence of lobbyists on the legislature (from "too strong" to "very weak"). A large plurality of respondents rated the influence as "moderate" (48.7 percent). In the remaining responses, perceptions of strong influence outnumbered those of weak influence by three to one. Suspicion of special interests is endemic to a certain degree in the population. After the successful referrals of several tax and morality issues in the 1989 special elections, an opinion frequently voiced by people who voted for the referrals was that they felt that the legislature had caved in to special interests.[52]

Extralegislative Activity

Since the legislature meets 80 days for only every two years, attention must also be given to interest group interaction with the executive branch and the judiciary. Abney and Lauth ranked North Dakota 23d among all states in group influence on the governor and 26th in group influence on state agencies.[53] Nevertheless, all lobbyists of major interests reported increased executive agency interaction in the 1980s decade as interests have had to grapple with agencies on technological and economic issues. The greatest involvement has concerned the expansion of the energy industry.[54]

One area where interest group influence in the executive branch has been institutionalized is in the regulatory boards and commissions. The state has some one hundred boards, commissions, and advisory bodies, many of which have statutorily guaranteed representation for special interest groups. For example, the Health Council has legislatively required representatives from the State Medical Association, the State Hospital Association, the State Nurses Association, and the State Pharmaceutical Association. The twenty-eight-member Manpower Services Council requires the governor to appoint members from agriculture, labor, business, low-income groups, the League of Cities, and the Association of Counties and to include American Indians and women. Many of the agricultural boards also mandate appointment of members from named associations.

The governor has the authority to appoint a majority of members of twenty-six different boards and a complement of members for all others. With changes in administration, a great deal of aggressive campaigning and competition takes places among interests as they nominate people for vacancies. Competition can become quite intense among the various banking interests seeking representation on the Banking Board or wildlife and sports groups as they compete for positions on game and fish advisory boards. Gubernatorial transitions generally mark a time of concerted pressure on the governor.[55]

Most advisory boards and commissions represent an amalgam of department agency heads, interest group representatives, and citizens. The political culture of the state seems to expect these nonpaid "citizen" and interest group administrators to provide needed expertise, particularly in the areas of health, human services, education, and water management. These board members are nonsalaried and are reimbursed only for traveling expenses.

There has been little involvement of interest groups with the judiciary. The North Dakota Trial Lawyers Association, the North Dakota Press Association, and the North Dakota Broadcasters Association have on occasion presented amicus briefs before the state Supreme Court (generally on open records issues). The North Dakota Education Association and its auxiliary, the N.D. Higher Education Association, underwrite about a dozen employee rights suits a year on behalf of members.

Some organizations have in effect bypassed the state's legislative arena to obtain their goals. The Audubon Society (the national parent organization) took the state and the federal government to court and was able to halt any progress of the Garrison Diversion project, thus frustrating the congressional delegation and most political interests in the state. The Association of Retarded Citizens (ARC), unable to get legislative support for its programs for deinstitutionalization of residents, filed suit in federal court and obtained decisions that mandated actions costing the state over $200 million since 1982.[56] The ARC continues to play a role in monitoring compliance with court orders.

Power of Interest Groups in North Dakota

In measuring the relative influence of different interest groups in North Dakota, one can develop several criteria. Power can be measured along various dimensions: by power base of a group, through political linkages, and by the scope of issue involvement by the group (which can range from single issues to broad spectrum issues).[57] In North Dakota a strong power base can be assumed for the farm organizations, the energy companies, the rural electric cooperatives, the North Dakota Education Association, and the GNDA. All have large memberships or have financial resources to maintain staffs for research and legislative affairs. All have a strong economic role in the state. In terms of political linkages, the Farmers Union and labor groups presided over the birth of the Dem-NPL party, and the North Dakota Farm Bureau and the GNDA have a broad overlap with the Republican donor community. The two major farm groups and the GNDA have traditionally operated as broad spectrum groups indicating stands on a wide range of issues.

An early ranking of interest groups in North Dakota was done by Sarah Morehouse.[58] She assessed North Dakota as a weak interest group state with the following strong groups: (1) education lobby (NDEA, PTA, school boards, Dept. Public Instruction), (2) farm group (Farmers Union, Farm Bureau, N.D. Stockmen's Assoc.), (3) rural cooperatives.

A journalistic assessment published in 1977 listed the top ten political influences in the state and ranked both interests and political personages. Interests included were the North Dakota Farmers Union (1st); the rural electric cooperatives (3d); the media (5th); the GNDA (7th); the NDEA (8th); and the N.D. AFL-CIO (9th).[59]

In 1981 and again in 1985, legislators were polled on identification of the lobbyist organizations exerting the most influence on the legislature (Table 10.5). The results confirm previous rankings.

These polls also asked legislators to rate the lobbying groups in terms of which ones provided the most reliable information and capacity for mobilizing the grass roots. In 1981 the most reliable information was seen as coming from the Farm Bureau (1st), the NDEA (2nd), and the utilities and energy interests (3rd). In 1985 the most reliable information was seen as coming from (1) Farm Bureau, (2) the NDEA, and (3) the

Table 10.5. Organizations exerting most influence on North Dakota Legislature, as evaluated by legislators, 1981 and 1985

1981 (N = 126)			1985 (N = 129)		
Organization	No.	%	Organization	No.	%
1. North Dakota Education Association	51	40.2	1. Education group	44	34.1
2. Utilities, energy	34	26.8	2. Utilities, energy	15	11.6
3. Farm Bureau	6	4.7	3. Retailers	10	7.8
4. Retailers	4	3.1	4. Greater North Dakota Association	8	6.2
5. Rural electric co-ops	5	2.4	5. Farm bureau	5	3.9
6. Greater North Dakota Association	3	2.4	6. Bankers	5	3.9
7. Business groups	3	2.4	7. Public employees	4	3.1
8. School boards	2	1.6	8. Other	15	11.6
9. Other	15	12.0	9. No response	23	17.8
10. No response	3	2.4			

Source: Author's interviews.

retailers. A slightly different alignment emerged in terms of mobilizing grass roots. In the 1981 legislature the most effective groups were NDEA (1st), the rural electric cooperatives, (2nd), and the utilities and energy group (3rd). In 1985 the ranking was (1) the education lobby, (2) the Farmers Union (2nd), and senior citizens (3rd).

Interviews with twenty-four lobbyists in 1987 indicated that the groups with the popular reputations had maintained their rankings. The lobbyists were asked to rank some twenty-four different groups and associations from very effective to not effective. Effectiveness scores are listed for the top ten groups in Table 10.6. A separate question was asked about effectiveness at election time. Here several groups not rated highly during the legislative session were given high marks. The North Dakota Education Association, the AFL-CIO, and the Farmers Union (which does not have a PAC) were rated first, second, and third. The contemporary ranking of North Dakota's most influential groups adduced on the basis of composite indicators is presented in Table 10.7.

Table 10.6. Interest group effectiveness in North Dakota, as indicated by key lobbyists

Interest Group	Mean Rank[a]
1. North Dakota Education Association	1.52
2. State universities	1.61
3. Medical group	1.71
4. Lignite Council	1.8
5. Rural electric co-ops	1.94
6. Greater North Dakota Association	2.05
7. Agricultural coalition	2.05
8. Public utilities	2.1
9. School Boards Association	2.16
10. Farm Bureau	2.21

[a]Range is from 1 (very effective) to 5 (not effective).

Table 10.7. Lobbyists' ranking of most influential interests in North Dakota

1. Education lobby (N.D. Education Association, N.D. School Boards Administration, Department of Public Instruction)
2. Energy group (Lignite Council, Petroleum Council, Basin Electric, Mon-Dak Utilities, Northern States Power, Ottertail Power)
3. Business groups (Greater North Dakota Assoc., N.D. Bankers Assoc.), U.S. West Communications
4. Farm groups (N.D. Farm Bureau, N.D. Farmers Union, N.D. Assoc. of Rural Electric Cooperatives, AG Coalition)
5. Medical group (N.D. Medical Assoc., N.D. Hospital Assoc., Blue Cross/Blue Shield of North Dakota, Nursing Home Assoc., N.D. Long Term Care Assoc., N.D. Nurses Assoc.)
6. Universities, colleges, and public employees' associations

This particular ranking does not include the referral and popular initiative interests, whose nebulous organizations and abstention from traditional lobbying activities put them outside of traditional classifications of interest groups. Yet it would be very difficult to deny that the messages they openly send the legislature make them highly active participants in the political process.

In assessing the strength of interest groups in North Dakota, Morehouse categorized the state as a weak interest group state. North Dakota's political setting and the research done on the state indicate otherwise. Legislators and lobbyists, while maintaining ethical restraints in their relationships, also exhibit symbiotic dependencies. There is a great deal of mutual respect between legislators and lobbyists, as can be expected to develop with close interaction extending over many sessions.[60] It should also be noted that almost all of the legislators are members of the main interest groups that are represented before the legislature, and many are local or state officers in those groups. The following groups had directors, officers, or members in the 1989 legislature: the Farmers Union (22), the Farm Bureau (19), rural electric co-ops (8), water management districts (9), the NDEA (8), the Stockmen's Association (15), and the GNDA (5). There is a shared sense of representation, and if there is an iron triangle in North Dakota politics, it involves linkages among interest groups, coupled constituencies, and the legislature.

This is not to suggest that interest groups can dictate to the legislature. Interviews with legislative leadership people indicate that lobbyists' influence is less successful in co-opting the legislative leadership. As one legislative leader indicated, the longer legislators serve, the more confident they become and the less dependent on lobbyists. Lawnmakers also develop and trust their own sources of information, such as the staff of the Legislative Research Council, the Office of Management and Budget, and the Tax Department, as well as research commissioned to consultants and legislative interns. Leadership people who carry out trustee roles in working out the critical omnibus spending and tax measures have indicated that they often have to fight off the efforts of interest groups. As special interests push for budgetary indulgences, leadership people feel that they need to neutralize this influence through caucus briefings.

Abney and Lauth rated North Dakota 23rd in the nation in terms of interest group influence on the governor.[61] Special interests seem to upset the finely tuned budgets and programs submitted by the executive branch. As one spokesperson of the governor's office commented, "They try to carve out exemptions for their interests and start an unraveling process." Many interests are also seen by the governor's office as exhibiting a great resistance to change. Such groups are often strong voices of parochialism, and it is difficult for them to see a broader public interest. Because the legislative leadership and the governor's office appear to act with some sense of removal from interest group pressures, we can more accurately define interest group strength in North Dakota as moderate, which is coincident with the public's view.

Conclusion

In reviewing the role of interests in North Dakota's political processes, one notes that few outside interests become involved in the state's politics. Local parochial interests predominate, and out-of-state corporations rely on indigenous associations (such as the N.D. Petroleum Council) to provide them with local legitimacy. A group such as the Audubon Society, which did involve itself in a major state issue in federal litigation, avoids direct contact with the North Dakota Legislature.

One also finds that constituency coupling is a prerequisite for successful lobbying. Major groups have memberships that blanket the state, and they pursue issues that affect significant populations and communities over the entire state. Even the medical interests embrace their patients and insurees as constituents. The environmentalists were able to achieve some measure of legitimacy only after they created their own indigenous organization (DRC). The members of the energy group have the hardest case in identifying with a constituency, but they compensate for that by forging intersector alliances with labor, the rural electric cooperatives, and the GNDA and by presenting a desperately sought-for alternative to the state's agricultural economy.

Finally, one notes that change is occurring in the lobbying process. Interest groups have become very professionalized with the use of phone trees, action calls, polls, and computer tracking of legislation. Increased professionalization has also been indicated in the greater activity before interim committees that meet between sessions. In spite of a significant increase of PAC formation since 1985, financial support of legislators is still at very modest levels. There has also been a proliferation of new groups seeking access. The number of public employee, medical interest, and public interest groups has tripled since 1984. Some interests, however, have splintered as groups with variant policy outlooks have sought to work directly with decision makers instead of through the associations that traditionally represented them.

Notes

1. North Dakota is 5th in the nation (after West Virginia, Vermont, South Dakota, and Maine) in percentage of rural residents. It is 2d in the nation (after South Dakota) in percentage of persons who reside on farms. *Statistical Abstract of the United States 1986* (Washington, D.C.: Bureau of the Census, 1985), 26, 651.

2. In the 1989 legislature 49 percent of both House and Senate members were farmers, ranchers, or hyphenated farmers.

3. Blue collar and trades include mining and oil-field workers (2 percent); construction (3 percent); manufacturing (4.5 percent); and transportation and utilities (5.9 percent). See Table 5.02 in *Statistical Abstract of North Dakota,* prepared by the Bureau of Business and Economic Research, University of North Dakota (3d ed., 1988), 129.

4. Elwyn Robinson, "Themes of North Dakota History," *North Dakota History* 26 (Winter 1959), 12–24. Robinson's themes have been assessed for contemporary relevance and generally found as valid at present as they were thirty years ago. D. Jerome Tweton, "The Future of North Dakota – An Overview," *North Dakota History* 56 (Winter 1989), 7–14.

5. See Virginia Gray, "Innovations in the States: A Diffusion Study," *American Political Science Review* 67 (December 1973), 1174–85; Jack Walker, "The Diffusion of Innovations among the American States," *American Political Science Review* 63 (September 1969), 880–99; Frank M. Bryan, *Politics in the Rural States: People, Parties and Processes* (Boulder, Colo.: Westview Press, 1981), 65.

6. For a discussion of dependence and the "conspiracy theory" that it spawned, see Robert P. and Wynona H. Wilkens, *North Dakota: A Bicentennial History* (New York: W. W. Norton, 1977), 122–36.

7. For a long-range assessment of the state's economy, see Scot Stradley, "A Staple Perspective on Economic Development in North Dakota," *North Dakota Economic Studies* No. 28 (Grand Forks: Bureau of Business and Economic Research, 1981).

8. This attitude mirrors the "drought mentality" of South Dakota's politicians reported by Robert Burns and Herbert Cheever in "South Dakota: Conflict and Cooperation among Conservatives," this volume, Chapter 13.

9. The 1984, 1986, and 1988 elections changed North Dakota from one of the most Republican states in the nation to one that reflects maximum party competition (score of 0.500 from 1981 to 1988). John F. Bibby, "Electoral Change in the Midwest: Presidential Republicanism and Counter Realigning Forces at the State Level" (Paper presented at the annual meeting of the American Political Science Association, September 2, 1989, Atlanta).

10. For an account of the fusion and the role of interest groups in it, see Lloyd Omdahl, *Insurgents* (Brainerd, Minn.: Lakeland Press, 1961).

11. University of North Dakota Bureau of Governmental Affairs polls for 1990 show identification levels of 25 percent for Democrats, 38 percent for Independents, 28 percent for Republicans, and 9 percent "Don't Know," "Undecided," or "Other."

12. The east-west cleavage is explored in terms of ballot issues in Theodore Pedeliski, Robert Kweit, Mary Kweit, and Lloyd Omdahl, "Cleavages on Recent Ballot Measures: The Two States of North Dakota" (Paper presented at the annual meeting of the American Political Science Association, September 1987, Chicago).

13. John W. Kingdon, *Congressional Voting Decisions* (New York: Harper & Row, 1981), chaps. 2 and 5.

14. Daniel Elazar, *American Federalism: A View from the States* (New York: Thomas Crowell, 1972), 96–114. Elazar's attributes of the political culture of the prairie states also apply to North Dakota. See Daniel Elazar, "Political Culture on the Plains," *Western Political Quarterly* 11 (July 1980), 261–83.

15. Since 1982, nine ballot measures on gaming, Sunday opening, and lotteries have been put on the ballot. Victory in the legislature does not ensure final resolution of such issues, as unsatisfied groups have the option of pursuing referrals, counterinitiatives, or initiatives aimed at repeal.

16. Glen Abney and Thomas Lauth, "Interest Group Influence in the States: A View of Subsystem Politics" (Paper presented at the 1986 meeting of the American Political Science Association, August 1986, Washington, D.C.).

17. Robert Wilkens, "Alexander McKenzie and the Politics of Bossism," in Thomas W. Howard, ed., *The North Dakota Political Tradition* (Ames: Iowa State University Press, 1981), 3–39.

18. Albert Irving Peterson, "The North Dakota Taxpayers Association (Ph.D. dissertation, University of North Dakota, 1946). For the role of the railroads, see 54–56.

19. For the story of the North Dakota Farmers Union, see Charles and Joyce Conrad, *Fifty Years: The North Dakota Farmers Union* (Bismarck: Conrad Publishing, 1976).

20. See Conrad and Conrad, *Fifty Years,* 63–73. Also see Theodore Saloutos, *The American Farmer and the New Deal* (Ames: Iowa State University Press, 1982), chap. 12.

21. Omdah, *Insurgents,* chaps. 3, 7, 9.

22. See Reed Karaim, "The Changing of the Guard," *Ag Week,* December 1, 1984, pp. 38–41.

23. A family voting membership provides voting rights to both spouses and to children between the ages of sixteen and twenty.

24. See G. J. Stafne, *History of the North Dakota Farm Bureau, 1942–1965* (Fargo: North Dakota Farm Bureau, 1967).

25. The FmHA was required to meet many new due process requirements after the decision in *Coleman v. Block,* 580 F. Supp. 194 (1984).

26. For a history of organized labor in North Dakota, see Henry R. Martinson, *History of North Dakota Labor* (Fargo: Labor Temple, 1970), and D. Jerome Tweton, *In Union There Is Strength* (Grand Forks: North Dakota Carpenter Craftsman Heritage Society, 1982).

27. These groups proliferated in the 1989 legislative session. They include the North Dakota Public Employees Association, the Association of Federal, State, County and Municipal Employees (AFSCME), the Independent North Dakota State Employees, the North Dakota Council of Public Employees, the Association of Former Public Employees, and the Society of Higher Education Professionals (SHEP).

28. North Dakota in 1985 had some 44,000 state and local employees.

29. Mike Dorsher, "The Teacher Equation: Why the Education Lobby Has a Lock on Votes," *Bismarck Tribune,* February 26, 1989, pp. D1, D7.

30. The constituency coupling changes. On the funding issues the relevant constituency includes the entire elementary and secondary parent population. On the teachers' rights issues the constituency reduces itself to about 8,000.

31. The permissive home school law was passed in the face of polls that indicated that 71.8 percent of the state's residents disapproved of home schools and 90.7 percent felt that home schoolteachers should be required to meet the same certification standards as public schoolteachers (Bureau of Governmental Affairs poll, November 1985).

32. Tracy Shatek, "New Lobbying Strategies May Be Paying Off," *Grand Forks Herald,* March 19, 1989.

33. Robert Engler, *The Politics of Oil: A Study of Private Power and Democratic Directions* (Chicago: University of Chicago Press, 1961); see chap. 1, "A Portrait in Oil," for a case study on North Dakota. Also see Ross Talbot, "Political Impact," in *The Williston Report: The Impact of Oil on the Williston Area of North Dakota* (Grand Fors: University of North Dakota Press, 1958).

34. For a history of political issues in mining and energy conversion, see Colleen A. Oihus, *A history of Coal Mining in North Dakota, 1873–1982* (Grand Forks: North Dakota Geological Survey, 1983), and Mike Jacobs, *One-Time Harvest: Reflections on Coal and the Future* (Jamestown, N.D.: North Dakota Farmers Union, 1975). A detailed record of environmental issues was covered in *The Onlooker,* an environmental newspaper published at Mandan, N.D., 1976–1981.

35. When the 1989 legislature held hearings on a proposal to merge the Game and Fish Department with the Departments of Tourism and Parks and Recreation, these interest inundated the capitol and packed halls and hearing rooms with angry constituents. As one legislator commented, "They made us feel as if we were the game and the season would open on election day."

36. In a 1989 referral campaign the North Dakota Education Association's receipt of $50,000 from the National Education Organization, the pro-seatbelt interest's receipt of $270,000 from national auto safety groups, and the YESS (You Expect State Services) expenditure of $100,000 on media advertising were used to discredit the organizations as "buying the election." The more the traditional organizations spent, the lower went the standing of their ballot positions in the polls.

37. 1911 N.D. Laws, chap. 182.

38. 1941 N.D. Laws, chap. 218.

39. 1975 N.D. Laws, chap. 465.

40. 1981 N.D. Laws, chaps. 243, 244.

41. For a journalistic assessment of the hospitality issue and the institutional norms, see Chuck Haga, "Lobbyist: Handouts Give Lobbyists Bad Public Image Elsewhere but in Bismarck, Legislators Say They Are Respected," *Grand Forks Herald,* December 15, 1974, pp. 13–14. Also see N.D. Cent. Code, Sec. 54.05-1-05.

42. Larry Dreyer, "Legislator and Lobbyist Views of Improper Lobbying in North Dakota," Special Report No. 40 (Grand Forks, N.D.: Bureau of Governmental Affairs, 1973). Also see Morgan Olson, "Legislative Perceptions of Lobbying in the North Dakota State Legislature" (Independent study, Department of Political Science, University of North Dakota, 1982).

43. "Legislative Perceptions of Lobbying," 15–17.

44. Bureau of Governmental Affairs poll conducted for the Farm Bureau (March 1985). The survey did reveal differences among Democrats and Republicans, with 22.9 percent of Democrats favoring more regulation.

45. The figures for registered lobbyists for the 1977–89 legislative sessions are 1977, 562; 1979, 568; 1981, 512; 1983, 461; 1985, 461; 1987, 390; 1989, 399.

46. The number does not include the PACs that registered to make contributions to the state's congressional candidates. It is not uncommon for several hundred PACs to register their contributions for U.S. Congress or U.S. Senate campaigns.

47. Pam Schmid, "N.D. Legislature Phone Operators' Days Aren't Dull," *Grand Forks Herald,* April 3, 1989.

48. Keith Hamm, Charles Wiggins, and Charles Bell, "Interest Group Involvement, Conflict and Success in State Legislatures" (Paper presented at the annual meeting of the American Political Science Association, September 1983, Chicago).

49. Thomas Quentin Jones, "Factors Leading to Interest Group Success in the North Dakota Legislative Process" (M.A. thesis, University of North Dakota, Grand Forks, 1977).

50. Poll conducted for the North Dakota Farm Bureau by the Bureau of Governmental Affairs, University of North Dakota, February 1987. Providing needed testimony was seen as an important service by 37.2 percent, helping legislators to understand issues, 31.8 percent; answering questions of legislators, 10.1 percent; and informing legislators of stands of their members, 5.4 percent.

51. Bureau of Governmental Affairs poll, March 2–4, 1987.

52. "Here's What the Election Means as Readers See It," Special letters section, *Grand Forks Herald,* December 17, 1989.

53. Abney and Lauth, "Interest Group Influence in the States," Table 3.

54. Basin Electric, which operates numerous power plants and the coal gasification plant, noted extensive contacts with the Public Service Commission, the State Water Commission, the tax commissioner's office, Job Service, the Department of Labor, the Economic Development Commission, the Department of Health, the Energy Impact Office (intense involvement), the attorney general's office, and the Industrial Commission (interview with author).

55. Theodore B. Pedeliski, "The Gubernatorial Transition in North Dakota, 1984–1985: Battling It Out in the Budgetary Badlands," in Thad Beyle, ed., *Gubernatorial Transitions: 1983–84 Elections* (Durham, N.C.: Duke University Press, 1988), 140–42.

56. *Association of Retarded Citizens v. Allan Olson* 561 F.Supp. 470 (1982).

57. See Sarah McCally Morehouse, *State Politics, Parties and Policy* (New York: Holt, Rinehart & Winston, 1981), 101–7.

58. Ibid., 111–12. Morehouse based her information on the narrative in Neal Peirce, *The Nine Great Plains States* (New York: W. W. Norton, 1973), 151–73.

59. Hal Simons, "They Influence North Dakota Government," *Fargo Forum,* October 23, 1977, D1–D3.

60. This finding parallels that of Harmon Zeigler and Michael Baer for Oregon (also a state with a moralistic political culture). See their *Lobbying: Interaction and Influence in American State Legislatures* (Belmont, Calif.: Wadsworth, 1969), 86.

61. Abney and Lauth, "Interest Group Influence in the States."

OHIO

A Plethora of Pluralism

FREDRIC N. BOLOTIN

Although not great in size (only 41,330 square
miles—the 16th smallest state), Ohio is very diverse in terms of population, economy, culture,
and politics. The types and influence of interest
groups are equally diverse. Although such diversity often is associated
with a weak interest group system, Ohio does not precisely fit this mold.
The pluralistic nature of Ohio politics may prevent dominance by any
particular group, but it has not limited the cumulative effect of group
efforts at influencing the policy process. The keys to understanding the
politics of Ohio and the role of interest groups in the political process are
the various aspects of the state's demographic and economic diversity.

Ohio is perceived as being a major industrial state, especially in the
Midwest. While manufacturing has been, and still is, an important part
of the economy, Ohio ranks 12th among the states in agricultural production. It is a major producer of corn, oats, and soybeans. The overall
economy, as far as income and employment are concerned, has declined
in relation to that of the nation as a whole and even compared to that of
the Great Lake states since 1970.[1] Per capita income in Ohio is less than
the national average.

The deterioration of the economy can be attributed to several factors, most of them related to its reliance on manufacturing. Industry and
people have migrated to the Sunbelt. Employment in the manufacture of
durable goods, on which Ohio has been quite reliant, has declined even
when output has grown. Manufacturing jobs in the state decreased by
more than 8 percent from 1970 to 1977[2] and continued to skid in the
1980s.

243

As a result, many of the major industrial areas in Ohio are trying to transform themselves into service centers. For example, the labor force in Akron, once the rubber capital of the world, is composed mainly of white-collar workers. Columbus is developing as a research and technology center,[3] and the abandoned industrial warehouses in Cleveland are being redeveloped into lofts and retail boutiques.

The socioeconomic composition of the state, however, is anything but homogeneous. Ohio often is described as consisting of four regions, delineated along north-south and east-west dimensions.[4] The northeast is the most industrialized part of the state. Its location along Lake Erie provided the area with an important source of transportation in its early settlement. The building of the Ohio-Erie Canal and later development of land transportation (e.g., railroads and highways) enhanced the region's value for industrial and commercial growth.[5] Cleveland is the dominant city in this area, serving as the center of industrial, commercial, and financial activity.

The northwest region is primarily rural. The fertile land accounts for the fact that much of the state's agriculture is located here. Toledo, the largest city in the area, has developed as an industrial site as well as being the commercial center.

Transportation channels help to explain the development of the southwest territory. The Ohio River and the old National Road provided the access necessary to make this area the first important commercial and agricultural center in the state.[6] The region has become highly industrialized and urbanized. Three of the six largest cities in the state—Columbus (the state capital), Cincinnati, and Dayton—are located here. Over 80 percent of the region's population lives in urban areas.

Finally, the southeast is the most rural, economically depressed region of Ohio. Located along the West Virginia border, this area shares its neighbor's persistent problems of unemployment and poverty. Much of the land is ill-suited for agriculture. The natural resources (coal, iron ore, and limestone) of the area provided the impetus for some small factories, but depletion and a drop in demand, have taken their toll on the economy and the population. Only two of thirteen counties here are located in a Standard Metropolitan Statistical Area (SMSA); in both instances, the central city is in West Virginia.

Ohio is thought of as a largely urbanized state; in 1980 more than 73 percent of the population lived in urban areas. However, this figure represented a decline of nearly 1.5 percent from the previous census—the first such decline in the state's history. The decline can be attributed to population loss in the major urban areas (population greater than 100,000). Population in the medium and small urban areas increased during the 1970s. Much of this migration is due to the perceived deterioration of economic and social conditions in the large cities and the relocation of business and industry away from the cities to save on taxes and other costs.[7]

Ohio's population has been described as "that of a patchwork quilt of different racial and ethnic groups sewn together by the state's economy and public institutions."[8] About 40 percent of geographic Ohio lies in the Appalachians. This large proportion and the mobility of the region's people to other parts of the state have produced an Appalachian subculture characterized by belief in hard work, justice, and fundamentalist religion.[9] The overall population includes over 12 percent foreign stock (people born in a foreign country or whose parents were born in another country). Most tend to be concentrated in the major urban areas. Ethnic groups in Ohio, not unlike those in other states, tend to segregate into communities within the urban areas. The principal ethnic groups are German, Italian, Polish, British, and Slovak. There is also a growing number of Hispanics moving to Ohio.

According to the 1980 census, approximately 10 percent of Ohio's population is black. As with the people of foreign stock, blacks are concentrated in the major cities. For example, blacks constitute nearly 40 percent of the population in Cleveland. There is a great deal of residential segregation. Such racial concentrations make blacks much more of a factor in politics on the local level than on the state level.

In the state as a whole the population has remained fairly static, increasing 1.3 percent from 1970 to 1980. Population projections through the end of the century indicate a slight increase, of 3.9 percent, from 1980 through 2000.[10] This pattern is typical of most Frostbelt states, in contrast to the southern and western states, where population increases were much greater. One result has been a decrease in Ohio's congressional influence in Washington. In 1982 Ohio lost two members from its delegation of twenty-three in the House of Representatives. It lost two more seats after the 1990 census.

The Politics of Government
and the Governing of Politics

It is difficult to discuss an overall political culture in Ohio. Elazar describes the state as having an individualistic culture with a strong moralistic strain.[11] It is characterized by strong party cohesiveness, patronage, and a government that serves as a marketplace in responding to demands. Although he classifies the state's political culture as individualistic, Elazar makes special note that Ohio has "strong traces of M[oral-istic dominant culture] in [its] northern counties and T[raditionalistic dominant culture] in [its] southern counties."[12] He basically groups political culture in Ohio with that of most of the other northern industrial states.

In another sense, however, the political culture in Ohio differs greatly from the liberal or progressive behavior one would expect from urbanized, industrial states. Ohio has, overall, a conservative political climate. Hibbeln stresses the importance of tradition in explaining Ohio's political behavior.[13] Gargan and Coke attribute it to "settlement patterns, ethnicity, urbanization and moralism."[14] The result is a somewhat parochial, antigovernment attitude.[15] Again, it would be a mistake to apply this generalization equally throughout the state. The northern (especially the northeastern) region is more liberal than the rest of the state.

Something of a discrepancy, however, exists between the overall political culture and the behavior of the electorate over the 1980s. Although Ohio voted Republican in every presidential election from 1976 to 1988, no Republican won a statewide (nonjudicial) election after 1978 until George Voinovich was elected governor in 1990. James A. Rhodes, the last Republican governor before Voinovich, was soundly defeated in his 1986 attempt to regain the office.

The current partisan political situation in Ohio is both advantageous and limiting to interest groups concerned with influencing legislation. Although conservative in nature, Ohio is not a one-party state. On the one hand, this situation provides interest groups with multiple points of access in the political system. On the other hand, a group cannot assume that a legislative coalition that it shapes today will remain intact for long.

The increasing competition within the strong two-party system is evident in the shifts of one-party control. One party has controlled both houses of the legislature during thirty-six years since 1945. In twenty-six of those years the Republicans controlled the legislature, as compared with only ten years of Democratic control. Since 1973, however, there has been one-party control in eight years—all Democratic. Although one might conclude that a realignment took place which resulted in a shift to one-party Democratic control, consideration of control of the executive branch refutes that suggestion. In only sixteen years since 1945 was there total one-party control (governor and both houses of the legislature) of state government, with twelve of those years under the Republicans. Since 1973, however, total control was achieved in only one election, by the Democrats from 1983 to 1984.

Strong interparty competition often has been associated with weak interest groups.[16] Although parties want the electoral support of interest groups, they must build the broadest coalition possible. That reduces the influence of interest groups somewhat. As with most other things, it would be a mistake to assume that Ohio fits the general pattern with regard to the relationship between party competition and interest group strength. The political process that operates in the state Senate differs greatly from that in the House.

The Democrats have controlled the Ohio House of Representatives since 1973, usually with a comfortable majority of the ninety-nine seats. Vernal G. Riffe has been Speaker of the House since 1977. Because of this majority and Riffe's unchallenged position, the party is fairly cohesive. The Speaker is able to exercise a great deal of control over the Democrats because of his influence in committee assignments and a variety of other political amenities he can use as incentives. He is able to keep the Democrats generally accountable to the party position. In addition, the safe advantage over the Republicans in the House can accommodate limited dissent within the party ranks without jeopardizing the party stand. This factor can be especially important when constituent opinion on an issue in a particular district differs from the party platform. In such instances the legislator can vote the local interest, which will help his or her reelection chances, without alienating the party leadership.

In contrast, the majority party in the Ohio Senate has changed three times since 1980. In 1985 the Republicans held a majority of one in the thirty-three-seat upper house. It often is a difficult task for Majority Leader Paul Gillmor to hold the Republican coalition together. Senators can exert more influence and independence than can state representatives. Gillmor must be willing to compromise to meet the needs and demands of all Republicans because any dissent threatens the party position. Thus he cannot control the Senate in the same way that Speaker Riffe controls the House.

Another important point of access for interest groups is in the executive branch. Although the overall formal powers of the office have been rated as moderate by Beyle,[17] the governor plays a major role in the policy process. Perhaps most important to interest groups, the governor has complete responsibility and control—not unlike the case in most states—over the formulation of the state budget. Before the legislature begins debate on the budget, interest groups present and lobby their agendas to the individual agencies and the governor. Interest groups have a much greater chance of achieving their goals if they can persuade the governor to include them in his or her budget than if they must try an "end run" by going over the governor's head to the General Assembly.

Two other powers of the governor make him or her a very important target of interest groups and their lobbyists: veto and appointment. The governor may veto any measure passed by the General Assembly and has line-item veto power over appropriation bills. A three-fifths vote of each house is required to override. Interest groups are thus provide with a second chance if they are unsuccessful at preventing the legislature from passing a bill.

For example, a major lobbying effort by organized labor and consumer groups, led by the Ohio Public Interest Campaign, was able to delay, but not prevent, the legislature from passing a Tort Reform Bill (which limits awards in work-related and other injury claims). These groups then successfully lobbied Governor Richard Celeste for a veto of the bill. Of course, groups are not always successful in securing a gubernatorial veto. Despite another strong effort, which included a personal appeal from Ralph Nader, Celeste signed into law a revised version of the Tort Reform Act in October 1987.

Also of major concern to interest groups is the governor's substantial power of appointment. The governor (with consent of the Senate) appoints the head of all but one of the twenty-three departments within the executive branch. In addition, he or she appoints members of most of the boards and commissions and some of the heads of divisions within the departments. Much effort is expended by major interest groups in influencing gubernatorial appointments.

During transitional periods between the election and the start of a new governor's term, and whenever a vacancy occurs during a term, relevant groups seek meetings with the governor to provide input into the appointment process. Many appointments are made to appease interest groups or to reward individuals or groups for electoral support. Such practice at times has resulted in controversy and embarrassment for the governor. James E. Rogers, a supporter of Celeste and a former director of the 21st District Caucus, was given a cabinet post as head of the Department of Youth Services (DYS). Less than two years later he was forced to resign after it was discovered that he had awarded contracts to his friends and had hired convicted drug felons for jobs in DYS.[18]

The Regulation of Interest Groups and Lobbying Activity

The General Assembly in Ohio has the authority to regulate interest groups and lobbyists within the state. In reality, this regulation is limited almost exclusively to monitoring. Individuals who lobby the legislature are required to register with the clerk of the Ohio Senate in even-numbered years. New lobbyists must register within ten days of employment. Lobbyists must register as individuals and also in the name of the person or group on whose behalf lobbying will be done. The registration rules are quite comprehensive. Legislative agents from government agencies, those representing not-for-profit groups, and even individuals who lobby on their own must register, in addition to those lobbying on behalf of for-profit causes. There is one major restriction in regard to who can act as a lobbyist: elected state officials are prohibited from lobbying for one year after leaving office. This provision in the Ethics Law was designed to prevent even the appearance of a conflict of interest.

In addition to registering, lobbyists must report a specific list of amounts spent on government officials, as well as total expenses. There are, however, no limits on the amount that can be spent. One of the only substantive restrictions is that lobbyists are prohibited from working on a contingency fee.

As in most states, interest groups attempt to influence electoral outcomes by donating money to those seeking office. Corporations and groups in Ohio are prohibited from using funds from their treasuries to support candidates. They must establish political action committees (PACs) to collect and disseminate funds. As with the laws concerning lobbying, the laws governing PACs monitor rather than regulate or restrict campaign funding. There is no limit on the amount that a PAC can donate to a candidate seeking state office. PACs are required to file reports listing contributions received and donations made to all campaigns. These reports are filed and, in general, forgotten. There is, in reality, minimal regulation of interest group or PAC activity.

The Universe of Groups

Interest groups are numerous and quite diverse in Ohio. As of March 12, 1987, there were 651 groups with registered legislative lobbyists, ranging from the American Automobile Association to the Youth Services Department of Ohio. Table 11.1 lists the number of groups and the number of lobbyists by interest area.

Fifteen percent of the groups represent business (24 groups) and industry (72 groups). These groups are represented by 159 lobbyists. The groups vary from interest-wide coalitions such as the Ohio Manufacturers' Association to groups representing specific corporations such as the Ford Motor Co. Many of the groups representing specific companies

Table 11.1. Number of groups and lobbyists of Ohio interests represented by ten or more lobbyists, by type of interest, 1987

Interest	No. of Groups	No. of Lobbyists
Industry	72	113
Labor/Professional groups	65	139
Medical/Health care	44	110
Education	40	72
State government agencies	25	168
Business	24	46
Banking/Finance	23	42
Insurance	20	29
State government boards	19	47
Single-interest groups	16	25
Law/Lobby/Public relations	15	45
Mining Petroleum	15	26
Communication	15	23
Recreation/Leisure	15	19
Political/Public interest	14	34
Automobile	13	31
Local governments	13	28
Utilities	13	28
Law enforcement/Justice	11	27
Construction	10	19
Agriculture/Dairy	10	17
Transportation	7	15
Alcohol/Liquor	7	13
Media/Press	7	13
Environment	4	33
Chamber of Commerce	4	11
Mentally retarded	3	10
Federal agencies	1	23
Governor's office	1	13
Self-employed	--	24

Source: Joint Committee on Agency Rule Review, 117th Ohio General Assembly, March 12, 1987.

devote most of their lobbying efforts to obtaining legislation or contracts promoting a particular company, rather than broader legislation beneficial to industry or business in general.

The second largest category comprises labor unions (25 groups) and professional and trade associations (40 groups). These groups range from the Ohio AFL-CIO and Ohio D.R.I.V.E. (the Teamsters' PAC) to the Air Transport Association and the Ohio State Medical Association (OSMA). The trade associations include such groups as the Ohio Coin Dealers' Association and the Ohio Brewers' Association. In all, 139 people are registered to lobby on behalf of the groups in this category.

Two other issue areas are each represented by more than 5 percent of the total number of groups. There are 44 medical/health-related groups, which range from the Ohio Nurses Association to the Cleveland Clinic Foundation, one of the country's most highly regarded hospitals. It should be noted that groups such as the OSMA were included with medical/health groups as well as with professional associations. Education, with 40 groups, is the other interest represented by more than 5 percent of all groups.

Another major category is made up of government and public sector groups. The most active and largest in number are the state agencies and departments: 168 people are registered as legislative liaisons on behalf of 25 government departments. In addition, 19 state government boards have legislative liaisons. The most visible agencies, as measured by the number of lobbyists, are the Department of Natural Resources (25), the Office of Budget and Management (24), and the Department of Mental Health (21). On the other hand, the Department of Education has only 1 liaison, probably because the issues relating to this department can be promoted by the 40 education-oriented interest groups that can exert a cumulative influence on the legislature. The number of government liaisons need not determine the success of the department's legislative efforts.

Local governments (cities and counties) also have taken to lobbying the state legislature. The competition for state funding of local projects has developed to the point where 17 local governments and local governmental boards have liaisons registered with the General Assembly.

A conglomeration of nonprofit, public interest, and special interest groups can be classified as the citizens' lobby. This lobby includes groups such as the Ohio Public Interest Campaign and Common Cause, as well as the Ohio Chapter of the Association for Retarded Citizens and the Ohio Right-to-Life Society. Such groups consist mainly of volunteers and rely heavily on the grass-roots efforts of members as well as registered lobbyists.

Finally, there are the self-employed or individual lobbyists. These are people who lobby for personal or pet projects on their own. Twenty-four people are registered as self-employed lobbyists. Their influence on major public policy is, of course, minimal.

Ohio's Lobbyists

As of March 12, 1987, there were 1,027 registered legislative agents authorized to lobby at the capital. This number includes those who work full time in the capitol or other government offices in the capital and also those who may never journey to Columbus. As in many other states, lobbyists can be classified into five categories: contract lobbyists, in-house lobbyists, legislative liaisons, citizen/public interest lobbyists, and individuals. The last two categories were discussed above, and thus the first three categories are given attention here.

The most noticeable, in influence if not in number, are the contract lobbyists. These people make themselves available for hire to groups seeking help in influencing policy. More and more, the story of interest group politics in Ohio is becoming the story of the contract lobbyist. There are fifty contract lobbyists who represent two or more interests. Although they account for only about 5 percent of all registered lobbyists, they (collectively) represent more than 315 groups (nearly 50 percent of all groups).[19] This figure is somewhat overstated in that some groups are represented by more than one of these contract lobbyists. A consulting firm that is hired by a group may register more than one of its people as lobbyists for the group. For example, Success Marketing, Inc., has three of its lobbyists registered to lobby for Blue Cross and Blue Shield of Ohio, and five for Local 11 of the Ohio Civil Service Employees Association (OCSEA). Some are retained on a continuous basis, and others are contracted only to lobby for one particular bill.

Table 11.2 lists the major contract lobbyists according to the number of groups they represent. Twelve of these lobbyists represent at least ten groups; four top the list, claiming sixteen different interests as clients.

The second category comprises the in-house lobbyists. This group consists of people whose duties as employees or members of an organization include lobbying. The extent of the lobbying effort put forth varies from those hired primarily (or exclusively) to lobby, such as John C. Mahoney, Jr., of the Ohio Council of Retail Merchants, to those who receive no compensation for lobbying, such as members of the Ohio Public Interest Campaign, a citizens' group.

Table 11.2. Number of groups represented by multiclient contract lobbyists in Ohio, 1987

Lobbyists	No. of Groups
Michael Bateson	16
Neil S. Clark	16
Stephen C. Landerman	16
Dennis L. Wojtanoski	16
Howard R. Collier	15
Eugene O'Grady	14
N. Victor Goodman	13
Keith H. Brooks	12
James F. DeLeone	12
Kevin L. Futryk	11
William P. Lewis	10
Kent B. McGough	10
Joseph F. McKeon	9
Edward J. Orlet	9
Paul Tipps	9
John Gilchrist	8
Robert C. McEaneney	7
Gordon M. Scherer	7

Source: Joint Committee on Agency Rule Review, 1987.

Legislative liaisons, a third category, often are not thought of as lobbyists either by legislators or even by the liaisons themselves. Of the nongovernmental liaisons, some may have no contact with policy makers if no issues of concern are raised during the year. In addition, most who do not live in the Columbus area never travel to the capital for personal contact with policy makers.

Included among liaisons are many of the 212 (more than 20 percent of all registered lobbyists) representing state agencies. The role of the liaison varies across government agencies; many liaisons play primarily an informational role. Liaisons monitor the progress of bills affecting their agencies. Some represent agency interests to both the legislature and the governor. In some cases they work with or even coordinate lobbyists whose groups share goals with those of an agency. For example, liaisons from the Department of Education often work in cooperation with groups such as the Ohio Education Association (OEA, made up of teachers and school personnel) in promoting education interests in the state legislature.

Lobbying in Ohio is still very much a male-dominated world. Three out of four registered lobbyists are men. Among contract lobbyists the distribution is skewed even more—only 4 percent are female. These women represent only eight groups, about 2 percent of all groups represented by contract lobbyists. Most of the female lobbyists represent government agencies.

Among contract lobbyists, many have had experience as lobbyists for a particular group before going out on their own. Increasingly, some of the most successful come from within the legislature itself—either as elected representatives or as members of a legislative staff.

Background within the legislature provides a significant advantage. As one legislative aide describes it:

> [T]hese people know the capitol like the back of their hands. They know the legislative process as well as anyone and know what strings to pull, when. After working with a person for so long, you develop a friendship, or at least mutual respect. These relationships and knowledge aren't left at the clerk's office when you leave the legislature. It provides a tremendous advantage to the legislative aide turned lobbyist.

Some of the staff members interviewed commented that there seems to be an increased tendency for highly skilled people to spend four or five years working in the legislature to gain experience and then make the jump to the more lucrative part of the political process—lobbying. The ethics law requiring a one-year hiatus for those wishing to become lobbyists is applicable only to elected officials, not to members of legislative staffs. A legislative aide could quit one morning and come back to the same office after lunch as a lobbyist.

In general, legislators view lobbyists favorably. They are looked to as information sources. As a leader in the Republican caucus in the Ohio Senate explained it, the legislature has an underdeveloped partisan staff. There also is almost no legislative oversight in the form of program analysis. Lobbyists who provide honest information about policy impact perform a service both to the legislature and to themselves. Alternatively, as one legislator remarked, lobbyists who provide false or inaccurate information don't last long. Their credibility, and thus their effectiveness, vanishes quickly.

Group Lobbying Tactics

In all states the goal of lobbying is to influence policy. In most respects, the methods used by interest groups in Ohio are the same as those employed by groups in any state. Success usually depends on information, organization, and resources. Nevertheless, several tactics, although not necessarily unique to Ohio, distinguish the role of Ohio interest groups.

Interest groups play an important role in the electoral process, especially those with sizable financial resources. There is no limit to the amount of money that a candidate can spend running for office or a group can donate to a campaign for state office. Interest groups donate generously through PACs. Most legislators, however, find interest groups to be more reactive than proactive. Contributions tend to come to incumbents who have supported a group's position rather than as an incentive to change positions. The fact that contributions are not limited, as they are in federal elections, provides groups with a powerful tool. It is difficult to estimate which particular groups play the biggest role in the electoral process, however, because there is no compilation of PAC expenditures, either individually or in the aggregate.

Political contributions help to provide another explanation for the success of the contract lobbyists. Contract lobbyists collect money (for campaign expenditures) from their various clients. As a result, each of these lobbyists has a large pool of money to distribute among candidates. For example, Robert C. McEaneney, a major contract lobbyist, donated a total of $24,250 to Governor Celeste and Speaker Riffe from 1982 to 1986.[20]

Resources in terms of numbers (which can translate into votes) and, especially, money still reign supreme. Interest groups spend a great deal of time and money entertaining policy makers. The tactics employed have been limited since 1970 as ethical issues have gained more attention. "Dinners and receptions have replaced hotel suites and women," according to a ten-year veteran at the capitol. It is not uncommon, especially near the close of a session, for legislators to have their choice of dinner invitations every night of the week. Such invitations may be arranged to discuss specific legislation, to provide information, or even to furnish a demonstration of some new service or product by a specific business or corporation. AT&T, for example, has at times invited groups of legislators and/or bureaucrats to receptions at which new telecommunications systems were demonstrated.

Groups attempt to influence the executive branch in a variety of ways. In addition to campaign contributions and their efforts to affect administrative appointments, as discussed earlier, groups provide information to agencies and often work with them to achieve legislative results. The OEA joins with the Department of Education, for example, in attempting to procure favorable budgetary decisions from both the governor and the General Assembly.

Groups also have been successful in lobbying for particular benefits. In what has developed as a scandal and an embarrassment to the governor, it has been discovered that Tele-Communications, Inc. (TCI), was granted some no-bid contracts to install telephone systems totaling more than $8 million in at least five administrative agencies and commissions since 1985.[21] These contracts were awarded despite rules requiring competitive bidding and despite the fact that agencies were being charged in some cases three times the price that other firms would have charged. Robert C. McEaneney, a lobbyist under contract with TCI, was employed as a consultant by the Ohio Bureau of Employment Services (OBES), which gave TCI $5.2 million worth of no-bid contracts. It has been reported that McEaneney was instrumental in introducing the chairman of TCI to officials at OBES.[22] An official at OBES, however, said that Governor Celeste's office had sent TCI to OBES.[23] The son-in-law of TCI's chairman "donated $50,000 to the reelection campaign of . . . Celeste last year and gave the Ohio Democratic Party, which was helping to finance Celeste's campaign, $100,000 more."[24] In addition, as stated above, McEaneney made significant contributions to the governor's campaign.

The executive/administrative branch also is involved in lobbying the legislature. The legislative liaisons from the governor's office and the state agencies often work closely with those at the capitol, testifying at hearings, monitoring the progress of bills, providing information, and persuading legislators on certain issues. The Office of Budget and Management's twenty-five registered liaisons explain the administration's budgetary decisions and advocate the approval of the governor's budget.

Another, although much more limited, point of access for interest group influence is the judicial system. Judicial interpretation can have a profound effect on policy. In addition to filing amicus briefs, groups can promote litigation by providing legal support to parties involved in judicial action. The AFL-CIO, the Teamsters, and other labor groups have been quite successful in obtaining favorable policy rulings from the Ohio Supreme Court regarding workers' compensation.

Interest group influence on the judiciary also is possible through the electoral process. In Ohio all state judges are elected by the people. PACs can play as important a role in supporting judicial candidates as they do with legislative candidates. Labor PACs, such as Ohio D.R.I.V.E. (Teamsters), were quite strong in their support for the reelection of Supreme Court Chief Justice Frank Celebreeze in 1986. The public, however, reacted negatively to reports of financial support from individuals and groups who had received favorable rulings from Celebreeze or who likely would be involved in Supreme Court litigation; Celebreeze was defeated.

Taking the Case Straight to the People

Interest groups have a potentially powerful tool at their disposal: direct democracy. Ohio offers the process of referendum as a means of preventing a newly enacted law from going into effect. Except for emergency legislation, which takes effect immediately, all laws become effective ninety days after approval. During this period, opponents of the law can circulate petitions to bring the statute to a vote of the electorate; if signatures are obtained totaling 10 percent of the vote in the previous gubernatorial election, the statute is suspended until the next statewide election, at which time the voters either approve or reject it.

Ohio also allows direct democracy to operate in the form of the initiative petition. In a manner similar to the referendum, if 10 percent of the registered voters sign the petition within ninety days, the question goes on the ballot in the next election. If approved, it becomes law. Ohio also has an indirect initiative by which a petition first forces the legislature to act on the issue. If the legislature rejects or significantly amends the initiative proposal, it then can be brought to the full electorate. Ohio is one of only four states that provide for both types of initiative and permit initiatives for both statutes and constitutional amendments.

The initiative and referendum were established to limit or counter the influence that special interests have on the legislature. It was argued that special interest lobbyists could ensure or block passage of legislation to the detriment of the general public. These efforts at direct democracy were seen as the poor man's lobby.[25]

Ironically, however, interest groups are a dominant force in the initiative and referendum. Organizing a petition drive is difficult and can be costly. Strong, wealthy groups are much better able to finance such an effort by employing people to circulate petitions. If an issue does get on the ballot, it is usually accomplished only by those groups that have the resources to launch a full media campaign in favor of or against the proposition.

The initiative has not been used very often in trying to amend the state constitution (thirty-eight times from 1898 to 1979) or statutes (eight times during that period). During this time period only 24 percent of the propositions were successful.[26] Initiatives may be the way to counter interest group influence on the legislature, but intensive efforts on the part of these groups seem very successful in influencing the electorate to reject the initiatives.

The most recent attempt at a constitutional initiative concerned the selection of state Appellate and Supreme Court judges. The League of Women Voters played a major role in coordinating the signature effort for placing the initiative for merit selection (rather than popular election) of judges on the November 1987 ballot. This controversial proposal received bipartisan opposition by the state political party organizations as well as a variety of powerful interest groups, such as the AFL-CIO. A major media campaign was launched to defeat the initiative under the auspices of a coalition of groups that organized as Ohioans for the Right to Vote. It was estimated that more than a million dollars was spent by the two sides.

Interest Group Power and Effectiveness

The true power of an interest group lies in its success in achieving its goals. Although groups may have a variety of goals, this chapter continues to focus on the effectiveness at achieving public policy goals in Ohio. The first observation to be made is that no interest group dominates the political scene. The 651 groups are indicative of the pluralistic nature of group politics in Ohio. This is not to say, however, that no groups are influential or that all groups are equally effective.

Interviews were conducted in 1987 with a nonrandom but cross-sectional (according to party and geographical area of representation) sample of both houses of the General Assembly and legislative staff members concerning the interests in which groups were most effective and the most influential groups overall. When asked to identify the interests in which group and lobbying efforts were most successful, respondents consistently acknowledged five types of interests (Table 11.3).

Table 11.3. Most influential interests lobbying the Ohio Legislature

Interest	No. of Groups Representing Interest	No. of Registered Lobbyists	% Identifying Interest as Influential[a]
Education	40	72	100
Business	24	46	89
Banking/Finance	23	42	83
Labor	24	65	78
Insurance	20	29	62

Source: Interviews with legislators and staff members, 1987.
[a]Percentage of those interviewed who listed the interest as among the five most influential.

Education was the only interest that was cited unanimously. This result is not surprising; as one senator remarked, "Who would be against education?" Seventy-two registered lobbyists represent forty interest groups concerned with education. In addition, local governments often lobby for education. The more programs and financial aid provided by the state, the lower the property taxes can be kept at the local level.

Somewhat surprising is the fact that no group representing education was cited as being among the most effective. Nevertheless, according to many at the capitol, that is an asset to supporters of education. The groups reinforce and strengthen each other. If one group loses favor, another can keep the interest promoted. A case in point concerns the OEA. In 1986 the OEA fought hard to defeat Bill Hinig, chairman of the House Finance and Appropriations Committee. The group was unsuccessful, as Hinig won reelection. As a result, however, the OEA is out of favor both with Hinig and, more important, with his supporter, Speaker Riffe. The other groups, though, can continue to promote policies in this issue area. Thus, though the OEA has lost much of its influence, the education lobby is still strong.

In contrast to education, which is concerned with relatively few policy issues, the next three most successful types of groups (Table 11.3) all are concerned with a broader range of issues. It is not surprising that business (24 groups), banking and finance (23 groups), and labor (24 groups) were ranked highly in an urbanized state. The interest that finished 5th, but significantly below labor, was insurance. There was little consistency among either legislators or their aides in identifying other powerful interests in Ohio.

Table 11.4 lists the specific interest groups that most frequently were

Table 11.4. Most influential interest groups in Ohio

Group	No. of Lobbyists	% Identifying Group as Influential
Ohio Council of Retail Merchants	5	95
Ohio State Medical Association	8	88
Ohio Bankers Association	3	63
Ohio Manufacturers Association	16	47
Ohio Association of Realtors	4	42

Source: Interviews with legislators and staff members, 1987.

mentioned as being the most influential by legislators and staff members. This list provides another indication of the cumulative as opposed to individual impact of interest groups in Ohio. Of the five most successful groups, only two represent interests that appear in Table 11.3.

The Ohio Council of Retail Merchants (OCRM) is the trade association for retailers throughout Ohio. Although it was cited most often as being successful, this result may be attributable simply to general sympathy in the legislature toward the interest in general. It is an umbrella organization with members in every legislative district. It also is *the* group representing retail merchants. Influence in this case may be a function more of the group's resources (size and financial) than of the skill of an individual lobbyist. A significant number of those interviewed commented that John C. Mahoney, Jr., OCRM's chief lobbyist, was not well regarded for his lobbying skill. Two legislative aides (representing different political parties) suggested that OCRM was effective despite, not because of, Mahoney's efforts.

Of the other groups mentioned most often, only the Ohio Bankers Association represented one of the interests rated as most influential. The Ohio State Medical Association, the professional association of doctors, was very influential in lobbying for the Tort Reform Act discussed earlier. This group is also represented by members in every community in the state. In fact, it is not unusual for legislators' personal physicians to lobby informally on behalf of the group. The Ohio Manufacturers Association (OMA) has been active in lobbying for economic development policies. In the mid-1980s it was successful in securing passage of revisions to the laws governing the establishment of PACs which now allow for corporation funds to be used to pay the costs of setting up a PAC.

Significantly, when asked to identify both the most important interests and the most effective groups, respondents placed the general category of contract lobbyist—neither an interest nor a group—at or near the top of every list. Previous relationships with the legislature were cited consistently as a primary reason for the success of contract lobbyists. Since this "group" was seen as being very influential, legislators were asked to identify up to five contract lobbyists that they rated as most powerful (Table 11.5). There were no unanimous selections. Since many found it unrealistic to distinguish rank within their own lists, the order of mention was not used in compiling these results. Dennis L. Wojtanoski, a former state representative, was mentioned most often. It should be noted that, as either a possible cause or effect of his success, no other contract lobbyist is registered as representing more groups (16) than Wojtanoski.

Table 11.5. Most influential independent lobbyists in Ohio

Lobbyist	% Identifying Lobbyists as Influential[a]
Dennis L. Wojtanoski	95
Paul Tipps	89
Robert C. McEaneney	82
Eugene P. O'Grady	78
Harry J. Lehman	76

Source: Interviews with legislators and staff members, 1987.

[a]Percentage of those interviewed who listed the lobbyist as among the five most influential independent lobbyists.

It is interesting to juxtapose Table 11.5 with Table 11.2 and note that three of the contract lobbyists rated as most effective in Table 11.5 do not rank high in Table 11.2. Paul Tipps represents nine groups; Robert C. McEaneney, seven; and Harry J. Lehman, only six. This result tends to indicate that having a large number of clients is neither necessary nor sufficient for maximizing influence on the legislative process. Indeed, some legislators cautioned that a lobbyist could lose effectiveness if he took on too many clients.

The ability of contract lobbyists also becomes apparent when it is noted that certain interest groups with their own lobbyists on occasion employ one of these major lobbyists on contract to lobby for specific policies or legislation. For example, included among the sixteen lobbyists of the Ohio Manufacturers Association is William D. Kloss, a contract lobbyist who represents five different groups. According to most legislators, the growth of independent lobbyists since the mid-1970s, at least in part, has redesigned the role of interest groups in Ohio politics. Legislators expect the role of contract lobbyists to continue to expand.

Conclusion

Morehouse described Ohio as a state in which pressure groups are moderately strong.[27] This claim could still be made; however, such an oversimplified categorization might lead to an assumption that interest group strength and activity has remained stable. It would be more accurate to describe Ohio as a state where groups have significant influence, but where no single group or set of groups dominates the policy process. Morehouse identifies five groups (actually some groups and some interests) as being significant.[28] Of those five, four were identified as being among the most influential interests in the present research. Two of Morehouse's interests (banking and savings and loan associations) fall within one category—banking/finance—used in this chapter. Another (Chamber of Commerce) is included here as part of business interests. Missing from her list are labor and the interest found to be the most influential—education. One reason for this difference may be that no education interest group is particularly powerful, but collectively the forty groups lobbying for education have achieved great success.

Ohio is a pluralistic state in every sense of the concept. The economic, geographic, political, and social diversity makes it difficult for an interest group to establish predominance throughout the state. The existence of a large number of groups is a response to this diversity. The trend toward the professionalization of lobbying, however, as indicated by the noted importance of the contract lobbyist, appears to represent a shift in tactics and effectiveness. The lobbyist, rather than the interest, is being recognized for his or her success. The total amount of resources made available to the contract lobbyist by the groups he or she represents facilitates effectiveness. This development, combined with the cumulative effects of a large number of groups associated with the same interest, suggests that group politics can be influential even though groups are only moderately strong.

Notes

1. Carl Lieberman, "Ohio: The Environment for Political Activity," in Carl Lieberman, ed., *Government and Politics in Ohio* (Lanham, Md.: University Press of America, 1984), 9.

2. Ibid., 10.

3. Ibid., 8.

4. See, for example, Joseph Spinelli and Sherstha Mohan, "The Many Faces of the State," in William O. Reichert and Steven O. Ludd, eds., *Outlook on Ohio: Prospects and Priorities in Public Policy* (Palisades Park, N.J.: Commonwealth Books, 1983), 4–32, and Donald J. Bogue and Calvin L. Beale, *Economic Areas of the United States* (New York: Free Press, 1961).

5. Spinelli and Mohan, "Many Faces of the State," 5.

6. Ibid.

7. Ibid., 12–22.

8. Kent Schwirian, "The Socio-Cultural Groups in Ohio," in Reichert and Ludd, eds., *Outlook on Ohio*, 33.

9. Ibid., 34.

10. Ohio Data Users Center, *Population Projections, Ohio and Counties, by Age and Sex: 1980 to 2005* (Columbus: Ohio Department of Development, 1982).

11. Daniel J. Elazar, *American Federalism: A View from the States,* 3d ed. (New York: Harper & Row, 1984), 135–36.

12. Ibid., 136.

13. H. Kenneth Hibbeln, "The Political Decision Making Process in Ohio," in Reichert and Ludd, eds., *Outlook on Ohio,* 198–216.

14. John J. Gargan and James G. Coke, "The Study of Ohio Government and Politics," in John J. Gargan and James G. Coke, eds., *Political Behavior and Public Issues in Ohio* (Kent, Ohio: Kent State University Press, 1972), 16.

15. Hibbeln, "Decision Making Process," 198.

16. L. Harmon Zeigler, "Interest Groups in the States," in Virginia Gray, Herbert Jacob, and Kenneth N. Vines, eds., *Politics in the American States,* 4th ed. (Boston: Little, Brown, 1983), 97–132.

17. Thad L. Beyle, "Governors," in Gray, Jacob, and Vines, eds., *Politics in the American States,* 202.

18. *Plain Dealer* (Cleveland), May 4, 1985, 1A.

19. Joint Committee on Agency Rule Review, "List of Legislative Agents" (117th Ohio General Assembly).

20. *Plain Dealer,* September 21, 1987, 1A.

21. Ibid., October 10, 1987, 11.

22. Ibid., October 5, 1987, 1A.

23. Ibid., October 10, 1987, 1A.

24. Ibid., 8A.

25. Michael J. Ross, *State and Local Politics and Policy: Change and Reform* (Englewood Cliffs: Prentice-Hall, 1987), 76.

26. David Magleby, *Direct Legislation* (Baltimore: Johns Hopkins University Press, 1984), 71.

27. Sarah McCally Morehouse, *State Politics, Parties and Policy* (New York: Holt, Rinehart & Winston, 1981), 110.

28. Ibid.

OKLAHOMA

Group Power
in Transition

ROBERT E. ENGLAND
and DAVID R. MORGAN

In his early study of lobbyists in Oklahoma, political scientist Samuel Patterson posits a symbiotic relationship between interest group representatives and legislators: "One of the most crucial relationships in the American political system is that between the lobbyist and the legislator. . . . The lobby role is functional for the maintenance of the legislative system."[1] Survey data collected in 1986 from members of the state legislature and registered lobbyists in Oklahoma suggest that the legislator-lobbyist nexus continues to be salient. Group representatives, for example, report that about 82 percent of their lobbying time is directed toward the state legislature. In turn, state policy makers rate the influence of interest groups on the legislative process as "crucial" (10 percent), "very important" (44 percent), or "important" (42 percent).[2]

What *has* changed over time in Oklahoma is the relative influence of various pressure groups. In fact, it is our thesis that group power in Oklahoma is currently in a state of transition. While the influence of some historically powerful interests remains entrenched, other groups seem to either be declining in influence or changing their primary locus of attention from Oklahoma City to Washington, D.C. Also, new "brokers of power" appear to be emerging concomitant with the changing Oklahoma social, economic, and political milieu. To better understand past and present interest group power in the Sooner state, a brief overview of the socioeconomic and political environment is required.

Socioeconomic and Political Environment

Oklahoma is a state of competing images. The Bureau of the Census classifies the state as southern. For others, Oklahoma is part of "Middle America," characterized by agribusiness and a people who epitomize the traditional American virtues of family, church, and independence.[3] Still others contend that the state is in the midst of social, economic, and political transition. Kirkpatrick Sale, for instance, includes Oklahoma as part of the contemporary "power shift" from the eastern establishment to the newly emerging, economically and politically powerful Sunbelt.[4] Perhaps H. Wayne Morgan and Anne Hodges Morgan are correct in their assessment that Oklahoma is "one of those states without any intense sense of place in national thinking."[5] As a relatively new state that joined the Union only in 1907, Oklahoma is still in the process of development and maturation. Historically, the people of the state have had strong ties to the land through either agriculturally related endeavors or mineral extraction activities. These traditionally dominant economic interests are giving way, however, as the state becomes more urban and an attempt is made to diversify its economic base. Nevertheless, the rural frontier nature of Oklahoma has significantly affected the character of the state.

The Character of the State: A Traditional View

Historical, social, economic, and demographic characteristics of a state help shape its political outlook and behavior.[6] Daniel Elazar, for example, contends that such factors help to explain the presence of "political subcultures" among the states. He refers to Oklahoma's political culture as predominantly "traditionalistic" in nature, one that "retains some of the organic characteristics of the preindustrial social order."[7] The role of government is to maintain the status quo. A single political party usually dominates state politics, but party cohesion is weak, politics are personal, and politicians are personalities.[8]

The traditionalistic political culture is quite evident in Oklahoma's politics and history. Although the state is usually divided into a Republican north and Democratic south,[9] since statehood Oklahoma has remained a one- or modified one-party state controlled by the Democrats.[10] With respect to party cohesion in the state legislature, Stephen Jones asserts that "Oklahoma is a state in which the influence of pressure politics and local issues is greater than party cohesion or national issues."[11]

As a state with strong ties to the land, Oklahoma lacks much of the diversity associated with more urbanized, heterogeneous states. In 1980 Oklahoma ranked 25th among the states in percentage of population living in urban areas (67.3 percent).[12] In many respects, the state can be viewed as a collectivity of preurban, agriculturally based, small communities. The state contains only two moderately large cities: Oklahoma City and Tulsa. Of the remaining 579 municipalities, only 15 have 25,000 or more residents. Racial, ethnic, and religious differences in the state are minimal. Approximately 86 percent of the population is white (6.7 percent black, 5.7 percent Indian, and 1.9 percent Hispanic).[13] Not only is Oklahoma largely white, it is overwhelmingly Protestant, mostly fundamentalist. According to a religious census taken in 1971, about 33 percent of the state's population can be classified as fundamentalist, one of the highest percentages of any state in the Union.[14]

As in its sister states in the Deep South, where the traditionalistic political culture is also dominant, income in Oklahoma is maldistributed. In 1970, the most recent date such information is reported, Oklahoma ranked 9th in the nation in income concentration or inequality among its populace.[15] The state does not compare well to the rest of the nation on other important socioeconomic indicators. For instance, the combination of a high farm population (4.29 percent, 15th rank nationally), an annual value of less than $10,000 for products sold by about 60 percent of state farms, a low percentage of high school graduates (66 percent, 35th rank nationally), and a high percentage of persons aged 65 years or older (11.9 percent, 21st rank nationally) has not produced a prosperous citizenry. Oklahoma ranks 26th among the states in per capita personal income, 35th in median family income, and only 14 states have a higher percentage of persons living in poverty.[16]

Oklahoma's economy has always been heavily dependent on energy-related activities, first involving coal and later oil and natural gas. In 1982 Oklahoma ranked 5th and 3d nationally in crude petroleum and natural gas production, respectively. In the same year the value of mineral fuels to the state was a little more than $10.5 billion (5th rank nationally).

What does this overview of the traditional character of the state have to do with interest group activity? Previous research suggests that many of the characteristics associated with Oklahoma's socioeconomic and political environment should give rise to strong interest group power. Specifically, a rural agricultural economic base as opposed to a more urbanized industrial base, significant inequalities in the distribution of income among a state's populace, the presence of a limited number of dominant economic interests, and the general lack of wealth and interparty competition are conditions often positively correlated with

interest group influence.[17] In Oklahoma a few interest groups historically have played a prominent role in state affairs. Moreover, groups that
have traditionally been categorized as influential, such as the oil lobby,
agriculture, the Baptist church, and local officials, are still formidable
forces. But an important caveat is in order. Just as Oklahoma is under-
going tremendous social, economic, and political change, the interest
group universe is also in transition. We might contrast this transitional
theme with the more traditional perspective of the state outlined above.

The Character of the State: A Transitional Perspective

In a book entitled *Oklahoma: New Views of the Forty-Sixth State,*
Jerome O. Steffen and Douglas Hale in separate chapters attempt to
detail the changing nature of Oklahoma and its people. After tracing
stages of development in the state's history, Steffen concludes that, like
other states in the Southwest, "Oklahoma is on the verge of experiencing
a major growth period."[18] Recent data show that Oklahoma ranked 9th
nationally in net migration during the period 1980–86.[19] Steffen also
asserts that Oklahoma is becoming more urban and industrialized. He
traces, for instance, the growth of the two major metropolitan areas in
the state, Tulsa and Oklahoma City. The state's industrial base has expanded as well; data indicate that 15 percent of the nonagricultural
workforce was employed in manufacturing in 1985, compared to a figure of only 9.8 percent in 1950.[20]

Hale's message is quite similar: transitional Oklahoma is much different than traditional Oklahoma. After highlighting three previous
phases of development, he contends that the state at present is in an
"Age of Resurgence." This era began in the 1950s, following the difficult
years of the dust bowl and "Okie" out-migration. According to Hale,

> The primary thrust for this expansion was provided by the long-delayed
> emergence of a substantial manufacturing industry and the increasing influ-
> ence of the governmental sector of the economy. By 1980 manufacturing
> contributed more to the gross state product than any other enterprise. In the
> process of growth it diversified. No longer concentrated in the processing of
> primary products like food and petroleum, the state has shifted into the
> high-income production of machinery, electronics equipment, and fabri-
> cated metals.[21]

In brief, Oklahoma is changing. Economic development is the
"buzz" word among state and local officials. Interparty competition is
increasing; voters in 1980 elected only the third Republican governor in
the state's history. Education has become a central issue as the state

attempts to attract industry and diversify its economic base. Concerns related to the manufacturing sector such as tort reform and right-to-work legislation are quite salient in transitional Oklahoma. Population changes, urbanization, and changing economic patterns have brought new heterogeneity to a once-placid agrarian state. Associated with heterogeneity, of course, is conflict and diversity of opinion. Russell L. Hanson hypothesizes that migration trends toward states in the Sunbelt "could transform their political institutions and policies."[22] Oklahoma certainly seems to be a state in which the interest group universe is expanding, where old, traditional groups must now compete with new, developing lobbies. Before examining the current group universe in the state, let us turn to the legal and political contexts of lobby activity in Oklahoma.

The Legal and Political Environment of Interest Group and Lobby Activity

The Legal Environment

When compared to those of the other forty-nine states, Oklahoma's laws regulating lobbying activities are probably best classified as only moderately stringent. They basically involve two requirements: registration and disclosure of expenditures.[23] Under state statutes passed in 1978, any person (1) who spends in excess of $250 in a calendar quarter for lobbying activities, (2) who receives compensation in excess of $250 in a calendar quarter for lobbying services rendered, or (3) whose employment duties in whole or part require lobbying regardless of whether the individual is compensated for the service above normal salary must register each year with the Oklahoma Ethics Commission.[24] Employees of state agencies and local governments, however, are not included in the definition of lobbyists and are therefore not required to register to lobby. In April 1986, 343 lobbyists were registered in Oklahoma representing more than three hundred different organizations. The total number of registered lobbyists for 1986 is up 313 percent from ten years earlier; in 1976 only 83 were registered.

All registered lobbyists must file expenditure reports semiannually with the State Ethics Commission any time an expenditure on any one member of the legislative, executive, or judicial branch exceeds $37.50, or $300 in the aggregate, during the twelve months preceding the first day of the reporting period. Activity reports are due between the first and tenth day of January and June of each calendar year. One provision of state law makes it a felony for lobbyists to receive fees contingent on the passage or defeat of legislation, the issuance of an executive order, or the approval or denial of a pardon or parole by the governor.

Every candidate for state or local office and every political party and organization that receives campaign contributions exceeding $200 must also file an itemized report with the Ethics Commission. Anonymous donors, corporations, and regulated industries and utilities are prohibited from making donations. Contributions are limited to $5,000 by an individual, corporate or labor political action committee, or political party for state offices, and $1,000 for local offices.[25]

Unfortunately, neither the State Ethics Commission, which was created in 1986, nor its predecessors provide published records of lobbyist or PAC contributions. All required expenditure forms are placed in file cabinets or large cardboard boxes that, of course, are available for public inspection.

The Political Environment

In 1986 state legislators were asked to characterize lobbyists in the Oklahoma political system along several dimensions such as honesty, acting in the public interest, and so on. Table 12.1 summarizes responses of legislators to five such questions.

Most state lawmakers hold positive attitudes about the honesty of lobbyists and feel that accurate information is supplied by group representatives. Legislators are less sure, however, that such groups act in the public interest. Additionally, some legislators are suspect of the influence

Table 12.1. State legislators' attitudes about lobbyists in Oklahoma (N = 87), 1986 (Percentage)

Lobbyists	Very	Somewhat	Uncertain	Somewhat	Very	Lobbyists
Are honest	22	64	7	7	0	Are dishonest
Provide accurate information	17	62	8	13	0	Provide inaccurate information
Have positive influence overall	13	49	19	12	7	Have negative influence overall
Are not overly influential	8	34	12	24	22	Are overly infuential
Generally act in the public interest	5	28	15	32	20	Generally do not act in the public interest

Source: 1986 survey of state legislators.

of groups; 46 percent felt that pressure groups are "somewhat" or "very" overly influential. This response may help explain why 61 percent of the state legislators either strongly agreed (28 percent) or agreed (33 percent) that stricter regulations governing the area of lobbying are needed. Not surprisingly, when registered lobbyists were asked the same question, 35 percent disagreed and 15 percent strongly disagreed that stricter regulations are required.

In sum, attempts to regulate lobbying and campaign financing in Oklahoma are relatively recent, and the agency charged with monitoring activities is currently underfunded and understaffed. Hence, interest groups in the state operate in a largely laissez-faire environment, with legislators acknowledging their value but at the same time expressing concern over their considerable influence.

The Group Universe in Oklahoma

When Patterson undertook his 1961 study of lobbying in Oklahoma, he found that the largest number of lobbyists (40 percent) represented business associations, followed at some distance by labor (19 percent), agriculture (16 percent), and government (16 percent).[26] The interest group universe has certainly expanded since then. Based on 1986 data, Table 12.2 provides a breakdown of the types of interests the 343 registered lobbyists in Oklahoma represent. The table also shows for each interest group category three indicators of group power: the total number of organizations represented, the total number of lobbyists employed by the organizations, and the ratio of lobbyists to organizations.

Formal interest group representation in Oklahoma can be organized into twenty-two categories. As in Patterson's earlier findings, business enterprises dominate, with about 17 percent of the total group universe ($N = 314$). Other business-related interests are prominent as well, including realtor/insurance, banking/finance, petroleum/mining, and industrial. All of these lobbies employ twenty or more group representatives. Banking and finance, in fact, has the highest ratio of lobbyists to organizations. In contrast to Patterson's earlier findings, in 1986 farm and labor interests are not as salient; they appear to be in the middle of the pecking order of organization-lobbyist strength.

To gather more specific information about group representatives in the state, in the summer of 1986 a survey questionnaire was mailed to each of the 343 registered lobbyists; 171 (54 percent) individuals returned the questionnaire. Most of the lobbyists reported either that they represent from one to twenty organizational members (33 percent) or that

Table 12.2 Interest group representation in Oklahoma, 1986

Lobby Type	No. of Organizations Represented	No. of Lobbyists	Ratio of Lobbyists to Organizations
Business	52	74	1.42
Realtors/Insurance	39	46	1.18
Banking/Finance	18	40	2.22
Petroleum/Mining	25	31	1.24
Education	14	30	2.14
Human services	21	30	1.43
Political/Public interest	22	28	1.27
Industrial	20	25	1.25
Professional groups	19	24	1.26
Labor	12	23	1.92
Utilities	13	19	1.46
Agriculture	9	15	1.67
Transportation/Communication	14	14	1.00
Environmental	9	11	1.22
Public employees	5	9	1.80
Senior citizens	3	5	1.67
Construction	5	5	1.00
Women	4	4	1.00
Press/Media	3	4	1.33
City/County officials	3	4	1.33
Consumer	2	3	1.50
Church	2	2	1.00
Total	314	446[a]	1.42[b]

Source: 1986 Oklahoma Lobbyists' Registrations (April 23, 1986).

[a]Total equals more than 343 because some lobbyists serve more than one type of interest.

[b]Mean ratio of lobbyists to organizations.

their constituency is comprised of more than five hundred members (43 percent). Almost 87 percent of the lobbyists represent only one organization, 8 percent represent two, and 5 percent lobby for three or more interests. The number of individuals that lobby full versus part time is evenly divided at 50 percent. Approximately 78 percent engage in lobbying between legislative sessions.

Most lobbyists in Oklahoma are organizational representatives such as trade executives from business or paid professionals who pursue the interests of the AFL-CIO, Oklahoma Education Association, and so on. A very few group representatives, however, are classified as contract lobbyists. These individuals are "at the top of the heap"; they are the "heavy hitters" who hire out as "free-lancers" to "do the big 'explaining' jobs." According to a 1987 assessment, four contract lobbyists stand out. Kenneth Nance, a lawyer and former state representative, represents ten clients, including oil, wine, tobacco, and the state's biggest public utility, Oklahoma Gas and Electric. Richard Huddelston is a former House administrator whose services are employed by thirteen groups, among which is the Anheuser-Busch brewing company and the DeBartolo Corporation (which recently secured the rights to build a multimillion-dollar pari-mutuel betting horse track in Oklahoma City). The third so-called heavy hitter is former congressman and one-time President Pro Tempore of the state Senate, Clem McSpadden, who speaks for agricultural groups, insurance interests, and Oklahoma Natural Gas. Finally, the only woman in this group of elite lobbyists is Otie Ann Carr. Her clients are health and hospital groups, including the powerful Oklahoma Medical Association. "Many legislators say she is the most effective woman who ever offered a viewpoint." These contract lobbyists are paid well. "The going Oklahoma price for a lobbyist on retainer is $1,200 to $1,500 per month per client, plus expenses. The pay is year round. On a single, controversial issue, a lobbyist may hire out for that alone, and draw $25,000 to $35,000."[27]

Interest Group Tactics

Lobbyists, PACs, and Elections

One of the principal resources lobbyists can offer elected public officials, of course, is money for campaign financing. Discussing this aspect of lobbying in Oklahoma, Ralph Sewell and Jim Young note that if "lobbyists work for a group with a political action committee, it makes the job easier, for the committee may make a campaign contribution."[28] The role of lobby and PAC money in Oklahoma politics is extremely hard to gauge. As noted above, summaries of expenditures of lobbyists and PACs are not published. In fact, PACs were not even required to register as lobbyists until 1985; all they had to do under law was report expenditures.

According to the State Ethics Commission, no information is currently available on PACs. Data are not even available on the number of PACs registered. We paid a visit to the State Ethics Commission to examine files. The receptionist/file clerk was quite hospitable and showed us the cabinet where lobbyist expenditure reports were filed. Information was tabulated for the total amount of reported expenditures by lobbyists from July 1984 to July 1986. During this two-year period lobbyists reported expenditures totaling only $18,670. Four major interests constituted 84.7 percent of all reported spending by registered lobbyists: business groups, $8,110; labor, $4,000; banking/finance, $1,887; and public interest groups, $1,818. Clearly, something was amiss! Lobbyists spent only about $19,000 in two years to affect public policy? We hypothesized that perhaps lobbyists used PACs as conduits for spending and asked to see campaign finance reports. We were directed to a room containing stacks of boxes. With a gleam in our eyes we began the process of calculating expenditures disaggregated by PACs. We quickly gave up, however. Since spending reports are required before primary and general elections and after the general election, there were literally hundreds of expenditure reports. Instead, we used an article published in the Oklahoma City newspaper to get a feel for the influence of PACs in Oklahoma.

In the fall of 1986 the *Daily Oklahoman* gathered information on the amount of PAC money spent by groups favoring and opposing tort reform, one of the hottest political issues of the past few years. The battle over tort reform has erupted around the nation as the result of rising costs and decreasing availability of liability insurance. Proponents of tort reform blame high jury awards in personal injury lawsuits and want to limit the amount of money defendants can be awarded. On the other hand, those who oppose tort reform (for example, trial lawyers) blame bad investment practices by insurance companies for recent losses and claim that the tort reform movement seeks to deprive citizens of their access to the courthouse. Anyway, according to the article in the *Daily Oklahoman,* the PAC of the Oklahoma Trial Lawyers Association, which opposed significant change in the existing law, contributed $187,200 to political candidates in 1986. Nineteen PACs that lined up favoring the tort reform issue donated some $316,538 to political candidates for that same year. Among the larger PACs or groups supporting tort reform and contributing to Oklahoma candidates in 1986 were United Community Bankers PAC, $46,537; Oklahoma Medical Association PAC, $38,000; Oklahoma Realtors PAC, $34,500; Oklahoma Independent Petroleum Association PAC, $36,050; and Certified Public Accountants PAC, $28,652.[29] In the 1986 legislative session tort reforms were made. Legislation was passed that limits damages and allows the prevailing party to recover costs and fees if the court finds the claim asserted by the nonprevailing party to be in bad faith or not grounded in fact or warranted by law.

In addition to contributing money, lobbyists in Oklahoma employ a wide variety of other techniques in their effort to influence public policy. Overwhelmingly, the locus of attention is on the legislative branch. Respondents to our lobbyist survey indicated that almost 82 percent of the time spent lobbying is directed toward the legislature, with another 15 percent devoted to administrative agencies and less than 1 percent aimed at the judiciary.[30]

Legislative Lobbying

Following the lead of Kay Schlozman and John Tierney,[31] we asked lobbyists in Oklahoma to indicate whether or not they used twelve specific techniques to advance their legislative goals. They were also asked to assess the effectiveness of each tactic. Table 12.3 (first two columns) organizes lobbyists' responses into three basic categories — legislator-assisting, influence-seeking, and organizational-directed. (Information presented in the second two columns of the table is addressed below under administrative lobbying.)

Lobbyists employ most of the twelve techniques quite frequently. With the single exception of using the press, more than two-thirds of the group representatives rely on each of the lobbying strategies. Personal contact with legislators is the most widely used tactic (97.7 percent), and it is also rated as the most effective by lobbyists. Of the three *types* of lobbying behavior, legislator-assisting techniques, which include helping

Table 12.3. Lobbying techniques used by Oklahoma lobbyists (N = 168) and state agency officials (N = 53), 1986

Type of Activity and Technique	Lobbyists		Agency Officials	
	% Using Technique	Mean Effectiveness[a]	% Using Technique	Mean Effectiveness[a]
Legislator-assisting				
Helping draft legislation	85.1	4.0	86.8	4.0
Appearing before committees	86.9	3.5	98.1	3.9
Presenting research results	81.6	3.5	81.1	3.6
Mean scores for 3 techniques[b]	**84.5**	**3.6**	**88.6**	**3.8**
Influence-seeking				
Personal contacts with legislators	97.7	4.2	90.6	4.3
Personal contacts with elected/politically appointed executive personnel	85.1	3.7	67.9	3.6
Supporting a legislator at election time	82.0	3.7	17.0	4.0
Using the press	62.5	3.1	34.0	2.9
Mean scores for 4 techniques[b]	**81.8**	**3.7**	**52.4**	**3.7**
Organizational directed				
Mobilizing public opinion behind a bill	69.7	3.7	32.1	3.9
Letter-writing campaigns	80.3	3.6	32.1	3.1
Joint lobbying by several organizations	84.6	4.0	45.3	3.8
Using clients to lobby legislators	82.8	3.9	47.2	3.9
Mounting grass-roots lobbying efforts	74.5	4.0	26.4	3.7
Mean scores for 5 techniques[b]	**78.4**	**3.8**	**36.6**	**3.7**

[a]Range is from 1 (ineffective) to 5 (very effective).
[b]Mean scores are for each lobbying activity area. Scores are calculated by summing percentage usage and effectiveness and dividing by the number of techniques in activity area.

draft legislation, appearing before committees, and presenting research results, receive the highest mean frequency of usage (84.5 percent). But the second and third most effective tactics are found in the organizational-directed category. Joint lobbying by several organizations and mounting grass-roots lobbying efforts are rated by lobbyists as productive strategies. More than four-fifths of the lobbyists use other grass-root tactics such as letter-writing campaigns and having clients lobby legislators to reach their goals.

Administrative Lobbying

Lobbyists also engage in extensive personal contacts with elected and politically appointed executive personnel to advance their legislative objectives. In fact, this particular tactic is tied with helping draft legislation as the third most important lobbying technique (85.1 percent). Five techniques, however, receive higher mean effectiveness scores than administrative lobbying. One close observer of Oklahoma politics feels that lobbying directed at the bureaucracy has increased in recent years, but no one can document exactly how much. The State Corporation Commission seems to be an especially favorite target of utility group representatives.[32]

Though lobbying the executive branch is generally conceded to have increased in recent years at all levels of government, another, less well understood manifestation of interest group politics is lobbying *by* agency officials. In the fall of 1986 a questionnaire was mailed to seventy-eight major state agencies, boards, and commissions requesting information about legislative-directed activities. Officials from fifty-six (72 percent) different state executive organizations responded. Sixteen (30 percent) of the agencies have at least one full-time employee designated (officially or unofficially) as a legislative liaison. Survey findings suggest that the interests agencies pursue are not limited to those on the governor's agenda. For instance, when asked the extent the agencies efforts to influence legislation were limited to only those matters approved by the chief executive or those consistent with the governor's explicit program or priorities, 17 percent of the respondents replied "rarely or never," 21 percent said "some of the time," and the remaining 62 percent said "most of the time" (28 percent) or "almost all of the time" (34 percent).

Agency officials were also asked to identify techniques used to advance their legislative goals and the perceived effectiveness of these strategies. In contrast to lobbyists, a majority of agency officials rely on only five specific techniques: appearing before committees (98.1 percent), personal contact with legislators (90.6 percent), helping draft legislation

(86.8 percent), presenting research results (81.1 percent), and personal contact with other executive personnel (67.9 percent) (see Table 12.3, second two columns).

The greatest differential in strategy usage between lobbyists and agency officials concerns the degree to which they support legislators at election time. This technique is employed by only 17 percent of the agency representatives, compared to 82 percent of the lobbyists. Organizational-directed, grass-roots techniques are practiced much less frequently by agency officials than by lobbyists.

The mean effectiveness scores in Table 12.3 show considerable consistency across the two groups. Both agree that two strategies are particularly effective: personal contact with legislators and helping draft legislation. Finally, of the three types of interest group activities, legislative-assistance techniques seem to be the most frequently employed by both groups. The mean usage score for lobbyists is 84.5 percent; for agency officials the score is 88.6 percent.

Judicial Lobbying

Lobbyists can affect judicial decisions in one of several ways. They can offer an *amicus curiae* (friend of the court) brief, initiate and/or finance litigation, or seek an injunction to stop a governmental action. The extent of judicial lobbying in Oklahoma is a mystery. As noted previously, lobbyists indicated that less than 1 percent of their time was directed at judicial officials. A recent controversy concerning the sale of wine coolers in the state's grocery stores, however, illustrates that interest groups do become involved in judicial politics.

In July 1987 District Judge Jack Parr overturned Attorney General Robert Henry's opinion that wine coolers, similar to 3.2 percent beer, should not be classified as intoxicating and could therefore be sold in grocery and convenience stores. Judge Parr commented: "I am of the opinion the state should have stricter regulation of these so-called wine coolers because I assume they are also intoxicating. Anyone who has handled drunk driving cases knows for a fact that 3.2 percent beer is intoxicating."[33] The decision by Judge Parr came in response to a lawsuit filed against the Oklahoma Tax Commission and the Alcoholic Beverage Laws Enforcement Commission by the League of Bottled Beverage Retailers. This trade group represents licensed liquor store operators.

Interest Group Power in Oklahoma

Sarah McCally Morehouse, a student of interest group politics, poses an important question: "How do you go about measuring the power of pressure groups?"[34] Findings are likely to be divergent, based on the respondent — political analysts of the state, legislators, lobbyists, and so on. Perhaps there are no absolute answers. Interest group power may vary according to organization size, fiscal resources, lobbying skill, and frequency of contact. Similarly, legislators' representational role orientations may affect their responsiveness to pressure group activities. Since the legislative agenda is dynamic, interest group involvement in politics may vary over time as well. With these caveats in mind, in this section we identify groups claimed to be powerful in state politics in previous studies, rank interests powerful in the current group universe based on legislators' perceptions, and offer our assessment of the groups most powerful in the state.

Group Power in the Past

Previous research suggests that a limited number of pressure groups have played a prominent role in Oklahoma politics. In 1947, for example, American journalist John Gunther identified five groups that he claimed "all . . . [had] something to do with running Oklahoma": the Baptist church, oil interests, the aged (the welfare lobby), education, and local officials.[35] Similarly, writing about Oklahoma politics in the 1960s, Jones surmised that these five groups were still dominant and added two new powerful interests: labor unions and newspapers.[36] As discussed above, Patterson found that lobbyists registered with the House of Representatives in 1961 primarily represented business, farm, labor, and governmental groups.[37] Finally, in her comparative interest group study Morehouse asserted that oil interests, local officials, power companies (utilities), and transportation associations are the power brokers in Oklahoma.[38]

Only Patterson's assessment is based on empirical data. Gunther isolated salient groups on his travels through the state in the early 1940s. Jones's analysis of group power in the 1960s is an extensive elaboration of Gunther's earlier work but still largely impressionistic in nature. Morehouse identified significant groups according "to the judicious consideration of . . . available evidence."[39] Perhaps a more appropriate way to measure group strength is to ask legislators, the principal target of lobbying efforts, to list and rank the most influential interest groups in the state. We did just that. In the summer of 1986, surveys were mailed to the 101 members of the House of Representatives and the 48 members of the Senate; 87 responses were returned, for a response rate of 58 percent.

Present Group Power in the Legislature

To compare interest group power past and present, members of the state legislature were asked to list and rank the most influential or successful interest groups in recent legislative sessions. A total of sixty-four specific groups (such as the AFL-CIO, Oklahoma Education Association, and Trial Lawyers Association) or general lobbies (such as the news media, senior citizens, and farmers) were identified. As in Table 12.1, groups mentioned were categorized by type of interests represented (Table 12.4).

Four lobbies emerge as the most powerful. In rank-order by their weighted influence scores, they are education, labor, professional groups, and banking/finance. Only two of these lobbies have been deemed significant in previous analyses of interest groups in Oklahoma: education and labor. Banking/finance and professional groups seem to be new power brokers. Also, every lobby, with the single exception of church interests, identified as prominent in the past has been influential

Table 12.4. State legislators' perceptions of influential lobbies in Oklahoma (N = 87), 1986

	Legislators' Rankings[a]				
Lobby	No. of 1st Rank Mentions	No. of 2d Rank Mentions	No. of 3d Rank Mentions	No. of 4th Rank Mentions	Weighted Influence Score (WIS)[b]
Education	54	10	12	8	278
Labor	7	16	14	10	114
Professional groups	4	16	12	15	103
Banking/Finance	7	13	5	5	82
Public employees	2	6	5	2	38
Oil	2	2	7	8	36
Business	3	4	2	6	34
Agriculture	2	1	6	6	29
Realtors/Insurance	3	1	3	3	24
Human services	0	3	3	4	19
Transportation/ Communication	0	4	2	0	16
Utilities	1	1	2	4	15
Senior citizens	0	2	2	3	13
City/County officials	0	2	2	1	9
Media	0	1	1	2	7
Construction	1	0	0	1	5
Other[c]	0	0	3	2	8

Source: 1986 survey of state legislators.

[a]Total number of times each lobby was ranked 1st through 4th most influential in recent legislative sessions by state legislators.

[b]Derived by multiplying number of 1st rank mentions times 4, 2d rank mentions by 3, 3d rank mentions by 2, and 4th rank mentions by 1 and summing products.

[c]Environmental, WIS = 3; Women, WIS = 2; Public Interest, WIS = 2; and Industrial, WIS = 1.

in recent legislative sessions. Given present legislative rankings, however, it seems that the traditionally accorded status of some groups is questionable. For example, oil and agriculture are in the middle of the influence hierarchy. Other interests, such as transportation, utilities, senior citizens, local officials, and the media (newspapers), though still successful, have low aggregate influence scores.

Two generalizations seem plausible from these findings. First, in support of our original thesis, the interest group universe in Oklahoma appears to be in transition. Second, and highly related, the power of *some* traditionally influential groups in the state is changing, either in intensity or in locus of attention.

The Most Powerful Groups in Oklahoma

Based on previous studies, recent findings from our survey of state legislators, and our own understanding of state politics, we argue that the "influential group universe" in Oklahoma consists of ten groups. They can be organized into three categories: traditional, continuing power; traditional, declining power; and nontraditional, emerging power.

TRADITIONAL, CONTINUING POWER GROUPS. Four groups belong to the traditional, with continuing power category: education, labor, newspapers, and local officials. According to Jones, education "is probably the strongest lobby or pressure group" in Oklahoma.[40] We concur. The education lobby received fifty-four first-rank mentions as the most influential group in the state by legislators, almost eight times the number of its closest rivals—labor and banking/finance. Education's power expressed as a weighted influence score also suggests that the interest is in an "influential class" all by itself.

The power of education in public affairs is somewhat paradoxical. Oklahoma does not rate particularly high nationally on educational policy indicators. For example, in 1984 Oklahoma ranked 31st among the states in per pupil expenditure for elementary and secondary schools and tied for 39th in average annual salaries for public elementary and secondary classroom teachers.[41] As a functional interest, moreover, education has historically been engaged in an ongoing battle with welfare forces for scarce resources. Jones argues that the state legislature is often forced into two blocs—education versus welfare.[42] In recent years education has clearly been the victor, as legislators and state leaders increasingly acknowledge its importance in economic development. Education's political muscle cannot be ignored either. In 1947 Gunther commented that teachers in Oklahoma are "sophisticated politically and highly vocal."[43] Nothing has changed in recent years. Approximately 20 percent of the delegates at the 1984 state Democratic convention, for instance, were active or retired teachers.[44]

Although Oklahoma seems an unlikely state where labor should be powerful—it ranks 43d nationally in percentage of nonagricultural employees belonging to labor organizations—labor interests have a long and active history in state politics.[45] For a number of years labor has been the beneficiary of sympathetic support from key leadership in the state legislature.[46] Important legislative leaders, for example, helped defeat right-to-work legislation in 1961 and more recently in the 1986–87 legislative session.

The third group in this category is newspapers. Although Table 12.4 shows a low weighted influence score for the media, as Frosty Troy, editor of the *Oklahoma Observer* and longtime commentator on state politics surmises, "There is not a lobby more feared among legislators than the newspapers."[47] Particularly influential is the *Daily Oklahoman*. E. K. Gaylord, founder and publisher of the newspaper, is considered one of the state's patriarchs. Until his death in 1974 at the age of 101, Gaylord played an important role in state affairs. In 1947 Gunther went as far as to assert that Gaylord was "the nearest thing to a boss the city [Oklahoma City] has."[48] Similarly, commenting on the power of Gaylord through the 1960s, Jones claims,"Whatever position Gaylord supports usually wins."[49] The domineering and much-feared titan was succeeded by his son, E. L. Gaylord, who has carried on his father's powerful influence.

The final group is local officials. Associated with Oklahoma's traditionalistic political culture is the importance of local interests in state politics. The power of local officials appears quite stable and may even be increasing. Despite the fact that county government was recently the focus of national attention in the wake of widespread corruption, county commissioners remain a political force. The influence of local officials has been enhanced by several developments. First, more former city officials than ever are now numbered among members of the state legislature. Second, federal programmatic decentralization has caused local elected officials to recognize that funds from "above" are less and less likely to come automatically, requiring instead more effort on their part to get their cities' share from state government. Finally, groups such as substate (regional) planning districts and the Oklahoma Municipal League articulate well the views of local officials.

TRADITIONAL, DECLINING POWER GROUPS. Historically, three other groups have been especially prominent in state affairs. They continue to be important, but their influence seems to be diminishing or changing in locus. Perhaps the most apparent is the Baptist church. In Oklahoma, a state with a strong fundamentalist religious orientation, the Baptist church has been a powerful force in state and local politics. But church interests seem to be losing vitality. In recent years voters approved liquor-by-the-drink (1984) and pari-mutuel betting (1985), long opposed by the Baptists and other conservative Protestant denominations. Voting patterns in the growing metropolitan areas of the state were crucial for the passage of both moral issues. There also seems to be much support for a state lottery despite opposition by religious groups. One commentator on state politics suggests that a state lottery question would have passed in the 1986 general election if the question had appeared on the ballot.[50]

Two other groups are also categorized as traditional but declining in influence: agriculture and the energy lobby. These two interests represent, of course, the paramount economic interests of the past. Since 1982 the oil industry in Oklahoma has been in a deep recession, or the "Black Gold Blues," as one major television station refers to the current situation in the oil patch. Agricultural interests have fared similarly. The influence of both groups, however, may not be attenuating as much as it is changing location. Jones argues, for example, that "the influence of oil in Oklahoma is more readily evident on the national scene . . . than on the state scene."[51] A brief excerpt from a recent article published in the *Washington Post* underscores the importance of national politics to Oklahoma oil interests.

> In 1980, when Ronald Reagan won the presidency and the GOP took over the Senate, the most important sources of large contributions to the Republican Party were oil men in Texas, Oklahoma, and to a lesser extent, Louisiana. In 1981 and the first half of 1982, Texas and Oklahoma, with 7.8 percent of the population, produced far more large donations per capita to the RNC than any other state. Out of $7.1 million from contributors across the country, $1.74 million, or nearly 25 percent, came from Texas and Oklahoma.[52]

The article concludes, however, that given the current recession in the petroleum industry, oil interests may be waning in influence.

Because agricultural policy, like energy legislation, is in many respects nationally defined, the hypothesis that agribusiness interests have been nationalized could be advanced. Regardless of whether one accepts our argument, there is no doubt that agriculture and mineral extraction activities no longer hold the premier positions of power they enjoyed in the past. Both groups, however, continued to be ranked as influential by state legislators in 1986; oil had the 6th highest weighted influence score and agriculture the 8th. In contrast, new groups seem to be growing in power along with Oklahoma's transitional economy.

NONTRADITIONAL, EMERGING POWER GROUPS. Three groups are included in this nontraditional, emerging power category: professional groups, banking/finance, and business. The three types of interests were ranked by legislators in 1986, respectively, as the 3d, 4th, and 7th most influential lobbies in Oklahoma. Only one of the groups, business, has been mentioned in previous research as important. The emerging power of these three lobbies illustrates the thesis that interest group power in Oklahoma is in transition. The fact that legislators rank these types of interests as influential adds support to Steffen's and Hale's contentions that the state is in the midst of economic change. As the economic base of the state moves from a reliance on activities tied to the land to one on manufacturing and services, lobbying activities by business interests and service-oriented professional groups that are regulated by state laws are likely also to increase.

That state legislators consider banking/finance as an important lobby is not surprising, given recent state developments. Since the failure of the Penn Square Bank in 1982, more than fifty other banks in the state have either failed or been declared insolvent, more than twenty alone in 1987. The troubles of banking and finance enterprises have been directly linked to the sagging oil and agriculture economies in the state. In response, the state legislature has been heavily involved in matters of concern to financial interests. Out-of-state ownership of local banks and branch banking, for instance, were recently approved by lawmakers.

Conclusion

Oklahoma has been characterized as a "strong" pressure group state, where a few "significant groups" in the past have been successful in achieving favorable policy responses.[53] We agree with this characterization of interest groups in the Oklahoma political system. Survey data presented here indicate that groups deemed influential in the past are currently actively engaged in lobbying and that legislators rate the influence of interest groups in the legislative process as important. A sizable number of legislators, in fact, expressed concern that pressure groups were overly influential in state politics.

Disagreement would surely arise over which interests in the state are the most powerful. Most observers over the years have recognized education as one of the strongest state lobbies. The Oklahoma Education Association, with its membership of 47,000 teachers and administrators, in particular, has long been identified as among the most active groups in the state. Education was also singled out by legislators as the overall most influential pressure group in recent legislative sessions. Labor was number two, followed by professional groups and banking/finance. The latter two interests have not been recognized previously as among the state's more potent groups. Even though Oklahoma still depends quite heavily on oil and agriculture, the appearance of these two new powers suggests that the state has indeed been caught up in the overall national trends toward a service and information economy. Such issues as branch banking and tort reform have forced financial and professional interests to engage in legislative battles as never before. And though these particular issues may recede, it seems likely that state interests organized around the service, financial, and information sectors of the economy will remain powerful forces for some time to come.

Oil still pays a large part of Oklahoma state taxes and no one doubts agriculture's critical contribution to the state's economy, but these traditional interests no longer dominate the policy agenda at the state capital. Energy companies direct most of their effort toward Washington; farmers likewise recognize that their economic fate is tied far more closely to decisions made by Congress than to those made by the state legislature. No doubt, as the state's economy is transformed, the interests represented in the halls of the legislature will also change. In fact, Governor Bellmon proposed that a cap be placed on the amount of petroleum-related tax dollars that can be allocated to the state's annual budget. He feared that as oil prices made a resurgence, state policy makers would once again over-rely on this volatile industry to finance public services.

How long Oklahoma will remain a strong interest group state is a question of debate. The interest group universe continues to expand. Some interests persist; education, labor, newspapers, and the power of local officials as traditional lobbies remain prominent. Church interests, however, seem to be declining. But as new interests and new demands related to the state's changing economy make their presence felt, group influence is likely to become more diversified and pluralistic—characteristics often associated with moderate or low interest group power in state affairs.

OKLAHOMA

283

Notes

1. Samuel C. Patterson, "The Role of the Lobbyist: The Case of Oklahoma," *Journal of Politics* 25 (February 1963), 72.

2. Registered lobbyists and state legislators were surveyed by mail in the late summer and early fall of 1986.

3. William Sweet, "The Plains States: World's Breadbasket," in Hoyt Gimlin, ed., *American Regionalism: Our Economic, Cultural, and Political Makeup* (Washington, D.C.: Congressional Quarterly Press, 1980), 155–71.

4. Kirkpatrick Sale, *Power Shift* (New York: Random House, 1975).

5. H. Wayne Morgan and Anne Hodges Morgan, *Oklahoma: A Bicentennial History* (New York: W. W. Norton, 1977), xiv.

6. See David R. Morgan, *Handbook of State Policy Indicators,* 4th ed. (Norman: Bureau of Government Research, University of Oklahoma, 1982), 1–15.

7. Daniel J. Elazar, *American Federalism: A View from the States,* 3d ed. (New York: Harper & Row, 1984).

8. Ibid., pp. 118–19.

9. See V. O. Key, Jr., *American State Politics: An Introduction* (Westport, Conn.: Greenwood Press, 1983), 220–22.

10. See Samuel A. Kirkpatrick, David R. Morgan, and Thomas G. Kielhorn, *The Oklahoma Voter: Politics, Elections, and Parties in the Sooner State* (Norman: University of Oklahoma Press, 1977), chap. 1; John F. Bibby, Cornelius P. Cotter, James L. Gibson, and Robert J. Huckshorn, "Parties in State Politics," in Virginia Gray, Herbert Jacob, and Kenneth N. Vines, eds., *Politics in the American States: A Comparative Analysis,* 4th ed. (Boston: Little, Brown, 1983), 59–96.

11. Stephen Jones, *Oklahoma Politics in State and Nation* (Enid, Okla.: Haymaker Press, 1974), 181.

12. Morgan, *Handbook of State Policy Indicators,* 21.

13. U.S. Bureau of the Census, *County and City Data Book, 1983* (Washington, D.C.: Government Printing Office, 1983), 2. *Indian* includes American Indian, Eskimo, and Aleut.

15. Douglas Johnson, Paul Picard, and Bernard Quinn, *Churches and Church Membership in the United States* (Washington, D.C.: Glenmary Research Center, 1971).

15. David R. Morgan, *Handbook of State Policy Indicators,* 3d ed. (Norman: Bureau of Government Research, University of Oklahoma, 1978), 24.

16. U.S. Bureau of the Census, *Statistical Abstract of the United States: 1985* (Washington, D.C.: Government Printing Office, 1984), 633, 637, 135, 29, 440, 450, 457.

17. See L. Harmon Zeigler, "Interest Groups in the States," in Gray, Jacob, and Vines, eds., *Politics in the American States,* 97–131; Sarah McCally Morehouse, *State Politics, Parties and Policy* (New York: Holt, Rinehart & Winston, 1981).

18. Jerome O. Steffen, "Stages of Development in Oklahoma History," in Morgan and Morgan, eds., *Oklahoma: New Views of the Forty-Sixth State,* 29.

19. State Policy Research, Inc., *State Policy Data Book 1987* (Alexandria, Va.: State Policy Research, Inc., 1987), Table A-9.

20. U.S. Bureau of the Census, *Statistical Abstract of the United States: 1987* (Washington, D.C.: Government Printing Office, 1986), 395.

21. Douglas Hale, "The People of Oklahoma: Economics and Social Change," in Morgan and Morgan, eds., *Oklahoma: New Views of the Forty-Sixth State,* 77.

22. Russell L. Hanson, "The Intergovernmental Setting of State Politics," in Gray, Jacob, and Vines, eds., *Politics in the American States,* 33.

23. See Council of State Governments, *Book of the States, 1986–87* (Lexington, Ky.: Council of State Governments, 1986), 140–43; Council of State Governments, *Campaign Finance, Ethics & Lobby Law Blue Book, 1986–87* (Lexington, Ky.: Council of State Governments, 1986).

24. *Oklahoma Statutes,* 1986 Supplement, Title 74, section 4206.

25. See *Campaign Finance, Ethics & Lobby Law Blue Book.*

26. Patterson, "Role of the Lobbyist," 81.

27. Ralph Sewell and Jim Young, "Courts Again Frustrate State's Efforts to Enforce Law: Capitol Comment," *Norman Transcript,* July 26, 1987.

28. Ibid.

29. "Tort Reform Issue Spurs Level of Giving by PACs," *Daily Oklahoman,* October 31, 1986.

30. The percentages do not add to 100. Lobbyists indicated that about 2 percent of the their time spent lobbying was directed at some "other" institution than the legislature, bureaucracy, or judiciary.

31. Kay Schlozman and John Tierney, "More of the Same: Washington Pressure Groups' Activity in a Decade of Change" (Paper presented at the annual meeting of the American Political Science Association, Denver, Colo., September 1982).

32. Telephone interview with George G. Humphreys, director, Research Division, Oklahoma House of Representatives, July 30, 1987.

33. "Judge's Ruling to Keep Coolers in Liquor Stores," *Daily Oklahoman,* July 28, 1987.

34. Morehouse, *State Politics,* 101.

35. John Gunther, *Inside U.S.A.* (New York: Harper & Brothers, 1947), 880.

36. Jones, *Oklahoma Politics,* 174.

37. Patterson, "Role of the Lobbyist," 81.

38. Morehouse, *State Politics,* 109.

39. Ibid., 112.

40. Jones, *Oklahoma Politics,* 176.

41. *Statistical Abstract of the United States: 1985,* 143, 141.

42. Jones, *Oklahoma Politics,* 176.

43. Gunther, *Inside U.S.A.,* 881.

44. Dorothy K. Davidson and Deborah Rugs, *Election '84: The Oklahoma State Party Convention Delegates* (Norman: Bureau of Government Research, University of Oklahoma, 1985), 38.

45. *Statistical Abstract of the United States: 1985,* 424.

46. Jones, *Oklahoma Politics,* 180; Samuel C. Patterson, "Dimensions of Voting Behavior in a One-Party State Legislature," *Public Opinion Quarterly* 26 (Summer 1962), 197.

47. Telephone interview, January 9, 1987.

48. Gunther, *Inside U.S.A.,* 881.

49. Jones, *Oklahoma Politics,* 187.

50. Telephone interview with George Humphreys, August 21, 1987.

51. Jones, *Oklahoma Politics,* 175.

52. "Business Chiefs Put Heart into Their Donations to Republican Party," *Washington Post,* August 29, 1986.

53. Morehouse, *State Politics,* 107–12.

SOUTH DAKOTA

Conflict and Cooperation among Conservatives

ROBERT E. BURNS
and HERBERT E. CHEEVER, JR.

South Dakota politics are best characterized as a form of moderate conservatism. This, we believe, is a reflection of the relative absence of sharp contrasts and extreme differences within South Dakota's physical, economic, and social setting.

South Dakota is a physically large state. It is 16th in size among the fifty states, running approximately 375 miles east to west and 205 miles north to south. In contrast, South Dakota is a small state in terms of population, its 690,768 citizens ranking it 45th among the fifty states. These facts about South Dakota are obvious. What is less obvious is that South Dakota is the biggest little state in the Union for anyone with a public profile.[1]

An interlocking web of personal relationships stretches across the miles and emptiness of South Dakota and creates a much smaller community than physical size would indicate, where anonymity for elected and appointed governmental officials and private sector leaders and spokespersons is impossible. Successful governmental and private sector participants in the state's political process understand that their daily behavior, both public and "private," affects their political careers. Those who fail to understand that are generally unsuccessful. Politics are clean and noncorrupt as a result of the small, interconnected community that exists.

South Dakota is an agricultural state. It ranks 6th among the fifty states with respect to land dedicated to farming, 23d in gross farm income, and 43d in percentage of the labor force employed in manufacturing. Corn, beans, feed grains, hogs, and feeder cattle are major products in the eastern counties. Moving west toward and across "The River," one increasingly encounters wheat and cattle range country and fewer cornfields, and the number of cities and towns decreases.

A greater population density in the Black Hills in the west compared to the central plains partially balances the higher population density of the eastern counties. Since 1920 South Dakota's representation in the U.S. House of Representatives has decreased from three to one. During this same time people have been leaving the farms, small towns, and central portion of the state and moving to the larger cities and towns near the eastern and western borders or leaving the state entirely.

South Dakota's small population is relatively homogeneous. The major exception to this homogeneity are the 45,000 Native Americans, who constitute 6.5 percent of the population. The homogeneous nature of the population does contribute to the presence of moderate as opposed to sharp political conflict in the state. Sharp conflict between the Native American population and the white population rarely surfaces in the state political process. Native American participation in state, county, and municipal politics frequently takes a back seat to participation in tribal reservation government (exempt from the state's jurisdiction) and federal bureaucratic politics, involving the Bureau of Indian Affairs and the Indian Health Service. That is not to suggest, however, that real conflict between the Native American and white population does not exist. We simply observe that the state's electoral and public policy-making processes are not frequently used as vehicles for resolving these conflicts.

Ethnic minorities other than Native Americans constitute less than 1 percent of the population. The vast majority of South Dakotans are of Northern European, English, or Irish ancestry. Most are mainstream Christians. Christian fundamentalism is not clearly visible in the state.

In an effort to capture the essence of South Dakota politics, much has been written about East versus West River interests, city versus farm and ranch interests, Sioux Falls municipal and labor interests versus small-town main-street business interests, and tourism versus mining interests. It is true that these competing interests are present in South Dakota. It is also true that some large, wealthy corporate interests, such as Homestake Mining Corporation, Citibank, and Bell Telephone, have been and will continue to be participants in the public policy-making process. However, the identification of all of these general and specific interests that participate in politics must be understood within the reality that South Dakota is a rural state with limited wealth. Urban interests are really urban interests within a rural setting. The wealthy interests are really wealthy interests within an environment of limited wealth.

Newcomers to South Dakota observe that there is a moderate brand of political conservatism that affects state elections and public policy making. Some of the state's conservatism can be viewed as a "drought mentality." The term implies that even during good agricultural years in South Dakota, when sales tax collections go up, there is a reluctance to increase state spending for fear that a drought might visit the state the following year.

South Dakota's total budget, including all state and federal revenues, was approximately $1 billion in FY 1988. South Dakota ranked 49th in the nation in total combined state and local expenditures. The state constitution requires state government to operate in the black. This limited state tax revenue (South Dakota ranked 38th in the nation in per capita tax revenues) means limited state government. Fiscal conservatism exists as a matter of law and philosophy, and interest groups must function within that reality.

South Dakota's moderate conservatism is opposed by a moderate form of liberalism. The state's two incumbent U.S. senators as of 1987, Larry Pressler (R) and Tom Daschle (D), reflect these moderate forms of conservatism and liberalism. Two earlier U.S. senators from South Dakota, Karl Mundt (R) and George McGovern (D), were less reflective of the moderate political views of the state's voters and appear to have earned their political success in the state through excellent organization and strong personal qualities that compensated for their less moderate views. South Dakota liberalism does address social justice, education, labor, and environmental issues, but these issue areas are approached by liberals within the parameters of a limited state revenue base and a state government of limited activity.

Moderate conservatism ordinarily prevails over moderate liberalism, and the Republican party and its candidates benefit. Between 1938 and 1988, Democrats controlled the Senate for only six years, the House of Representatives for two years, and the governorship for ten years. The extent of Republican domination in legislative politics is emphasized by the fact that Democrats have held more than one-third of the membership in the Senate only six additional years and in the House only ten additional years.[2] Republicans have controlled the governorship and both houses of the legislature by more than a two-thirds margin about three-fourths of the time. It should be noted, however, that Democrats have won half of the races for congressional offices and the state Public

Utilities Commission, with its significant regulatory powers, since 1970. Conservative views might be overrepresented in the South Dakota Legislature because of the peculiarities of localized legislative elections. Interest groups, however, must function within the reality of conservative strength in the legislature. The great equalizers in South Dakota are the initiative and the referendum. If the more conservative oriented legislature behaves in a manner that is clearly at odds with less conservative voters, the voters might organize and rely on the referendum to "undo" unpopular legislation or the initiative to "do" popular legislation. Direct democracy is particularly threatening to the legislature in South Dakota because the state ranks consistently in the top five with respect to percentage of voting age population casting votes in general elections.

The Chem-Nuclear and Bell Telephone deregulation controversies are excellent examples of the strength of direct democracy. When the more conservative, business-oriented legislature seemed ready to approve locating a nuclear dump site in South Dakota, an environmental group sponsored an initiative that blocked the legislative action. Likewise, when a referendum on a proposal to allow deregulation of Bell Telephone in South Dakota was threatened during the 1987 legislative session, the deregulation sponsors agreed to postpone any final vote until after a summer interim study.

Interest Group Activity

Lobbying tactics started to change in South Dakota when "sunshine" came to the South Dakota Legislative Assembly in the early 1970s. At this time the Democratic party was making politics in South Dakota a two-party affair. The arbitrary power of committee chairs was lessened, committee meetings were opened to the public, committee agendas were published in advance of meetings, votes were taken in public, and the amount of testimony from the public was expanded. These changes, along with better transportation, better newspaper and television coverage, and the expansion of state government activities during the 1960s and 1970s, prompted an expansion of the number of interest groups, lobbyists, and citizens who lobby and closely observe the legislature.

During the 1987 legislative session 289 different paid lobbyists representing 262 different interests registered with the secretary of state as required by law. There were a total of 406 registrations in 1987, since many lobbyists represented more than one group, and many groups were represented by more than one lobbyist. In addition, 214 public employee lobbyists registered with the secretary of state. Many of the lobbyists appeared at the session for only a brief time. However, a normal day finds 70 to 100 public and private lobbyists at work in the corridors of the legislature.

Comparing the numbers of lobbyists and organizations active during past legislative sessions is difficult because of changes in laws affecting lobbyists and changes in the nature of compliance with those laws. Long-time observers of the legislature, however, note a steady increase in the number of groups and lobbyists present during legislative sessions since 1960. New issues and increased concerns with governmental activity account for much of this increase.

Most of the public employees who lobby the legislature are ranking members of their department, agency, board, commission, college, or university. Many of these lobbyists are at the session because they are required to be present. Others, particularly those representing the governor and his or her cabinet officers, are lobbying on behalf of the governor's program. Their problem is to get the job done without causing an undercurrent of resentment in the legislature by seeming to be excessively omnipresent and overbearing.

Most of the lobbyists representing private interest groups at the legislative session are executive directors, employees, or members of an association or organization. However, approximately 50 of the 289 different lobbyists, representing about 150 of the 406 registrations with the secretary of state, are contract lobbyists hired by the organization or corporation to lobby the legislature. Many are lawyers or former executive branch employees. Based on our assessment, the contract lobbyists include among their number many of the most influential lobbyists. Interestingly, few former legislators return to Pierre to lobby the legislature.

Relatively few laws regulate lobbying and other interest group activity in South Dakota.[3] Paid lobbyists must register with the secretary of state and pay a $10 registration fee for each organization they represent. Public employees who lobby must also register. Lobbyists must wear name badges while in the capitol building. They are prohibited from bribing or threatening legislators. They must file an expense account for nonpersonal expenses incurred for the purpose of influencing legislators. Lobbyists are prohibited from being hired on a contingency fee basis, according to which their pay depends on their success in getting legislation passed or defeated. Legislators and full-time state employees who were confirmed in their positions by the Senate are prohibited from serving as nonpublic employee lobbyists for one year after they serve in such positions.

In addition, organizations that hire a lobbyist must register that information with the secretary of state and file a list of expenses with that office. Political action committees are not limited in the amount of money they may contribute to state, local, or legislative candidates. PACs must file reports with the secretary of state listing their contributions to candidates. Persons, committees, and organizations that spend money to influence constitutional amendments or initiated or referred measures must also file reports with the secretary of state. Unions and corporations are prohibited from making contributions to candidates but may become involved in campaigns concerning amendments or initiated or referred measures.[4]

Bills that might limit PAC contributions to legislative candidates or require that the salaries or fees received by lobbyists be disclosed have fared poorly in recent legislative sessions. Given the squeaky clean image of lobbyists and the limited impact of PACs at the present time, it does not seem likely that laws regulating lobbyists and PACs will be changed in the near future.

The techniques that interest groups use to influence public policy in South Dakota include "down home" grass-roots lobbying, legislative lobbying, executive branch lobbying, judicial activity, electioneering, and involvement in initiatives and referendums.

Grass-Roots Lobbying

South Dakota's thirty-five senators and seventy representatives are elected for two-year terms from thirty-five legislative districts each with a population of approximately 20,000. Most citizens know one or more of the legislators and find it easy to gain access to them. Interest groups with members spread throughout the state are able to contact legislators all during the year, and especially during the legislative session, with a grass-roots lobbying effort.

Grass-roots lobbying is facilitated by the fact that "cracker barrel" sessions are held in many legislative districts on Saturdays during the legislative session. Legislators report on what is happening in Pierre, answer questions, and listen to constituents' opinions. Many of the effective interests use these sessions and other opportunities to contact legislators and often orchestrate such contacts, preferring not to leave what is heard by legislators back home to chance.

Citizens also travel to Pierre during the session. So many interest groups and organizations want to sponsor some sort of social hour for legislators that the Legislative Research Council finds it hard to schedule all the activities. On a given day all legislators may find themselves invited to a lunch sponsored by the State Extension Homemakers on their annual "Plunge to Pierre"; invited to the capitol rotunda to have an afternoon snack of homemade rolls, locally made cheese, and other items, sponsored by the City of Milbank Chamber of Commerce; and invited to a dinner held by the South Dakota Automobile Association. Unlike the situation in the late 1950s, when many legislators drank and ate their evening meals in one of the hospitality rooms set up by lobbyists in the St. Charles Hotel, lobbyists today may experience difficulty in finding a legislator who does not already have a meal engagement.

Interest Groups and Elections

Election campaigns in South Dakota are largely personal efforts by candidates. Interest groups ordinarily do not become involved in the recruitment of candidates. However, individual realtors, bankers, retail merchants, lawyers, doctors, and others are often an important part of these efforts. This involvement by individuals, along with contributions and perhaps even some volunteer time, places many of these groups in the best possible position to lobby these candidates if and when they are elected.

Political action committees do not have a long history of making major contributions to legislative or, for that matter, gubernatorial or other candidates for state office. As late as 1980, based on our own experiences in legislative campaigns, the number of interest groups and PACs making contributions to legislative campaigns was small. That pattern is changing, however. In the 1986 general election, PACs contributed $162,051 to legislative candidates, for an average of $871 per contested candidate.[5] These PAC donations amounted to 28 percent of the contributions received by legislative candidates in 1986. The PAC contributions were most frequently directed to incumbents, legislative leaders, and majority party candidates. Bob Mercer, an *Aberdeen American News* reporter who recently investigated the subject, stated that PACs "concentrated their efforts on the Republican power structure."[6] In addition to PAC contributions, individual lobbyists make contributions to candidates, again most often to incumbents.

The PACs that gave the most money in 1986 were associated with the following groups: South Dakota Realtors, $13,750; S.D. Education Association (SDEA), $13,725; S.D. Medical Association, $13,650; Northwestern Bell Telephone, $13,300 (to 104 candidates, several uncontested); and S.D. Life Underwriters, $12,450. Contributions ranging from $5000 to $7,650 were made by S.D. Chiropractors, Black Hills Power and Light, Citicorp, Rural Electrification, S.D. Hospital Association, S.D. Retail Beverage Dealers, and the National Rifle Association.[7]

Three interesting observations can be made about this list of contributors. First, "large" contributions do not necessarily translate into influence. Some of the big contributors, such as the SDEA, are not always perceived as the most effective by legislators. Second, some of the large contributors had relatively few legislative concerns in the 1987 legislative session. Third, PAC leaders and legislators are totally united in their belief that "you don't buy votes in the legislature." Gary Hanson, a state senator and realtor, commented, "Our industry is so affected by what government does that we feel if we elect people who are responsible legislators, it's going to benefit our industry."[8] On the other hand, in our research survey conducted during the 1987 legislative session, legislators and lobbyists acknowledged that money helps make a group effective, allowing it to secure good lobbying efforts and to make contributions to legislative campaigns. One lobbyist said, "A legislator who receives a contribution from a PAC finds it harder to say no, not impossible or even difficult, but harder."

Interest Groups and the Initiative and Referendum

Between the mid-1970s and the mid-1980s, various interest groups effectively used both the initiative and referendum for their causes. From 1978 to 1986 seventeen constitutional amendments and nine initiated or referred measures were placed on the general election ballot. Some were approved; others were defeated. Significant interest group activity supported and opposed such diverse measures as establishment of a statewide lottery, the loaning of nonsectarian textbooks to nonpublic schools, establishment of Memorial Day on the last Monday in May (as in the rest of the U.S.), stricter regulation of the manner in which a nuclear waste dump site could be established, a requirement that public schools begin after Labor Day, endorsement of a nuclear arms freeze, establishment of single-member Senate districts throughout South Dakota, limiting real property taxes along the lines of California's Proposition 13, allowing dove hunting, regulating electric rates, repealing the dairy marketing act, and defining and regulating obscenity. Several of the bills concerned major issues. Others concerned minor issues that were important to only a small segment of the population.

Many of the interests involved in initiative and referendum drives have been temporary, loose, ad hoc groups that formed to push a particular proposal. The Dakota Proposition proposal, modeled after California's Proposition 13, was supported primarily by a group of citizens who had not been heavily involved in politics before 1980. Likewise, the regulation of obscenity was advocated by persons from outside the mainstream churches who had not been involved before 1978. Both efforts were defeated by coalitions of groups and citizens who were more established in the political structure.

In 1984 an environmental group led the fight to strictly regulate nuclear waste dump sites. Their poorly funded but well publicized effort was successful and effectively shut out Chem-Nuclear Corporation's efforts to establish a major, low-level nuclear dump site in southwestern South Dakota. Chem-Nuclear had previously won some major victories in the legislature. It spent a significant amount of money in an effort to defeat the initiated measure. As in many other initiated or referred measure elections, voters were reacting to the issue on a strongly emotional as well as intellectual basis.

Interest Groups and the Executive Branch

During the summers of 1971 and 1984 Robert Burns was employed by the governor's office to conduct executive branch reorganization research as a part of executive reorganization initiatives made by former Governors Kneip and Janklow. Burns prepared and supervised interviews of all state department and agency heads as part of the research. One of the questions asked each agency head to identify interest groups with which the agency had a working relationship. In 1971 and 1984 the executive officials identified a large and diverse number of interest groups in response to this question. The responses given in 1971 are similar to those in 1984 with respect to what interests tend to lobby what departments or agencies.

The pluralistic model of interest group activity appears to apply in the realm of executive agency-interest group relations. Burns's interviews show that specific interest groups try to influence specific agencies. There is no evidence that a single private interest group effects an ongoing relationship with a large number and diverse array of executive agencies or departments.

Other scholars have introduced us to the "iron triangle," or tripartite power relationship, in the national public policy-making process. The "iron triangle" refers to carefully cultivated political and personal relationships between executive agency heads, congressional standing committee chairs and members, and private interest group leaders. This tripartite relationship is identified by several leading students of American government as one of the most vital relationships in American politics. We have no evidence that the iron triangle is at work in South Dakota.

Interest groups do effect relationships with executive agencies and legislators, but the tripartite power relationship does not form for several reasons. First, legislative committees do not have executive turf to protect in South Dakota, as is true of congressional committees at the national level. Further, the South Dakota Legislature has a much higher turnover in membership every two years than is true of the U.S. Congress. Both the motive and the opportunity to cultivate and nurture the tripartite power relationship are lacking in South Dakota politics.

Examples of interest group activity in relation to the administration include insurance corporations and interests actively lobbying the Department of Commerce's Division of Insurance; sporting groups working to affect decisions in the Department of Game, Fish and Parks; a coalition of highway users and the Associated General Contractors dealing with the Department of Transportation concerning planning decisions and how and where contracts are let for highway construction; and mining corporations and interests and environmental groups lobbying the Department of Natural Resources.

South Dakota executive agencies have been subject to the provisions of the South Dakota Administrative Procedures Act since the mid-1970s. This legislation imposes basic prior notice and fair hearing requirements on executive agencies as they exercise rule promulgation and rule adjudication authority. Interest groups do attempt to influence administrative decision making. Success or failure appears, in part, to be a matter of knowing how the administrative rule making and adjudicating process works and of participating effectively in that process. Interested, narrow, private groups maintain a close watch over notices of administrative hearings and dedicate the time, money, and resources necessary to prepare testimony for the hearings. The less organized, disinterested general public rarely does the same, and citizen groups, though interested, often lack the money and resources to participate effectively.

Since the legislature must review all rules promulgated by the executive branch, private groups that are displeased with a rule may lobby the legislature to defeat that rule. Indeed, the legislature has been protective of its prerogative and does not hesitate to defeat executive rules that are in conflict with the prevailing political sentiments of the legislature.

Interest Groups and the Courts

Groups, corporations, and other interests attempt to use the courts
to influence public policy in South Dakota when the opportunity exists.
A quiet but prominent policy dispute that has prompted court activity
since the mid-1970s involves public and private schools. They have been
in conflict concerning legislation that required public school boards to
furnish secular textbooks to private schools. This legal controversy was
resolved in 1986 with the popular approval of a constitutional initiative.
Other interest group activity before the judiciary certainly occurs, but
such opportunities are relatively rare.

Interest Groups and the Legislature

The South Dakota Legislature meets annually for alternating forty-
and thirty-five-day sessions. The part-time legislators are relatively low
paid and do not consider themselves to be professional politicians, as
almost all of them have other full-time employment. There is normally a
turnover of 25 percent to 35 percent every two years, most of it due to
voluntary retirement. Legislators are served by a small staff of fifteen
professionals of the Legislative Research Council. As in other states with
a similar situation, strictures of time and resources on the legislature
tend to increase the need for legislators to rely on executive agencies and
lobbyists for expert information.

The range of interest groups active in lobbying the legislature is
typical of most states. The number of groups in various categories and
their power configuration reflect the realities of South Dakota. We have
divided the 262 different interests represented by paid lobbyists during
the 1987 legislative session into eleven categories (Table 13.1).

It is obvious from Table 13.1 that the business community is well
represented before the legislature. Not only does this group have a great
deal at stake, but most business organizations find the conservative nature of the legislature to their liking. The groups in the professional
category could also be considered a part of the business community. The
South Dakota Education Association, which might be put into either the
professional group or labor union category, has been included among
the educational groups. Agricultural groups include rural utilities such
as the Rural Electric Association as well as various organizations concerned with water and irrigation. Government groups include both organizations representing counties, townships, and cities as well as those

Table 13.1. South Dakota interest groups represented by paid lobbyists, by category of interest, 1987

Category	No. of Lobbyists Registered[a]
Business associations	70
Business corporations	64
Professional groups	22
Education groups	22
Social justice groups	21
Agricultural and rural utility groups	20
Government groups	19
Labor unions or employee groups	8
Recreation or sporting groups	7
Environmental groups	6
Veterans' groups	3

Source: South Dakota Secretary of State's Office, 1987.
[a]Two hundred fourteen public employees registered as lobbyists representing most agencies of state government. Their registrations are kept on a separate list by the secretary of state and are not included in this table.

representing officeholders in these jurisdictions, such as sheriffs. Labor unions include the AFL-CIO, some specific unions, and the State Employees Organization, which, though not a union, is concerned with many of the same labor issues. Recreation, environmental, and veterans' groups are self-explanatory.

We conducted a mail survey in 1987 of the state's 105 legislators and 64 selected full-time lobbyists representing the better-known interest groups in South Dakota. Responses were received from 43 legislators and 22 lobbyists. We admit to the tentativeness of the conclusions that can be drawn from the questionnaire.

In the first question, legislators and lobbyists were asked to rate groups in terms of whether they believed the group is ordinarily successful in winning legislative approval for its proposals (Table 13.2). Legislators and lobbyists had similar perceptions of the relative effectiveness of the different specific groups, but the perceptions are not identical. We emphasize that these responses reflect perceptions and should not be read as a performance evaluation of individual lobbyists or groups. A low effectiveness rating might reflect philosophical differences of the majority party with that interest group.

Question two asked legislators and lobbyists to list, in rank order, the five most powerful specific interest groups in South Dakota in terms of their overall impact on state politics and government policy. Legislators listed thirty-eight different interest groups. More than 50 percent of the responses were limited to the following seven interest groups in rank order: South Dakota Bankers Association, S.D. State Bar, Wholesale Liquor Dealers, the governor's office, Northwestern Bell Telephone, S.D. Medical Association, and the Investor Owned Utilities Association.

Lobbyists listed twenty-nine different groups. Forty percent of the lobbyists' responses were limited to four groups that they ranked significantly higher than any others. The four interests in rank order are the governor's office, S.D. State Bar, S.D. Municipal League, and S.D.

Table 13.2. Interest group effectiveness in South Dakota, as ranked by legislators and lobbyists, 1987

Type of Interest	Legislators		Lobbyists	
	Score[a]	Rank	Score[a]	Rank
Business groups				
S.D. Bankers Association	1.97	1	1.61	1
S.D. Press Association	2.13	2	2.14	3
Investor Owned Utilities Association	2.15	3	1.68	2
Industry and Commerce Association of S.D.	2.28	4	2.50	7
S.D. Automobile Dealers Association	2.29	5	2.36	5
Associated General Contractors	2.36	6	2.75	11
S.D. Broadcasters Association	2.38	7	2.61	9
S.D. Mining Association	2.41	8	2.47	6
S.D. Trucking Association	2.43	9	2.33	4
S.D. Retail Association	2.47	10	2.55	8
S.D. Innkeepers Association	2.70	11	2.61	9
S.D. Association of Realtors	2.74	12	3.00	12
Black Hills, Badlands & Lakes Association	2.80	13	3.06	13
S.D. Music and Vending Association	3.16	14	3.29	14
Business corporations				
Northwestern Bell Telephone	1.75	1	1.72	2
Citibank	1.78	2	1.75	4
Homestake Mining	2.13	3	1.47	1
John Morrell & Company	2.33	4	1.73	3
Northern States Power Co.	2.58	5	2.44	5
Burlington Northern (railroad)	3.12	6	2.91	6
Scientific Games, Inc. (lottery)	3.25	7	4.00	7
Professional groups				
S.D. State Medical Association	2.05	1	1.68	2
S.D. State Bar Association	2.10	2	1.28	1
S.D. Nurses Association	2.61	3	2.94	5
S.D. Dental Association	3.00	4	2.92	4
S.D. Chiropractors Association	3.05	5	2.50	3
Liquor groups				
Wholesale Liquor Dealers	1.89	1	1.78	1
S.D. Retail Beverage Dealers	2.07	2	2.21	3
S.D. Beer Wholesalers	2.30	3	2.05	2
S.D. Association of 3.2 Dealers	2.50	4	3.21	4
Agricultural groups and rural utilities				
S.D. Rural Electric Association	2.36	1	1.63	1
S.D. Water Congress	2.62	2	2.61	4
S.D. Farm Bureau Federation	2.89	3	2.58	3
S.D. Association of Telephone Co-ops	2.90	4	1.81	2
S.D. Wheat Growers	2.93	5	2.75	5
S.D. Stockgrowers	3.16	6	3.11	7
S.D. Farmers Union	3.48	7	3.05	6
Education groups				
School Administrators of S.D.	2.36	1	2.73	3
Associated School Boards of S.D.	2.40	2	1.90	1
S.D. Student Federation	2.97	3	3.75	4
S.D. Education Association	3.10	4	2.68	2

(Table 13.2 continued)

Type of Interest	Legislators Score[a]	Rank	Lobbyists Score[a]	Rank
Veterans' groups				
S.D. American Legion	2.55	1	2.44	1
S.D. Veterans of Foreign Wars	2.62	2	2.61	2
Disabled American Veterans	2.69	3	2.72	3
Labor groups				
S.D. State Employees Organization	2.62	1	2.95	1
S.D. AFL-CIO	3.59	2	3.57	2
Government groups and executive branch				
Governor's office	1.42	1	1.18	1
S.D. Municipal League	1.82	2	1.45	2
Governor's cabinet	1.94	3	2.00	3
S.D. Association of County Commissioners	2.51	4	2.71	5
State Board of Regents	2.58	5	2.70	4
Social welfare environment recreation				
American Association of Retired Persons	2.66	1	3.05	3
S.D. Right to Life	2.76	2	2.84	1
S.D. Wildlife Federation	2.87	3	2.88	2
National Women's Political Caucus	3.16	4	3.47	5
League of Women Voters	3.42	5	3.05	3
S.D. Peace and Justice Center	3.78	6	4.06	7
S.D. Resources Coalition	3.93	7	3.81	6

[a]Range is from 1 (most effective) to 5 (least effective).

Bankers Association. Question three asked legislators and lobbyists to rate the general categories of interests in terms of their effectiveness (Table 13.3).

Finally, question four asked legislators and lobbyists to list the four categories of interests which they felt were most powerful in South Dakota, in terms of overall impact on South Dakota politics and government policy, using the list of twelve categories in Table 13.2. Legislators ranked agricultural groups, government groups and the executive

Table 13.3. Effectiveness of South Dakota interest group categories, as ranked by legislators and lobbyists, 1987

Category	Legislators Score[a]	Rank	Lobbyists Score[a]	Rank
Government groups and executive branch	1.97	1	1.72	4
Business corporations	2.11	2	1.76	5
Professional groups	2.21	3	1.61	1
Business association groups	2.21	4	2.00	7
Liquor and beer interests	2.30	5	1.83	6
Agricultural groups	2.67	6	1.61	1
Agricultural related utilities	2.70	7	1.68	3
Education groups	2.85	8	2.61	8
Veterans' groups	2.87	9	2.70	9
Social welfare/Justice groups	3.52	10	3.94	10
Labor groups	3.82	11	4.00	12
Environmental groups	3.90	12	3.94	10

[a]Range is from 1 (most effective) to 5 (least effective).

branch, and business association groups at the top, followed closely by professional groups, liquor and beer groups, and business corporations. Lobbyists ranked agricultural groups, government groups and the executive branch, business association groups, and professional groups at the top, with other groups following far behind.

Reviewing the survey results and the personal interviews with lobbyists and legislators, we find that no single interest group dominates the legislative process. Interest group activity in the legislature can be best understood by viewing it as pluralistic, with groups focusing on fairly narrow policy areas that concern them directly. From time to time, however, interests may form coalitions and work with one of the political parties and/or the governor's office to influence public policy.

Interest Group Effectiveness

Since the governor and more than two-thirds of the legislators have been Republicans for the last ten annual sessions, the most effective groups are likely to be those that have a normal affinity with the Republican party. A review of the ratings in Tables 13.1 and 13.2 and of the responses to other questions substantiates that supposition. Most business association groups, corporations, and professional groups have a close working relationship with the Republican party. Many environmental groups, labor organizations, and social welfare groups either have ties with the Democrats or at least have no ties with the Republicans. These groups generally do not do as well in the legislature or in politics in general as do those from the business community.

The governor and his or her cabinet are influential forces within the legislative process (Table 13.2)[9]. With Republican party domination of both branches, with a strong governor system of state government, and effective governors, such as Janklow and Mickelson, the influence of the executive branch relative to the part-time legislature comes as no surprise.

Many business, liquor, and professional groups and corporations rank either high or moderately high (Table 13.2). These general interests join ranks almost annually to form a formidable coalition of conservative interests dedicated to protecting the status quo of the local and state taxation system. The taxation system at present places heavy emphasis on the real property tax at the local level and the sales tax at the state level and excludes any personal or corporate income tax. In contrast to business and professional groups, social welfare, social justice, environmental, labor, and education groups rank low (Tables 13.2 and 13.3).

Agricultural groups and rural utilities are not especially influential (Table 13.2)[10]. This is the most surprising finding of this research. One explanation for this limited influence might be found in the fact that the agricultural community has been making unusually high financial demands on the legislature because of the bad economic times faced by many farmers. These demands are not perceived as legitimate by most lawmakers and do not square with fiscal conservatism. From a historical point of view, agricultural interests suffered a dramatic loss of influence in the legislature when legislative districts were redrawn in 1965 to conform to the one-person, one-vote rulings of the U.S. Supreme Court. In addition, since about 1960, farmers have become increasingly specialized in their agricultural production. Commodity interests have replaced general agricultural interests. Commodity interests are not only divergent interests, they are also often conflicting interests. The disunity within agriculture accounts, in part, for its declining influence. Nonetheless, agriculture, as a category of general interests and especially when acting in a reasonably united fashion, as it does through the coalition organization known as Ag Unity, is still a powerful, albeit diminishing, force in South Dakota politics.

Another general category of interests that fares poorly in terms of their perceived effectiveness is education. The South Dakota Education Association (SDEA) represents both public elementary and secondary (K–12) schoolteachers and public higher education faculty. Through a close working relationship with former Governor Janklow, the SDEA was successful from 1979 to 1986 in winning significant increases in state aid to K–12 education. Given the fact that K–12 teacher salaries still average the lowest in the United States, one might conclude that the SDEA has been more effective in helping property owners keep real property taxes low at the local level than in increasing teacher salaries. The present rating of the SDEA and other education groups by legislators and lobbyists also reflects the fact that public education, both K–12 and higher education, is likely to fare poorly when increased financing is sought in a conservative, rural state during difficult times in the agricultural and rural economies.

Labor unions and the South Dakota State Employees Organization rank relatively low in terms of effectiveness (Table 13.2). The weakness of the labor lobby is also manifested in the overall status of labor law in South Dakota, which is generally antilabor in its orientation and even has a right-to-work provision in the state constitution. This is another reflection of the rural, nonindustrialized character of South Dakota.

Veterans' groups rank only as moderately effective (Table 13.2), perhaps reflecting the fact that the legislature does not have to deal annually with major issues of concern to veterans. On the other hand, the liquor lobby, relatively united, monied, and with numerous retail business members, ranks as very effective today as well as in the past.

We have no reason to question the assessment of interest group power presented by Sarah McCally Morehouse for an earlier period.[11] Our survey, however, indicates that the effectiveness of and power wielded by interest groups have changed considerably since the late 1960s in South Dakota. Among interests listed as significant by Morehouse, the agricultural groups (Farm Bureau, Farmers Union, South Dakota Stockgrowers, and S.D. Wheat Growers Association) are no longer especially effective unless acting as a coalition along with other agricultural groups. Further, Northern States Power Company and the Industry and Commerce Association of South Dakota (into which the former Chamber of Commerce merged), which were identified in the Morehouse study as very effective, are now only moderately effective. Only rural utilities, the Bankers Association, Homestake Mining Company, and the liquor lobby continue as effective groups in their narrow areas of concern. The Bankers Association and the liquor lobby, including the Wholesale Liquor Dealers, are identified as powerful in influencing state politics overall.

Interest Group Tactics

Successful lobbyists in South Dakota reflect the positive images one has of the role of lobbyists in the political process. Jeremiah Murphy, a thirty-year veteran of lobbying and the South Dakota "King of Lobbyists," frequently shares his techniques with students and others. His "Murphy's Laws" of effective lobbying are paraphrased below, albeit without his eloquence, grace, and style.[12]

Murphy has told all who wish to listen: Be honest. If you discover that you have given out wrong information, backtrack and tell people that you were in error. Educate yourself on a multitude of issues. Many things affect your clients, and you need to be well informed about a variety of issues. When you lobby a committee or a legislator, give both the pros and cons in a case. Better they hear the negatives from you than someone else. Integrity is the only thing you have over the long haul. Be helpful. If I expect them to give me a minute of their busy time to listen to my position, then I can give them some of my time. If someone needs an amendment or bill drafted, help him with it even if you don't support that particular amendment. Better that it be a well-drawn amendment than a poorly drawn one if it becomes law. Know the rules and how to use them. You can often help a legislator with this knowledge. Be a source of ideas, of facts. If you can, bring some pressure on legislators from constituents. The ones that are most influential back home are the ones that have helped the legislator with campaigns.

Murphy has also insisted that it is important to work hard: Diligence will pay off. Know the bills you are working on inside out. Be aware of every bill that affects your client in any way. Be personable. Know the legislators as people. Be able to work with other groups. A lot of the effective lobbying today is done through coalitions. Know when to convince your client to compromise. Be articulate. Be able to explain your position to a legislator or committee in ten minutes—or in two minutes if two minutes is all the time you get. Especially be able to explain what the bill will do to your client and others. Bring pressure on the legislator [he smiles]—sometimes by logic, sometimes through his or her conscience. If legislators have doubts about a bill, you hope they will express those doubts so that you can deal with the negatives.

Our mail questionnaire included an open-ended question that asked legislators and lobbyists to identify the personal factors and interest group characteristics that account for the effectiveness of the successful interest groups in South Dakota. The responses reinforced and added to the formula for success prescribed by Jeremiah Murphy. The additional factors identified as contributing to the success of an interest group are not unlike the factors identified by many other students of interest group politics. The existence of a permanent organization, large group membership spread throughout the state, articulate and informed spokespersons, adequate wealth to support year-round activities, and interest group goals that are perceived as the legitimate business of South Dakota government are among the ingredients identified by the respondents as a part of the recipe for success.

Some respondents obviously gave this question considerable thought and provided lengthy, meaningful analysis. Some of the more interesting responses we received include, "Hard to fight your doctor and banker when they have your life and purse strings"; "Failure of South Dakota media to discuss issues . . ."; "Tenacity is acceptable— redundancy is rude"; and "Friendly people who are able to communicate."

Conclusions

Political conflict is moderate in South Dakota. Politics is essentially clean and honest. Interest groups do not succeed as a result of back-room, under-the-counter deals. Interest groups succeed with information; moderate, legitimate demands; friendly, cooperative mannerisms; and persistence.

We are convinced that the pluralistic model best characterizes South Dakota politics. Agricultural interests do not dominate a wide spectrum of state government policy decisions. Indeed, it appears that the influence of agricultural interests is on the decline. The influence of government officials, especially the governor and the cabinet, is considerable. No one private general interest or specific interest group is successful in influencing public policy making that affects many and diverse public issues. Our study does not even suggest that any general or specific private interest attempts to dominate the process. There are indications that those few groups that attempt to influence policy beyond their primary concerns are perceived negatively by other interest group leaders and legislators. The most effective lobbyists and interest groups mind their own business.

We comment again on the relatively frequent resort to direct democracy in South Dakota. Less conservative and less well financed and organized interests have secured gains through the use of the referendum and initiative. Generally, however, the more conservative and more well organized and financed interest groups, relying on a primary strategy of lobbying the legislative and executive branches with legal, nonthreatening, nontheatrical practices, succeed in influencing the policy decisions of particular interest to them.

Notes

1. Linda Baer, "Significant Rankings Among Fifty States—South Dakota," data sheet shared with authors by the Department of Rural Sociology, South Dakota State University, Brookings, S.D.

2. Alan L. Clem, *South Dakota Political Almanac* (Vermillion, S.D.: Dakota Press, University of South Dakota, 1969), 26; data from S.D. Secretary of State, "Official Election Returns and Registration Figures for South Dakota: General Elections (for 1978, 1980, 1982, 1984, and 1986)," State Capitol Building, Pierre, S.D.

3. *South Dakota Codified Laws,* Title 2-12 (dealing with lobbyists).

4. *South Dakota Codified Laws,* Titles 2-12 and 12-25 (dealing with lobbyists and campaign financing, respectively).

5. Bob Mercer, *Aberdeen American News* (S.D.), February 8, 1987, p. 1. Other articles on PAC activity appeared in the paper on January 26 and 27, 1987.

6. Interview with Bob Mercer, February 19, 1987.

7. Bob Mercer, *Aberdeen American News,* February 8, 1987, p. 1.

8. Ibid., 3.

9. *Sioux Falls Argus Leader* (S.D.), March 8, 1987, p. 11A. The headline of colum-

nist David Kranz's story at the conclusion of the legislative session read, "Lawmakers Gave Mickelson Most of What He Wanted."

10. *Sioux Falls Argus Leader,* March 9, 1987, p. 2B. The headline of an article by Steve Erpenbach read, "Session Unproductive for Farmers, Some Say."

11. Sarah McCally Morehouse, *State Politics, Parties and Policy* (New York: Holt, Rinehart & Winston, 1981), 110.

12. Jeremiah Murphy has lectured about lobbying to groups of students from South Dakota State University on several occasions since the mid-1970s. The following comments draw on those lectures.

WISCONSIN

Pressure Politics and a Lingering Progressive Tradition

RONALD D. HEDLUND

To understand politics and government in Wisconsin, it is essential to appreciate the role of the Progressive movement. From its emergence in the 1890s, the Progressive movement profoundly affected citizen views of politics, the procedures used to make public decisions, the policies made by state government, and Wisconsin's political and governmental institutions. Although its direct influence has waned, the Progressive tradition continues to have an impact on the Wisconsin political scene. Progressivism's distrust of big business and skepticism about the consequences of pressure politics created an atmosphere of public wariness regarding special interest groups and their "pressure-bringing" activities which lingers in the state.[1]

This continuing impact can be illustrated by events that unfolded in 1986 and formed one of the more ironic twists of political fortune in the state's history. As earlier, the role of special interests and their representatives were at the core. A century after Progressive leader Robert M. "Fighting Bob" La Follette, Sr., began his political career by opposing special interests that obtained political favors via "gifts," his grandson, and contemporary standardbearer, was reprimanded by the Wisconsin Ethics Board and fined the legal maximum, $500, for actions involving a well-known lobbyist, James Boullion. Specifically, Wisconsin attorney general Bronson La Follette admitted to one violation of the ethics code and to permitting "the appearance of impropriety" to develop in his "official" actions.[2] Ten months later, after having suffered an unaccustomed electoral defeat, La Follette, the lobbyist, one lobby group (the Tavern League of Wisconsin), and Wisconsin treasurer Charles P. Smith were sued by the Wisconsin secretary of state for lobby law violations. The complaint charged that La Follette (1) accepted an unsecured, personal loan of $3,000 from the lobbyist (repaid after the Ethics Board finding); (2) accepted a free plane trip to Minnesota; (3) "suggested" (in jest, he maintained) that a lobbyist purchase a product from a company he partially owned; (4) announced at a Department of Justice meeting (again in jest) that a company should consider purchasing this same product; and (5) knew that a company he partly owned received a loan and a loan guarantee from a group that employed the lobbyist.

As this crisis was passing, revelations in mid-1988 about unethical and unlawful lobbying practices began an onslaught of new investigations that made the 1986 events seem pale. Within twelve months (1) eight legislators, one former legislator, and one legislative officer had paid civil fines for accepting gifts (e.g., food, drink, lodging) from lobbyists; (2) one legislative leader was ordered by the state Ethics Board to pay forfeitures for accepting a free vacation from a lobbyist; (3) several legislators and former legislators, including the governor and attorney general, admitted accepting free meals and so on from lobbyists but were not charged because of the minor nature of their actions (accepting a can of soda) or the passage of time; (4) two lobbyists were charged with felonies for illegal campaign contributions (in one case $3,255, and in the other, $640); (5) four lobbyists and three groups faced civil fines for providing something of value to state officials; (6) one group and its president paid fines for felony charges involving "laundered" campaign contributions; (7) one legislator was charged with felonies for "stealing" from his own campaign funds and accepting money from a lobbyist.

Many of the practices that led to these charges are "tolerated" in other states, but the consequences in Wisconsin were far reaching: (1) La Follette—a popular, well-known state official, reelected to the same office on four occasions—was fined and defeated and left public office under a cloud of suspicion; (2) several legislators, including three holding chamber leadership positions, paid fines and faced public embarrassment and potential electoral defeat for their behavior; (3) Boullion, a widely known, influential lobbyist, was fined, lost his sponsoring groups, and agreed not to seek a lobbying license for three years; (4) two influential lobbyists, Gary Goyke and James Hough, and one associate, Carl Otte, faced career-threatening consequences; (5) the sizable and influential Tavern League, as well as Pfizer Pharmaceuticals, Inc., and the Wisconsin Utilities Association, were fined and suffered a "tarnished image"; and (6) widespread demands were voiced to "reform and cleanse" lobbying activities in Wisconsin. These examples illustrate the high level of attention given special interest activities in Wisconsin; the potentially grave consequences for public officials, individuals, and groups associated with "transgressions"; the open atmosphere in which the public's business is transacted in the state; and the high standard for conduct expected of Wisconsin public officials. All are legacies from the Progressive tradition.

Wisconsin: A Political History of Change and Progressivism

From its admission to the Union as the 30th state in 1848 until 1856, Wisconsin was politically Democratic.[3] The increasing number of Yankees, however, together with immigrants from northern Europe, especially Germany and Scandinavia, pushed the state toward the Republicans. The Civil War firmly placed Wisconsin in Republican hands, where it remained for the rest of the nineteenth and much of the twentieth century. The only exceptions were brief periods of Democratic (and later Progressive) control of the state legislature and the governor's office from 1891 to 1895 and 1933 to 1938.[4]

The most enduring political element of the late 1800s and early 1900s was the emergence of the Progressive movement and its champion, "Fighting Bob" La Follette. The state was controlled by a conservative Republican political machine whose abuses of power included patronage, dispensation of special privileges, and domination by special interests (railroads, lumber barons, and utility companies). When these factors combined with economic uncertainties in agriculture, growing urban centers, and the changing economic base (the growth of foundries, machine shops, and manufacturing, especially in Milwaukee), an opportunity was created for a new force in state politics: progressivism. It began as a movement within the Republican party and later achieved a separate partisan identity.[5] In describing Wisconsin progressivism, noted historian Robert S. Maxwell stated:

> Thus the Wisconsin population from whom came the most fundamental and thoroughgoing of the state progressive movements did not differ noticeably from its neighbors in the other north-central states. The program developed in Wisconsin was distinguished from the reforms of other states chiefly in that it was more comprehensive and far-reaching rather than more radical. As elsewhere, Progressivism in Wisconsin was neither left-wing

agrarian nor socialistic. It was moderate, pragmatic, and non-doctrinaire in approach, including agricultural, industrial, and intellectual elements in its appeal. As the movement developed and unfolded, powerful and able leaders emerged to give it direction.[6]

Among its long-term consequences for the state were (1) an enduring penchant for innovation in the public sector, represented in Wisconsin's motto, "Forward"; (2) initiation of numerous public services such as railroad and utility regulation, workers' compensation, unemployment compensation, and state-sponsored insurance; (3) inauguration of reforms in political institutions, including municipal home rule, nonpartisan local elections, presidential primaries, and legislative representation based on population; (4) provision of a high level of public services to all citizens, with a fair distribution of costs; (5) establishment of "clean government," based on citizen consultation and involvement; (6) a suspicion of special economic interests, especially railroads, public utilities, big corporations, and economic institutions; and (7) protection of individual rights against special interests and government.[7] In summarizing, Maxwell noted that progressivism "included the idea of placing more of the machinery and functions of government under the direct control of the electorate and a demand for the removal of corrupt influences from positions of power. Progressivism also envisioned the expansion of government to curb special-interest groups and to promote the economic and social well-being of the individual citizen."[8]

In the early twentieth century, immigration continued but the countries of origin changed to southern and, especially, eastern Europe. Large numbers of Poles, Czechs, Russians, and Italians located in Milwaukee and southeastern Wisconsin. These newcomers affected not only the social and economic patterns where they settled, but also the political ones, and a stronger base for the Democratic party began to emerge. During the 1930s both the Democrats and Progressives (now a separate party) experienced brief rejuvenations, but they began to fade after the 1936 election. Emigration from the southern United States, Mexico, and Puerto Rico occurred after World War II, but the numbers of minority residents in the state remains low—5.6 percent nonwhite, according to 1980 census figures. As with previous groups, these minorities tended to live (not always by choice) in segregated neighborhoods, which limited their political impact. Their predisposition in politics was clearly Democratic and mainly liberal. By the late 1960s Wisconsin was becoming a competitive two-party state, with the Democrats holding the governor's office from 1959 to 1965 and controlling both legislative chambers since 1975. Three Republicans and three Democrats have been governor since 1965. Against this backdrop, contemporary Wisconsin-style interest group politics emerged and matured.

Policy Making and Economic Sectors in Wisconsin

With Lake Superior to the north and Lake Michigan to the east, Wisconsin's proximity to the Great Lakes has been an important factor in the state's history, economy, and interest group development and has augmented the development of its agricultural and manufacturing sectors.[9] The fertile land encompasses more than 82,000 farms (covering almost half of Wisconsin's land area), which are known for the production of dairy products (ranking 1st nationally), cattle, corn, hogs, and vegetables. Although productive acreage and the number of farms have declined, the agricultural component of the state's economy places Wisconsin 8th in terms of farm marketing.

At times, agriculture's hold on state politics has been substantial. Wisconsin was the last state to permit sale of colored oleo margarine (1967), and this approval stipulated a special tax, targeted to support research on dairy farming. Dairy interests had long controlled key legislative positions, from which they defeated efforts to permit the sale of yellow oleo margarine. The growing urbanization of the state had diminished rural sectors, but not their dominance. It took the 1964 reapportionment to remove some rural leaders from their positions of influence, allowing the legislature to respond to public pressure for changing state statutes. The agricultural interests have not been able to reestablish their dominance of state government in part because two-thirds of the population lives in metropolitan areas.

The abundance of highly skilled labor, together with a convenient rail and water transportation system, fostered the development of the machine, tool and die, and manufacturing industries in the state. The availability of agricultural products and timber were critical for food processing and paper production. As a consequence, labor unions have been an important interest group, which in 1982 had membership estimated at 24.5 percent of total nonagricultural employment. Though such membership has decreased from former levels, a substantial proportion of the population continues to have some family member affiliated with a union. Both unions and corporate leadership influence public policy, as seen in the former's success in obtaining legislative support (but a governor's veto) for a higher minimum wage three times in 1987–88, and in the latter's ability to preserve a liberal capital gains tax provision via a governor's veto in 1987. One reason for Republican Governor Thompson's actions on both of these issues was his close association with business and industry leaders and their representatives, especially Wisconsin Manufacturers and Commerce (WMC), who took strong stands on each.[10]

At one time, forests covered more than 85 percent of the state. As a consequence, lumber and related industries have a long history of political involvement in Wisconsin. Frequently, early politics revolved around the twin forces of lumbering and railroading. Indeed, one primary target of the Progressives was wealthy lumber barons who continued to dominate politics in the 1890s despite a decline in their share of the state's economy. Today forests cover about 40 percent of the state, but political domination by lumber interests is long gone. Two legacies of this abundance of timber are tourism and a large paper industry.

The political sensitivity of tourism needs resulted in successful legislation, in 1985, to prevent the state university system from beginning its fall semester until after September 1 (the resort industry had sought a post–Labor Day date) so as not to deprive resorts of one primary source for seasonal labor.[11] The argument accepted by legislators from tourism lobbyists was that establishing this start date would not harm the university system and would assist an important economic sector in keeping its guests as long as possible. Progressives might question the propriety of the state's imposing policies on an agency to aid private business.

Wisconsin's diverse economy has not insulated the state from recent economic recessions. Like most states in the region, Wisconsin has been especially hard hit in its "rusting" manufacturing segment, as well as in its agricultural economy. These events have made state government a target for appeals requesting policies that foster economic development, a "probusiness" climate, and financial relief for farm operators. For example, in 1986 the financially troubled American Motors Corporation (AMC), with strong support from the United Auto Workers (UAW), sought and received state legislative support for a $3 million retraining program for workers on a new assembly line to be operated for Chrysler Corporation. In the 1987–89 budget the Wisconsin Development Fund committed $5 million for retraining at Chrysler and $9 million for General Motors. When the Wisconsin Finance Development Board, the committee responsible for formally distributing these funds, proposed reducing the amount committed to GM by $3.6 million, the governor quickly intervened, explaining that "an agreement had been made."[12] The use of public money to assist companies, even through worker training programs, would not be a strategy advocated by Progressives. Further, the brouhaha over Chrysler's 1988 closing of its Kenosha assembly line after having been promised state support and providing reassurances to state officials created even more skepticism about state support for private enterprise.

The continuing plight of the state's farmers led to a flurry of activity during the 1985–86 legislative session, with part or all of two special sessions devoted to this problem. Laws were enacted which provided agricultural loan guarantees and interest rate reductions and created a farm mediation and arbitration program to resolve disputes with creditors, helping to prevent foreclosures. Though many public officials and observers conceded that these actions would have a modest impact at best, these enactments were visible signs that the legislature and governor were concerned about agricultural issues.

Together these state actions suggest that Wisconsin public officials have been sensitive and responsive in their decision making to the policy needs of economic sectors in the state, although in manners sometimes at variance with those championed by Progressives. In these instances it became apparent that some action by state government was desired to assist these important economic sectors. The Progressive movement never denied that a state could or should initiate action to protect its economic sectors; however, the methods used to determine which sectors to protect, how, and at what costs were important considerations to Progressives. This dilemma of state help to economic sectors is intensified when one focuses on the attention being given by government to narrow special interest groups active in state politics.

The Interest Group Setting in Wisconsin

Although some of the actions initiated by Wisconsin government to protect and advance interests have been taken because of the advocacy of public officials and interested citizens, many have been enacted at the urging of narrowly organized special interest groups. To understand how this influence takes place, Zeigler and van Dalen proposed that attention be given to the effects of the social and political setting as it affects groups and government.[13] This area of study includes how group activities are regulated, how factors from the environment affect group fortunes, and how group characteristics advance or retard group success.

State Regulation of Pressure Group Activity

Like all other states, Wisconsin regulates the activities groups use to influence policy making through both state statutes and administrative rules. The official philosophy, adopted from the Progressive tradition, is stated in the statutes and indicates that regulations have been adopted to ensure an open, honest, and responsible government. The means for achieving this goal involve disclosure of information about influence and lobbying activities and monitoring of activities by a variety of state agencies. As a consequence, the regulations require that both lobbyists (agents) and the principals (organizations) they represent register with the secretary of state and report on their influence activities. Exempted are activities on one's own behalf and in a public hearing. Any other attempt to influence action by state officials—legislative or administrative—by direct communication is defined as lobbying, and receipt of a salary, fee, or retainer for seeking to influence classifies one as a lobbyist.[14] This definition reflects the Progressive approach, which protects individual and "grass-roots" organizational contact with state government.

Representatives from state agencies and public employees must also register and report their activities if a part of their regular duties includes efforts to influence legislative activity. Even the governor's office is not exempt from this ruling and must register and report its lobbying expenditures. Representatives from other levels of government may be exempt if they exercise their influence via a public forum or are furnishing requested information; however, many choose to register, thus avoiding problems.

Both lobbyists and principals are required to file reports every six months describing their activities and indicating expenditures. Although it is not required, organizations and individuals may register at committee hearings, indicating their positions for or against the legislation under consideration, and most do. As a consequence, a great deal of information is available about the activities of special interest groups with regard to pending legislation in Wisconsin.[15] These requirements were basic provisions of Progressivism's approach for the conduct of governmental business.

In addition to registration and reporting requirements, the statutes set out several specific prohibitions concerning the activities of lobbyists, principals, state public officials, and even candidates for public office. These prohibitions are very restrictive with regard to certain lobbying activities (among the most restrictive in any state) and reflect the Progressive tradition. For example, lobbyists and principals cannot provide to any state employee, elected official, or candidate any gift having a pecuniary value, including lodging, transportation, food, meals, or beverages. If, however, food, meals, or beverages are furnished as part of a bona fide social function or regular meeting, they may be provided to state employees, elected officials, or candidates. Rumors persist and evidence emerged in 1988 about the degree to which this Progressive-influenced restriction is being eroded, as witnessed by the "entertaining" reputed at Madison establishments like Namio's and The Madison Club. One example involved Governor Thompson and two of his cabinet secretaries, who each agreed to pay $86.96 plus court costs to settle violations of this provision of the state lobby law. The transgression occurred when the two cabinet secretaries, before the new governor's inauguration, were having dinner with representatives from the Wisconsin Professional Police Association. The governor-elect stopped at the table to say hello and then remained for a brief conversation. In its report of expenditures to the secretary of state, the group listed this meeting and indicated the expenditures. Since it was a prohibited activity, the secretary of state sued the individuals plus the organization in a civil case and obtained a forfeiture via a stipulated agreement. From July 1987 to July 1988 the secretary of state's office filed twenty-one civil lawsuits regarding similar violations in the lobby law. This effort illustrates the degree to which the restrictions exist and are enforced, as well as the completeness of the records filed as a part of lobbying regulations.

Restrictions also exist governing the lobbying profession. Lobbyists are prevented from initiating action, either legislative or administrative, that might assist them in obtaining employment by groups. Further, lobbyists are prohibited from negotiating a contingency fee contract with the principal to receive compensation depending on the success or failure of administrative or legislative actions. These regulations are in addition to the prohibitions against providing anything of value to state employees and to making campaign contributions during legislative sessions. In short, the regulation of lobbying in Wisconsin is intended to maintain an open and honest atmosphere surrounding this activity, and the widespread consensus is that these goals are largely achieved, in spite of recent revelations.

The primary exception in terms of providing anything of value to candidates or elected public officials is the ability of lobbyists and principals to give campaign contributions to candidates. This practice is explicitly permitted in the statutes, although time limits are imposed to prevent contributions from being made at the same time that legislative or administrative actions by elected officials are being initiated. As a consequence, fund-raising events by campaign committees and by the leadership of all caucuses take place in Madison, with the largest number of attendees typically being lobbyists, principals, and PAC representatives.

Recent difficulties with existing laws and administrative rules have led the legislature to make several changes in the lobby law. Such changes revised various definitions to remove existing ambiguities; clarified the reimbursement provisions to permit candidates and elected officials to accept speaking engagements; expanded the scope of reported activities and expenditures to include time and money spent on "research"; and shifted the responsibility for enforcing lobby laws from the secretary of state to the Ethics Commission.

External Setting Factors

The nature of the general political, social, and economic setting, together with the level of public support held for policy alternatives, has a great deal to do with the impact of an interest sector or pressure group on decision making. For example, the widely reported declining strength of the U.S. industrial and manufacturing sector has increased public awareness of and support for governmental efforts aimed at protecting and stimulating this sector of every state's economy. As a consequence, a variety of governmental policies more favorable to business and industry are being proposed and implemented nationally and in the states.

In Wisconsin, Democratic governor Earl, on taking office in 1983, signaled the importance he attached to this effort by appointing his lieutenant governor to head the Department of Development; calling two special legislative sessions to consider economic development issues in 1984–85; proposing several initiatives to assist business, including legislation to enhance interstate banking and to permit utility holding companies; and creating a business permit information center (to reduce red tape) and a business development fund. Nonetheless, Earl found himself under heavy attack from the business sector during his 1986 reelection bid. His opponent, Republican Tommy Thompson, had a strong probusiness legislative record, an impressive array of business connections (including WMC, the realtors, the roadbuilders, and the corporate medical people), and almost unanimous endorsements from the business community. As a consequence, one of the major campaign issues was the need for state government to be more "probusiness." This example illustrates how public support permitted and even forced both gubernatorial candidates to advocate policies supporting business and industry. As a consequence, regardless of who was elected governor in 1986, business interests would fare better than ten or fifteen years earlier when public support favored interests such as energy conservation and environmental protection.

The extent to which state government was willing to go to support state business was tested in the fall of 1987. Australian billionaire Alan Bond initiated an "unfriendly takeover" bid for the last sizable independent Wisconsin brewer—G. Heileman Brewing Company, the 4th largest U.S. brewer. Immediately, the company countered with several "protective actions" and an impressive public relations campaign to win support from key groups and individuals. One of the more interesting was an announcement of support from Governor Thompson and an offer to call a special legislative session. It became clear that the governor was prepared to do almost anything Heileman requested in order to protect a "home-grown" industry.[16] One strategy involved legislation that made takeovers without corporate board approval much more difficult.[17] The legislation, prepared by Heileman's attorneys, was introduced to a special session less than two weeks after the takeover was announced. With lobbyists and observers for both sides crowding the chambers, the legislature convened. Amendments to the proposed legislation sought by Bond were introduced, but the Heileman version passed overwhelmingly and was signed by the governor within three days of its introduction.

The company then formally rejected Bond's offer but invited a friendly takeover bid at a higher selling price and with certain conditions. Although Bond threatened court suits, he raised his offer; Heileman quickly accepted. This turnabout was too much for several legislators, who immediately questioned the legislation and attacked what had been passed less than one week earlier. These doubts proved well founded when a federal district court ruled Wisconsin's antitakeover legislation unconstitutional within twenty-four months. Regardless of the facts, it was widely perceived that one company had been able to obtain specific actions by state government to be used for a stronger bargaining position in a private transaction that worked largely for private benefit. Such a role for state government was clearly at odds with what the Progressives would have advocated. The key elements to the success of this strategy were widespread concern about a hostile takeover; broad-based public support for Heileman, orchestrated by the company; and adroit strategy by the Heileman "team" to a receptive state government.

The absence of support for a policy or program can also be a factor in public decision making. In response to escalating health-care costs in Wisconsin, the Democratic governor proposed a Hospital Rate Setting Commission in his 1983–85 budget bill. The purpose of the commission was to review and approve all rate increases for hospitals throughout the state. The Democratic legislature approved, in deference to the governor, but without enthusiasm. In passing the legislation, lawmakers established a "sunset" for the commission for June 30, 1987.[18]

As the time approached for commission reauthorization, the new Republican governor, with long and close ties to the hospital industry, including substantial campaign support, let it be known that he was prepared to let the commission end. The Wisconsin Hospital Association strongly opposed the commission and debated its supporters across the state on whether state government should protect consumers or permit hospital costs to be established by competition. A loose coalition of senior citizens' groups (especially the American Association of Retired Persons), consumer groups, and certain unions supported continuing the commission. The governor's opposition to the commission probably doomed its continuation, but an absence of strong legislative support was also obvious. Consequently, it went out of existence with little public outcry largely because its main proponent (the Democratic governor) had been defeated.

These cases show how public opinion, the tenor of the times, and the broad public setting can affect the fortunes of policy proposals. Supporters of the Progressive tradition certainly recognized how the broader social and economic environment affected government and supported public decisions consistent with the public's will. Yet many would have opposed efforts by state government to act on behalf of a private interest even if the public supported it. Certainly the state's entrance into the Heileman effort would have been resisted. This change probably reflects a dimming adherence to Progressive tenets of governing in Wisconsin.

Group-Based Factors

David B. Truman argued that a third set of environmental factors important in policy making relate to the group itself—its resources and internal organization.[19] These factors are especially important to narrowly focused interest groups since such groups do not represent either a sufficient number of people or a substantial economic sector so that they could expect to be effective simply by publicizing and pressing their needs. Instead, these groups must rely on their resources, internal organization, and cohesiveness. And although internal organization alone is not sufficient to ensure access to decision makers, it is an important ingredient that should not be minimized.

The Wisconsin Education Association Council (WEAC) is generally reputed to be one of the most effective special interest groups, if not the most effective, in the state. Beyond recognition of the current importance placed on education, legislators, lobbyists, and other public officials have repeatedly pointed out that WEAC has done a very good job in organizing itself to be effective.

This effectiveness became clear when, during the 1987 legislative session, proposals were presented to alter the state's public employee retirement system. Because of the successful investments of retirement funds, a surplus of more than $2.6 billion was projected at the beginning of 1987. Several plans were presented and discussed to resolve this situation, including increasing pension benefits for retirees; permitting a "window" of early retirement to reduce the size of the more expensive, senior ranks of public employees; returning a portion of the earnings to local units of government; and cutting the costs of retirement contributions required from units of government. However, the Republican governor made it clear that he would veto any bill that did not liberalize the binding arbitration provisions covering public employees. Needless to say, public employee unions and the Democratic legislature, both of which had played important roles in securing the arbitration provisions, were opposed to linking changes in one to changes in both. A stalemate seemed inevitable, yet the governor sought a way around the impasse which involved direct negotiations with WEAC.[20] These negotiations were rumored to have begun months earlier and generated considerable discussion once they became public. During legislative debate on altering the retirement provisions, members in both chambers noted that the manner in which the agreement was reached was one reason for opposing linkage of the two issues. Opposition developed to the governor's proposal, and the legislature passed its version, which was vetoed by the governor. The important feature of this case was the governor's decision to attempt resolving the issue via direct negotiations with one special interest group while excluding the legislature. Two subsequent attempts to liberalize public employee retirement without altering the arbitration procedures in 1987–88 were also vetoed. Finally, in 1989, WEAC reached an accommodation with its opponents (largely outside state government) regarding public employee retirement. Although this understanding was disavowed by legislators, a new bill was passed and signed into law in a very short period of time.

Another narrow interest group noted in Wisconsin for its organizational strength and judicious resource use is the Wisconsin Chiropractic Association (WCA). While relatively small in numbers, chiropractors have become very effective on a narrow range of topics, much more so than the state medical society. As one legislator said, "I can always count on them to help me during my campaign. They're not arrogant or pushy and don't expect a lot. They know what they're doing [in a campaign] and do it very well." Their continuing strength in Wisconsin is traceable not only to their organization, but also to their concentration on a single, easy-to-understand issue. For almost twenty years they sought a statutory requirement that insurance providers cover chiropractic services on a basis comparable to physician and hospital fees. Opposition by doctors and hospitals was widely portrayed as a selfish effort by a special group to maintain its own preferred position. Successive legislatures had passed bills requiring the insurance coverage, only to have the governor veto them. This repeated scenario did not deter the chiropractors, but only intensified their efforts to unite their members and to continue their support of legislative candidates. In 1987 they finally succeeded when

Republican governor Thompson did not veto this provision in the budget bill. (The governor's secretary of administration, James R. Klauser, was the former lobbyist for the WCA, and their political conduit contributed $6,185 to Thompson's 1986 campaign.) Persistence, a strong base of support for a tightly knit group, and active involvement in political campaigns were the primary reasons for their ultimate success.

When asked about special interests that suffered because of the absence of a strong organizational base, several legislators mentioned the contemporary standing of most unions in the state. These respondents indicated that many union leaders have aged and grown out of touch with their membership and with the contemporary economic and social situation. With weakened ties to rank-and-file union members, little agreement on agenda items has been apparent. The unions, especially the AFL-CIO, are not the potent force they once were in Wisconsin politics. Even obtaining legislative support for a higher minimum wage in 1987 and again in 1989 didn't mean much because everyone knew the governor would veto it and that a successful override was not likely. Similarly, the governor's veto of a liberalized plant-closing bill thwarted another policy initiative sought by unions. Thus, while labor continues to be a primary source of electoral funds for Democratic candidates, its ability to convert this support into political clout has waned. A possible mitigating factor, offered by one legislator, is that Wisconsin unions have accomplished much of their agenda and are in a period of transition until future issues and priorities emerge. Such is clearly the case with unemployment benefits, an area in which the unions have been very successful in defending the status quo.

Wisconsin Lobbyists

Time and again, public officials, when talking to the author about interest groups in Wisconsin, noted that perhaps the single most important factor affecting success is the person(s) representing the group before state government. A good lobbyist with access to decision makers, when complemented by the factors elaborated above, can materially affect a group's fortunes. The characteristics of the lobbyist are important regardless of whether attention is directed to the legislature or to an agency. In fact, discussions with lobbyists indicate that they tend to represent their clients before all units of state government, not just the legislature.

Lobbyist Traits

Several themes are apparent with regard to the attributes and approaches of people sought as lobbyists. Of primary importance in Wisconsin, as elsewhere, is honesty. Public officials often use lobbyists for information, especially on the impact of proposed decisions, and expect lobbyists to tell the truth, even if it is to the group's disadvantage. The most effective presentation, according to legislators, is one that provides a balanced set of facts and figures both supporting and opposing the group's position. Lobbyists interviewed pointed out the steps they take to ensure balance, accuracy, and a quick response. One reason for this attention is that information remains a primary means whereby Wisconsin lobbyists can gain access to public officials for influence. A common response was that information from "good" lobbyists is better than that provided by regular staff. Every public official and lobbyist interviewed stated that a single purposeful lie or misleading statement will probably prevent a lobbyist from every being effective again.

A second important lobbyist attribute is access to and knowledge of state government. Persons with prior experience in state government are widely viewed as having an inherent advantage as lobbyists. One study in 1986 found that 14 of the 317 lobbyists registered were former legislators (4.4 percent), but that they represented more than one-third of the 450 registered clients.[21] In addition, two former governors registered in 1989–90. This domination of lobbying by former legislators clearly indicates the degree to which prior experience and contacts in state government serve as an important base for access and influence.

In assessing lobbying tactics, legislators, public officials, and lobbyists all stressed the importance of the approach and attitude taken by group representatives. "Bashing" legislators or agency staff (i.e., attacking them sharply with little pause) based on party identification, type of district, personal philosophy, or anything else was seen as "dangerous" to the positions being advocated. Every official interviewed was able to cite examples of how some group had attempted to use embarrassment, confrontation, "unfounded attack," or name calling to aid its cause. Four groups received more mention than others: the Wisconsin Action Coalition (a "left-wing" group that lost its credibility with legislators because of rude and confrontational tactics as well as inaccurate information), the National Rifle Association (which "attacked" legislators personally and "distorted" member policy positions), WMC (a conservative business organization that was seen as "needlessly assaulting" Democrats),[22] and unions (some of which were always attacking and "baiting" Republicans, regardless of the issue). These tactics are the opposite of efforts used by most lobbyists to build warm and cordial relations with public officials.[23]

Lobbyists and Pressure Groups

The number of private lobbying groups registering has climbed steadily between 1979 and 1986 from 314 to 485 (a 54 percent increase), surpassing only slightly the growth of public agencies, 28 to 41 (46 percent) (Table 14.1). During the 1987–88 legislative session 612 groups registered, as did 34 state agencies. The most dramatic growth has been among health/insurance, transportation/recreation, government/education, and issue/miscellaneous groups. Although no type of organization has experienced a decrease in numbers, the growth patterns have been smallest for labor/professional, environmental, commerce/industry, and banking groups. In 1985–86, business interests (banking, commerce, industry, health, and insurance) comprised more than 40 percent of all private groups registering, compared with 17 percent for labor and professional groups; 40 percent is probably a conservative estimate because some energy, transportation, and recreational groups are also businesses.

As for lobbyists, there are approximately three to four times the number of lobbyists registered as there are legislators. Although not all lobbyists attend every legislative function, this comparison illustrates the attention being given to lobbying. The 1985–86 figures represent a 30 percent growth in private lobbyists since 1979–80 and a 37 percent increase for public. A total of 434 lobbyists registered for private groups in 1987–88, while 149 registered on behalf of public agencies. Across-year expenditure comparisons are invalid because of changes in reporting requirements; however, one interesting observation is that almost half (49 percent) of all expenditures in 1985–86 were reported by business interests.

The inclusion of public agencies in the registration and reporting requirements underscores the degree to which state agencies pay attention to lobbying activities before the legislature. Table 14.1 also provides an indication of their attention level to this aspect of policy making. During the first six months of 1986 the governor's office reported spending more than $69,000 on legislative lobbying. One state agency considered by many to be an effective interest group is the University of Wisconsin system. This entrance of state agencies into lobbying would be suspicious to the Progressives.

Table 14.1. Group representation in Wisconsin lobbying activities 1979-80, 1981-82, and 1985-86

Organizations	1979-80 N	%	1981-82 N	%	1985-86 N	%
Private groups						
Agriculture	8	3	10	2	14	3
Banking	16	5	22	5	20	4
Commerce/Industry	83	26	114	28	111	23
Energy	11	4	16	4	17	4
Environment	7	2	10	2	9	2
Government/Education	39	12	49	12	69	14
Health/Insurance	29	9	32	8	66	14
Issues/Miscellaneous	35	11	60	15	64	13
Labor/Professional	69	22	68	17	82	17
Transportation/ Recreation	17	5	21	5	33	7
Total	314	99	402	98	485	101
All groups						
Private groups	314	92	402	92	485	92
Public agencies	28	8	37	8	41	8
Total	342	100	439	100	526	100

People	N	%	N	%	N	%
Private lobbyists	284	73	333	68	369	72
Public lobbyists	104	27	158	32	142	28
Total	388	100	491	100	511	100

Expenditures[a]	$	%	$	%	$	%
Private groups						
Agriculture	62,715	3	82,064	4	59,770	2
Banking	170,015	8	188,141	9	327,207	11
Commerce/Industry	492,585	24	467,307	22	894,860	29
Energy	31,258	2	77,088	4	150,334	5
Environment	41,696	2	33,496	2	70,763	2
Government/Education	351,950	17	377,460	18	397,257	13
Health/Insurance	163,407	8	120,784	6	319,300	10
Issues/Miscellaneous	192,102	9	228,331	11	275,949	9
Labor/Professional	467,486	23	442,060	21	499,081	16
Transportation/Recreation	86,920	4	73,600	4	95,346	3
Total	2,060,133	100	2,090,322	101	3,089,867	100

Source: Compiled by Michael P. Wenzel from records kept by the Wisconsin secretary of state and Biennial Reports. Entries are groups and individuals officially registered as lobbyists and principals.

[a]In 1984 the secretary of state's office began new reporting procedures for groups. As a consequence, comparisons of dollar amounts across years are not meaningful. Further, for these three sessions, if a group spent less than $250 on lobbying in a six-month period, it was not expected to report expenditures. Groups spending between $250 and $500 could file a "special verified statement" that did not list expenditures. Thus, expenditure data are approximations.

Megalobbyists

Since 1983, the Wisconsin legislative lobbying scene has witnessed the emergence of a new approach to lobbying—interest group representation by megalobbyists. Though contract lobbyists have a long history in the state, the domination of lobbying efforts by a relatively few persons is unprecedented. Of the 136 lobbyists in the 1986–87 "Directory of the Association of Wisconsin Lobbyists," 22 percent were listed as contract lobbyists. These lobbyists have large numbers of clients (Gary Goyke, a former senator, had more than twice as many—sixty vs. twenty-five—as his nearest competitor, Bill Broyderick, a former representative), have become very visible in the legislative process, and are reputed to be very effective on behalf of their clients. The exact number of megalobbyists in Wisconsin is open to some debate, but the consensus is that there are at least six and perhaps as many as fifteen. They tend to be former legislators or to have had government experience, they are aggressive and outgoing, and they are known for their "good access to legislators" and state agency personnel. Their continued access, however, depends on their maintaining good relations with officials and providing excellent, well-documented information and a new perspective on a problem. One megalobbyist stated that the election of a "new breed" of legislator has resulted in a change in the type of information he provides: "Since more and more legislators are being elected right out of college or from legislative staff positions, they lack many real life experiences and have difficulty assessing the impact of various proposals on those affected. Consequently, much of the information I'm now providing indicates *how* a bill will affect various people in the state." In spite of recent revelations, wheeling and dealing are insufficient for applying influence in Wisconsin, even if you're a megalobbyist.

The concentration of lobbying and access to public officials in a few hands would be strongly resisted and even attacked by the Progressives, but this position holds little sway in contemporary Wisconsin. Legislators report that the appearance of megalobbyists has added to the level of information provided and to the general professionalism of lobbying. An initial explanation for increases in this type of lobbyist includes their close ties to Democratic leaders in the legislature and their ability to deliver legislative access to their clients.

Most of these megalobbyists have formed their own service corporations rather than joining existing law and public relations firms involved in lobbying. Though the involvement of law and public relations firms in lobbying has a long tradition in Wisconsin, there is no indication that their role has become greater or more dominant in recent years, unlike trends reported in other states.

Several concerns have been expressed about the trend toward megalobbyists in Wisconsin. Perhaps the greatest is the potential for domination. Some fear that lobbying will become a "one-stop shopping" activity in which a very few lobbyists will represent the entire spectrum of interests, thus restricting the diversity of views being presented to legislators. A second concern relates to the costs incurred by such representation. Contract lobbyists can be expensive, thus limiting their use to wealthy interests. Questions have also been posed about the resources that megalobbyists can command, especially during reelection efforts. For example, a lobbyist representing several organizations may be able to direct substantial individual, conduit,[24] and PAC contributions from each of the several organizations he or she represents to candidates. In a state legislative election this type of funding could easily be the difference in obtaining the necessary campaign financing. Finally, two of the so-called megalobbyists have been charged with a variety of violations in the state's ethics code and lobbying regulations. No one believes that the large scope of their lobbying activities had any role in the difficulties they now face, but some clients sought other contract lobbyists in 1989.

Having discussed the interest group setting and lobbyists in Wisconsin, it is now important to consider how groups representing important economic and social sectors as well as narrow special interests "press their case" for favorable policy decisions by Wisconsin state government. Even though the Progressive legacy opposed political responsiveness to special interests and advocated measures to distance such interests from the conduct of public business, such groups have developed strategies for approaching government.

Interest Group Tactics

Pressure and influence tactics directed toward public officials are important forces in public policy making. Key, Milbrath, and Zeigler and Baer have argued that by focusing attention on the communications and interactions among group representatives and public officials, one can develop an understanding of group effectiveness.[25] In Wisconsin these tactics and methods have evolved against a background of the Progressive tradition and consequently are open to public view, sometimes to the chagrin of many participants. Thus, much information is available to the ordinary citizen about group pressure and influence activities.

Grass-Roots Efforts

In Wisconsin, elected public officials expend great efforts to establish and maintain close ties to their constituents. Legislative candidates in many districts campaign door to door and attend a multiplicity of public meetings. Even legislative committees have a long tradition of citizen testimony and have recently increased the number of hearings held across the state. In short, elected public officials adhere to the Progressive norms of public contact and accessibility. Similar predispositions, but much less evidence, are reported for state agency officials.

One consequence is that public officials are very accepting of information and influence from the public. Evidence indicates that much communication takes place between the public (especially interested citizens) and officials on the entire range of issues. Although routine letter-writing and telephone campaigns have a limited impact on most issues, a relatively small number of thoughtful letters or personal visits can be very persuasive, according to legislators and staff.

One example of a decision reflecting grass-roots sentiment was approval for a state lottery and parti-mutuel betting. The 1848 Wisconsin Constitution prohibited the legislature from authorizing any lottery in the state. The provision was so restrictive that a constitutional amendment was passed in 1975 to permit the use of bingo by nonprofit religious, charitable, service, fraternal, and veterans' organizations. Popular wisdom held that the moral, family-oriented predispositions of Wisconsin residents would make the acceptance of lotteries and other games of chance highly unlikely. However, the fact that well over half of the states permit lotteries and/or betting with few apparent difficulties, plus the fact that Wisconsin was an "island" surrounded by states with lotteries, created a situation in which public opinion became supportive for a lottery and pari-mutuel betting.[26] The almost unanimous and constant opposition of newspapers caused what one lobbyist called heightened public awareness, which eventually back-fired and built support for gaming.

Several legislators who had long supported lotteries took the initiative and in 1986 secured initial legislative passage of a constitutional amendment permitting both lotteries and pari-mutuel betting. This success was followed in early 1987 by a second legislative approval (as required by the constitution), this time by a two-thirds majority. In April 1987 voters supported both measures. Interestingly, organized groups were not very active on any side of the issue during either legislative consideration. Public hearings were held and both sides presented evidence and opinion, but there were no intense lobbying or public relations efforts. In fact, the primary lobbying effort appeared late during the legislature's second consideration when passage by a two-thirds majority was needed to ensure an early vote. The overwhelming legislative sentiment was to let the public decide. Only when this amendment was nearing the public vote did opponents begin to organize seriously. In this instance, a state decision was made largely in the absence of strong pressure from organized groups, with officials deferring to a public vote.[27] Such deference to public wishes is very consistent with the Progressive tradition.

Legislative Lobbying

Although much legislation has its origins outside the legislature, a bill must be prepared by the Wisconsin Legislative Reference Bureau and officially introduced into the Senate or Assembly. In many instances the bill as introduced is formulated elsewhere (e.g., the governor prepares the first version of the budget bill), but once introduced, the bill is subject to review and alteration by each chamber. Thus, both chambers as well as individual legislators become targets for pressure from special interest groups, public officials, and citizens. In Wisconsin the budget bill has become a primary goal for attention because (1) virtually all actions by state government involve public money, (2) substantive policy is increasingly placed in the budget bill, and (3) the process of writing the legislative budget is especially susceptible to individual and group influence.

The saga of special interest group influence begins as the legislation is being planned because it is most advantageous to have the bill as introduced reflect a group's wishes. Ample opportunity exists for such influence because group representatives in Wisconsin have invested efforts in getting to know legislators and staff likely to be involved in formulating bills of interest to them.

On introduction, bills are referred to the appropriate committee(s), and public hearings are scheduled on nearly every one. The tradition of citizen input is long standing, but the influence of state agency personnel and registered lobbyists is considered much more important. For example, a 1980 study of legislative committees in Wisconsin found that the position taken by extralegislative groups had a substantial relationship to the decisions made by a committee on a bill. Absence of opposition at committee hearings by pressure groups was related to a favorable recommendation by that committee.[28] Regarding the impact of lobbyists, interviews with several committee members in 1987 indicated that (1) lobbyists provided much information and helped organize it for legislators; (2) lobbyists, who had good information and access, were able to get many of their provisions included; and (3) lobbyists conducted negotiations to help legislators secure compromises with one another.[29]

Once the committee has concluded its deliberations and forwarded its recommendations to each chamber, the majority party caucuses become involved if the bill is of partisan interest. For the budget bill, the majority party caucus is an especially important step. The strategy traditionally has been to prepare a bill that will be supported on the floor by enough members of that caucus to ensure the bill's passage.[30] A budget bill practice has evolved known as "decorating the legislative Christmas tree." Though some of this "decoration" takes place in committees, the practice has been honed to a fine edge in the majority caucuses. Such inclusion of pet provisions has become an important strategy for special interests and an anathema to Progressives. This practice led Assembly Speaker Loftus to describe the 1989–91 state budget as a "flypaper" bill because it attracted everything.

In Wisconsin the governor has general and line-item veto powers, providing an important opportunity to affect decisions. A Wisconsin Supreme Court decision described the line-item veto as "writing with an eraser" because it has been used to remove words, letters, and even numbers from a bill.[31] In 1987 this practice reached a new plateau when Governor Thompson exercised 290 partial vetoes in the budget bill, altering several provisions and even inserting some of his own. (This action, challenged in the courts, was upheld as constitutional.) This veto power has been used by governors to aid economic sectors as well as special interest groups, to the chagrin of Progressives.

Campaign Contributions

As elsewhere, election and reelection campaigns in Wisconsin are increasing in cost and in effort required from candidates. In urban legislative districts the amount of money required for a campaign keeps many persons from seeking office.[32] Thus, substantial contributions are required for a candidate to be successful; and as public officials continually point out, campaign contributions are one of the best strategies for ensuring access to a candidate after his or her election.

Using officially reported figures from the Wisconsin State Elections Board, Table 14.2 lists information about the recipients of campaign contributions for both individual candidates and political organizations. Across-time variation is one of the obvious characteristics in these figures. (Since there was no election for statewide office in 1979–80, the contributions for this period were quite different.) Among candidates, the division in contributions between the major parties had varied considerably with the election. The 58 percent growth in contributions to Republicans from 1981–82 to 1985–86 is in sharp contrast to the 10 percent growth for Democrats. This difference is due primarily to important contested races for governor and attorney general in 1986, both of

Table 14.2. Recipients of campaign contributions in Wisconsin 1979-80, 1981-82, and 1985-86

Recipients	1979-80 $	%a	1981-82 $	%a	1985-86 $	%a
Candidates						
Democratic	1,244,790	32	3,392,931	49	3,747,363	41
Republican	1,375,840	35	2,767,485	40	4,379,224	48
Others	8,988	-	30,120	-	11,661	-
Nonpartisan	1,293,661	33	692,774	10	966,563	11
Total	3,923,279	100	6,883,310	99	9,104,811	100
Statewide	131,679	3	2,933,695	43	4,315,859	47
Judicial	1,280,500	33	534,949	8	952,063	11
Legislative	2,511,100	64	3,414,666	50	3,836,889	42
Total	2,923,279	100	6,883,310	101	9,104,811	100
Incumbent	1,165,462	30	1,337,587	19	3,718,586	41
Nonincumbent	1,652,008	42	4,911,280	71	4,688,225	52
Continuing	1,105,809	28	634,443	9	698,000	8
Total	3,923,279	100	6,883,310	99	9,104,811	101
Winner	1,565,425	40	2,572,773	37	4,263,197	47
Loser	1,252,045	32	3,676,094	53	4,143,614	46
Continuing	1,105,809	28	634,443	9	698,000	8
Total	3,923,279	100	6,883,310	99	9,104,811	101
Political Party Committees						
Democratic	703,320	22	1,511,666	39	1,576,283	40
Republican	2,442,193	77	2,374,525	61	2,322,808	59
Others	20,977	1	17,410	-	21,379	1
Total	3,166,490	100	3,903,601	100	3,920,470	100
State	1,762,219	56	1,838,428	47	1,752,555	45
County	1,086,696	34	1,115,291	29	1,376,546	35
Local	102,002	3	83,066	2	72,705	2
Other	215,573	7	866,816	22	718,664	18
Total	3,166,490	100	3,903,601	100	3,920,470	100
Summary						
Candidates	3,923,279	34	6,883,310	42	9,104,811	55
Political party committees	3,166,490	27	3,903,601	24	3,920,470	24
Political action committees	4,498,121	39	5,500,187	34	3,397,847	21
Total	11,587,890	100	16,287,089	100	16,423,128	100

Source: Taken from appropriate years, Wisconsin State Elections Board, Biennial Reports of Wisconsin State Elections Board: Part II

aA (-) indicates that the dollars constitute less than 1 percent, and a (0) indicates no dollars received.

which were won by Republicans over incumbent Democrats. In each of these races the Republican challengers received more contributions than did their predecessors four years earlier. The election of 1982 is at variance in that more contributions went to Democratic than to Republican candidates.

Regarding the trends among statewide, judicial, and legislative positions, the most dramatic growth has been in increased contributions made to statewide candidates, which is expected given the increased contributions to the Republican gubernatorial and attorney general candidates noted above. The more modest growth in legislative contributions (12 percent) may indicate that these contributions have leveled off from earlier growth.

Table 14.2 also tabulates information on support for incumbents/ nonincumbents and winners/losers. Of great interest is the degree to which nonincumbents received support. Their higher contributions in 1981–82 (more than 3 to 1), resulted because both gubernatorial candidates in 1982 were nonincumbents. In general, it appears that challengers have been able to garner significant contributions in Wisconsin. Also interesting is the finding that substantial contributions were given to candidates who ultimately lost. Though only one period, 1981–82, showed more contributions for losers than winners, the percentage differences are not as great as might be expected.

As far as political organizations are concerned, Republican party committees have fared much better than Democratic ones in their receipt of campaign contributions. Although the disparity between the two has closed somewhat in recent years, Republican organizations continue to have a sizable edge over Democrats. Some of this increase may be due to the growth in the number of political party committees receiving campaign contributions. One example has been the appearance of campaign committees for each party caucus in each chamber of the legislature, presumably to compensate for the lack of attention given legislative candidates by the regular party organizations.[33] Perhaps the most important trend discernable in Table 14.2, however, is found in the summary section, indicating a sizable across-time shift in contributions to candidates. In 1985–86, 55 percent of all contributions were reported to candidates, compared with 34 percent in 1979–80. Most of this trend is attributable to increasing dollar contributions made to candidates directly and through group conduits, and to decreasing contributions to political action committees. Lobbyists contributed $61,092 to legislative fundraisers during the first six months of 1987.[34]

Regarding the type of contributor, Table 14.3 presents information on the sources of contributions for individuals and parties. These data indicate the degree to which candidates (and parties) rely on individuals, parties, PACs, and public funding in financing their campaigns. Interest group contributions are likely to appear as part of individual, PAC, and party committee funding. The only certainty is that candidates and public officials know the source of these funds and the groups, if any, represented. This became very evident during the fall of 1987 when the Democratic Assembly caucus held a rare closed session to discuss special legislative election campaign contributions from several lobbyists and their groups. The Republican victory—aided by these contributions—prompted an uproar among Democrats and led to a call for an audit of the activities of one group whose lobbyist was identified with these contributions. The publicity was sufficient warning about future campaign contributions. An effort by Assembly Republicans in 1988 to pour large amounts of money into a few marginal districts did not produce the defeats of incumbent Democrats desired.

Regardless of candidate or party, contributions from individuals compose a larger portion of all contributions than any other source—from 40 percent to 91 percent. Thus, contributions from individuals remain an important factor in financing campaigns in Wisconsin. Public funding has become an increasingly important source of funds and is most evident for legislative candidates (28 percent in 1985–86). It is viewed as a way of neutralizing the influence formerly felt from interest groups and individuals and was supported in Wisconsin by the remaining elements of the Progressive party. Enacted in 1977, Chapter 107 created a state fund into which individuals having a tax liability or refund may specify that $1.00 be donated. (Only 12.8 percent of all state taxpayers for 1986 agreed to the check-off.) The fund thus created is available to candidates for statewide office after their primary election if they receive a specified number of votes and raise an initial number of private contributions in amounts less than $100. Campaign spending limits as well as restrictions on public funds use are imposed, under certain conditions, if public funding is accepted. In summary, candidates have been very reliant on contributions from individuals and public funding, with PACs being next in importance; however, the pattern of contributions varies with the candidate type and party.

Table 14.4 presents contributions by interest giving source. Much of the funding from Table 14.3 cannot be identified by source in Table 14.4. Over 50 percent of all 1985–86 contributions to statewide and legislative candidates, which could be identified, were from business-related sources. Most contributions in judicial races were from attorneys, as might be expected. Party contributions varied by interest sector, too. Labor and education in Wisconsin contributed much more to the Democratic party, and business to the Republican.

PAC contributions have decreased in dollar amount and as a percentage of all contributions for judicial and legislative candidates (Table 14.3). Further, legislators indicated that PAC contributions have become less important to them, while public funding and individual contribu-

Table 14.3. Recipients of campaign contributions (candidates and parties) in Wisconsin, by type of contributor, 1979-80 and 1985-86

Recipients — Candidates

Type of Contributor	Statewide 1979-80 $	%a	Statewide 1985-86 $	%a	Judicial 1979-80 $	%a	Judicial 1985-86 $	%	Legislative 1979-80 $	%a	Legislative 1985-86 $	%a
Individuals	102,389	58	2,694,323	62	626,013	48	506,307	53	1,000,594	40	1,786,690	47
Self	19,233	11	131,647	3	513,536	40	428,878	45	183,807	7	82,708	2
PACs	11,085	6	643,628	15	48,323	4	14,972	2	610,939	24	530,172	14
Public funding	-556b	*	668,786	15	98,344	8	0	0	494,771	20	1,057,632	28
Party committees	42,895	24	126,019	3	850	-	100	-	203,833	8	313,839	8
Candidate committees	2,407	1	59,396	1	2,825	-	1,321	-	10,118	0	13,847	-
Miscellaneous	-45,774b	*	-7,940b	*	-9,391b	*	485	-	7,038	0	52,001	1
Total	178,009	100	4,315,859	99	1,289,891	100	952,063	100	2,511,100	99	3,836,889	100

Parties

Type of Contributor	Democratic 1979-80 $	%	Democratic 1985-86 $	%	Republican 1979-80 $	%a	Republican 1985-86 $	%	Other 1979-80 $	%a	Other 1985-86 $	%
Individuals	444,109	63	584,517	37	2,071,620	85	1,739,558	75	19,054	91	970,406	55
PACs	57,886	8	397,676	25	95,513	4	201,404	9			196,846	11
Party committees	121,853	17	256,863	16	101,196	4	199,367	9	574	3	368,883	21
Candidate committees	30,207	4	41,625	3	11,295	-	18,610	1	0	0	18,795	1
Miscellaneous	46,265	7	295,602	19	165,569	7	163,869	7	1,349	6	219,004	12
Total	703,320	99	1,576,283	100	2,442,193	100	2,322,808	101	20,977	100	1,773,934	100

Source: Taken and adapted from appropriate years, Wisconsin State Elections Board, Biennial Reports of Wisconsin State Elections Board: Part II.

aA (*) indicates a negative number, a (-) indicates that the dollars consitute less than 1 percent, and a (0) indicates no contributions from that source.

bNegative numbers indicate for public funding that more money was returned than was accepted during the time period and for miscellaneous that loan repayments exceeded contributions. These entries were excluded in determining totals and percentages.

Table 14.4. Recipients of campaign contributions (candidates and parties) in Wisconsin, by interest giving source, 1979-80 and 1985-86

	Recipients											
	Candidates											
	Statewide				Judicial				Legislative			
	1979-80		1985-86		1979-80		1985-86		1979-80		1985-86	
Interest Giving Source	$	%a	$	%a	$	%a	$	%a	$	%a	$	%a
Agriculture	306	1	39,967	2	585	-	700	-	3,997	3	9,838	1
Attorneys	2,720	11	168,605	8	67,689	34	49,689	30	3,632	11	46,803	6
Education	1,000	3	144,292	6	12,322	6	6,023	4	939	1	60,876	8
Finance	3,396	10	276,640	12	7,246	4	2,232	1	4,320	4	125,867	15
Health care	975	3	130,713	6	5,403	3	8,337	5	8,921	7	96,762	12
Insurance	4,200	13	36,641	2	1,605	1	1,280	1	3,920	3	31,935	4
Labor	585	2	152,929	7	0	0	11,144	7	0	0	62,643	8
Manufacturing	6,026	18	263,597	12	12,598	6	3,379	2	18,992	16	65,792	8
Mercantile	0	0	50,104	2	3,397	2	5,930	4	3,508	3	19,338	2
Other business	10,578	32	399,024	18	26,688	14	32,073	20	26,587	22	115,973	14
Realtors	2,435	7	96,374	4	7,687	4	2,170	1	2,912	2	40,483	5
Transportation	250	1	34,174	2	650	-	200	-	820	1	27,058	3
Utilities	0	0	42,783	2	1,165	1	585	-	775	1	45,459	6
Miscellaneous	-23,720	*	386,432	18	50,146	25	40,783	25	31,660	26	67,350	8
Total	33,471	101	2,213,275	101	197,081	100	164,525	100	120,983	100	816,177	100
% Total contributions	10		69		56		5		34		26	

Source: Taken and adapted from appropriate years, Wisconsin State Elections Board, Biennial Reports of Wisconsin State Elections Board: Part II.

a A (*) indicates a negative number, a (-) indicates that the dollars constitute less than 1 percent, and a (0) indicates no contributions from that source.

b A negative number indicates that loan repayments exceeded contributions. This entry was excluded in determining totals and percentages.

(Table 14.4. continued)

Interest Giving Source	Parties											
	Democratic				Republican				Other			
	1979-80		1985-86		1979-80		1985-86		1979-80		1985-86	
	$	%	$	%	$	%a	$	%	$	%a	$	%
Agriculture	1,123	1	1,736	-	7,505	1	7,536	1	265	4	5,631	1
Attorneys	8,380	9	31,710	6	29,394	6	41,127	6	0	0	43,580	6
Education	4,223	4	36,402	7	3,500	1	9,258	1	0	0	17,986	2
Finance	2,609	3	58,622	12	40,834	8	81,032	11	0	0	35,102	5
Health care	20,722	21	23,720	5	23,160	4	23,175	3	0	0	19,380	3
Insurance	3,623	4	11,305	2	23,460	4	27,917	4	0	0	17,239	2
Labor	798	1	104,679	21	0	0	1,641	-	0	0	31,031	4
Manufacturing	2,876	3	9,322	2	130,300	24	144,988	19	0	0	112,201	16
Mercantile	1,890	2	8,900	2	22,523	4	18,533	2	121	2	12,240	2
Other business	29,835	31	37,016	7	115,222	22	162,907	22	388	6	140,122	19
Realtors	2,222	2	18,170	4	14,819	3	21,589	3	0	0	10,269	1
Transportation	0	0	3,450	1	9,330	2	8,724	1	0	0	3,575	-
Utilities	200	0	19,245	4	5,416	1	28,166	4	0	0	7,600	1
Miscellaneous	18,515	19	133,834	27	107,343	20	177,769	24	5,411	87	264,484	37
Total	97,016	100	498,111	100	532,806	100	754,362	101	6,185	99	720,440	99
% Total contributions	15		25		84		38		1		37	

Source: Taken and adapted from appropriate years, Wisconsin State Elections Board, Biennial Reports of Wisconsin State Elections Board: Part II.

aA (*) indicates a negative number, a (-) indicates that the dollars constitute less than 1 percent, and a (0) indicates no contributions from that source.

bA negative number indicates that loan repayments exceeded contributions. This entry was excluded in determining totals and percentages.

tions have become more important. As the role of PACs has changed, their numbers have decreased. Of the 742 PACs ever registered in Wisconsin, more than two of every three (68 percent) are no longer active (Table 14.5). Several reasons may be cited for this erosion: PAC contributions proved to provide less access to and influence on legislators than did contributions from other sources, especially individuals and conduits, and the record keeping required discouraged many smaller groups. Consequently, many former PAC contributions now come from individuals who identify themselves with a group, or from a conduit rather than from a group-based PAC.

Table 14.5 Wisconsin PACs, by registration status, 1979-87, in percent

| | | PAC Registration Status[a] | |
PAC Type	Currently Active	Active in Past Inactive Now[b]	Total
Agriculture	1	1	1
Attorneys	2	-	-
Education	13	18	16
Financial	10	3	5
Governmental	3	10	8
Health care	5	2	3
Insurance	4	1	2
Labor, general	17	32	27
Labor, governmental	3	2	3
Manufacturing	7	4	5
Mercantile	2	2	2
Other business	12	6	8
Resources	3	-	1
Real estate	3	0	1
Single issue	5	10	8
Transportation	3	-	1
Utilities	5	-	2
Miscellaneous	3	8	6
Total %	101	99	99
Total N	240	502	742

Source: Compiled by Karen M. Hedlund from records kept by the Wisconsin State Elections Board.
[a]As of September 1, 1987.
[b]A (-) indicates less than 1 percent, and a (0) indicates 0 percent.

The largest percentage of currently registered PACs, 17 percent, is labor based; 32 percent of those registered at one time but no longer active represented labor. If one combines all business PACs (financial, insurance, manufacturing, mercantile, other business, real estate, and utilities), their current predominance, 43 percent, is evident. Business-type PACs also show consistently lower numbers in past than in current registration, thus indicating greater staying power, as well as increases, than for labor or education PACs. Overall, then, we see high but changing levels of PAC and group involvement in Wisconsin campaign financing, with especially high levels for business and industry. The recent erosion of PAC contributions to legislators and the increasing use of public funding would be applauded by Progressives, but the wholesale entry of special interest money into campaigns would not.

Protests

At times, certain types of groups have used "unconventional" pressure methods involving protests and confrontations to present their cases to Wisconsin state government. During activist eras (the late 1960s and 1970s) and periods of severe economic distress, "dispossessed" and "ignored" groups have sometimes entered the political arena attempting to influence policies via confrontation. The effectiveness of these tactics has been questioned in Wisconsin and elsewhere, but many groups persist.

In 1969 the conservative-dominated legislature passed a state budget that reduced by $33 million some types of state aid to families with dependent children (AFDC). These reductions were especially hard on minority residents in Milwaukee's inner city. In August 1969 Father James Groppi, an acknowledged leader and prime advocate for the affected citizens, announced that a group of welfare mothers would march from Milwaukee to the state capitol at an upcoming special legislative session to press their demands for a restoration of the payments. On the day the legislature was to convene, the marchers, including large numbers of university students, broke down a door, entered the assembly chamber, and demanded an opportunity to be heard. After two hours of speeches by welfare mothers, an agreement was reached in which the assembly could convene. Speaker Froehlich quickly convened and then adjourned the chamber. Prevented from presenting their case officially, the marchers decided to take over the chamber to pressure public officials to listen and respond to their needs. In the words of Father Groppi, "We have captured the Capitol and we intend to stay here until we get what we want."[35] Eleven hours of demonstrator control over the assembly chamber was ended when the demonstrators were "tricked" and left the capitol. Father Groppi was cited by the assembly for contempt and jailed.[36] The welfare cuts were not restored by the legislature.

With one exception,[37] subsequent use of confrontation has not involved a chamber takeover; however, visible protests have continued. Pressure from several forces on the state retirement system encouraging the divestment of its investment funds from companies doing business in South Africa resulted in the construction of a "shanty town" on the capitol grounds in 1984. Another time, a small group of farmers camped on the capitol grounds, accompanied by a herd of cattle. Although confrontation activities have been discouraged because of their ineffectiveness, public demonstrations by groups having few conventional resources have served to call public attention, via press accounts, to less salient issues.

Influence via the Courts

Increasingly, interest groups have used the courts in their efforts to secure favorable decisions. The basic requirement is that the resolution being sought is amenable to litigation. Groups have found that Wisconsin courts, like the other branches of state government, have developed an activist image and a reputation for aggressiveness.[38] Not unlike state courts elsewhere, the Wisconsin courts have played an ongoing role in interpreting and setting boundaries for state policies through their decisions. In this role the courts are called on to determine if the actions of officials and private citizens correspond with the Wisconsin Constitution, state statutes, judicial precedents, and common law principles.

One example of a special group using the courts to affect its future occurred in 1986. After the Milwaukee Brewers Baseball Club lost a heated legislative battle in 1983 regarding the siting of a state prison, it successfully sued the Department of Health and Social Services, preventing the siting action from moving forward. Specifically, the state Supreme Court ruled that when the legislature forbade the department from using the normal hearing procedures (a "contested case" format) for the environmental impact statement regarding the location of the prison in close proximity to Milwaukee County Stadium (home of the Brewers), the legislature had violated the equal protection clause of the Wisconsin Constitution.[39]

Another situation evolved in 1980 when Republican governor Dreyfus unilaterally reduced state aid to local governments (including school districts) by 4.4 percent. Although state statutes permit a reduction in state appropriations whenever a deficit is anticipated, eight municipalities and one school district filed suit against state executive officials, charging that they lacked the power to take such action. The Wisconsin Supreme Court agreed, ruling that only the legislature could reduce state aid to local governments. These judicial actions are typical of many court decisions and may not be recognized as interest group influence tactics, yet they are instances in which interest groups used the courts to obtain favorable decisions.

Administrative Agencies

Many agency personnel have natural ties to the groups interested in their programs and interact constantly with the affected groups. Such interactions are widespread and have been identified by Lowi, Fiorina, and others as a key element in policy making by subgovernments.[40] Since public employees in Wisconsin are widely respected for their honesty and expertise, the interaction takes the form of information and suggestions, not necessarily public or private pressure. The concerns expressed by group members to agency representatives may find their way into policies, decisions, and rules.

One example of agency policy making via group interaction occurred with regard to environmental issues. The Wisconsin Department of Natural Resources (DNR) works with a multiplicity of disparate groups representing both corporate and environmental protection interests in fulfilling its environmental regulation duties. The cumulative impact of group interactions can be seen in a series of decisions by the DNR concerning the issuance of permits for the discharge of waste water into the state's rivers and streams. Since paper manufacturing involves the disposal of considerable amounts of conventional and toxic liquid wastes, resolution of this issue was vital to the future of a state industry employing more than 47,000 people and producing 11 percent of all paper products in the United States—over 3.7 million tons annually, more than any other state. Using Environmental Protection Agency guidelines based on the federal Clean Water Act, the DNR promulgated regulations in 1981 for the discharge of conventional wastes. These administrative rules (NR 212) were especially important for the lower Fox River (the location of ten pulp and paper mills and four municipalities) because this part of the state has been a target for efforts to improve water quality.

During most of the 1970s much environmental rule making involving the DNR and the paper industry, as well as companies in general, was tumultuous and confrontational. State bureaucrats were labeled obstructionist and narrow, and the industry was called a self-centered and profit-dominated special interest group. A gradual change occurred, within a context of new leadership and an altered business and economic climate. The process became more consensual. Representatives from environmental groups, industry, and the DNR discussed and sought to resolve differences regarding policies and enforcement via working groups and committees before formal rule making.[41] Although this practice did not alter DNR, legislative, or gubernatorial roles, the consensus-building process permitted policies to be formed based on commonality and compromises reached largely outside the glare of public debate. As a result, the 1981 DNR rules allocated portions of the total permissible discharge to companies and municipalities and allowed them to trade their shares (or parts thereof) as their needs changed, so long as the maximum discharge level was not exceeded. Such a policy introduced greater flexibility to the companies, municipalities, and even the DNR regarding the operation of this discharge system.[42] Other often-cited examples of decision making with substantial group involvement in Wisconsin include road building, nursing home regulation, and professional licensure. Although the public is represented in this decision making, old-line Progressives would be very dubious about policies formulated via discussions with those whose interests are being "regulated."

An Assessment of Group Power

Group Power in the Past

In her 1981 analysis of parties and pressure groups at the state level, Morehouse listed the following "significant" pressure groups: AFL-CIO, United Auto Workers, business interests, Farmers Union, liquor lobby, and local public officials.[43] Some of these groups continue to be effective in Wisconsin, but as we have seen, other groups have emerged. Both Democratic and Republican legislators noted that unions (including the AFL-CIO and UAW) have lost much of their clout in the legislative process. Ardor for their causes has waned. Though unions still make substantial financial contributions to many Democratic candidates and to the party itself, their influence on decision making has diminished, as indicated above, with the notable exception of public employee unions. They continue to be able to protect many of their earlier gains and to influence decisions that protect and enhance jobs in the state, but the influence they had on state politics in Wisconsin is not as strong as it once was.

In spite of the key role played by agricultural sectors in the state's economy, farm organizations have not been able to regain the influence lost during the increasing urbanization of the state in the 1960s. Though a succession of legislators and governors has responded to agricultural crises and established new state programs, some of these would probably have been implemented without the existence of organized groups. Even legislators from rural and agriculturally dominant districts pointed out the relatively low level of lobbying success attached to farmers' organizations.

Before the demise of independent breweries in Milwaukee and throughout the state, liquor interests, especially the Wisconsin State Brewers Association and the Tavern League of Wisconsin, were important groups for influencing public policy regarding their interests, especially taxes on their products. The loss of brewing capacity through the sale and takeover of Wisconsin-based breweries plus problems encountered by the Tavern League (indicated above) have led to a weakened position from what had formerly been the case. The emergence of new leadership for the Tavern League plus the hiring of a new lobbyist have led to a perceived rejuvenation of the brewing and tavern influence. Although it is premature to place them back in the top group of Wisconsin lobbying organizations, these interests are experiencing a strong revival.

Local public officials have always been a very important source of influence in state decision making, as Morehouse suggested, but the levels have changed in Wisconsin in recent years. State programs for returning revenue to local communities and the natural relationships between state and local governments have cemented this interdependency. At the same time, recent budget crises have led to reevaluations of the state's role in funding local programs and to program curtailments. As a result, local public officials appear to have lost some influence.

The Most Powerful Groups in Wisconsin

As previously noted, WEAC is widely considered to be the strongest and most effective special interest group in the state. Its large membership (approximately 50,000) is distributed in sizable numbers throughout the state (unlike members in most other groups), thus providing a strong, grass-roots base. In addition, WEAC has been very successful in mobilizing its members to become involved in issues and election campaigns (spending more than $700,000 on all campaigns in 1985–86 and approximately $350,000 on state legislative races in 1988). This involvement has included not only contributions, but also member assistance to candidates during their campaigns, a tactic often overlooked by groups. WEAC has also developed a strong and responsive leadership, skilled in its interaction with state officials and effective in presenting the teachers' case.

Second is probably the WMC and related business groups and companies. These organizations have developed long and close ties to the Republican party, especially to recent Republican governors. These governors have worked closely with business leaders in advancing business causes and have gladly protected business interests via the veto, even when a bill had bipartisan legislature support.[44] Given the broad interpretation noted above about how the veto can be used, this practice has become a significant weapon. In addition, these organizations have raised sizable campaign funds and have been able to take advantage of recent public opinion supporting economic development in the state. One recent assessment concluded that these groups and the Republican governor have succeeded in elevating economic development to a protected status above the political fray, so that it is no longer seen as a narrow business lobby issue.[45] Further, recent growth in Wisconsin's manufacturing sector has added to the clout held by these interests.

The Wisconsin Realtors Association has maintained a low profile but is considered to be one of the more influential organizations affecting many state policies. Not only are its members distributed throughout the state, but it has raised significant funds for campaigns (primarily for Republican candidates) and has concentrated its efforts on a relatively few issues. Resources, the ability to mobilize its members, and the development of ties to important governmental leaders have resulted in a potent group in state politics.

The University of Wisconsin system has become a very effective state agency influencing education policies. Its thirteen four-year campuses, thirteen two-year centers, and extension services located throughout the state have helped the university develop a broad base of public support. Its reputation for education, research, and public service is widely recognized and endorsed. Further, large numbers of state officials have a pro-university predisposition because they are graduates and continue to be interested in the university.

Another effective group is the Wisconsin Academy of Trial Lawyers. Although the membership is relatively small, it is an influential and articulate group that has focused its attention on a narrow set of issues, including tort reform. The organization has been very successful in mobilizing members and in presenting its concerns to state decision makers, especially legislators.

In addition, there is a secondary level of single-issue groups, with varying amounts of influence. Environmental groups have experienced a decline in impact during recent years. In the 1970s they had considerable influence on both the legislature and state agencies in the development of many state policies related to environmental protection. They contributed significantly to the election of Democratic governor Earl in 1982 by providing many grass-roots workers. Recently, the changing economic situation plus continuing pressure to liberalize some of the restrictive environmental policies have created a more difficult situation for these groups. Many companies, once locked in battle with environmental groups, have succeeded in replacing the adversarial proceedings used for decision making and have become more effective in countering environmentalist strategies. The Wisconsin Chiropractic Association and its successful techniques of achieving influence on a very narrow issue were discussed above. Another group, often mentioned for its effective influence, is the Wisconsin Road Builders Association.

The Wisconsin Safety Belt Coalition, a group of organizations largely responsible for the 1987 seatbelt law, provides an example of a different approach by a single-issue interest group. With substantial funding from the automobile manufacturers and great success in enlisting the medical establishment, insurance groups, law enforcement officials, the WMC, and a large number of health and safety organizations, this coalition became a formidable force on the side of the mandatory seatbelts. Such broad-based support and the advocacy of newspapers throughout the state helped this group to be very effective on its single issue. Now that that issue has been passed (even though there is a three-year sunset on the legislation), it is doubtful if the organization will continue to exist.

Overall Group Strength in Wisconsin

As we have seen, interest groups press their cases effectively to Wisconsin state government. Thus, the state must be reclassified from the "weak" category of Morehouse[46] to one in which pressure groups are "moderately strong." The number of cases in this chapter describing pressure group activity on a variety of issues documents the important role played by interest groups in public decision making. In addition, legislators themselves, as well as others, point to the changing level of reliance state decision makers have on pressure groups as a source of information. Lobbyists have become more sophisticated and professional in their approach to legislators and other state officials, and these officials have become more reliant on lobbyists. Though wining and dining have never been the centerpieces of influence, as sometimes was the case in other states, there appears to have been a general increase in all types of interaction between lobbyists and legislators, resulting in better access, better information, and more influence.

Conclusion

As the subtitle of this chapter indicates, interest group activity in Wisconsin reflects a lingering Progressive tradition. The Progressive movement has continued to play an important role in shaping the views of Wisconsinites on politics and government and in the form and operation of political institutions. This chapter has shown that the Progressive norms of openness, honesty, and high expectations that public officials will act on behalf of the public still characterize Wisconsin government and politics; at the same time, however, there has been erosion in other aspects of the Progressive tradition. For example, the wariness and "arm's length" relationship the Progressives held toward special interests, especially corporations and utilities, has diminished greatly. Like public officials everywhere, Wisconsin's political leaders have been willing participants in creating public policies that protect and advance the state's dominant economic interests. Even when it appears as if state government is being used by special, narrow interest groups to gain an advantage, public officials have been willing to listen and, frequently, to act in a supportive manner.

The compelling need that elected public officials have for campaign contributions because of escalating election costs has provided group representatives with an important opportunity to develop access in Wisconsin. Public financing offers one means to blunt this trend in a manner consistent with the Progressive tradition, but the reluctance to embrace this concept fully means continuing access for special groups via campaign contributions.

In addition, there is a growing tendency for private interests to seek direct representation in the state capitol. More and more corporations and businesses are hiring lobbyists or sending their own officers to advance their own special interests. The consequences is not only better access for them, but a gradual movement of state government toward decision making that advances and balances narrow interests. Although this development is not necessarily bad, it does represent a major departure from the Progressive philosophy.

The Progressive belief that openness, together with minimal regulation, is sufficient to ensure proper conduct between government and interest groups also has been replaced with a more detailed, regulation-oriented atmosphere. Though there is no indication that the Progressive norms will disappear, many former state officials express distress about the current closeness between decision makers and group representatives. Lobbyist clout is perceived to be at an all-time high, and alarm over this prospect is not widespread. As a consequence, while Wisconsinites continue to revere and respect their Progressive political legacy, in actual fact much political practice is at great variance with Progressive philosophies, norms, and approaches to governing. The Progressive tradition lingers but is not the pervasive, vital driving force it once was.

Notes

The author is grateful for the assistance of a number of people who provided essential information in the preparation of this chapter, including several legislators, public officials, lobbyists, and colleagues. The author alone assumes responsibility for all interpretations.

1. Frederick I. Olson, "Introduction," in Wilder Crane et al., *Wisconsin Government and Politics,* 4th ed. (Milwaukee: Department of Governmental Affairs, University of Wisconsin-Milwaukee, 1987), 1–10; David Stoeffler, "State Pushes, Pulls Progressivism," *Wisconsin State Journal,* July 19, 1987, p. 1; David P. Thelen, *Robert M. La Follette and the Insurgent Spirit* (Boston: Little, Brown, 1976).

2. Daniel W. Hildebrand, "Report to the Ethics Board" (Madison: State of Wisconsin Ethics Board Report on Attorney General Bronson La Follette, October 13, 1986).

3. All statistical information reported in this section is taken from Bureau of the Census, *Statistical Abstract of the United States: 1987* (Washington, D.C.: Government Printing Office, 1987).

4. Olson, "Introduction," 6–8.

5. Thelen, *La Follette;* Robert M. La Follette, *La Follette's Autobiography* (Madison: University of Wisconsin Press, 1911).

6. Robert S. Maxwell, *La Follette and the Rise of the Progressives in Wisconsin* (Madison: State Historical Society of Wisconsin, 1956), 8–9.

7. Olson, "Introduction," 2.

8. Maxwell, *Rise of the Progressives,* vii.

9. For additional elaboration regarding the development and political role of these economic sectors, see Mordecai Lee, "Interest Groups," in Crane et al., *Wisconsin Government and Politics,* 79–92.

10. "Businesses Provide Thompson with the Veto Hit-List," *Milwaukee Journal,* July 26, 1987, part A, p. 19; Chuck Martin, "Business Leaders Find Budget Vetoes Pleasing," *Milwaukee Journal,* August 2, 1987, part A, p. 12; Avrum D. Lank, "Pro-business Attitude May Have Reached Peak with Heileman," *Milwaukee Sentinel,* October 2, 1987, part 2, p. 7.

11. Wisconsin Legislative Reference Bureau, "The University of Wisconsin System Fall Semester Starting Date," Brief 85-2 (Madison, November 1985).

12. Chuck Martin, "GM Grant Rekindles Furor," *Milwaukee Journal,* October 6, 1987.

13. Harmon Zeigler and Hendrik van Dalen, "Interest Groups in State Politics," in Herbert Jacob and Kenneth N. Vines, eds., *Politics in the American States: A Comparative Analysis,* 3d ed. (Boston: Little, Brown, 1976), 94; Zeigler, "Interest Groups in the States," in Virginia Gray, Herbert Jacob, and Kenneth N. Vines, eds., *Politics in the American States: A Comparative Analysis,* 4th ed. (Boston: Little, Brown, 1983), 111–17.

14. Wisconsin Legislative Council, "The Wisconsin Lobbying Regulation Law," Staff Brief 86-5 (Madison, July 15, 1986).

15. Similar disclosure is not required for contacts with administrative agencies. While expenditures and areas of interest would be covered under the disclosure, the same information regarding contact on specific matters is not available.

16. "Thompson Offers Help for Heileman," *Milwaukee Sentinel,* September 9, 1987, part 2, p. 4.

17. Wisconsin joined with fourteen other states in this effort to regulate unfriendly

takeovers of state companies. John W. Kole, "States Protected Their Companies," *Milwaukee Journal*, January 3, 1988, part D, p. 5.

18. Jarel Barliout, "Hospital Rate-Setting Commission," report (Madison, Legislative Fiscal Bureau, January 1987).

19. David B. Truman, *The Governmental Process: Political Interests and Public Opinion* (New York: Alfred A. Knopf, 1951), part 2.

20. This case is not the first or only example of negotiations taking place between the governor and interest groups on the content of legislation. In 1985, negotiations between Democratic governor Earl and the Tavern League of Wisconsin on liability for liquor servers were widely reported in the press. Matt Pommer, "Tavern League, Earl Aides Reach Liability Deal," *Capitol Times* (October 28, 1985).

21. James Rowan, "Ex-legislators Becoming Top Lobbyists in 1 Easy Step," *Milwaukee Journal*, June 10, 1986.

22. Chuck Martin, "Business Lobby Antagonizes Democrats," *Milwaukee Journal*, December 20, 1987.

23. Arthur L. Srb, "Former Legislators Find Success as Lobbyists," *La Crosse Tribune*, May 29, 1985; David Dishneau, "Lobbyists Find They Need Facts to Make Points," *La Crosse Tribune*, May 31, 1985; Cliff Miller, "The Season Has Come to 'Snuggle Up' in Politics," *Green Bay Gazette*, June 29, 1986.

24. Conduits are funds set up by special-interest groups and companies in which individuals pool their contributions, which are then directed toward specific campaigns. Though only twenty-six conduits are listed with the Wisconsin Elections Board, they are seen as an important development in the state and are being regulated like PACs.

25. V. O. Key, Jr., *Politics, Parties, and Pressure Groups*, 4th ed. (New York: Thomas Y. Crowell, 1958), chap. 6; Lester W. Milbrath, *The Washington Lobbyists* (Chicago: Rand McNally, 1963), chap. 2; Harmon Zeigler and Michael A. Baer, *Lobbying Interaction and Influence in American State Legislatures* (Belmont, Calif.: Wadsworth, 1969), chaps. 1–3.

26. Wisconsin Legislative Reference Bureau, "Pari-Mutuel Betting on Horse Racing," Information Bulletin 86-IB-1 (Madison, April 1986); Wisconsin Legislative Reference Bureau, "Beyond Bingo: The State Lottery Experience," Information Bulletin 85-IB-2 (Madison, November 1985).

27. After public approval, however, the lobbying activity increased dramatically. All types of gaming and racing interests secured lobbyists and became very active in trying to influence the legislative committees preparing the regulations to implement the constitutional amendments. Neil H. Shively, "Gaming Lobbyists Gearing Up for Big Push," *Milwaukee Sentinel*, February 26, 1987.

28. Keith E. Hamm, "U.S. State Legislative Committee Decisions: Similar Results in Differing Settings," *Legislative Studies Quarterly* 5 (February 1980), 31–54.

29. Doug Mell, "From Health to Yachts, Lobbying Affects Budget," *Wisconsin State Journal*, July 19, 1987, p. 1.

30. This practice underwent a major change in 1987 when the Democratic Assembly caucus reported out a budget bill without sufficient votes for passage. Support from Republicans was needed to pass the bill. Steve Schultze, "A Budget Born of Late Nights, Compromise," *Milwaukee Journal*, June 5, 1987.

31. "State Supreme Court Throws Light on 'Pork,' " *Milwaukee Sentinel*, May 15, 1986.

32. One hotly contested Senate race in 1984 for Milwaukee County reputedly cost approximately $200,000.

33. Ronald D. Hedlund, "The Wisconsin Legislature," in Crane et al., *Wisconsin Government and Politics*, 93–132; Gail B. Shea, "Legislative Campaign Committees: The

Wisconsin Experience," report prepared for Common Cause in Wisconsin (Madison, 1986); Elizabeth G. King and David G. Wegge, "The Rules Are Never Neutral: Public Funds in Minnesota and Wisconsin Legislative Elections" (Paper presented at the Annual Meeting of the Midwest Political Science Association, Chicago, April 1984).

34. "Lobbyists Contribute $61,092," *Wisconsin State Journal,* September 24, 1987.

35. John Patrick Hunter, "Groppi's Welfare Marchers Occupy the State Capitol, Knowles' Speech Delayed," *Capitol Times,* September 29, 1969.

36. On appeal, the U.S. Supreme Court, *Groppi v. Leslie* 404 U.S. 496 (1972), ruled that the use of this procedure by the assembly denied the plaintiff due process. Ralf R. Boer, "Constitutional Law–Due Process–Power of a Legislature to Punish for Contempt," *Wisconsin Law Review* 259 (1973), 268–79.

37. In 1972 about two hundred beer bar owners occupied the floor of the assembly, preventing the legislature from convening into a special session. Their issue was a proposal to permit 18–21-year-olds to be served "hard liquor." Though the duration of this occupation, three hours, was much shorter than in the welfare case, the outcome was the same. They were forced to leave the floor under threat of arrest and saw the legislature act contrary to their wishes.

38. Fred A. Wileman, "The Wisconsin Judiciary," Crane et al., *Wisconsin Government and Politics,* 175–86.

39. 130 Wis. 2nd 79, 387 N.W. 2nd 254 (1986).

40. Theodore J. Lowi, *The End of Liberalism* (New York: W. W. Norton, 1969), chap. 3; Morris P. Fiorina, *Congress: Keystone of the Washington Establishment* (New Haven: Yale University Press, 1977), chap. 7.

41. Though citizen representatives from various environmental groups sit on these committees and panels, this step has not necessarily led the groups to abandon their opposition to company actions or to forego use of litigation against the state and companies.

42. William O'Neil, Martin David, Christina Moore, and Erhert Joeres, "Transferable Discharge Permits and Economic Efficiency: The Fox River," *Journal of Environmental Economics and Management* 10 (1983), 346–55.

43. Sarah McCally Morehouse, *State Politics, Parties and Policy* (New York: Holt, Rinehart & Winston, 1981), 112.

44. Chuck Martin, "Thompson Is All Business: But Strategies Must Aid State Economy to Succeed," *Milwaukee Journal,* December 27, 1987, part D, p. 1.

45. Chuck Martin, "State Backed Business," *Milwaukee Journal,* January 3, 1988, part D, p. 1.

46. Morehouse, *State Politics,* 107–13.

The Changing Nature of Interest Group Activity in the Midwestern States

RONALD J. HREBENAR

As was observed in the opening chapter, because of its special blend of demographic and economic patterns, the Midwest is a microcosm of the nation. A complete range of interests and interest groups is found among the various economies and peoples of the thirteen midwestern states. Those quintessential midwestern interest groups and their state-by-state patterns have been analyzed in Chapters 2 through 14.

It is obvious from the preceding chapters that significant changes have occurred in the interest group scene in all midwestern states since the mid-1960s. Yet at the same time, there has been considerable continuity in the conservative nature of midwestern politics. This pattern of change in terms of technology and technique within a context of the continuity of long-term political traditions and style is a central theme in our analysis of midwestern interest groups.

This chapter synthesizes the information from the individual state chapters to identify regional characteristics in such areas as the types of groups that are active, lobbyists, group power, and group tactics. These data are then used to discuss the question, In what ways do midwestern interest groups differ from their counterparts in other regions of the nation? To answer these questions, we refer to the analytical framework we developed in Chapter 1.[1]

The Changing Lobbying Game in the Midwest

The greatest change in midwestern interest groups since the 1960s has been a significant expansion in three dimensions of interest group activity: (1) the number of groups active in state lobbying, (2) the range of groups, and (3) the frequency and intensity of lobbying activities.

These changes in interest group activities have not occurred in a political vacuum. Broader political changes have swept the Midwest which have affected the interest group system in various degrees. For example, the relative decline of agriculture in all the midwestern states has resulted in the reduction of agricultural interest group activity and power in the state capitals. The causes of the decline range from climatic changes to internal migration for better-paying urban jobs, but the effect is fairly constant—the farmers and their allies no longer dominate midwestern state legislatures. A second major change has been the emergence of a more balanced two-party system in most of the Midwest. Political scientists have long contended that the relationship that exists between political parties and interest groups and any changes in the former are quite likely to influence the latter and vice versa. The reapportionment revolution that occurred during the late 1960s and early 1970s throughout the nation also contributed to a broadening of interests being represented in midwestern capitals and hastened the decline of agricultural interests. The diminishment of agriculture was also associated with the increased economic diversity and the growing urbanization of midwestern states. These developments, in turn, resulted in growing demands on state and local governments for additional services, greater tax revenue, and larger budgets. Government and its clients became more important in states that had long-term traditions of relatively insignificant public sectors. Power has shifted in most of the midwestern states, and now widely diversified urban and public sector interests tend to dominate legislative debates.

The rise of public sector groups representing state and local employees and public schoolteachers has changed the balance of power in state legislatures across the region. Public employee associations and education groups have in some states become the most powerful lobbies. All this increased government activity has also brought an array of often nonregistered government agencies onto the lobbying scene at both the state and local level.

In every state of the region the loopholes of existing lobby registration laws result in the serious underreporting of governmental lobbyists. All of the midwestern states have provisions for registering lobbyists and requiring reporting of some types of lobby expenditures. Most have some provisions for the regulation of campaign finance and conflict of interest. In the post-Watergate era of political reform some of the upper midwestern states such as Wisconsin and Minnesota were in the forefront of this movement. However complex, these laws usually have as their primary objective the disclosure of interest group activities, rather than the restriction or prohibition of most activities. The relative comprehensiveness of midwestern lobbying laws, as compared to those found in the South, is largely a function of the region's moralistic political culture, which views politics as the legitimate activity of amateurs and also has as a central imperative, the desire to clean up unethical political activities.

Overall, the aforementioned changes have tended to promote a more competitive group style of politics in the Midwest than before, and that enhanced competition has required an increased sophistication in lobbying strategies and tactics that have manifested themselves in all midwestern state capitals. This professionalization has occurred in terms of interest group organizations, the skills of the lobbyists, and the range of lobbying techniques used to influence public policy.

Major Interests Active in the Midwest

Since the 1960s significant changes in group activity have occurred in the Midwest as a result of the developments mentioned earlier. As noted above, there has been a considerable expansion in the number and range of groups seeking to influence state government. Many new interests, including social-issue, public interest, and single-issue groups, have entered the political arena while other more traditional interests have proliferated. Business and local government lobbies have become more specialized and numerous in most midwestern states. This is because specific groups do not see their specific interests as being fully served by their umbrella groups such as the Chamber of Commerce or a league of cities. The third dimension of this expansion is that groups are lobbying more intensively than was the case in the 1970s or even the early 1980s. They have more regular contact with public officials and use more sophisticated techniques.

Midwestern interests have been aggregated and presented in Table 15.1 on the basis of their overall effectiveness as lobbying organizations and the extent of their presence in the thirteen midwestern states. The

Table 15.1. Most effective midwestern interests, by number of states

Interest	No. of Midwestern States where Interest Is Judged To Be Most Effective	No. of Midwestern States where Interest Is Judged To Be of Second Level of Effectiveness	Total Rank
1. Schoolteachers' organizations	10	1	21
2. Bankers' associations (includes savings and loan associations)	8	5	21
3. Labor associations (includes AFL-CIO)	8	2	18
4. General business organizations (chambers of commerce)	7	4	18
5. Lawyers (bar association/ trial lawyers' organizations)	4	7	15
6. General farm organizations (mainly farm bureaus)	3	9	15
7. Doctors	4	4	12
8. Labor (individual unions, Teamsters, UAW, etc.)	5	1	11
9. Manufacturers	4	3	11
10. Retailers (companies and associations)	4	3	11
11. Utility companies and associations (electric, gas, telephone, and water companies)	3	5	11
12. Health care groups	2	7	11
13. Individual banks and financial institutions	2	6	10
14. Realtors' associations	3	3	9
15. Insurance	1	6	8
16. K-12 education interests	3	1	7
17. Universities and colleges (institutions and personnel)	2	3	7
17. General local government	2	3	7
19. Antiabortion groups	2	2	6
20. State and local government employees	2	1	5
21. Liquor, beer, and wine	1	3	5
22. Mining companies and associations	1	3	4
23. Agricultural commodity organizations (stock growers, grain growers, etc.)	1	2	4
23. Oil and gas companies and associations	1	2	4
25. Environmentalists	1	1	3
25. Taxpayers' groups	1	1	3
28. Truckers/Private transportation	1	0	2
28. State agencies	1	0	2
28. Sporting, hunting and fishing, and antigun control groups	1	0	2
31. Senior citizens	0	2	2
31. Railroads	0	2	2
33. Gaming interests (racetracks, casinos, and lotteries)	0	1	1
33. Newspapers/Media	0	1	1
33. Tourist industry	0	1	1

Note: Scores were calculated by allocating 2 points for each "most effective" ranking and 1 point for each "second level of effectiveness" placement and adding totals. Where a tie in total points occurs, interest are ranked according to the number of "most effective" placements (where possible). Placement of interests in "most effective" and "second level effectiveness" categories was determined by authors of the individual state studies in this volume.

top six interests listed are active and influential in at least ten of these states. However, only banking interests are effective lobbying organizations in all the region's states. Organizations representing farm, labor, lawyer, teacher, and general business interests are slightly less comprehensive in terms of their effectiveness in the region. The interests in this table represent the "power elite" of interest group politics in the midwestern states. We estimate that as much as three-quarters of the lobbying effort in terms of time and money is attributable to the top fifteen or twenty interests listed in the table.

One interesting tendency in the midwestern states is the increasing prominence of lobbies representing individual cities, special local government districts, and state agencies. The most prominent of state agencies in all states are the departments of education or public instruction, transportation, and welfare, in addition to state universities and colleges. Associated with this rise of government lobbying has been the increased prominence of public sector unions, particularly those of state and local employees and of teachers. Ideological groups, which are also often single-issue groups, such as prolife organizations, have also become quite active in recent years. Public interest organizations, groups promoting good government, senior citizens' associations, and, increasingly, environmentalist groups are other forces that now have a presence in all midwestern state capitals.

The range of interests displayed in Table 15.1 is extremely broad. It is important to note that each state has its own unique collection of interest groups. It is also important not to equate presence with power. Just because a group or interest is active in a midwestern state does not by itself ensure power or success.

Interest Groups and Public Policy in the Midwest

Group power in this study is used in two distinct but interrelated ways. It may refer to the power of specific or individual groups, interests, or lobbies, or to the power or impact of interest groups as a whole on the political system of a particular state. With regard to the dimension of specific interest group influence, we focused on the ability of a group to achieve its self-defined goals. We recognize how difficult it is to measure individual group power definitively, for numerous variables or influences are involved, several of which are extremely volatile or dynamic in nature, such as the political climate, public opinion, and power relationships between public officials.

Assessment of Individual Interest Group Power

To assess the power of the midwestern interest groups, we used a combination of quantitative and qualitative techniques. In Table 15.2 we

Table 15.2. Most effective interest groups in the thirteen midwestern states: An alternative assessment to Morehouse

Morehouse Assessment	Hrebenar and Thomas Assessment
Illinois	
Illinois Manufacturers Assn; Illinois Chamber of Commerce; coal operators; insurance companies (State Farm, Allstate); Illinois Education Assn[a]; Illinois Medical Society[b]; AFL-CIO unions (Steelworkers); retail merchants; racetracks; Farm Bureau; *Chicago Tribune.*	Illinois Medical Society; Illinois Education Assn; Illinois Manufacturers Assn; AFL-CIO; Illinois Chamber of Commerce; Illinois Assn of Realtors; Illinois Bankers Assn. Illinois Trial Lawyers Assn; retail merchants; Illinois Farm Bureau
Indiana	
AFL-CIO; Indiana Farm Bureau; Indiana State Teachers Assn; Chamber of Commerce.	Indiana State Teachers Assn; Indiana Chamber of Commerce; Indiana Trial Lawyers Assn; AFL-CIO and individual unions; Indiana Manufacturers Assn; Indiana Farm Bureau. Insurance industry (individual companies and assns); Indiana Medical Assn and other health care groups (esp. Indiana Hospital Assn, Indiana Health Care Assn); banks (Independent Bankers Assn of Indiana, Indiana Bankers Assn, and individual banks); public utilities; senior citizens' groups (American Assn of Retired Persons, Indiana Retired Teachers Assn); state universities.
Iowa	
Farm Bureau Federation; truckers.	Iowa Farm Bureau; Iowa State Education Assn; Iowa Assn of Business and Industry; Iowa Federation of Labor (AFL-CIO); Iowa Bankers Assn. Iowa Academy of Trial Lawyers; insurance companies; realtors; contractors; savings and loans; retail merchants.
Kansas	
Banks; power companies; pipeline companies; railroads; Kansas Farm Bureau.	Banks (esp. Kansas Bankers Assn, Independent Bankers Assn); agriculture (esp. Kansas Farm Bureau, Kansas Livestock Assn); education (esp. Kansas-NEA, Kansas Assn of School Boards). Kansas Chamber of Commerce and Industry; utilities (Kansas Power and Light, rural electric co-ops, Southwestern Bell); lawyers (Kansas Bar Assn, Kansas Trial Lawyers Assn); Kansas Medical Society; insurance; local govt groups and individual cities; oil and gas.

(Table 15.2 continued)

Michigan	
General Motors; Ford; Chrysler; American Motors; United Automobile Workers; AFL-CIO.	United Auto Workers; AFL-CIO; automobile manufacturers; Michigan Manufacturers Assn; Michigan United Conservation Clubs; City of Detroit; Michigan Education Assn; Michigan taxpayers' interest.
	Michigan Hospital Assn; Michigan Chamber of Commerce; Michigan Farm Bureau; Michigan Milk Producers Assn; state universities and colleges; local govt assns (esp. Michigan Townships Assn) and individual local govt units; insurance (esp. Blue Cross/Blue Shield of Michigan); banks; oil interests; public utilities; senior citizens; Michigan Beer and Wine Wholesalers Assn; tourist industry; Right to Life; Michigan Auto Dealers Assn.

Minnesota	
Railroads Assn; 3M; Dayton Hudson Corporation; Northern States Power Company; Honeywell; Northwestern Bell Telephone; banking; beer; iron mining; liquor; Minnesota Education Assn; Teamsters; Minnesota Assn of Commerce and Industry; AFL-CIO; Minnesota Farm Bureau; Farm Union; League of Women Voters.	Chamber of Commerce; The Business Partnership; realtors; automobile dealers; utilities (esp. Northern States Power, Minnesota Power, U.S. West[c]; schoolteachers (American Federation of Teachers and NEA); state employees; AFL-CIO and traditional labor unions; National Federation of Independent Business; doctors; Minnesota Citizens Concerned for Life.
	Banks; large business corporations (3M, Dayton-Hudson [department stores], etc.); farm groups (esp. Minnesota Farm Bureau, Farmers' Union, and commodity groups); dentists; lawyers ; railroads.

Missouri	
Missouri Farmers' Assn; AFL-CIO; Missouri Bus and Truck Assn; Teamster; Missouri State Teachers Association; brewers.	Missouri Farm Bureau; Missouri State Labor Council (AFL-CIO); Missouri Bankers Assn; Missouri Citizens for Life; Missouri Bus and Truck Assn; Missouri Bar Assn.
	Missouri State Teachers Assn; Missouri Farmers Assn; Missouri Assn of Realtors; Missouri Hospital Assn; Missouri Assn of Trial Attorneys; Taxpayers Research Institute of Missouri (TRIM).

Nebraska	
Nebraska Farm Bureau; Omaha National Bank; Northern Natural Gas Company; Union Pacific Railroad; Northwestern Bell Telephone; education lobby.	Nebraska State Teachers Assn; Nebraska Bankers Assn; Nebraska Chamber of Commerce and Industry; AFL-CIO (and labor in general); University of Nebraska; Nebraska League of Municipalities/Assn of County Officials; Nebraska State School Boards Assn.
	Nebraska Railroads Assn; Nebraska Farm Bureau; Nebraska Assn of Public Employees; Assn of Mental Health Providers; Nebraska Medical Assn; Nebraska Bar Assn; Nebraska Telephone Assn; Nebraska Public Power Assn.

(Table 15.2 continued)

North Dakota	
Education lobby: North Dakota Education Assn, PTA, school boards, Department of Public Instruction; Farmers Union; North Dakota Farm Bureau; North Dakota Stockmen's Assn; Assn of Rural Cooperatives.	Education (esp. North Dakota Education Assn, but also North Dakota School Boards Assn and school administrators); energy (esp. Lignite Council, energy conversion co-ops, oil and gas, utilities, rural electric co-ops); U.S. West[c]; business (esp. Greater North Dakota Assn; bankers, retail merchants); North Dakota Medical Assn; North Dakota Hospital Assn; Blue Cross/Blue Shield; sportsmen's groups. North Dakota Farm Bureau; Farmers Union; Agricultural Coalition; North Dakota League of Cities; County Commissioners Assn; water users' lobby; AFL-CIO; public employees; state universities; Right to Life.

Ohio	
Insurance; banking; utilities; savings and loans; Chamber of Commerce.	Education lobby (esp. Ohio Education Assn); Ohio Council of Retail Merchants; Ohio State Medical Assn; Ohio Health Care Assn; Ohio Bankers Assn; AFL-CIO and traditional labor unions; Insurance Federation of Ohio and individual insurance companies. Ohio Savings and Loan League; Ohio Manufacturers Assn; Ohio Assn of Realtors; Chamber of Commerce; Ohio Academy of Trial Lawyers; Ohio Farm Bureau.

Oklahoma	
Phillips Petroleum, Kerr-McGee, other oil companies (Texaco, Mobile, Humble, Atlantic-Sinclair, Sun-Sunray, DX Division, Hess Oil); transportation companies, power companies, local public officials.	Education (esp. Oklahoma Education Assn, Oklahoma School Boards Assn); labor (esp. AFL-CIO), Oklahoma Public Employees Assn; newspaper interests (esp. Daily Oklahoma. Oklahoma Press Assn); banking and finance (esp. Oklahoma Bankers Assn and individual banks); lawyers (esp. Oklahoma Trial Lawyers Assn). Oil interests (esp. Oklahoma Independent Petroleum Assn, Kerr-McGee, Phillips Petroleum); agriculture (esp. Oklahoma Farm Bureau, Farmers Union); business groups (esp. Chamber of Commerce); medical groups (esp. Oklahoma Medical Assn, nursing homes); local govt (esp. County Commissioners Assn); utilities (esp. Southwestern Bell, Oklahoma Gas & Electric).

(Table 15.2 continued)

South Dakota	
Farmers Union; rural co-ops and rural electrification interests; South Dakota Farm Bureau; Chamber of Commerce; banks; South Dakota Wheat Growers Assn; South Dakota Stockgrowers Assn; Northern States Power; Homestake Mine; liquor lobby.	Governor's office and cabinet officials; South Dakota Bankers Assn; South Dakota State Bar Assn; liquor lobby (esp. Wholesale Liquor Dealers); South Dakota Municipal league; investor-owned utilities assn; rural telephone and electric co-ops; Homestake Mine.
	South Dakota Medical Assn; South Dakota Retail Beverage Dealers (bar owners); U.S. West[c]; Citibank; John Morrell & Co. (meat packers); South Dakota Press Assn; Industry and Commerce Assn; South Dakota Farm Bureau; Farmers Union; Ag Unity; insurance industry.

Wisconsin	
AFL-CIO; United Auto Workers; business interests; Farmers Union; liquor lobby; local public officials.	Wisconsin Education Assn Council; Wisconsin Manufacturers Assn; Chamber of Commerce; University of Wisconsin and state higher education system; Wisconsin Realtors Assn; Wisconsins Academy of Trial Lawyers.
	AFL-CIO; United Auto Workers; Wisconsin State Brewers Assn; Tavern League; farm interests; environmentalists; Wisconsin Chiropractic Assn; banking; gaming/state lottery interests.

Source: The Morehouse assessment is reprinted with permission from Sarah McCally Morehouse, State Politics, Parties and Policy (New York: Holt Rinehart & Winston, 1981), Table 3.2. The Hrebenar and Thomas assessment was compiled from survey research conducted by the authors of the individual state chapters in this volume.

Note: The first paragraph lists those interest groups assessed as being the most consistently influential during the 1980s. The second paragraph contains those interests declining in power, those rising in power but not yet in the first rank, and those that are ephemeral or only occasionally active. Abbreviations used in this table: Assn=Association; AFL-CIO=American Federation of Labor-Congress of Industrial Organizations; Govt=Government; NEA=National Education Association.

[a]The designation Education Association in the formal name of a group indicates a schoolteachers' organization.

[b]The designation Medical Association (or Medical Society) in the formal name of a group indicates a general practitioners' organization.

[c]Formerly Northwestern Bell Telephone.

compare the most influential interest groups in the thirteen midwestern states as listed by Sarah McCally Morehouse in 1981 with the findings from our study.[2]

By comparing these two sets of rankings, we can discern the changing influence of individual groups and interests in the Midwest. States that previously had been dominated by one or several powerful interests, such as Michigan, once dominated by labor unions and automobile manufacturers, have changed into pluralist interest group systems. Those interests that do exert considerable influence must share power with other groups. Because of increasing political pluralism, the days when one interest or a handful of interests could dictate policy on a wide range of issues appear to be gone.

As for the power status of the so-called traditional interests in the Midwest — business, agriculture, labor, education, and local government — three of these have maintained or enhanced their power, while two appear to have lost ground. Education interests (especially schoolteachers), local governments, and business remain very influential. Contrary to some predictions, increased political pluralism and interest group fragmentation within the business community does not appear to have significantly affected business influence overall. Certainly, some more traditional businesses may have declined, but they have been replaced by service and other businesses among the ranks of the most powerful groups. On the other hand, agriculture and traditional labor appear to have suffered some loss of power, even though they still rank among the most influential interests.

Teachers and, to a lesser extent, public employees are the new face of labor in the Midwest. The rise of state employees' associations is a noteworthy phenomenon in the changing configuration of group power in the region. It seems to be linked to the increased role of government since the 1960s, which also has enhanced the power of many state agencies, particularly departments of education and transportation and state university systems.

Less significant gains have been made by health care groups, environmentalists, and senior citizens. Additionally, single-issue groups, such as prolife groups in Missouri and Minnesota, have had a series of successes, although many of these groups are ad hoc in nature and appear and disappear as their issues ebb and flow.

The successes of these nonestablishment interests, including social-issue and minority groups, do not appear to have been significant enough across the midwestern states to have upset the relative influence of the traditionally powerful groups. Indeed, the changes in the hierarchy of group power across the Midwest, as in the other regions, has been far less dramatic since the mid-1960s than the major expansion in group activity might lead us to assume. This is not surprising, however, when we consider the factors that constitute individual group power. The players in the game may have changed by the addition of new groups, but the rules of success, particularly the command of resources and the building up of long-term relationships with public officials, remain virtually unchanged.

Evaluation of Overall Group Power

We define *overall group power* as the extent to which interest groups as a whole influence public policy when compared to other components of the political system, such as political parties, the legislature, the governor, and so on. Researchers have encountered the same types of problems in assessing this area as they have in evaluating individual group power. However, drawing on the research presented in this volume, we have classified the fifty states according to their impact on their respective state policy-making systems.

It is not an easy task to evaluate the overall group power within a given state. Other scholars have attempted to assess this aspect of group power. The various studies have had varying methodologies and mixed results and left many unanswered questions. The first such investigation, by Belle Zeller, was based only on the assessments of political scientists. The Zeller study argued that group strength was primarily a function of political party strength and was inversely proportionate to it.[3] Subsequent research explored this idea and attempted to develop it further. Work by Morehouse, for example, used measures of party strength to define the relationship more accurately.[4] Zeigler and van Dalen added the variable of economic and social development.[5] As we noted in presenting our analytical framework in Chapter 1, these theories predicted the gradual transformation of strong group systems into moderate and eventually weak systems as economic and social pluralism advanced.[6] The results from the present study enable us to suggest an alternative way of approaching an understanding of overall group power.

We find little to support the categorization of states into strong, moderate, and weak group systems. First, this categorization gives the incorrect impression that in some states groups are literally weak or powerless and thus of little consequence in state politics. Even in those states where groups are not all-powerful, certain interest groups, such as the UAW and the automobile makers in Michigan politics, have undeniable strength.

A more accurate and informative way to designate the overall impact of groups is to use a terminology that avoids the impression that groups are not important but communicates the degree of their significance in state policy making vis-à-vis other political institutions. We describe the impact of a particular group system as having a *dominant,* a *complementary,* or a *subordinate* impact in relation to other aspects of the system. We also provide two intermediate categories that are combinations of two of these pure types of interest group power systems.

It has already been noted in Chapter 1 that the inverse relationship between party strength and group impact does not always hold and that socioeconomic development and increased professionalization do not always lessen the impact of groups on a state's political system. This is not to argue that these variables are not significant. Rather it is to say that their effect on overall group power appears to be different than originally predicted. For instance, it is generally the case that party strength has considerable influence on the overall impact of groups. However, though weak party systems are invariably accompanied by dominant group systems, strong parties do not always mean weak group systems, as Illinois illustrates. Furthermore, increasing party strength may not result in a decrease in overall group influence, as recent developments in California demonstrate. We also suggest that there is no automatic progression from dominant to subordinate status resulting from socioeconomic development and increased professionalization of government. In fact, groups often increase their influence as such developments occur. All this leads us to conclude that party strength, socioeconomic development, and professionalization are not the only factors that influence overall group power. In some circumstances they may not even be the most important variables. What is clearly needed is a more sophisticated analysis of these relationships. Although we do not claim to have developed a definitive theory, a combination of quantitative and qualitative analysis of the data suggests that a more comprehensive understanding can be provided by reference to the components of our analytical framework, described in Chapter 1.

Each of the seven factors in our framework has some influence on overall group power. The problem is, however, that the impact of each appears to vary from state to state and from time to time within a state, and thus the combined influence of all seven factors varies accordingly. For example, the moralistic political culture apparently moderates group influence in North Dakota in a situation that with relatively weak parties and a fragmented policy-making system would otherwise mean that groups would be dominant. In contrast, the same political culture does not have a similar restraining influence on group power in Minnesota.

Table 15.3 lists the states according to overall group power. States listed in the "Dominant" column are those in which groups as a whole are the overwhelming and consistent influence on policy making. The "Complementary" column contains those states where groups tend to have to work in conjunction with or are constrained by other aspects of the political system. More often than not this is the party system, but it could also be a strong executive branch, competition between groups, the political culture, or a combination of all these factors. The "Subordi-

Table 15.3. Classification of the thirteen midwestern states, by overall impact of interest groups and in comparison with states in other regions

		States Where the Overall Impact of Interest Groups Is:		
Dominant	Dominant/ Complementary	Complementary	Complementary/ Subordinate	Subordinate
The Midwest				
	Nebraska	Illinois	Minnesota	
	Ohio	Indiana		
	Oklahoma	Iowa		
		Kansas		
		Michigan		
		Missouri		
		North Dakota		
		South Dakota		
		Wisconsin		
The West				
Alaska	Arizona	Colorado		
New Mexico	California			
	Hawaii			
	Idaho			
	Montana			
	Nevada			
	Oregon			
	Utah			
	Washington			
	Wyoming			
The South				
Alabama	Arkansas	North Carolina		
Florida	Georgia			
Louisiana	Kentucky			
Mississippi	Texas			
South Carolina	Virginia			
Tennessee				
West Virginia				
The Northeast				
		Maine	Connecticut	
		Maryland	Delaware	
		Massachusetts	Rhode Island	
		New Hampshire	Vermont	
		New Jersey		
		New York		
		Pennsylvania		

Source: Adapted from Clive S. Thomas and Ronald J. Hrebenar, "Interest Groups in the States," in Virginia Gray, Herbert Jacob, and Robert Albritton, eds., Politics in the American States: A Comparative Analysis, 5th ed. (Glenview, Ill.: Scott, Foresman; Boston: Little, Brown, 1990), Table 4.3.

nate" column represents a situation in which the group system is consistently subordinated to other aspects of the policy-making process. As we see from the absence of states in this column, groups are not consistently subordinate in any state. The "Dominant/Complementary" column includes those states whose group systems alternate between the two situations or are in the process of moving from one to the other. Likewise, the states in the "Complementary/Subordinate" column are those whose group systems alternate between being complementary and being subordinate.

Midwestern interest group systems exhibit the most complementary power pattern in the nation. Only one state, Minnesota, is found in the "Complementary/Subordinate" category, and only three states (Nebraska, Ohio, and Oklahoma) manifest a dominant aspect to a complementary pattern. The other nine midwestern states fall in the "Complementary" category. We have grouped the individual states by region in Table 15.3. In summary, the South has a strong pattern of dominant interest group systems; the West has largely a dominant/complementary type of interest group politics; the Midwest is overwhelmingly complementary; and the Northeast is basically complementary, with four states in the "Complementary/Subordinate" category. Clearly, the Midwest and the West represent the middle ground on the continuum of interest group power vis-à-vis other institutions such as political parties.

Lobbyists and Lobbying in the Midwest

Americans, in general, tend to be suspicious of interest groups and lobbyists. Especially in the midwestern states, the misuse of political power by railroad interests during the late nineteenth century contributed to a legacy of distrust among the public toward interest groups and particularly the lobbyists who represent them. Because of the often huge amounts of money at stake in many legislative battles, interest groups have used almost any means at their disposal, sometimes illegal ones, to secure access to public officials and to influence government decisions in their favor. Despite these perceptions, the world of lobbying on the state level has significantly changed with the passage of public disclosure laws and increased media monitoring of the interest group scene in most state capitals.

A lobbyist is a person designated by an interest group to represent it to government for the purpose of influencing public policy in that group's favor. Many, including the popular press and some academics, tend to group all lobbyists in the same stereotyped category. As we noted in Chapter 1, there are five major categories of lobbyists: contract, in-house, government lobbyists and legislative liaisons, volunteer or citizen, and hobbyist or self-styled. It is important, however, to distinguish among them because they have different strengths and weaknesses. The various categories are also perceived differently by public officials, and these perceptions determine the nature and extent of each lobbyist's power base.

Increased numbers and professionalism characterize the lobbyist corps in the Midwest since the 1960s. In terms of direct lobbying, the most common and still the most effective tactic is the use of lobbyists. Until very recently, it was the only tactical device used by the vast major-ity of groups, and it remains the sole approach used by many today.

Perhaps the greatest change has been the proliferation of profes-sional contract lobbyists and lobbying firms in many midwestern capi-tals. These lobbying firms often provide a wide variety of services and represent up to as many as twenty-five clients. Another trend is for more and more lobbyists to become specialists in a particular field of lobby-ing, reflecting the increased specialization of government. Typical of these specialists is Rich and Associates, a lobbying firm in Missouri, specializing in representing "liberal" groups such as the League of Women Voters; and Otie Ann Carr, in Oklahoma, whose clients are health and hospital groups. Additionally, in all midwestern states law-yers and law firms are increasingly moonlighting as lobbyists.

Clearly, the days of "booze and bribes" in most midwestern capitals are over. But the wheeler-dealers still exist in a more subtle manifesta-tion. Like their predecessors, the new breed of lobbyists realize the need for a multifaceted approach to establishing and maintaining good rela-tions with public officials. This strategy includes everything from partici-pating in election campaigns to helping officials with their personal needs. Even more important, the modern lobbyist is very aware of the increased importance of technical information, the increased profession-alism and changing needs of public officials, and the increased public visibility of lobbying. The result is a low-key, highly skilled, and effective professional who is a far cry from the old public image of the stereotype lobbyist.

New tactics have supplemented the traditional work of the lobbyist. Grass-roots lobbying, public relations, media campaigns, and, to a lesser extent, demonstrations and sit-ins are the major indirect tactics, whose ultimate purpose is to enhance direct access and influence. Other suc-cessful practices include building coalitions with other groups and con-tributing workers and especially money to election campaigns, particu-larly by establishing PACs. These tactics are viewed not as a substitute for a lobbyist, but as a means of enhancing the ability of the group's lobbyist to contact and influence public officials. Interest group leadership generally chooses the most cost-efficient and politically effective method to achieve its goals. Because of the high costs, the newer techniques are employed only if absolutely necessary. Despite these limitations, these new tactics are being widely and increasingly used on the state level.

Combined state- and national-level campaigns are often planned and implemented by interest groups. Many state groups have national affiliates. The National Education Association, for example, is an extensive and sophisticated national organization that provides all sorts of aid and advice to its local and state affiliates. When needed, state affiliates are sometimes activated to participate in lobbying in Washington, D.C. Large corporations set general policies on political involvement which are followed by the state offices of these organizations.

How Distinctive Are Interest Group Systems in the Midwest?

Midwestern interest group politics are both similar to and different from those of the other three regions in our study. First, we must conclude that no significant patterns are uniquely midwestern. Although there are certainly variations among the four regional systems and from state to state, they do not appear to be uniquely regional. Increasingly, state and regional interest group systems share patterns with each other and with the national pattern found in Washington, D.C.

Several patterns, however, appear to differentiate midwestern interest groups from those of other regions. These differences derive primarily from the nature of the midwestern economy, based as it has been on both agricultural and heavy industries, and the region's mixed traditions of fiscal conservatism and moralistic and individualistic styles of politics. Government has become a significant lobbying force recently, as have teachers and other public employees. The group systems as a whole are powerful but often are in competition with equally powerful institutions such as political parties in states such as Illinois, Indiana, and Michigan. The professionalization of lobbying in many midwestern capitals approaches that found in the nation's most professionalized lobbying corps, in Sacramento, California.

The established interests — business, labor, agricultural, and professional groups — as well as state and local government agencies, still dominate the political processes in most midwestern states. It is primarily their command of extensive resources that has enabled them to maintain and, in some cases, enhance their influence.

Overall in the Midwest the top-ranked interest groups or interests are not surprising: teachers, bankers, labor, business, lawyers, and doctors. Perhaps most interesting is the fact that teachers rank as the most effective interest group in three of the four regions – they are supplanted by business groups only in the northeastern states. Labor organizations are by far the strongest in the Midwest and, as we would expect from other data, weakest in the South and the West, both of which are regions of low unionization. All in all, a wealth of subtle differences exists among the various states in the Midwest, the fifty individual states, and the four regions. But in the final analysis (at least in this regional study) what is remarkable are the growing similarities among quite different states and regions as well as the increasing congruence of interest group politics on the state level with those on the national level. Perhaps it is predictable that the Midwest, the region that most closely approximates the rest of the nation, would best highlight these changes.

Notes

1. This chapter's data are based on the synthesized data contained in the individual chapters for the thirteen midwestern states and the other thirty-seven states contained in the Hrebenar-Thomas study. The most complete results for the fifty states published from this study to date can be found in Clive S. Thomas and Ronald J. Hrebenar, "Interest Groups in the States," in Virginia Gray, Herbert Jacob, and Robert Albritton, eds., *Politics in the American States: A Comparative Analysis,* 5th ed. (Glenview, Ill.: Scott, Foresman; Boston: Little, Brown, 1990).

2. Morehouse's assessment was based on thirteen books and one journal article on state politics. She relied heavily on the series of books on the subregions of the country by Neal R. Peirce. Sarah McCally Morehouse, *State Politics, Parties and Policy* (New York: Holt, Rinehart & Winston, 1981), 108–12. An updated version of the Morehouse table was produced by Michael Engel, *State and Local Politics: Fundamentals and Perspectives* (New York: St. Martin's Press, 1985), 241–42. Most of the updating, however, appears to be based on Neal R. Peirce and Jerry Hagstrom, *The Book of America* (New York: W. W. Norton, 1983).

3. Belle Zeller, *American State Legislatures,* 2d ed. (New York: Thomas Y. Crowell, 1954), 190–93 and chap. 13, "Pressure Group Influence and Their Control."

4. Morehouse, *State Politics,* 107–17.

5. L. Harmon Zeigler and Hendrik van Dalen, "Interest Groups in State Politics," in Herbert Jacob and Kenneth N. Vines, *Politics in the American States: A Comparative Analysis,* 3d ed. (Boston: Little, Brown, 1976), 94–110; L. Harmon Zeigler, "Interest Groups in the States," in Virginia Gray, Herbert Jacob, and Kenneth N. Vines, eds., *Politics in the American States: A Comparative Analysis,* 4th ed. (Boston: Little, Brown, 1983), 111–15.

6. Two other works have attempted to assess aspects of overall group power in the

fifty states but based their assessments on studies of only one aspect of the process. Francis concentrated on the legislature, and Abney and Lauth based their list on a survey of administrators. Wayne L. Francis, *Legislative Issues in the Fifty States: A Comparative Analysis* (Chicago: Rand McNally, 1967); Glen Abney and Thomas P. Lauth, "Interest Group Influence in the States: A View of Subsystem Politics" (Paper presented at the Annual Meeting of the American Political Science Association, Washington, D.C., August 1986).

APPENDIX: Methodological Guidelines

The general focus of the contributors' research was to be the organization, operation, and role of interest groups in each state. These findings were to be presented within the context of each state's particular political, social, and economic setting.

1. Use of Common Definitions.

   Each contributor was to use a common definition of *interest group, lobby, lobbyist,* and of *individual group, overall group,* and *lobby power.*

   a. An interest group = Any association of individuals, whether formally organized or not, that attempts to influence public policy.

   b. A lobby = One or more individuals, groups, or organizations concerned with the same general area of public policy but that may or may not be in agreement on specific issues.

   c. The power of any particular interest group or lobby = Its ability to achieve its goals as it defines them and as perceived by the various people directly involved in and observing the public policy-making process (e.g., present and former legislators, aides, bureaucrats, other lobbyists, journalists, etc.).

   d. Overall group power = The extent to which groups as a whole influence public policy when compared to other components of the political system, such as political parties, the legislature, the governor, etc.

2. Information and Data on Various Aspects of Interest Group Activity.

   a. General relevant social and economic environment of the state.
      (i) Social, ethnic, religious composition.
      (ii) Economic base and employment distribution.
      (iii) Regional variations within the state.

   b. Relevant background on the governmental and political system.
      (i) Legislative and executive organization.
      (ii) Role and strength of parties.
      (iii) Political culture, including public perception of interest groups.
      (iv) Relevant political history.
      (v) Principal past and current political issues.

   c. The legal setting of group activity.
      (i) Constitutional protections.
      (ii) Group and lobbyist registration requirements.
      (iii) PAC regulations.
      (iv) Reporting requirements for groups, lobbyists, and PACs.

d. Kinds of groups active.
   (i) Registered groups.
   (ii) Nonregistered groups.
   (iii) Changes over time, especially since the 1960s.
e. Lobbyists.
   (i) Types of lobbyists: contract lobbyists, in-house lobbyists, legislative liaisons, citizen or volunteer lobbyists, and private individuals.
   (ii) Educational and professional backgrounds.
   (iii) How lobbyists are perceived by elected and appointed officials.
   (iv) Lobbyists' views of their roles and most effective techniques.
f. Group and lobbying tactics.
   (i) Access through the election process: PACs, campaign support.
   (ii) Legislative lobbying.
   (iii) Administrative lobbying.
   (iv) Judicial lobbying.
   (v) Using direct democracy as a method of achieving group goals (i.e., initiative, referendum, and recall).
   (vi) Grass-roots techniques and networking.
   (vii) Coalition building.
   (viii) Trends in group tactics.
g. Interest group power.
   See next section.

3. Analysis and Assessment of Group Power.
    We asked each contributor to evaluate two aspects of group power: (a) to assess the power of individual groups and lobbies; (b) to assess the impact of groups as a whole on the political system, especially as actors in the public policy-making process.
   a. Individual group and lobby power.
      This concept was to be defined as set out in section 1, above. The assessment method was to be survey research combined with qualitiative investigations — namely, interviews and newspaper and magazine articles.
      For comparative purposes, we asked the contributors to assess the present validity of Morehouse's listings of the most significant groups and lobbies for their particular states. Where the authors came up with one or more different listings, we asked them to explain the reasons.
   b. Group power as a whole.
      Here we were concerned with three aspects of group power in each state:
      (i) The overall impact of groups on the public policy-making system. Morehouse categorizes this impact into *strong, moderate,* and *weak.*
      (ii) Whether this overall impact is increasing or declining, and why.
      (iii) The relationship of overall group power to party strength.
      The methodologies for assessing overall group power are at

present not well developed. Therefore, we gave the contributors instructions to develop their own approaches, although they were free to use the methods employed by Zeigler and by Morehouse.

4. Reference to Existing Research and Writing on State Interest Groups.
   Here we asked the contributors to consider the relevance, or lack of relevance, of:
   a. Previous research on interest groups in their states, if it existed.
   b. Previous research on interest groups in general in the fifty states.
   c. In particular, we asked them to assess for their states the applicability of various existing theories and propositions on interest groups in the fifty states, including:
      (i) The relationship between various economic and social variables and the interest group system.
      (ii) The relationship between the state's political culture and the interest group system.
      (iii) The relationship between interest group power and party strength.
   d. We also requested that they suggest modifications in old theories and propositions and develop new ones.

5. Development of Empirical Data.
   We requested that the aforementioned four areas of research be based on as much empirical data as possible.
   In particular, we requested that the contributors use survey research to develop data on group tactics, perceptions of lobbyists and groups by elected and appointed officials, group power both of individual groups and as a whole, and lobbyists. For this purpose, we circulated copies of the various surveys that we had used in researching our own Alaska and Utah chapters for *Interest Group Politics in the American West* (Salt Lake City: University of Utah Press, 1987).
   In addition, we requested that as much quantitative information as possible be generated from lobby registration lists and reports and from records relating to political action committees.

Index

AAA Auto Club, 170
Abney, Glen, 219, 238
Abortion. *See* Prochoice; Prolife
Access points, for lobbyists, 28, 247,
  256, 318, 322, 325
Administrative lobbying. *See* Executive
  branch lobbying
Advertising campaigns, 155. *See also*
  Media campaigns
A. E. Staley, 135
AFL-CIO, 41–43, 80, 87, 107, 120, 123,
  137, 150, 152, 153, 157, 159, 160
Agreed bill
  in Illinois, 35–40, 45
  in Indiana, 65–66
Agricultural Coalition, 221–22, 232
Agricultural/agribusiness lobbies
  in Illinois, 31, 41
  in Iowa, 87
  in Kansas, 94–96, 103–5
  in Michigan, 122, 128, 133–35, 137,
    138
  in the Midwest, 348, 354, 360–61
  in Minnesota, 151
  in Missouri, 185
  in Nebraska, 195, 202, 210–12, 214
  in North Dakota, 216–17, 220–22,
    230, 235
  in Oklahoma, 266, 269, 271, 276,
    280–82
  in South Dakota, 286–87, 300–301,
    303
  in Wisconsin, 309, 310–11, 334, 337
Agricultural sector, of state economy, 13
  in Illinois, 21
  in Indiana, 51–52
  in Iowa, 77, 79, 82, 87
  in Kansas, 94–96
  in Michigan, 119
  in Minnesota, 146
  in Missouri, 165

  in Nebraska, 193–94, 195
  in North Dakota, 216–17, 220–22
  in Ohio, 243–44
  in Oklahoma, 264–65
  in Wisconsin, 309
Ag Unity, 300
Aid to families of dependent children
  (AFDC), 334
Alcoholic Beverage Laws Enforcement
  Commission, 275
American Agricultural Movement, 105,
  221
American Federation of State, County,
  and Municipal Employees
  (AFSCME), 151
American Federation of Teachers, 101,
  137, 170
American Indian Affairs Commission,
  230
American Motors Corporation (AMC),
  310
Amnesty International USA, 102
Anheuser Busch, 100, 176, 270
Antitakeover legislation, 315
Association of Retarded Citizens (ARC),
  211, 234–35, 251
AT&T, 255
Audubon Society, 234
Automotive industry, in Michigan, 118–
  20, 133, 137

Baer, Michael, 130, 208
Bainbridge, Phillip, 50, 63
Banking/finance interests
  in Illinois, 32, 39–40, 41
  in Iowa, 80, 84, 88
  in Kansas, 96, 99, 103, 105
  in Michigan, 122, 128, 137
  in the Midwest, 348, 360–61
  in Minnesota, 146, 149–50, 158